Newcomers Navig

Experiences of Immigrants and Street-level Bu

MW01230314

NEWCOMERS NAVIGATING THE WELFARE STATE

EXPERIENCES OF IMMIGRANTS AND STREET-LEVEL BUREAUCRATS WITH BELGIUM'S SOCIAL ASSISTANCE SYSTEM

EDITED BY
HANNE VANDERMEERSCHEN, ELSA MESCOLI,
JEAN-MICHEL LAFLEUR, AND PETER DE CUYPER

LEUVEN UNIVERSITY PRESS

The research pertaining to these results received financial aid from the Belgian Science Policy Office according to the agreement of subsidy no. [BR /191/P3/BBOX]

Published with the financial support of KU Leuven Fund for Fair Open Access and the Belgian Science Policy Office according to the agreement of subsidy no. [BR /191/P3/BBOX]

Published in 2023 by Leuven University Press / Presses Universitaires de Louvain / Universitaire Pers Leuven. Minderbroedersstraat 4, B-3000 Leuven (Belgium).

ISBN 978 94 6270 382 7 (Paperback)
ISBN 978 94 6166 524 9 (ePDF)
https://doi.org/10.11116/9789461665249
D/2023/1869/22

NUR: 752
Layout: Crius Group
Cover design: Stéphane de Schrevel

TABLE OF CONTENTS

INTRODUCTION

ELSA MESCOLI AND JEAN-MICHEL LAFLEUR

The welfare state in Europe functions as a dynamic system of complex legal rules and practices, which, despite its high level of formalisation, often leads to unexpected and diverse outcomes for beneficiaries. When it comes to social welfare policies in Europe in particular, their implementation is frequently characterised by wide variations between and within states. One consequence of these variations is that there often exists a difference between 'rights on paper' and 'rights in practices' for potential beneficiaries.

With regards to immigrants as a specific subset of beneficiaries of welfare policies, the link between the welfare state and the governance of migration has been widely studied in the literature (see, for example, Geddes, 2003; Sainsbury, 2012; Lafleur & Vintila, 2020) and is further discussed in Chapter 1 of this volume. Indeed, when it comes to the provision of social assistance to immigrants, the implementation of legal provisions can lead to the seemingly arbitrary inclusion or exclusion of this population. To this end, the concept of discretion as a practice by states and institutions, but also by professionals on the ground is of critical importance for studying immigrants' access to welfare (van der Leun, 2006).

As shown in the literature on immigrants' access to welfare, the use of discretion is often based on moral judgements, stereotypes, personal experiences, and contextual social norms (Maynard-Moody & Musheno, 2012; Raaphorst & Groeneveld, 2019; Thomann & Rapp, 2018). These elements are used by street-level bureaucrats to assess not only the eligibility of applicants but also their deservingness of social assistance (Belabas & Gerrits, 2017; De Wilde & Marchal, 2019; Chauvin & Garcés-Mascareñas, 2012). For this reason, discretion carries the risk of discrimination and reproduction or reinforcement of social inequalities (Lotta & Pires, 2019), which, in turn, can create a perception of injustice in bureaucratic processes among immigrant beneficiaries (Lafleur & Mescoli 2018). By studying interactions in the application process for social benefits, one can therefore understand not only the differences in treatment and the motivations and rationale behind welfare decisions, but also the extent to which specific immigrant needs are met by the norms and administrative practices in place (Brussig & Knuth, 2013).

This book presents the results of a research project that carried out an analysis at three levels: the organisational level, the level of social workers implementing the policies, and the beneficiary level. Through this analytical process, we were able to achieve three goals. First, we mapped practices regarding the granting of rights and social activation interventions targeting newly arrived immigrants. Second, we shed light on the factors influencing social workers' choices and decisions regarding social benefits and social activation targeting newcomers. Third, we provided an analysis of the accessibility of social welfare for newcomers and of their experience with a European welfare state administration.

Aiming to contribute to the study of the intersection between the welfare state and migration governance, this book provides a thorough analysis of the specific case of Belgium. More precisely, we rely on original qualitative and quantitative data collected in Public Centres for Social Welfare (PCSWs) and with newcomers.[1]

Similar to the case of other EU member states, the issue of access to social assistance is often perceived as being of growing importance in Belgium. Indeed, the number of beneficiaries of one or another form of social assistance granted by the 581 PCSWs in Belgium has risen sharply over the past 10 years. Looking only at one specific scheme – the social integration income – the number of beneficiaries rose from about 80,000 in 2008 to 144,151 in 2019. Of these, 25,502 are allocated to recognised refugees or immigrants benefiting from subsidiary protection. While the issue of immigrants and refugees' access to social assistance is frequently discussed in public debates, it is however important to note that the Ministry of Social Integration communicated in 2019 that recognised refugees represented only 11.2% of the total population of social integration income recipients.

Several scholars have studied the provision of social assistance services by PCSWs in Belgium in the past decade. Among their most important findings, they showed that service provision differed across the 581 PCSWs that deliver social assistance across the country (see, for example, De Wilde & Marchal, 2019; Dumont, 2012; Driessens et al., 2015; Raeymaeckers & Dierckx, 2013). This body of literature showed that variations in the delivery of services depend both on the autonomy of each PCSW (even though they are bound by a common legal framework), and on the discretionary power of the agents. The factors influencing these variations are diverse and include the socio-economic and political characteristics of the local environment and institutions, the organisational characteristics of PCSWs, and the agents' approach.

Belgian PCSWs play a crucial role in granting access to social benefits to newcomers and, more generally, in their settlement and integration process. For many newly arrived immigrants,[2] contacts with social workers represent one of the first or most important interactions with the local society. In addition, decisions taken by the PCSW regarding the allocation or refusal of social benefits can have a long-term influence on the lives of newcomers. However, little is known about the practices and interventions with newcomers in PCSWs in Belgium, the policies that regulate them, and other factors that may influence them. With this case study, we will therefore not only contribute to document the specific national situation but also contribute to a broader understanding of the dynamics between immigrants, the welfare state, and street-level bureaucracy.

The general structure of the book is as follows. A first set of chapters (1, 2, 3) aims at introducing the theoretical framework, the context, and the methodological approach of our study. Then, Part I gathers the chapters (4, 5, 6) dedicated to the analysis of social assistance targeting newcomer beneficiaries from the point of view of PCSW staff members, including a focus on the organisation of service provision – and its challenges and pitfalls – and on labour market activation policies. Part II (Chapters 7, 8) looks in more detail at the decision-making process concerning the granting of social benefits to newcomer beneficiaries, describing its different stages and the role of a range of actors and social factors within it. Part III (9, 10, 11) brings the perspective of the newcomers themselves into the reflection, looking at their access to and experiences with PCSWs and how they cope with the challenges and opportunities they encounter. Finally, the conclusion brings together the main findings from all chapters and levels of analysis, in order to make some final analytical remarks, and in particular to combine and compare insights stemming from different perspectives, namely the point of view of institutions and agents with that of the newcomers.

DETAILED CONTENT OF THE BOOK

With the general framework presented above in mind, this volume is organised around the following chapters:

1. **Conceptualising immigrants' access to social assistance and their interaction with street-level bureaucrats**
    Chapter 1 presents the theoretical framework of our research, focusing on two main concepts: accessibility and street-level bureaucracy. Accessibility is conceived as a multi-dimensional analytical tool that allows for an account of both the ways in which services are organised and operate and the experience of beneficiaries, thus focusing on the 'degree of fit' between institutions and individuals. With regard to street-level bureaucracy, we first recall the main meaning of this concept as well as its emergence and the theoretical debates it generates. Second, we present a critical review of the literature that mobilises this analytical tool to study the ways in which the practices of street-level bureaucrats influence the access to rights of newcomer beneficiaries. This highlights how the regulation of access to social assistance functions as additional means of migration governance. We then also focus on the notion of (welfare) 'deservingness' as the main key to understanding the functioning of discretionary practices on the ground.

2. **Social assistance bureaucracies and new migrants: the Belgian context**
    Chapter 2 describes the specific context of our research, explaining the functioning of the social welfare system in Belgium and the role of PCSWs as key actors in this system. It also clarifies who is considered as 'newcomer immigrant' both in this study and in PCSWs. In addition, important changes in the approach to the provision of social assistance (in general and to immigrant beneficiaries in particular) are discussed. We highlight, for example, the shift towards reciprocity of rights and duties and the strengthening of the notion of individual responsibility in active welfare states. Attention is also paid to the large diversity in terms of policy orientations, organisational cultures, and policy instruments.

3. **Applying mixed-method design in the study of immigrant social protection**
    Chapter 3 illustrates the methodological approach adopted in our research and in the analysis of the data collected. We highlight, in particular, the relevance of a mixed-method approach. The quantitative and qualitative tools applied are presented in terms of their rationale, their practical implementation, their objectives and results, and the challenges they pose. In addition, we explain the reasoning behind the choice of case studies and the profiles of the research participants involved. Overall, the combination of these methodological tools allowed the collection of a rich variety of data from different research participants.

4. **Explaining variations in forms of service delivery for newcomers**
    Chapter 4 first describes how the provision of social assistance services targeting newcomers is organised in the PCSWs we studied. Two main approaches are examined: the 'specialised' approach and the 'generalist' approach. Second, the chapter also reveals what types of social assistance is provided to newcomers, and what the conditions of access are. Third, we study the extent to which there are differences in the provision of services to newly arrived immigrants compared to other recipients – with a focus on the 'tailor-made' approach. We also present the main forms of collaboration with partner institutions. The objective of this chapter is to better understand why PCSWs make certain choices in terms of service provision to newly arrived immigrants, what the underlying reasons are, and whether or not, and how, PCSWs perceive the (specific) needs of migrant beneficiaries.

5. **Understanding challenges and pitfalls in the service delivery to newly arrived immigrants**
    Based on the study of the organisation of service provision for newcomer beneficiaries presented earlier, Chapter 5 highlights the emerging challenges and pitfalls. In particular, we pay attention to the working conditions and structural constraints that weigh on social workers, as well as on the other difficulties they face in providing adequate social guidance and support to newcomers. We also focus on the 'understandability' of the Belgian welfare system for newcomers, highlighting language issues as one of the main factors affecting the accessibility of social services and social assistance rights. Finally, we highlight the existence of implementation gaps and unmet needs – 'blind spots' – in the provision of services to newcomers.

6. **Labour market activation and newly arrived immigrants**
   Chapter 6 focuses on labour market activation policies and practices
   targeting newcomers receiving social assistance in Belgium. Based on the
   assumption that social welfare institutions invest in citizens and promote
   social integration, especially through employment, we first investigate
   what is meant by 'socio-professional integration' in our case studies and
   what goals are set for (newcomer) social welfare beneficiaries. Second,
   we discuss the role of the PCSW and its social workers, as well as other
   relevant institutions, in terms of guidance towards socio-professional
   integration. Third, we analyse in detail how the assessment of the employability (disposition/readiness to work) of newcomers by PCSW social
   workers is conducted.

7. **The allocation of social assistance as a hierarchised decision-making
   process**
   This chapter follows a general introduction to Part II of this volume, which
   recalls the law and policy framework that establishes the functioning
   of PCSW in Belgium and constitutes the main context of the decision-
   making process. Such an introduction also highlights the possible room
   for manoeuvre and interpretation that institutions have (that is, the
   differences in the overall approach towards the demands of beneficiaries,
   migrants, and others). After this, Chapter 7 analyses the different steps of
   the decision-making process (described as a highly hierarchised process)
   concerning the allocation of social assistance to newcomer beneficiaries
   and the role of each social actor involved (staff members of PCSWs,
   including presidents, managers, committee members, and social workers)
   within it.

8. **The discretion of social workers towards newly arrived migrants**
   Drawing on the literature presented above and additional texts, Chapter 8
   examines how discretion operates in the field, particularly through the
   practices of social workers. Discretion emerges in a discursive context
   where the law governing social assistance is described as highly restrictive.
   Therefore, discretionary power functions as a set of often non-explicit
   micro-practices that take various forms. In this chapter, we also explore the factors that influence choices and decisions on entitlement
   – including 'cultural' skills and stereotypes – with a particular focus on
   the relationship between welfare workers and recipients and the process
   of assessing the deservingness of recipients. Finally, we analyse the extent
   and objectives of the sanctioning of newcomer beneficiaries.

9. **Pathways of access: analysing newly arrived immigrants' access to welfare services**

Chapter 9 examines the accessibility of PCSWs from the perspective of newcomers. It first looks at the emergence of the need for support, highlighting when this need arises, and which forms it takes in the case of newly arrived immigrant beneficiaries. Second, it examines the access to PCSWs and the use of the services themselves. Doing so, it highlights the factors that play a role in this respect – such as the language skills, knowledge, and social capital of newcomers. It also reveals the contextual elements and organisational characteristics of the institution, and the types of support experienced. Information provision, communication, and understandability issues are the central themes of this chapter.

10. **The newcomers' perception of social assistance provision and its organisation**

Following on from the previous chapter, Chapter 10 examines newcomers' perceptions of welfare provision and its organisation. The focus is on the system itself, but also, and in more detail, on the policy implementation practices operating on the ground (including controls, sanctions, and the discretionary power of social workers). This chapter highlights newcomers' self-perceptions as welfare recipients, and their views on the changes in their social status that this may entail. In addition, we analyse the notion of deservingness from the perspective of the beneficiaries' experience by highlighting the negotiations undertaken by them and accounting for the diverse aspirations and expectations of the social actors involved.

11. **Developing forms of agency: how do newcomers deal with difficulties in accessing PCSW services**

In the asymmetrical relationship between social workers and welfare recipients, the latter are not simply passive actors. Indeed, Chapter 11 explores how potential beneficiaries of social assistance cope with the difficulties they encounter when trying to access their welfare entitlements, as well as the strategies they may develop to 'navigate' the Belgian welfare system. These strategies are diverse, ranging from compliance and collaboration to assertiveness. Strategies also include different forms of non-take-up of welfare entitlements. In this last chapter, a particular attention is paid to the ways in which recipients cope with street-level bureaucracy, highlighting a typology of possible responses.

12. Conclusion

In a last concluding chapter, we come back to our research aims and shortly recapitulate the main conclusions with regard to each of them, bringing the perspectives of managers and staff as well as newcomer beneficiaries together. In addition, other main findings related to key themes that emerged from our study are also discussed, more particularly the question of equity and the high price of support.

NOTES

1. This data has been gathered within the framework of the project 'BBOX: OCMW/CPAS & new migrants/refugees: opening the black box of policy in practice', funded by BELSPO – Belgian Science Policy Office, coordinated by the Katholieke Universiteit Leuven (HIVA – Research Institute for Work and Society) in partnership with the University of Liège (CEDEM – Centre for ethnic and migration studies, Faculty of Social Sciences) and the University Saint-Louis Brussels (CESIR –Centre for Sociological Research and Intervention).
2. In Chapter 2, we provide a thorough discussion of the meaning of 'newcomers' in the framework of this research.

REFERENCES

Belabas, W., & Gerrits, L. (2017). Going the extra mile? How street-level bureaucrats deal with the integration of immigrants. *Social Policy & Administration, 51*(1), 133–150.

Brussig, M., & Knuth, M. (2013). Good intentions and institutional blindness: Migrant populations and the implementation of German activation policy. In E. Brodkyn, & G. Marston (Eds.), *Work and the welfare state. Street level organisations and workfare politics* (pp. 185–208). University Press.

Chauvin, S., & Garcés-Mascareñas, B. (2012). Beyond informal citizenship: The new moral economy of migrant illegality. *International Political Sociology, 6*(3), 241–259.

De Wilde, M., & Marchal, S. (2019). Weighing up work willingness in social assistance: A balancing act on multiple levels. *European Sociological Review, 35*(5), 718-737.

Driessens, K., Franssen, A., Méhauden, L., & Depauw, J. (2015). *Le projet individualisé d'intégration sociale recherche évaluative et prospective au sein des CPAS belges.* SPP Intégration Sociale.

Dumont, D. (2012). *La responsabilité des personnes sans emploi en question.* La Charte.

Geddes, A. (2003). Migration and the welfare state in Europe. *The Political Quarterly, 74*(s1), 150–162.

Lafleur, J.-M., & Mescoli, E. (2018). Creating undocumented EU migrants through welfare: A conceptualization of undeserving and precarious citizenship. *Sociology, 52*(3), 480–496.

Lafleur, J.-M., & Vintila, D. (2020). *Migration and social protection in Europe and beyond (volume 1): Comparing access to welfare entitlements.* Springer Nature.

Lotta, G., & Pires, R. (2019). Street-level bureaucracy and social inequality. In P. Hupe. (Ed.), *Research handbook on street-level bureaucracy. The ground floor of government in context* (pp. 86–101). Edward Elgar Publishing.

Maynard-Moody, S., & Musheno, M. (2012). Social equities and inequities in practice: Street-level workers as agents and pragmatists. *Public Administration Review, 72*(S1), 16–23.

Raaphorst N., & Groeneveld, S. (2018), Double standards in frontline decision making: A theoretical and empirical exploration. *Administration and Society, 50*(8), 1175–1201.

Raeymaeckers, P., & Dierckx, D. (2013). To work or not to work? The role of the organizational context for social workers' perceptions on activation. *British Journal of Social Work, 43,* 1170–1189.

Sainsbury, D. (2012). *Welfare states and immigrant rights: The politics of inclusion and exclusion.* Oxford University Press.

Thomann, E., & Rapp, C. (2018). Who deserves solidarity? Unequal treatment of immigrants in Swiss welfare policy delivery. *Policy Studies Journal, 46*(3), 531–552.

Van der Leun, J. (2006). Excluding illegal migrants in The Netherlands: Between national policies and local implementation. *West European Politics, 29*(2), 310–326.

CHAPTER 1
CONCEPTUALISING IMMIGRANTS' ACCESS TO SOCIAL ASSISTANCE AND THEIR INTERACTION WITH STREET-LEVEL BUREAUCRATS

ROBERTA PERNA AND HANNE VANDERMEERSCHEN

INTRODUCTION

The nexus between welfare states and migration policies is fundamental to understand the production of distinctive patterns of immigrants' social rights across countries (Lafleur & Vintila, 2020; Sainsbury, 2012). On the one hand, welfare systems are *'powerful institutional forces embodying ideas and practices associated with inclusion, exclusion, membership, belonging, entitlement and identity'* (Geddes, 2003, p. 152), delimiting the legitimate beneficiaries of social protection in a country. On the other hand, migration policies regulate immigrants' differential inclusion in society (Mezzadra & Neilson, 2013), setting the rules and norms that govern immigrants' possibilities to enter and reside in a country, and to participate in its economic, cultural, and political life. The interplay between these policy fields not only produces 'administrative slots' and hierarchies of statuses (for example, recently arrived versus long-term immigrants, refugees versus economic immigrants, documented versus undocumented immigrants), but also structures and gives legitimacy to differentiated entitlements to social protection for different immigrant groups.

Beyond formal entitlements, however, the actual possibility for immigrants to enjoy social rights depends on two key elements: the level of accessibility of welfare provisions, and the degree to which access is subject to bureaucratic discretion. Accordingly, the complex and multidimensional concept of accessibility is key to understand the dynamic interaction between welfare services and beneficiaries, which is influenced by the way in which service provision is designed and organised, by the global structure and logics of the welfare system, as well as by broader policy and societal dynamics.

Moreover, while official policies and programmes define 'migrant categories' more often depending on their residence status and their associated social rights in destination countries, the concrete responsibility to assess immigrants' eligibility to social protection is in the hands of 'street-level bureaucrats' (Lipsky, 1980/2010), the gatekeepers of welfare states. Understanding bureaucrats' daily practices in their encounters with immigrants is fundamental not only to identify the existence of any gaps between formal policies and actual practices, but also to grasp the process of socialisation that immigrants – and recently arrived immigrants in particular – undergo. As representatives of the state (Dubois, 2010), SLBs contribute to establishing the expectations – and self-image – of migrants in relation to that state; they *impact the socialisation of individuals into their role and category as immigrants* (Eule, 2014, p. 5).

This theoretical chapter situates the overall book's contribution to the study of immigrants' access to social protection at the intersection of the literatures on accessibility, street-level bureaucracy, and welfare deservingness. Among other considerations, it reviews the institutional, organisational and individual factors that shape the local provision of social services and the access to them. In doing so, it brings discretionary decisions and moral considerations about welfare deservingness to the fore to understand the dynamics of welfare provision towards immigrant beneficiaries. The different chapters in this book refer to and build upon the theoretical framework presented here, while also bringing additional theoretical inputs that interact more closely with the collected data.

1. WHAT SHOULD WE UNDERSTAND BY 'ACCESSIBLE' WELFARE PROVISIONS?

Accessibility is an important underlying concept in the design of our study on welfare policy practice towards immigrants. Indeed, one of the central research goals is to understand the accessibility of PCSWs based on the experience of newly arrived immigrants and the latter's perception of service delivery. Therefore, at the onset of this book, we need to dwell on the meaning and operationalisation of the concept of accessibility first.

The understanding of accessibility of services and its implication has been largely developed in the context of health care research – with or without a specific focus on immigrant groups and the specific barriers they may face. Although focusing on a different policy domain, borrowing insights from the broader health care literature proved helpful to develop a better understanding of the concept and its analytical scope, which will be further developed in following chapters with regard to the specific experience of newcomer beneficiaries of social welfare.

There is no consensus on a definition of accessibility. According to the World Health Organization (1978, pp. 58–59):

> Accessibility implies the continuing and organised supply of care that is geographically, financially, culturally and functionally within easy reach of the whole community. The care has to be appropriate and adequate in content and amount to satisfy the needs of people and it has to be provided by methods acceptable to them.

Similarly, Rogers, Flowers and Pencheon (1999, p. 866) state, '*Optimal access means providing the right service at the right time in the right place.*'

Across the large variety of definitions of accessibility in the academic literature, it is acknowledged that accessibility is a complex and multidimensional concept and various recurring elements can be identified. In what follows, we will summarise these main ideas.

1.1. 'Accessible services': the interplay between users, service deliverers, and the system

A first important element that can be found in many definitions of accessibility is the idea of a system corresponding to the needs and abilities of users or, put differently, a good 'match' between the system and its clients. This idea was already central in the seminal work of Penchansky and Thomas (1981, p. 128), who define access as:

> A concept representing the degree of 'fit' between the clients and the system. […]. Access is viewed as the general concept which summarises a set of more specific areas of fit between the patient and the health care system.

In other words, accessibility should not be seen as an 'absolute' characteristic of a service, but rather as the result of the interplay between a service on the one hand, and the users on the other, as well as the degree of fit between both. As argued by Russell *et al.* (2013, p. 61), this implies that policy interventions cannot merely target the 'supply side' (the characteristics of the service, 'the system'), but they always need to consider its interplay with the 'demand side' (the characteristics and needs of the population, 'the clients' or beneficiaries) as well.

Second, and closely related to the previous point, accessibility is the result of the interplay between multiple actors at different levels. For example, a distinction to make is between service providers (the so-called 'street level bureaucrats', who are in direct contact with the clients/users/beneficiaries), and the system itself (EXPH, 2016). At the level of service providers, elements such as staff composition (number, socio-economic and demographic characteristics, and so forth), their knowledge, skills, their preconceptions, perceptions, attitudes, and so on play a role in the accessibility of the service itself. Intercultural competences are also part of it. At the level of the system, factors to consider are, for example, the affordability, acceptability, or availability of the service (EXPH, 2016; cf. infra). In addition, other domains or components of society can play a role, such as the general attitude towards foreigners in society. Accessibility is influenced by the way in which service delivery is designed and organised (including the availability of resources, the working conditions, and so forth), by the global structure of the system (including how it was organised and institutionalised over the years, what responsibilities are placed in a same organisation, its public or for-profit nature, and so forth), and by the broader society (considering the impact of the policies of other overlapping or connected fields, the presence or absence of social support in society, and so forth) (Lammertyn, 1998). In sum, this second element shows that what is referred to as the 'system' should be further disentangled; it comprises different components, actors, and levels, interacting with one another.

Looking for applications of this concept in our field of research, a study of Koning and Banting (2013) stands out. These authors analysed forms of social exclusion in terms of welfare/social protection of immigrants in Canada, showing that the legal framework and regulations have a clear impact on accessibility. Koning and Banting mention, among other things, that practices of exclusion are structural in social protection systems due to what they call 'direct disentitlement', that is, not (yet) having the right to certain forms of protection or support as an immigrant compared to other citizens (the authors refer to regulations on the right to work, differences in social security entitlement, and so forth).

Particularly relevant in the context of our study is also the concept of 'administrative burden' (Burden et al., 2012; Moynihan et al., 2014), which can be defined as an individual's experience of policy implementation as onerous (Burden et al., 2012). These are costs that citizens experience when interacting with public administrations, and they have an impact on whether or not citizens can access and use these services. Administrative burden consists of learning costs, psychological costs, and compliance costs. Table 1.1 shows how the various components of administrative burden are defined.

Table 1.1 The components of administrative burden

Type of cost	Application to social policy
Learning costs	Citizens must learn about the programme, whether they are eligible, the nature of benefits, and how to access services
Psychological costs	Citizens face stigma of participating in an unpopular programme, as well as the loss of autonomy and increase in stress arising from program processes
Compliance costs	Citizens must complete applications and re-enrolments, provide documentation of their standing, and avoid or respond to discretionary demands

Source: Moynihan et al. (2014, p. 46)

Based on insights from behavioural economics, Moynihan *et al.* (2014) argue that individuals do not take a rational approach when it comes to these burdens; costs and benefits are not rationally weighed but rather experienced personally and emotionally: '*the impact of burdens depends on how individuals construct the world, not on objective measures of costs and benefits*' (Moynihan *et al.*, 2014, p. 46). For example, 'reasonable' burdens from a policy maker's point of view can have a major impact on citizens. In addition, there is a tendency to choose the present over the future, and avoiding burdens in the present may be preferred over significant benefits in the longer term (for example, not investing in a long application procedure in the present, whereas this would provide benefits in the future). In summary: small burdens can be a big deal, as Moynihan and colleagues phrase it (p. 47). The authors also emphasise that creating or reducing such burdens is often also a political choice; they speak of 'hidden politics' (p. 43), in which meaningful policy changes can take place relatively unnoticed; changes in regulations and the like can pass for technical matters while in fact they concern substantive, political choices concretely impacting on individuals' experience of the concerned system/services.

1.2. The multiple dimensions of accessibility

According to Penchansky and Thomas (1981), who had an important role in the conceptualisation of accessibility, the 'degree of fit' translates into a number of so-called 'areas of fit' (p. 128), or dimensions of access. These different dimensions are availability, accessibility,[1] accommodation,[2] affordability, and acceptability. These dimensions can be found in later work of many other authors, often in a modified or further developed form, and the definitions of the dimensions differ between authors as well (see, for example, Levesque *et al.*, 2013; Roose, 2003; Russell *et al.*, 2013; Thomasevski, 2001; Vandenbroeck & Lazzari, 2004). Russell and colleagues (2013) for example come to seven dimensions: the dimensions of availability, affordability, accommodation, and acceptability are retained, while accessibility (which is a dimension in the work of Penchansky and Thomas, among others) is captured here by timeliness and geography. They also add awareness as an extra dimension. Of particular interest in the approach of Russell and colleagues is the way they integrate the idea of 'degree of fit' (cf. supra) explicitly in their explanation of the different dimensions. Each dimension is explained as the degree of fit between system characteristics and population characteristics. For example, in their study – in the field of health care – geography is described as the fit between the proximity of providers to consumers (system characteristic) and the ease with which the population can transcend this space (population characteristic), while timeliness is explained as the fit between the time until health care can be provided (system characteristic) and the urgency of the need for health care (population characteristic). Similarly, accommodation is to be understood as the fit between the manner in which the supply resources are organised (system characteristic) and the consumers' ability to contact, gain entry to, and navigate the health system (population characteristic) (Russell *et al.*, 2013, p. 64).

It should also be noted that the terminology of degree of fit, or also degree of adjustment, implies that accessibility is a continuum. It is not a black-and-white story, but there are many shades of grey in between. In addition, Ricketts and Goldsmith (2005) underline that access is also a dynamic process *'where there is the potential for individuals and families to learn and modify their behaviour'* (p. 274). The authors speak of 'dynamic axes of learning and adaptation'. Clients or beneficiaries are, in a sense, consumers who learn from experience and act on that experience to choose whether or not to make use of a service. Yet, as argued by the authors, the dynamic nature of access is often not taken into account in research.

1.3. Criticisms and pitfalls in studying accessibility

In the literature on accessibility, many author stress the fact that the quality of the provided service should also be taken into account when studying this process, whereas this element often tends to be omitted (Goddard & Smith, 2001). Moreover, as pointed out by Goddard and Smith, the quality of services provided to users with supposedly identical needs can differ between population groups. In the context of this book, a relevant question is whether the quality of service delivery is different for newly arrived immigrants (or subgroups) compared to other beneficiaries of welfare services.

Second, there are the issues of the 'treatment gap' and that of the needs that remain unmet, which should also be taken into account when studying accessibility. In the context of mental health care, the WHO uses the term 'treatment gap' to denote the gap between the number of people with a particular condition and the number of people treated for it (Kohn *et al.*, 2004). In other words, this means *'the difference between the true prevalence rate and the proportion who receive any kind of treatment'* (Thornicroft & Tansella, 2013, p. 849). As for the concept of 'unmet need', it is a frequently used indicator for access within the health care sector. Both concepts are closely related to the concept of non-take-up of welfare provisions (see f.i. Bargain *et al.*, 2010; Bruckmeier & Wiemers, 2012), which occurs when individuals do not apply for support to which they are entitled, even if it would be of great benefit (see, for example, Observatorium voor Gezondheid en Welzijn Brussel, 2016, on non-take up of social rights within the Brussels region). Exploring and understanding non-take-up is an important element in analysing the accessibility of an organisation.

Third, and more fundamentally, accessibility as a concept also meets with a lot of criticism (see, among others, Coussée & Roets, 2011; De Bisschop, 2010; Van de Walle, 2011, all within a context of youth work). The core idea of these critics is that accessibility does not call into question the service offered itself. The offer is considered as given, and only the question of 'how to lead the target group to that offer' is studied, while the existing offer itself may not be the best possible option for the target group. The existing offer is not value-free. While we agree with this conclusion, in our opinion, this criticism can partly be addressed by – and at the same time it also points to the importance of – including criteria such as acceptability and appropriateness as dimensions of accessibility, and including the 'fit' between the needs of the target group on the one hand, and the offer on the other, in the analysis.

We end this section on the concept of accessibility by presenting an inspirational model of access, provided by Levesque *et al.* (2013), in which these points of concern are well addressed, and that brings together many important elements that have been raised throughout this section.

1.4. An inspirational model

Levesque, Harris and Russel (2013) present an inspirational model of access (in the context of health care), which actually provides a summary of this section on the concept of accessibility, as it comprises most of the key lessons we identified from the literature. The authors actually provide two complementary graphical representations, the first one (Figure 1.1) presented as the definition of access, the second presented as a conceptual framework by the authors, but both being helpful to understand and study the issue of access.

Figure 1.1 Graphical representation of 'access to health care'

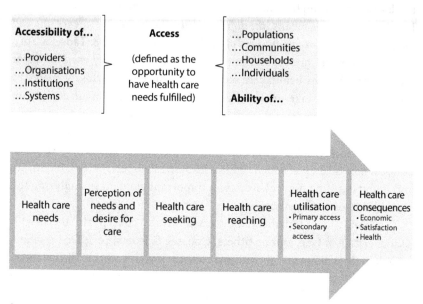

Source: Levesque et al. (2013, p. 4)

This first representation illustrates how access is the result of a degree of fit between the supply and the demand, with both sides consisting of different actors. It acknowledges the different layers in the supply side, such as providers, organisations, and systems. This representation also shows how 'seeking help' – in this model, seeking health care – is the result of a chain of actions, from the emergence/identification of a need to the use and benefit of a service.

However, these different steps require different abilities from the side of the user, and access is also determined by the characteristics of the supply, referring to the dimensions of approachability, acceptability, availability, accommodation, affordability, and appropriateness, as mentioned earlier. These factors are graphically represented in the second model (Figure 1.2), representing the theoretical framework of access to health.

Figure 1.2 Theoretical framework on access to health care

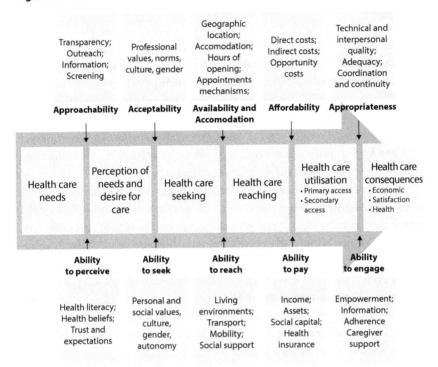

Source: Levesque et al. (2013, p. 5)

Throughout the different chapters of this book this framework will serve as an inspirational tool and an analytical grid to comprehend the data gathered through our research, exploring and analysing the multiple dimensions of service delivery towards newcomer beneficiaries, addressing newcomers' own experience of these services and, ultimately, analysing the degree of fit between welfare institutions and newly arrived migrant users.

In the next section, we delve into the notion of street-level bureaucracies, whose characteristics and dynamics are key to understanding the accessibility of a service in its daily functioning.

2. STREET-LEVEL BUREAUCRACY, WELFARE DESERVINGNESS, AND IMMIGRANTS' ACCESS TO SOCIAL PROVISIONS

Challenging the conventional perspective in public policy studies, which considered policymaking as a hierarchical and linear process following on from clear policy goals to coherent decisions to neutral implementation, Lipsky (1980/2010) coined the concept of 'street-level bureaucracy' (hereafter: SLB) as the common denominator for '*the schools, police and welfare departments, lower courts, legal services offices, and other agencies whose workers interact with and have wide discretion over the dispensation of benefits or the allocation of public sanctions to citizens*' (Lipsky, 1980/2010, p. xi).

A core proposition of Lipsky's approach is that certain structural conditions consistently characterise street-level work: ambiguous policy goals, insufficient resources, and complex demands on the side of users. To deal with these constraints and create a manageable workload, SLBs develop varieties of 'coping mechanisms' that indirectly but significantly shape policy on the ground. These include people-processing techniques aimed at standardising and simplifying the daily job, such as rationing services, routinising daily activities, creaming (give more attention to 'easy' clients), or shifting administrative costs to clients. Hence, SLBs are framed as rational actors, who attempt to cope with structural constraints while improving their working conditions.

Since Lipsky's seminal work, a range of empirical studies have extended the field, turning SLB into a key theme of public administration research (for elaborate overviews, see Brodkin, 2012; Hupe, 2019; Maynard-Moody & Portillo, 2010).

First, the conceptualisation of the nature of discretion has been extended. Rather than a dichotomous phenomenon (absence *versus* presence of discretion), it has been recognised as a graduated scale of freedom of bureaucrats to take binding decisions towards citizens, which range from formal autonomy 'granted' by decision makers to bureaucrats so they can do their jobs, to bureaucrats' informal use of the interstices between rules (Evans & Harris, 2004), thus calling for empirical, situated analyses of street-level work – as we will indeed do in the following parts of this book.

Second, focusing on the institutional and organisational constraints that shape SLBs' daily practices, another stream of research has devoted significant attention to the role played by organisations' management in orienting street-level work, particularly since the introduction of New Public Management principles in public administration (Brodkin, 2011a; Ellis, 2011; Riccucci *et al.*, 2004). High-level managers of public organisations have a significant power in orienting street-level practices, by (re-)interpreting legal rules in regard to organisations' priorities, defining workers' position within the organisation, organising, coordinating and distributing work, and holding prerogatives to reward or penalise staff using formal and informal incentives or sanctions (Brodkin, 2011b; Raeymaeckers & Dierckx, 2013).

Contrasting Lipsky's understanding of street-level practices as determined by structural constraints and work pressure, a third growing body of empirical studies have looked at street-level decisions as the result of a complex, multi-level negotiation process between bureaucrats and claimants (Dubois, 2010). As already mentioned in relation to the concept of 'accessibility' (Section 1.1 of this chapter), workers' individual characteristics, personal values, and professional identities matter to explain street-level dynamics in their encounters with welfare beneficiaries and the structuration of 'accessible services'.

To start with, empirical variation in street-level practices has been analysed in relation to bureaucrats' individual identity markers, such as gender (Saidel & Loscocco, 2005; Wilkins, 2007) and racial and ethnic background (Pitts, 2005; Wilkins & Williams, 2009). Addressing whether these attributes affect the distribution of outputs to claimants who share these same characteristics (the so-called 'active representative bureaucracy'), findings appear inconsistent in this regard. In relation to the dimensions of race and ethnicity, in particular, some studies found that bureaucrats belonging to ethnic minorities use their discretion to reduce the discriminatory treatment claimants of the same groups have historically received from public bureaucracies (Hindera, 1993; Selden, 1997), while others contend that the presence of officials with ethnic minority backgrounds may even increase racial disparities (Wilkins & Williams, 2009).

Focusing on the role of professional identity in service delivery, other studies have revealed how professional values and work ethics constitute a significant driver of discretionary decisions (Evans & Harris, 2004; Ellis, 2011; Taylor & Kelly, 2006). When professionals face tasks that contrast with their codes of conduct, discretion becomes an expression of a professional culture that guides and legitimises workers' practices (Ellis, 2011). From this perspective discretion is understood as a form of resistance against measures and policies that contradict professional ethics (Van der Leun, 2006).

Finally, research has focused on the key role played by bureaucrats' personal views and value judgements in orienting street-level practices. Accordingly, research has demonstrated that caseworkers' attitudes towards the policy goals to be implemented and towards claimants vary empirically and significantly influence street-level work (May & Winter, 2009; Tummers, 2013). Importantly, SLBs' decisions are particularly shaped by their personal beliefs about what is fair and unfair, and about which clients are deserving or undeserving of bureaucrats' concern (Maynard-Moody & Musheno, 2000, 2003, 2012; Zacka, 2017). Developing a 'citizen-agent' perspective (in contrast to Lipsky's 'state-agent' one), SLBs are deemed to first 'make moral judgments about the relative worthiness of the citizen client, and then they use rules, laws, and procedures to help those they consider worthy and punish those they deem unworthy' (Maynard-Moody & Musheno, 2000, p. 351).

Hence, SLBs are far more than mere technocratic and neutral actors implementing policies and delivering services. Rather, the decisions they make at the everyday level of practices contribute to the production of policies and of the normative value system regarding 'who gets what, when and how'.

2.1.   Street-level bureaucracy, welfare provision, and the 'activation turn'

Welfare provision is probably the domain where the SLB perspective has been taken up the most to understand SLBs' decisions and their effects on policy outcomes (for a recent review, see Nothdurfter & Hermans, 2018). Delving into the complexity of social work in practice, this stream of research has expanded since the late 1990s, in concomitance with the shift 'from the welfare to the workfare state' across Europe and the systematic introduction of activation measures in the areas of unemployment and social assistance (Borghi & van Berkel, 2007; Eichhorst et al., 2008; Rice, 2013).[3]

Accordingly, several studies have addressed the ways in which caseworkers deal with the double task of 'counselling' – that is, to support and advise unemployed users in their search for a job by building rapport and trust – and 'enforcing' – that is, to follow-up and eventually constrain beneficiaries' job-search behaviour by threatening them with sanctions (Ellis, 2007; Nothdurfter, 2016; Van Parys, 2016). While some argue for SLBs' capacity to balance these tasks (Van Parys & Struyven, 2018), the majority of empirical contributions contend that activation, which includes monitoring and sanctioning, conflicts with traditional social work repertoires of action (Brodkin & Marston, 2013; Hasenfeld, 2010).

Moreover, research has pointed out the contradictions that this system may create in terms of targeted beneficiaries and real outcomes (Brodkin 2011b; Brodkin & Marston, 2013; Ellis, 2007; Lindsay et al., 2015). The expansion of activation programmes has been associated with increased compulsion and conditionality, raising administrative barriers to access social benefits for the most vulnerable and disadvantaged groups. Moreover, the introduction of New Public Management approaches in public services has been accompanied by the development of performance systems that often evaluate workers' activity according to the achievement of beneficiaries' short-term job outcomes, rather than on the basis of responsiveness towards claimants' individual needs.

Focusing on migrant beneficiaries, Shutes (2011) analysed the impact of a job outcome-oriented performance system on the responsiveness of providers to the needs of unemployed refugees. She found that activation and integration programmes whose performance was assessed on the basis of short-term job outcomes reproduced labour market inequalities experienced by refugees. Accordingly, emphasis on short-term job outcomes conflicted with supporting refugees who were 'harder to help', particularly those with English language needs, and to access employment according to their skills and interests, encouraging caseworkers to focus on placing refugees in easy-to-access, low-skilled, and low-paid jobs. Similarly, Hagelund and Kavli (2009) analysed caseworkers' attempts at negotiating the tension between employment-based and social inclusion considerations in the implementation of a Norwegian activation programme for newly arrived refugees. Distinguishing between two distinct frameworks of interpretation – an activation discourse (which emphasises formal integration in the labour market), and a citizenship discourse (which broadens the meaning of 'participation' to include other forms of engagement) – the authors highlight how caseworkers pursued different goals depending on the frame mobilised. In the case of the former, they insisted on the importance of formulating precise employment goals, with the side effect of reducing activation to mere participation in the labour market. When a citizenship frame was invoked, caseworkers extended the concept of 'participation' to activities other than work; however, this could lead to the definition of too general goals, affecting the employment prospects of recently arrived refugees.[4]

As these studies suggest, New Public Management principles and workfare reforms have altered organisational and bureaucratic practices to emphasise workfare's harsher regulatory features while undermining its potentially enabling ones to the detriment of the most vulnerable welfare claimants, including immigrants.

2.2. SLBs' interactions with migrants and welfare deservingness on the front-line

Acknowledging the changing nature of European welfare states and its impact on street-level practice is fundamental not only to understand the context in which SLBs operate, but also the broader societal logics that orient caseworkers' decisions. These logics supply the *moral* categories SLBs refer to when assessing applicants' deservingness to welfare, and they legitimate bureaucrats' practices on the front-line (Altreiter & Leibetseder, 2015; Garrow & Grusky, 2013; Rice, 2013; Zacka, 2017). As Hasenfeld (2010, p. 97) argues,

> The very action taken on behalf of clients not only represents some form of concrete service, [...] but also confers a moral judgement about their social worth, the causation of their predicament, and the desired outcome.

Accordingly, public attitude research has consistently demonstrated that certain categories of welfare beneficiaries are more likely to receive support from society than others on the grounds of the so-called CARIN criteria (among others, see Kootstra, 2016; Laenen, 2018; van Oorschot, 2006; van Oorschot et al., 2017):

- control (the extent to which a person is responsible for her current situation of need: the less control, the more deserving);
- attitude (the behaviour of the person: the more complying with activation measures, the more deserving);
- reciprocity (the extent to which the person has already contributed to society: the more reciprocation, the more deserving);
- identity (whether the person is part of the 'in-group' or not: the closer to 'us', the more deserving); and
- need (the situation of need of the person: the greater the level of need, the more deserving).

Although welfare deservingness research has largely addressed public opinion, recent SLB studies have provided evidence that street-level decisions concerning welfare eligibility are partially driven by the same characteristics that guide public opinion's perceptions of deservingness (among others, see Adam et al., 2021; De Wilde, 2017; Einstein & Glick, 2017; Jilke & Tummers, 2018; Ratzmann & Sahraoui, 2021a, b). Claimants who are not considered especially needy, who repeatedly violate SLBs' expectations with regard to the willingness to work, who have not contributed enough to society, or who are perceived as not belonging to the 'in-group', are frequently perceived as less worthy of welfare support and more likely to be sanctioned.[5,6]

Endorsing this perspective, recent survey and experimental research has specifically addressed the impact of applicants' migration status, ethnicity, and race on welfare bureaucrats' decisions. For instance, Pedersen and colleagues (2018) found that caseworkers in Danish employment agencies were more likely to recommend sanctions for ethnic minority (Middle-Eastern origin) users than for Danish ones. Similarly, a study on activation policies in Germany indicates that migrants were subject to a more straightforward work-first regime than non-migrants and, more generally, that non-European migrants experienced harsher forms of activation than other applicants (Brussig & Knuth, 2013). Likewise, Hemker and Rink (2017) analysed German welfare offices' responses towards applicants of different ethnic backgrounds. Although they found no significant differences in response rates, non-German applicants received responses of significantly lower quality when compared to natives, potentially deterring the former from applying for benefits.

Theoretically grounded on the welfare deservingness heuristics, case studies and ethnographic research have enriched the understanding of SLBs' moral considerations and discretional decisions in their encounters with migrant claimants. Accordingly, a growing body of empirical studies has highlighted how SLBs may reproduce – or oppose – broader stigmatising discourses on migration and welfare, which may turn into discretionary practices of exclusion – or inclusion – on the front-line of welfare systems (among others, see Andreetta, 2019; Björngren Cuadra & Staaf, 2014; Bruquetas-Callejo, 2014; Dwyer et al., 2019; Lafleur & Mescoli, 2018; Marrow, 2009; Perna, 2019; Ratzmann & Sahraoui, 2021b; Van der Leun, 2006; Ventuyne et al., 2013). As these studies point out, SLBs may mobilise discourses concerning migrants' opportunistic behaviour and 'welfare shopping' strategies to legitimate the adoption of discretionary practices of exclusion, reproducing broader welfare chauvinist arguments (for a recent review on the concept and its determinants, see Careja & Harris, 2022). Simultaneously, they may adapt, bend, circumvent, and even subvert official policies and programmes to grant social benefits for the 'deserving immigrants'. Accordingly, SLBs may choose to make their jobs harder, and even put themselves at risk, to help those immigrants they deem morally deserving, grounding their discretionary decisions on the basis of service-oriented claims and professional ethics.

Overall, these studies reveal the existence of a structural tension between 'care' and 'control' that welfare bureaucrats are often confronted with in their everyday encounters with immigrants. This has resulted from the shift of migration control tasks to welfare state's actors, and the consequent contradictory logics and goals that SLBs have to deal with in their daily job, which originate from the overlapping of social policies and immigration policies (Ataç & Rosenberger, 2019; Lahav & Guiraudon, 2006; Van der Leun, 2006). In such context, discretionary decisions of SLBs – 'an inescapable feature' (Terum et al., 2018, p. 39) and a necessary component of social work for the definition of effective and tailored measures for the most diverse welfare claimants and needs (Tummers & Bekkers, 2014) – inherently carry a risk of differential treatment, or even discrimination, thus reproducing – rather than reducing – social inequalities (Lotta & Pires, 2019; Maynard-Moody & Musheno, 2012; Raaphorst & Groeneveld, 2019; Thomann & Rap, 2018).

CONCLUSION

This chapter summarised key findings from the literature on SLB and welfare institutions and presented important theoretical insights on the accessibility of institutions of care and welfare. Concerning the former, the literature on SLB offers a valuable lens to understand the everyday experiences of social workers as central actors in welfare institutions (Part I and II of this book), as well as the individual, organisational, and institutional factors shaping their decisions and practices on the front-line of welfare systems towards 'un/deserving' applicants. This theoretical perspective also allows to bring to the fore the central – and even determining – role of the social/case worker as experienced by (newly arrived) migrant beneficiaries, which will be addressed in detail from Part III in this book.

Shifting the focus from social workers and their managers only to all actors participating in the 'welfare state', however, it is key to study both the 'supply side' (the actions and perspectives of welfare institutions) and the 'demand side' (the users/beneficiaries, in this case more particularly newly arrived immigrants). The insights offered by the review of the concept of accessibility and its multiple dimensions presented in this chapter, and the emphasis on the idea of a good fit between system and users, allow for a deeper understanding of service provision as the result of the interaction of diverse actors. Moreover, the concept of administrative burden discussed in this chapter appears as an essential analytical tool to understand the issue of non-take up of benefits or services, as our findings based on the perspective of newcomers will reveal (Part III).

Although the 'SLB' and the 'accessibility' approaches stem from different streams in the scientific literature, bringing them together allows building a solid framework to develop a comprehensive empirical analysis of service provision to newly arrived migrant beneficiaries. The chapters in this book will build upon this framework to bring new theoretical and empirical insights on immigrants' access to social assistance and their encounters with street-level bureaucrats.

NOTES

1. Defined as the relationship between the location of supply and the location of clients, taking account of client transportation resources and travel time, distance, and cost.
2. Defined as the relationship between the manner in which the supply resources are organised to accept clients (including appointment systems, hours of operation, walk-in facilities, telephone services) and the clients' ability to accommodate to these factors and the clients' perception of their appropriateness.
3. This shift has also taken place in Belgian PCSW's, as will be discussed in Chapter 2.
4. See Chapter 6 for a discussion of how this applies in the case of activation in Belgian PCSWs.
5. Beyond nationality, race, or ethnicity, studies have emphasised other – yet intertwined – drivers of structural disadvantage, such as language proficiency. For instance, Holzinger (2020) and Adam and colleagues (2021) analysed discriminatory practices in welfare offices in Austria and Switzerland respectively, showing how claimants with limited knowledge of the German language were more frequently excluded from access to social benefits and labour market integration services compared to German-proficient applicants.
6. Interestingly, research has consistently demonstrated that 'invoking reciprocity' represents a key tool that immigrants rely on when claiming access to welfare on the basis of 'earned citizenship' (Kremer, 2016), pointing out their deservingness to access social provisions as a consequence of active participation in the labour market and social security contributions, while criticising entitlement to social rights immediately upon arrival for newly arrived immigrants (Albertini & Semprebon, 2018; Alho & Sippola, 2019; Chauvin & Garcés-Mascarenas, 2014; Lafleur & Mescoli, 2018; Osipovič, 2015).

REFERENCES

Adam, C., Fernández-i-Marín, X., James, O., Manatschal, A., Rapp, C., & Thomann, E. (2021). Differential discrimination against mobile EU citizens: Experimental evidence from bureaucratic choice settings. *Journal of European Public Policy, 28*(5), 742–760.

Albertini, M., & Semprebon, M. (2018). A burden to the welfare state? Expectations of non-EU migrants on welfare support. *Journal of European Social Policy, 28*(5), 501–516.

Alho, R., & Sippola, M. (2019). Estonian migrants' aspiration for social citizenship in Finland: Embracing the Finnish Welfare State and distancing from the 'non-deserving'. *Journal of International Migration and Integration, 20*(2), 341–359.

Altreiter, C., & Leibetseder, B. (2015). Constructing inequality: Deserving and undeserving clients in Austrian social assistance offices. *Journal of Social Policy, 44*(1), 127–145.

Andreetta, S. (2019). Writing for different audiences: Social workers, irregular migrants and fragmented statehood in Belgian welfare bureaucracies. *Journal of Legal Anthropology, 3*(2), 91–110.

Ataç, I., & Rosenberger, S. (2019). Social policies as a tool of migration control [Special Issue]. *Journal of Immigrant & Refugee Studies, 17*(1), 1–10.

Bargain, O., Immervoll, H., & Viitamaki, H. (2010). No claim, no pain: Measuring the non-take-up of social assistance using register data. *Journal of Economic Inequality, 10*(3), 375–395.

Björngren Cuadra, C., & Staaf, A. (2014). Public Social Services' encounters with irregular migrants in Sweden: Amid values of social work and control of immigration. *European Journal of Social Work, 17*(1), 88–103.

Borghi, V., & van Berkel, R. (2007). Individualised service provision in an era of activation and new governance. *International Journal of Sociology and Social Policy, 27*(9/10), 413–424.

Brodkin, E. Z. (2011a). Putting street-level organizations first: New directions for social policy and management research [Special Issue]. *Journal of Public Administration Research and Theory, 21*(2), 1199–1201.

Brodkin, E. Z. (2011b). Policy work: Street-level organizations under new managerialism. *Journal of Public Administration Research and Theory, 21*(2), 1253–1277.

Brodkin, E. Z. (2012). Reflections on street-level bureaucracy: Past, present, and future. *Public Administration Review, 72*(6), 940–949.

Brodkin, E. Z., & Marston, G. (2013). *Work and the welfare state: Street-level organizations and workfare politics.* Georgetown University Press.

Bruckmeier, K., & Wiemers, J. (2012). A new targeting: A new take-up? Non-take up of social assistance in Germany after social policy reforms. *Empir Econ, 43*, 565–580.

Bruquetas-Callejo, M. (2014). *Educational reception in Rotterdam and Barcelona: Policies, practices and gaps* (IMISCOE Research Series). Amsterdam University Press.

Brussig, M., & Knuth, M. (2013). Good intentions and institutional blindness: Migrant populations and the implementation of German activation policy. In E. Z. Brodkyn, & G. Marston (Eds.), *Work and the welfare state. Street level organisations and workfare politics* (pp. 185–208). Georgetown University Press.

Burden, B., Marx-Freere, M., & Soss, J. (2012). The effect of administrative burden on bureaucratic perception of policies: Evidence from election administration. *Public Administration Review, 72*, 741–751.

Careja, R., & Harris, E. (2022). Thirty years of welfare chauvinism research: Findings and challenges. *Journal of European Social Policy, 32*(2), 212–224.

Chauvin, S., & Garcés-Mascareñas, B. (2014). Becoming Less Illegal: Deservingness Frames and Undocumented Migrant Incorporation. *Sociology Compass, 8*, 422-432. https://doi.org/10.1111/soc4.12145

Coussée, F., & Roets, G. (2011). *Vrijetijdsbeleving van kinderen in armoede* [Leisure experiences of children in poverty]. Ghent University.

De Bisschop, A. (2010). Lokale netwerken in perspectief. Belangrijke tendensen in de historiek van armoedebestrijding [Local networks in perspective. Important tendencies in the history of poverty reduction]. *Momenten, 7*, 6–12.

De Wilde, M. (2017). Deservingness in social assistance administrative practice: A factorial survey approach. In W. van Oorschot, F. Roosma, B. Meuleman, & T. Reeskens (Eds.), *The social legitimacy of targeted welfare. Attitudes to welfare deservingness* (pp. 225–240). Edward Elgar Publishing Limited.

Dubois, V. (2010). *The bureaucrat and the poor: Encounters in French welfare offices.* Ashgate.

Dwyer, P. J., Scullion, L., Jones, K. & Stewart, A. (2019). The impact of conditionality on the welfare rights of EU migrants in the UK. *Policy and Politics, 47*(1), 133–150. https://doi.org/10.1332/030557318X15296527346800

Eichhorst, W., Kaufmann, O., & Konle-Seidl, R. (2008). *Bringing the jobless into work? Experiences with activation schemes in Europe and the US.* Springer.

Einstein, K. L., & Glick, D. M. (2017). Does race affect access to government services? An experiment exploring street-level bureaucrats and access to public housing. *American Journal of Political Science, 61*(1), 100–116.

Ellis, K. (2007). Direct payments and social work practice: The significance of 'street-level bureaucracy' in determining eligibility. *The British Journal of Social Work, 37*(3), 405–422.

Ellis, K. (2011). Street-level bureaucracy revisited: The changing face of frontline discretion in adult social care in England. *Social Policy and Administration, 45*(3), 221–244.

Eule, T. G. (2014). *Inside immigration law: Migration management and policy application in Germany.* Routledge.

Evans, T., & Harris, J. (2004). Street-level bureaucracy, social work and the (exaggerated) death of discretion. *British Journal of Social Work, 34*(6), 871–895.

EXPH [Expert Panel on Effective ways of investing in Health] (2016). *Access to health services in the European Union.* European Commission.

Garrow, E. E., & Grusky, O. (2013). Institutional logic and street-level discretion: The case of HIV test counseling. *Journal of Public Administration Research and Theory, 23*(1), 103–131.

Geddes, A. (2003). Migration and the welfare state in Europe. *The Political Quarterly, 74*(s1), 150– 162.

Goddard, M., & Smith, P. (2001). Equity of access to health care services: Theory and evidence from the UK. *Social Science & Medicine, 53,* 1149–1162.

Hagelund, A., & Kavli, H. (2009). If work is out of sight: Activation and citizenship for new refugees. *Journal of European Social Policy, 19*(3), 259–270.

Hasenfeld, Y. (2010) Organizational forms as moral practice: The case of welfare departments. In Hasenfeld, Y. (Ed.), *Human Services as Complex Organizations.* Sage, 97–114.

Hemker, J., & Rink, A. (2017). Multiple dimensions of bureaucratic discrimination: Evidence from German welfare offices. *American Journal of Political Science, 61*(4), 786–803.

Hindera, J. J. (1993). Representative bureaucracy: Further evidence of active representation in the EEOC district office. *Journal of Public Administration Research and Theory, 3*(4), 415–429.

Holzinger, C. (2020). 'We don't worry that much about language': Street-level bureaucracy in the context of linguistic diversity. *Journal of Ethnic and Migration Studies, 46*(9), 1792–1808.

Hupe, P. (2019). *Research handbook on street-level bureaucracy: The ground floor of government in context.* Edward Elgar Publishing.

Jilke, S., & Tummers, L. (2018). Which clients are deserving of help? A theoretical model and experimental test. *Journal of Public Administration Research and Theory, 28*(2), 226–238.

Kohn, R., Saxena, S., Levav, I., & Saraceno, B. (2004). The treatment gap in mental health care. *Bulletin of the World Health Organization, 82*(11), 811–890.

Koning, E. A., & Banting, K. G. (2013). Inequality below the surface: Reviewing immigrants' access to and utilization of five Canadian welfare programs. *Canadian Public Policy, 39*(4), 581–601.

Kootstra, A. (2016). Deserving and undeserving welfare claimants in Britain and the Netherlands: Examining the role of ethnicity and migration status using a vignette experiment. *European Sociological Review, 32*(3), 325–338.

Kremer, M. (2016). Earned citizenship: Labour migrants' views on the welfare state. *Journal of Social Policy, 45*(3), 395–415.

Laenen T. (2018). Do institutions matter? The interplay between income benefit design, popular perceptions, and the social legitimacy of targeted welfare. *Journal of European Social Policy, 28*(1), 4–17.

Lafleur, J.-M., & Mescoli, E. (2018). Creating undocumented EU migrants through welfare: A conceptualization of undeserving and precarious citizenship. *Sociology, 52*(3), 480–496.

Lafleur, J-M., & Vintila, D. (2020) (Eds.) *Migration and Social Protection in Europe and Beyond (Volume 1). Comparing Access to Welfare Entitlements.* IMISCOE Research Series, Springer Cham. https://doi.org/10.1007/978-3-030-51241-5

Lahav, G., & Guiraudon, V. (2006). Actors and venues in immigration control: Closing the gap between political demands and policy outcomes. *West European Politics, 29*(2), 201–223.

Lammertyn, F. (1998). Aspecten van (on)toegankelijkheid: een sociologische duiding [Aspects of (in)accessibility: A sociological interpretation]. In S. Opdebeeck, C. Van Audenhove, & F. Lammertyn (red.), *De toegankelijkheid van de voorzieningen in de welzijns- en gezondheidszorg. Visies uit de praktijk, het onderzoek en het beleid [The accessibility of welfare and health services. Views from practice, research and policy]*. LUCAS, s.l.

Levesque, J.-F., Harris, M. F., & Russell, G. (2013). Patient-centred access to health care: Conceptualizing access at the interface of health systems and populations. *International Journal for Equity in Health, 12*(18), 1–9.

Lindsay, C., Greve, B., Cabras, I., Ellison, N. & Kellett, S. (2015). Assessing the Evidence Base on Health, Employability and the Labour Market – Lessons for Activation in the UK. In C. Lindsay, B. Greve, I. Cabras, N. Ellison and S. Kellett (Eds.), *New Perspectives on Health, Disability, Welfare and the Labour Market*. John Wiley & Sons, 1-23. https://doi.org/10.1002/9781119145486.ch1

Lipksy, M. (1980/2010). *Street-level bureaucracy: Dilemmas of the individual in public services* (30th Anniversary Expanded Edition). Russel Sage Foundation.

Lotta, G., & Pires, R. (2019). Street-level bureaucracy and social inequality. In P. Hupe (Ed.), *Research handbook on street-level bureaucracy: The ground floor of government in context* (pp. 86–101). Edward Elgar Publishing.

Marrow, H. B. (2009). Immigrant bureaucratic incorporation: The dual roles of professional missions and government policies. *American Sociological Review, 74*(5), 756–776.

May, P. J., & Winter, S.C. (200). Politicians, Managers, and Street-Level Bureaucrats: Influences on Policy Implementation. *Journal of Public Administration Research and Theory, 19*(3), 453–476. https://doi.org/10.1093/jopart/mum030

Maynard-Moody, S., & Portillo, S. (2010). Street-level bureaucracy theory. In R. Durant (Ed.), *Oxford Handbook of American Bureaucracy*. Oxford University Press, 252–277.

Maynard-Moody, S., & Musheno, M. (2000). State agent or citizen agent: Two narratives of discretion. *Journal of Public Administration Research and Theory, 10*(2), 329–358.

Maynard-Moody, S., & Musheno, M. (2003). *Cops, teachers, counselors: Narratives of street-level judgment*. University of Michigan Press.

Maynard-Moody, S., & Musheno, M. (2012). Social equities and inequities in practice: Street-level workers as agents and pragmatists. *Public Administration Review, 72*, S16–S23.

Mezzadra, S., & Neilson, B. (2013). *Border as method, or, the multiplication of labour*. Duke University Press.

Moynihan, D., Herd, P., & Harvey, H. (2014). Administrative burden: Learning, psychological, and compliance costs in citizen-state interactions. *Journal of Public Administration Research and Theory, 25*, 43–69.

Nothdurfter, U. (2016). The street-level delivery of activation policies: Constraints and possibilities for a practice of citizenship. *European Journal of Social Work, 19*(3–4), 420–440.

Nothdurfter, U., & Hermans, K. (2018). Meeting (or not) at the street level? A literature review on street-level research in public management, social policy and social work. *International Journal of Social Welfare, 27*(3), 294–304.

Osipovič, D. (2015). Conceptualisations of welfare deservingness by Polish migrants in the UK. *Journal of Social Policy, 44*(4), 729–746.

Pedersen, M. J., Stritch, J. M., & Thuesen, F. (2018). Punishment on the frontlines of public service delivery: Client ethnicity and caseworker sanctioning decisions in a Scandinavian Welfare State. *Journal of Public Administration Research and Theory, 28*(3), 339–354.

Penchansky, R., & Thomas, J. W. (1981). The concept of access.: Definition and relationship to consumer satisfaction. *Medical Care, 19*(2), 127–140.

Perna R. (2019). Bound between care and control: Institutional contradictions and daily practices of healthcare for migrants in an irregular situation in Italy. *Ethnic and Racial Studies, 42*(12), 2103–2123.

Pitts, D. W. (2005). Diversity, representation and performance: Evidence about race and ethnicity in public organizations. *Journal of Public Administration Research and Theory, 15*(4), 615–631.

Raaphorst, N., & Groeneveld, S. (2018). Double standards in frontline decision making: A theoretical and empirical exploration. *Administration & Society, 50*(8), 1175–1201.

Raeymaeckers, P., & Dierckx, D. (2013). To work or not to work? The role of the organizational context for social workers' perceptions on activation. *British Journal of Social Work, 43*(6), 1170–1189.

Ratzmann, N., & Sahraoui, N. (2021a). Conceptualising the role of deservingness in migrants' access to social services. *Social Policy and Society, 20*(3), 440–451.

Ratzmann, N., & Sahraoui, N. (2021b). The (un)deserving migrant? Street-level bordering practices and deservingness in access to social services [Special Issue]. *Social Policy and Society, 20*(3), 436–439.

Riccucci, N. L., Meyers, M. K., & Jun Seop Han, I. L. (2004). The implementation of welfare reform policy: The role of public managers in front-line practices. *Public Administration Review, 64*(4), 438–448.

Rice, D. (2013). Street-level bureaucrats and the welfare state: Toward a micro-institutionalist theory of policy implementation. *Administration & Society, 45*(9), 1038–1062.

Ricketts, T. C., & Goldsmith, L. J. (2005). Access in health services research: The battle of the frameworks. *Nurse Outlook 2005, 53*, 274–280.

Rogers, A., Flowers, J., & Pencheon, D. (1999). Improving access needs a whole systems approach: And it will be important in averting crises in the millennium winter. *BMJ, 319*, 866–867.

Roose, R. (2003). *Participatief werken in de jeugdhulpverlening.* Academia Press.

Russell, D. J., Humphreys, J. S., Ward, B., Chisholm, M., Buykx, P., McGrail, M., & Wakerman, J. (2013). Helping policy-makers address rural health access problems. *Australian Journal of Rural Health, 21*(2), 61–71.

Saidel, J. R., & Loscocco, K. (2005). Agency leaders, gendered institutions, and representative bureaucracy? *Public Administration Review, 65*(2), 158–170.

Sainsbury, D. (2012). *Welfare states and immigrant rights: The politics of inclusion and exclusion.* Oxford University Press.

Saurman, E. (2016). Improving access: Modifying Penchansky and Thomas's theory of access. *Journal of Health Services Research & Policy, 21*(1), 36–39.

Selden, S. C. (1997). Representative Bureaucracy: Examining the Linkage between Passive and Active Representation in the Farmers Home Administration. *The American Review of Public Administration, 27*(1), 22–42. https://doi.org/10.1177/027507409702700103

Shutes, I. (2011). Welfare-to-work and the responsiveness of employment providers to the needs of refugees. *Journal of Social Policy, 40*(3), 557–574.

Taylor, I., & Kelly, J. (2006). Professionals, discretion and public sector reform in the UK: Revisiting Lipsky. *International Journal of Public Sector Management, 19*(7), 629–642.

Terum, L., Torsvik, G., & Overbye, E. (2018). Discrimination against ethnic minorities in activation programme? Evidence from a vignette experiment. *Journal of Social Policy, 47*(1), 39–56.

Thomann, E., & Rapp, C. (2018). Who deserves solidarity? Unequal treatment of immigrants in Swiss welfare policy delivery. *Policy Studies Journal, 46*(3), 531–552.

Thomasevski, K. (2001). *Human rights obligations: Making education available, accessible, acceptable and adaptable. Right to education primers, 3*. Swedish International Development Corporation Agency, Sida.

Thornicroft, G., & Tansella, M. (2013). The balanced care model for global mental health. *Psychological Medicine, 43*, 849–863.

Tummers, L. (2013). *Policy alienation and the power of professionals: Confronting new policies*. Edward Elgar Limited Publishing.

Tummers, L., & Bekkers, V. (2014). Policy implementation, street-level bureaucracy, and the importance of discretion. *Public Management Review, 16*(4), 527–547.

Van de Walle, T. (2011). *Jeugdwerk en sociale uitsluiting. De toegankelijkheidsdiscussie voorbij?* [Youth work and social exclusion. Beyond the accessibility debate?]. Academia Press.

Van der Leun, J. (2006). Excluding illegal migrants in The Netherlands: Between national policies and local implementation. *West European Politics, 29*(2), 310–326.

van Oorschot, W. (2006) Making the difference in social Europe: Deservingness perceptions among citizens of European welfare states. *Journal of European Social Policy, 16*(1), 23–42.

van Oorschot, W., Roosma, F., Meuleman, B., & Reeskens, T. (2017). *The social legitimacy of targeted welfare: Attitudes to welfare deservingness*. Edward Elgar Publishing Limited.

Van Parys, L. (2016). *On the street-level implementation of ambiguous activation policy. How caseworkers reconcile responsibility and autonomy and affect their clients' motivation* [PhD dissertation, KU Leuven].

Van Parys, L., & Struyven, L. (2018) Interaction styles of street-level workers and motivation of clients: A new instrument to assess discretion-as-used in the case of activation of jobseekers. *Public Management Review, 20*(11), 1702–1721.

Vandenbroeck, M., & Lazzari, A. (2014). Accessibility of early childhood education and care: A state of affairs. *European Early Childhood Education Research Journal, 22*(3), 327–335.

Vanthuyne, K., Meloni, F., Ruiz-Casares, M., Ruosseau, C., & Ricard-Guay, A. (2013). Health workers' perceptions of access to care for children and pregnant women with precarious immigration status: Health as a right or a privilege? *Social Science & Medicine, 93*, 78–85.

Wilkins, V. M. (2007). Exploring the causal story: Gender, active representation, and bureaucratic priorities. *Journal of Public Administration Research and Theory, 17*(1), 77–94.

Wilkins, V. M., & Williams, B. N. (2009). Representing blue: Representative bureaucracy and racial profiling in the Latino community. *Administration & Society, 40*(8), 775–798.

World Health Organization (WHO) (1978). *Primary health care: Report of the International Conference on the Primary Health Care*, Alma Ata, 6–12 September, Geneva (Switzerland).

Zacka, B. (2017). *When the State Meets the Street: Public Service and Moral Agency*. Harvard University Press.

CHAPTER 2
SOCIAL ASSISTANCE BUREAUCRACIES AND NEW MIGRANTS: THE BELGIAN CONTEXT

ABRAHAM FRANSSEN

INTRODUCTION

Our research project focuses on the policies and practices of social integration and activation implemented by the PCSW (called OCMW in Dutch, and CPAS in French) with regard to newcomers, that is to say people from non-European foreign nationality, legally present for less than five years on Belgian territory. In the context of the PCSW, a large part of this public of newcomers consists of recognised refugees or people who have been granted subsidiary protection.

In Belgium, the social assistance granted by the PCSW aims to enable everyone to lead a life in conformity with human dignity (Art. 1 of the Organic Law of the PCSW of 1976). This is subsidiary and residual aid, granted as a last resort, on the basis of the state of need, determined individually through a social investigation aimed at assessing the effective needs of the concerned person. This is why the PCSW agencies are considered to be the first and the last safety net, for those who do not have access to other forms of social protection or once the possibilities of applying to other social rights have been exhausted.

In order to clarify the context of this research, it is necessary to (1) elucidate the missions and operating principles of the PCSWs in the multi-level social protection system of Belgium as a federal state; (2) clarify the contours of the category of 'newcomer immigrants'; (3) identify the contemporary shift towards reciprocity of rights and duties and the strengthened notions of activation and individual responsibility in active welfare states; and (4) take into account the diversity of political orientations, organisational cultures, and services of the PCSW.

1.   THE ROLE OF PCSWS IN WELFARE PROVISION

In the complex, multi-level system of social protection and social assistance in Belgium – a federal state consisting of three regions – Flanders, Wallonia, and the Brussels Capital Region – and 581 municipalities, the PCSWs constitute both the first and the last level of social protection and assistance.

Historically, it is the first level, since the current PCSWs are the distant heirs of the public assistance commissions (PACs) set up in 1925 in each Belgian municipality with the mission of 'relieving and preventing misery', as well as 'hospitalising the indigent'. Unlike the charitable societies, the PACs were no longer aimed at the working class, which was now better protected by the rise in wages and the gradual acquisition of social rights, but at people 'in need', that is, those who could not provide for themselves. The relief granted by the PACs remained a favour, however, since they had the sovereignty to assess the state of indigence and the response, in the form of financial aid or aid in kind, to be given to each particular situation.

The gradual construction of the welfare state and the development of the wage society throughout the 20th century, and in particular after the Second World War, led to a decline in the role of social assistance, financed by taxation, in favour of social security, financed by contributions on work and that instituted a system of 'entitlements': rights to unemployment benefits, pension, income replacement and health care, and family allowances. It is through the wage relationship and through the social security rights linked to the status of worker that the integration and protection of people is conceived, particularly that of people from European and non-European immigration. This is the case for Italian, Turkish, and Moroccan workers who arrived in Belgium under the agreements for the import of labour established, with the consent of the social partners, between Belgium and Italy (1948), Spain (1956), Greece (1957), Turkey (1964), and Morocco (1964). At the time, the term 'immigrant workers' was used, not 'newcomers'. As for other categories of the population, recourse to the PAC was only in exceptional situations.

When in 1976 a new law established the PCSWs – which succeeded the former PACs – it affirmed the 'right of everyone to human dignity' and it instituted the principle of a 'minimum means of subsistence' (Minimex) for people who had no other means of subsistence. This Minimex only concerned 8,000 beneficiaries for the whole of Belgium.

The intervention of the PCSWs is indeed conceived as residual, that is, only for people who cannot benefit from social security rights (unemployment or sickness and disability benefits). It aims to complement social security coverage. In this respect, the PCSWs are the last social safety net.

The 1976 legislation also strengthens the autonomy of the PCSWs and their possibilities of action through the creation of service associations. Both institutionally and financially, the PCSWs are therefore local institutions, chaired by an elected municipal official and whose social assistance council – responsible for approving the aid granted to beneficiaries – is also made up of local elected officials, but that must comply with federal legislation, under the control of the Ministry of Social Integration and its inspection services (see also Chapter 7). In terms of their budget, the operating resources and the financial aid granted are mainly financed by the federal government, but part of it is paid for by the municipal budget.

While the initial aim of the PCSWs was to complement and universalise the social protection of the welfare state, it gradually became more and more important and was the subject of specific policies in the name of the fight against poverty. Over the last 40 years, the PCSWs have indeed been confronted with a significant increase and diversification of their public and their beneficiaries. From 8,000 beneficiaries of the Minimex in 1976, the PCSWs have increased to 76,000 beneficiaries of the Social Integration Income in 1996, to 111,000 in 2006, 139,000 in 2016, and 170,000 in 2021. Behind the increase in figures, we can observe a diversification of the profiles of the public receiving assistance from the PCSWs, with a significant proportion of young people under 25 years of age – especially students – plus the arrival of people excluded from the unemployment benefit system, low-income employees (working poor), and self-employed people following bankruptcy.

Among these new groups are newly arrived immigrants – that is, people from outside the European Union (EU) who have obtained a residence permit and are officially and legally established in Belgium, including people who have been granted refugee status following an asylum procedure.

This indicates that the PCSWs have a crucial role to play in ensuring that people who have no other resources have a minimum financial means of existence. In financial terms, the PCSWs can, under certain conditions, grant a social integration income to people who apply for it.

Amounts and conditions of the Social Integration Income

In 2022, the amount of the Social Integration Income is:
- For cohabitants (category 1): € 743,78/month.
  This means that if, for example, the household consists of two people, both of whom are cohabiting Social Integration Income beneficiaries, the household's income will be 2 x € 743.78, or € 1,487.56 in total.
- For single people (people living alone – category 2): € 1,115.67/month.
- For people living with their dependent family (category 3): € 1,507.77/month.
  To be included in this category, one must be the sole head of a family household with at least one unmarried minor child.

In order to be eligible for the right to integration, the applicant must meet the following conditions:
- He or she must have their effective residence in Belgium, which means that they must be habitually and permanently resident on Belgian territory.
- He or she must have Belgian nationality, or fall into one of the following categories: foreigners registered in the population register, recognised refugees or stateless persons.
- He or she must also be of age.
- He or she may not have sufficient resources, nor be able to claim them, nor be in a position to obtain them, either by personal effort or by other means.
- He or she must be willing to work, unless health or equity reasons prevent him or her from doing so.
- Finally, he or she must claim his or her rights to benefits that he or she can receive under Belgian or foreign social legislation. The right to social integration should be considered as the last resort.

Source: Belgian government, 2022

It should also be noted that the right to integration and the granting of a social integration income entails a series of benefits for the beneficiaries, such as guaranteed family benefits, health care insurance, a specific social tariff for electricity, water, and gas supplies, a social telephone tariff, and reductions in training and study fees.

As Jan Vranken points out (2014, p. 142), the 'direct' anti-poverty policy of the PCSWs now compensates for the shortcomings of 'indirect' policies that impact on poverty. By 'indirect' policies, Vranken is referring to the effects of all other policies in the field of employment or social security, but also housing, health care, and so forth.

2.   'NEWCOMERS', AN EMERGING AND FLUCTUATING CATEGORY IN PUBLIC INTEGRATION POLICIES

2.1.   Institutional divisions and resulting categories of migrant groups

The definition of the category of 'newcomers' relates to the different statuses of people of foreign nationality present in Belgium. It is the result of fluctuating institutional divisions and must be understood as an expression of political visions of immigrant integration in Belgium. 'Undocumented immigrants', 'applicants for international protection' ('asylum seekers'), 'recognised refugees', and 'newcomers' are seen as different (socially constructed) categories, but in the course of their migratory trajectory, immigrants can move from one status to another, each status being linked to specific rights, particularly in terms of access to social rights. It is therefore important to clarify these different institutional categories. Moreover, as we will see in what follows, not all 'newcomers' are entitled to an integration income.

The institutional category of 'newcomers' does not include all foreigners present in the country. In particular, it does not include 'undocumented migrants' who are present on the territory illegally and without a residence permit. These may be people who have entered the country illegally after crossing borders and who have never applied for asylum. Some of these people may have been illegally staying in Belgium for many years, as well as being 'transmigrants', that is, people for whom Belgium is a place of passage in their migratory journey, but who, due to the policies of closing the borders, sometimes find themselves permanently 'stuck' on Belgian territory. People considered as illegal residents can also be people whose asylum application has been refused and who have remained on Belgian territory despite an order to leave the territory. They can also be people who entered the territory with a temporary visa (tourist, student, or work visa), but who did not return to their country after the period covered by the visa. It is by nature difficult to estimate the number of 'undocumented' persons on Belgian territory. That said, a figure of approximately 80,000 to 110,000 undocumented migrants in Belgium is regularly mentioned by associations active in this field (Vertongen, 2022). This heterogeneous group of illegal residents, referred to as 'undocumented migrants', is a particularly vulnerable population who do not have the right to social assistance and do not receive any assistance from public social action centres, with the sole exception of emergency medical assistance (EMA). Yet, in certain circumstances and under certain conditions, illegal residents can have their residence regularised on humanitarian or medical grounds, based on an individual examination of their particular situation.

The institutional category of newcomers does not include 'applicants for international protection' (or 'asylum seekers') either who, having fled their country of origin, have submitted an application for protection in a third country under the 1951 Geneva Convention relating to the Status of Refugees and who are waiting for this application to be processed by the competent administration, that is, in Belgium by the Office of the Commissioner General for Refugees and Stateless persons (CGRS). While waiting for the procedure to be completed, asylum seekers are not entitled to financial assistance in principle, but they are entitled to material assistance from the moment they submit their application for asylum and throughout the procedure. Organised by Fedasil (the Belgian federal agency for the reception of asylum seekers) in the form of reception structures, this reception can also be organised by the PSCW in the form of local reception initiatives (LRIs), providing accommodation and social support for asylum seekers. At the end of an asylum procedure, either the asylum application is deemed inadmissible and is rejected, or it is accepted and the person is granted refugee status or subsidiary protection status. As soon as refugee status is recognised, the person is entitled to social integration, provided he or she meets the conditions.

The institutional category of 'newcomers' consists of people who, at the end of a migratory journey, that is, their recognition as refugees or a regularisation procedure, have obtained a residence permit and are officially and legally established in Belgium. This category of public action has been used since the implementation of specific policies dedicated to the integration of newcomers. Indeed, in line with the trend observed in several European states since the end of the 1990s to set up public policies dedicated to the reception or integration of migrants, we witnessed the establishment (and Brussels) of the 'inburgeringtraject' in Flanders since 2003. Similarly, in Wallonia we have seen the emergence of the parcours d'integration pour primo-arrivants since 2013, while in Brussels the BAPA (Bureau d'Accueil pour Primo-Arrivants, or Reception Office for newly arrived immigrants), a French-speaking reception programme for newcomers, has been operationalised since 2016 (Xhardez, 2016). These integration policies have specificities and differences according to the regions.

It should be noted that the category of newcomers as defined by the Walloon, Flemish, and Brussels decrees is not limited to recognised refugees, who constitute only a minority of newcomers (11%). The majority of non-EU newcomers concerned by the integration process are established in Belgium on the basis of a family reunification procedure, for reasons of studies or work contracts. For third-country nationals, family reasons are the main reason for migration (45%). These newcomers on the basis of family reunification are also subject to the obligation to follow an integration programme. However, they are not entitled to apply for and obtain social assistance from the PCSWs.

2.2. Newcomers as beneficiaries of the PCSWs

With the exception of newly arrived immigrants whose residence permit is linked to family reunification, study, or work contract, the newcomers have access to general social services and, in particular, they can claim to benefit from the financial and social assistance provided by the PCSWs under the same conditions as citizens of Belgian nationality. By virtue of their position in the social assistance system in Belgium and by their functions, the PCSW constitutes a key actor whose finalities, functioning, and services need to be studied in order to be able to understand the role and the impact of this institution on the integration of newcomers.

The statistics of the Federal Ministry of Social Integration do not record as such the number of newcomers who receive support from a PCSW. The estimate of the number of newcomers receiving PCSW support can be approached in two ways: on the one hand, by the number of non-EU foreign nationals receiving support; on the other, by the number of people with recognised refugee status receiving support (with the extension that these two categories partially overlap). In April 2022, among the 152,611 recipients of the Social Integration Income, there were 36,114 non-EU foreigners and 12,834 EU foreigners. In terms of geographical distribution, it should be noted that the proportion of non-EU foreigners, recognised refugees, or those under subsidiary protection who apply for PCSW assistance tends to be concentrated in the large urban PCSWs, and within conurbations such as Brussels, to be concentrated in a few PCSWs in particular. In 2022, there were 23,558 recognised refugees or refugees under subsidiary protection among the 152,611 RIS beneficiaries (SPP Social Integration, 2022a).

However, we must be precise that not all newcomers necessarily apply for the social integration income and the social benefits provided by the PCSW, either because they do not comply with the requested conditions of access to the concerned measures or because they are unaware that they could receive it, or because they deliberately decide not to resort to this kind of help or support (non-take-up). Regardless of the reason(s) for not applying – whether they do not need the social service, they do not know about it, or they do not want it – newcomers develop other ways and strategies of survival and integration (Gossiaux *et al.*, 2019), as is also established in Part III of this book. Particularly for some communities, informal, friendly, and family support and information networks play an important role in their integration process (Kasongo, 2015).

In summary, in the complex regime of foreigners' rights:

- Not all foreigners (outside the EU) who have been present on Belgian territory since then are considered as newcomers in the institutional sense. Indeed, undocumented immigrants are not taken into account and are not entitled to social assistance, but only to urgent medical assistance.
- All newcomers (non-EU) are covered by the integration pathway organised by the Regions, but not all newcomers are entitled to social assistance. People who have obtained a temporary residence permit on the basis of family reunification are not entitled to apply for and obtain social assistance from the PCSWs.
- Recognised refugees and refugees under subsidiary protection are new-comers, have the obligation or the possibility to follow an integration programme and are entitled to social assistance from the PCSWs. In practice, it is these recognised refugees who constitute the majority of their 'newcomer' public for the PCSWs.

2.3. PCSWs as part of a public action network

It is also important to specify that the PCSW is not the only institution concerned with the reception and integration of newly arrived immigrants. Depending on the status of the newcomer and their personal and family situation, other institutions such as municipal administrations, public em-ployment and training services, socio-professional integration services, educational institutions, youth support services, and ultimately all the institutions that deliver public policies may be called upon to intervene and impact the trajectories of newcomers (Adam *et al.*, 2018). It will therefore be necessary to take into account the connections and interactions between the various public and associative actors who constitute together the public action network and the 'multi-level' and 'multi-actor' system of governance of migration and integration issues in Belgium (Adam, Martiniello & Rea, 2018; Hondeghem, 2017; Van Heffen, Kickert & Thomassen, 2000) concerned with the issue of reception and integration of newcomers. For example, in terms of schooling, specific reception arrangements for newcomer pupils are organised and in place. Similarly, housing, training, and employment policies and actors are also concerned. However, explicit coordination between the various stakeholders involved in the integration of newcomers is often weak or non-existent. Partnerships and cooperation will be analysed and discussed in more detail in Chapter 4.

3.   THE STRENGTHENED NOTIONS OF ACTIVATION AND INDIVIDUAL RESPONSIBILITY IN ACTIVE WELFARE STATES

In order to understand the impacts and effects of the measures implemented by PCSWs with regard to newcomers, it is also necessary to take into account the characteristics of these policies and their recent evolution. Over the past 20 years, the PCSW as an institution has undergone considerable changes in its missions, organisation, service delivery, socio-political environment, and, as a consequence, in terms of the profiles of its beneficiaries. In Belgium, as in most Western countries, social policies have been characterised by a paradigm shift. The paradigm of 'assisted dependence' has been replaced by a paradigm of 'active participation of each individual', through the implementation of policies of activation, empowerment, and accompaniment, but also increased control of beneficiaries (Vielle *et al.*, 2005).

3.1.   The Right to Social Integration (2002)

Since the law of 2002 on the Right to Social Integration (DIS) (Loi du 26 mai 2002 concernant le Droit à l'Intégration Sociale), the general principle of socio-professional activation is an essential objective and condition of the assistance provided by the PCSW (Dumont, 2012). Social assistance is now underpinned by the purpose of integration through and into employment. As the explanatory memorandum to the 2002 law on the right to social integration explains: *'The right to social integration is guaranteed by the PCSW when it offers a job to a suitable person. In order to receive the living income, the person concerned must indeed be willing to accept a job.'* In French, the PCSWs – *Centre public d'aide sociale* – have been reclassified as *Centre public d'action sociale*, meaning that this institution should not only be the last bulwark against social exclusion, it must above all be a springboard towards 'social integration'. As Daniel Dumont notes, the leitmotif of the DIS law is to move from strictly financial assistance to social action (2012, p. 175).

Almost 20 years after its introduction, the principle of striving for social integration is now commonly accepted and firmly integrated in the functioning of the PCSWs. At the level of political actors and those in charge of PCSW, a broad consensus exists around the idea that the merely granting of social allowances (the PCSW as '*Bancontact* for the poor') does not suffice to counter the phenomenon of social exclusion, which is a multi-dimensional and multi-factorial phenomenon.

3.2. Between employment and social activation

Along the same line, the PCSW have considerably strengthened their
socio-professional integration tools through a wide variety of organisational
forms and professional practices, in particular through the development of
socio-professional integration services and opportunities for the employment of beneficiaries under the Art. 60§7[1] contract. The latter is the main
form of employment used by the PCSW insofar as the institution directly
manages it by acting legally as an employer. Individuals benefiting from
this measure can be working in the PCSWs' own services or at third-party
services or companies. Besides this tool, PCSWs also offer, in principle,
through services devoted to socio-professional integration, a support to job
search and other steps of the path toward the insertion into the labour market,
through individual counselling or other collective projects (see Chapter 6).

If socio-professional integration and employment are the goals that are
put forward through these measures, it should be noted that for a majority
of PCSW users, these goals remain distant, even elusive. For example, in
the Brussels-Capital Region, data for 2013 indicate that only a third of the
beneficiaries of the integration income are the subject of support in terms
of socio-professional integration, and the proportion of those who actually
integrate in employment (mainly and temporarily via Art. 60 jobs) is even
more reduced (Degraef & Franssen, 2013).

> The limits and difficulties in socio-professional integration have led many
> PCSWs to develop specific social activation programs and measures.
> These activation measures imply a greater individualisation in the social
> support of the beneficiaries. The term 'social activation' labelling these
> measures refers to a category that allows for the financing of activities
> implemented by the PCSW through the Participation and Social Activation
> Fund provided for by the SPP Social Integration and it has been the subject
> of circulars setting the criteria of subsidisation. However, a study carried
> out in 2012, commissioned by the SPP Social Integration, highlighted the
> large diversity of social activation practices among PCSWs: 'Under the
> term "social activation", a wide range of activities is offered, ranging from
> training projects such as language and computer courses to activities offered
> in a day centre, socio-cultural activities and recreational, support groups,
> *arbeidszorg*, etc. Volunteering can also be part of it.' (Franssen *et al.*, 2013)

Chapter 6 will go deeper into current practices in the field of social activation
and socio-professional integration in PCSWs. It should also be noted that

in recent years the Federal Ministry of Social Integration has promoted the implementation by the PCSWs of social activation projects specifically aimed at newcomers (SPP Social Integration, 2022b).

Due to the diversity in prospective beneficiaries and services delivered, categorising and orienting users has become a central task of the PCSW (as organisation) and of social workers (as fields agents).

3.3. The Individual Social Integration Project as a central instrument for the action of the PCSW

The individualisation of support which follows from the focus on activation has been further reinforced by the generalisation of the Individual Social Integration Project in the social support and counselling of beneficiaries. Indeed, since September 2016, the PCSW has been required to formalise an Individual Social Integration Project (ISIP, or PIIS in French, GPMI in Dutch) with all beneficiaries of the Social Integration Income, except when considered not desirable/applicable for reasons of equity and health (as appreciated by the PCSW). The ISIP represents a 'contract' established between the PCSW and the beneficiary of the aid, specifying the objectives of social integration (engaging in studies or training, active search for employment, and so forth) pursued by the user with the support of social workers from the PCSW. In other words, the ISIP is presented as a contract that lists the mutual rights and duties of the beneficiary and the competent PCSW. Whereas until 2016 it was only used for young people under 26 who relied on the PCSW, at present it is compulsory for everyone. Non-compliance with the signed contract may result in a penalty of one month's withdrawal of the integration income (three months in case of recurrence).

The establishment of the ISIP ensures a certain formalisation of the objectives and the means implemented in the support of each user. For this reason, accounting for this measure is crucial to analyse PCSWs' practices. Notwithstanding the aim of formalisation of the PIIS, previous research (Franssen *et al.*, 2015) highlighted the large diversity of the types of ISIP (which are generally based on standard models that are personalised: ISIP-project determination, ISIP-study, ISIP-training, ISIP-house search, ISIP-professional insertion) and their implementation. Some PCSWs have thus developed a 'ISIP-newcomer' model, which provides for the monitoring of the 'Integration path' implemented by the Regions.

In several PCSWs, the follow-up of the integration path (*'inburgeringst raject'/'parcours d'intégration'*) becomes an action to be carried out in the framework of the social integration project contracted between the beneficiary and the PCSW. As the CRACS-CBAI[2] annual report 2021 states with regard to the integration path for newcomers:

> The fact that the PCSWs indicate the integration trajectory as an action to be carried out within the framework of the ISIP and thus make the granting of a social integration income conditional on participation in the integration path, creates a form of indirect obligation to follow the integration path. (CBAI-CRACS, 2021, p. 15)

The use of the ISIP contract in practice will be discussed in Chapter 8.

4.   THE DIVERSITY OF POLITICAL ORIENTATIONS, ORGANISATIONAL CULTURES, AND SERVICES OF THE PCSW

The diversity of the practices of the PCSW and their social workers is linked to the autonomy of the PCSW. Despite a trend towards the standardisation of procedures – through the standards set by the PPS Social Integration (POD Maatschappelijke Integratie/SPP Intégration Sociale) and verified by the inspection services, and also through the implementation of IT tools (for example, management of files) – each of the 581 PCSWs in Belgium constitutes a specific organisation,[3] the characteristics of which are determined by several factors, which will be described in the next sections of this chapter.

4.1.   Philosophical differences in the interpretation and application of legal and regulatory frameworks

Despite a convergence on the principle of activation, we observe divergences between PCSWs' actors who place a focus on rights and those who place it more on the duties of the beneficiaries. Practices and discourses oscillate between these two poles. In the first case, the actors tend to limit the requirements of the contractualisation of the integration income, which they consider to be unconditionally due to anyone whose state of need has been proven and objectified by the social enquiry ('enquête sociale'). These PCSWs also tend to implement their integration mechanisms on a voluntary, non-binding basis, taking the demands, needs, and desires of the person as a starting point. In the other case, it is considered that in exchange for the integration income (RIS/Leefloon), the user is bound to a series of legitimate obligations and that, in the event of non-compliance with these conditions, the integration income can be withdrawn (Driessens et al., 2016).

A crucial point influencing the approach of each PCSW concerns the willingness to work of its beneficiaries. As we will see in Chapter 8, this notion is also the subject of divergent interpretations, ranging from strict to broad interpretations and resulting in varying requirements from one PCSW to another, especially in terms of 'proofs' of the implemented measures/received benefits. The same variety of approaches also concerns the assessment of possible exemptions on grounds of 'equity and health'. Some PCSWs establish guidelines in this area while others stress the non-generalisable nature of these criteria, which by definition must be assessed on a case-by-case basis (Driessens *et al.*, 2016).

4.2. The differences in the programmes and measures provided

There are important differences between PCSWs from the point of view of the range of services that can be offered to users and the ways in which the trajectories are organised. While all the PCSWs have a general social service, in accordance with the legal prescription, the vast majority of the PCSWs also have a service for socio-professional integration (sometimes reduced to a part-time staff of social workers and limited to the possibility of offering certain users an Art. 60 job) (see also Chapter 6). The range of services also depends on the resources of the local network and on the partnerships established by the PCSW with other operators (working in specific domains such as alphabetisation and language learning, education/training, and social participation).

In other words, the PCSW functioning has moved gradually, depending on the size of the agency and the local political and organisational dynamics:

1. From a PCSW providing 'a basic service': granting of financial assistance (social integration income, equivalents, one-off social assistance), with more or less regular monitoring by the social worker of reference.

2. To a PCSW proposing/imposing for some of the users to take part to a trajectory in view of socio-professional integration, which may lead, for some of them, to employment – possibly via an Art. 60. Depending on the size and organisational development of the PCSW (presence or not of an offer of 'orientation and project determination', of training, of 'employment tables', and so forth), this support for socio-professional integration can itself be more or less concise or on the contrary complete. It can be slightly differentiated (that is, only consisting in global monitoring) or on the contrary highly specialised (organised in several modules and stages).

3. To PCSWs that have developed a 'holistic', '360 degree' offer and approach, ideally covering all users (those in great social distress as well as those

ready for employment) and the various dimensions of their social and professional integration. Beyond the variety in the range of services, the integration trajectory of users is therefore organised in a variable manner. The degree of systematicity and specialisation of the trajectories varies mainly according to the size of the PCSW and the available staff.

Thus, in some large PCSWs, we can observe a very sequenced and linear organisation of the services or programs, where the user, in the course of their trajectory, passes from one service to another and from one referent to another and where their file, computerised, is accessible to all workers of the agency. Other PCSW agencies opt for much more integrated follow-ups, where the user keeps the same referent throughout their trajectory (Driessens *et al.*, 2016; Degraef & Franssen, 2013). Chapter 4 will go into the organisation of service delivery specifically for newly arrived immigrants.

4.3.   Organisations under pressure from their environment

Finally, we must also take into account the increased pressures weighing on the PCSWs. The PCSWs, and therefore primarily their staff, have experienced a strong intensification of work over the past 20 years, leading to a scarcity of time and resources, among other things (see also Chapter 5). PCSW staff complain, on the one hand, about the lack of time and resources and, on the other, about the lack of recognition of the scale and complexity of their work. Action-research carried out in 2013 with the PCSW agencies of the Brussels Region has already highlighted the pressures of the social, legal, and political environment on their functioning, leading them to be confronted with a *triple 'crisis' and mutation* (Degraef & Franssen, 2013):

1.   **A permanent change in their users and their needs.** The number of beneficiaries of one or another form of social assistance granted by the 581 PCSWs in Belgium has increased very sharply over the past 10 years. The number of beneficiaries of a Social Integration Income increased from approximately 80,000 beneficiaries in 2008 to 144,151 in 2019. Of these, 25,502 integration incomes are allocated to recognised refugees or in subsidiary protection (SPP Social Integration, 2022). In addition to the continuous increase in the number of beneficiaries, their problems and issues are evolving as well: from the residual populations of the 'old poor' to 'new poor' (young people, newcomers, people excluded from unemployment benefits, students, working poor, and so forth), and from the need for assistance and material repairs to 'multiple and

complex' difficulties. These pressures related to the quantity and diversity of the beneficiaries are particularly exacerbated in the context of large cosmopolitan cities.

2. **A change in its mission.** In addition to the changes already mentioned above, the autonomy of the PCSWs have led to the continuous definition of new goals and services (such as housing, energy, young people, social remobilisation, training, citizenship, and culture).

3. **A change in its organisation.** Although local contexts are heterogeneous, the PCSW does not escape the widespread transversal trends and demands of 'managerial modernisation' and the 'new public management' of public action, relying on computerisation and evaluation, constitution of the user as 'client', professionalisation and systematisation of procedures, and so forth (Degraef & Franssen, 2013).

These factors and characteristics are all variables to be taken into account when analysing the practices of PCSW and their actors towards their audiences in general. It will be necessary to analyse whether and how these variables influence the practices with regard to newcomers.

NOTES

1. By working under an Art. 60 contract, the beneficiary can acquire professional experience as well as recover their right/or have access to unemployment. The duration of the contract corresponds in fact to the necessary duration that the beneficiary needs to be entitled to unemployment at the end of their employment contract. One of the criticisms generally leveled at the Art. 60 mechanism is that it does not allow lasting integration into employment.
2. Centre régional d'appui en cohésion sociale (CRACS) – Centre Bruxellois d'action interculturelle (CBAI)
3. Even though in Flanders, the PCSWs are now merged into the municipality.

REFERENCES

Adam, I., Martiniello, M., & Rea, A. (2018). Regional divergence in the integration policy in Belgium: One country, three integration programs, one citizenship law. In A. Rea, E. Bribosia, I. Rorive, & D. Sredanovic (Eds.), *Governing diversity. Migrant Integration and Multiculturalism in North America and Europe* (pp. 235–256). ULB Press.

Belgian Government (2022). *Droit à l'intégration sociale.* https://www.socialsecurity.be/citizen/fr/aide-cpas/aide-financiere/droit-a-l-integration-sociale

Centre régional d'appui en cohesion sociale – Centre Bruxellois d'action interculturelle (CRACS-CBAI) (2022). *L'impact du parcours d'accueil dans l'installation des personnes migrantes à Bruxelles* (Synthèse du rapport de recherche – 2021). CRACS–CBAI.

Degraef, V., & Franssen, A. (2013). *Recherche-action sur l'accompagnement des personnes dans les CPAS bruxellois.* Section CPAS de l'Union des Villes et Communes de la Région de Bruxelles capitale, http://hdl.handle.net/2078.3/147215

Driesssens, K., Franssen, A., Depauw, J., & Mehauden, L. (2016). *Het Geïndividualiseerde Project voor Sociale Integratie: Formaliteit, ondersteunend kader of begeleidingsinstrument?* Annuaire Fédéral de la Pauvreté 2016. https://www.mi-is.be/fr/etudes-publications-statistiques/annuaire-de-la-pauvrete-en-belgique-2016

Dumont, D. (2012). *La responsabilité des personnes sans emploi en question.* La Charte.

Franssen, A., Méhauden, L., Driessens, K., & Depauw, J. (2015). *Le projet individualisé d'intégration sociale. Recherche évaluative et prospective au sein des CPAS belges.* Karel De Grote Hogeschool/Université Saint-Louis. Bruxelles: Rapport de recherche pour le SPP Intégration Sociale.

Franssen, A., Van Dooren, G., Kuppens, J., & Struyven, L. (2013). Les ambivalences de l'activation sociale. In W. Lahaye, I. Pannecoucke, J. Vranken, & R. Van Rossem (Eds.), *Pauvreté en Belgique: annuaire 2013.* (pp. 205-226). Leuven: ACCO.

Gossiaux, A., Mescoli, E., Riviere, M., Petit Jean, M., Bousetta, H., Fallon, C., & Fonder, M. (2019). *Évaluation du parcours d'intégration et du dispositif ISP dédiés aux primo-arrivants en Wallonie* (No. 33). IWEPS. https://www.iweps.be/publication/evaluation-parcours-dintegration-dispositif-isp-dedies-aux-primo-arrivants-wallonie/, 23 Mai 2019.

Hondeghem, A. (2017). De bestuurskunde als discipline. In A. Hondeghem, W. Van Dooren, F. De Rynck, B. Verschuere, & S. Op De Beeck (Eds.), *Handboek bestuurskunde. Organisatie en werking van het openbaar bestuur* (pp. 37–70). Vanden Broele.

Kasongo, P. (2015). L'intégration socioculturelle des migrants d'origine congolaise à Bruxelles dans *Diversités & Citoyennetés, 40–41, 9–12.*

SPP Social Integration (2022a). *Revenu d'intégration (RIS) – refugiés reconnus (RR) et personnes en protection subsidiaire (PS).* https://stat.mi-is.be/fr/dashboard/recognized_refugees?menu=drilldown

SPP Social Integration (2022b). *Outil activation sociale primo-arrivants.* https://www.mi-is.be/fr/outil-activation-sociale-primo-arrivants?page=1

Van Heffen, O., Kickert, W., & Thomassen, J. (2000). Introduction: Multi-level and multi-actor governance. In O. Van Heffen, W. J. M. Kickert, & J. J. A. Thomassen (Eds.), *Governance in Modern Society.* Library of Public Policy and Public Administration, Vol. 4 (pp. 3–11). Springer.

Vertongen, Y. L. (2022). *Pratiques collectives au sein de la mobilisation en faveur de la régularisation des sans-papiers en Belgique (2014-2020). Tactiques, autonomie et articulations entre acteurs avec et sans papiers* (Phd thesis, Université Saint-Louis).

Vielle, P., Pochet, P., & Cassiers, I. (Eds.) (2005). *L'état social actif: vers un changement de paradigme?* PIE Peter Lang.

Vranken, J. (2014). Combattre crise économique en fournissant des efforts d'austérité en politique sociale? In I. Pannecoucke, W. Lahaye, & J. Vranken (Eds.), *Pauvreté en Belgique, annuaire 2014* (pp. 297–322). Academia Press.

Xhardez, C. (2016). The integration of new immigrants in Brussels: An institutional puzzle. *Brussels Studies, 105*(2), 1–20.

CHAPTER 3
APPLYING MIXED-METHOD DESIGN IN THE STUDY OF IMMIGRANT SOCIAL PROTECTION

ELSA MESCOLI, ANGELIKI KONSTANTINIDOU, MARIJE REIDSMA
AND JÉRÉMY MANDIN

In order to study immigrants' access to social assistance and the functioning of welfare policies and related decision-making processes on the ground, we adopted a mixed-methods design, combining both qualitative and quantitative research tools, as well as accounting for the perspective of a variety of stakeholders and social actors involved. Mixed methods have proved efficiency as the weaknesses of each single method could be compensated by 'the counter-balancing strengths of another'; moreover, '[m]ixed methods can serve a transformative purpose for vulnerable populations' (Stewart *et al.*, 2008, p. 1407; also see Beiser & Stewart, 2005; Creswell, 2003; Tashakkori & Teddlie, 2003). This is particularly relevant in policy evaluation research, which aims to assess the effect of measures implemented on the ground in relation to the experience of specific groups – which is the case for our study. Combining data collected through a mixed-methods approach – particularly through quantitative and qualitative research tools – can serve a range of analytical purposes, including triangulating data; generating complementary data; expanding data (Greene *et al.*, 1989). We considered these objectives throughout our analysis. First, while the low response rate in the quantitative part does not allow us to treat those results as equal to the qualitative findings, their comparison still helped in gaining a better understanding of our research results. Moreover, the complementarity of the applied research tools allowed us to assess different components of our object of study and aims, as well as to complexify the interpretation of the collected data – without necessarily looking for convergences on each of the assessed topics. Lastly, the use of mixed methods led to extend the scope of our research, which is beneficial for both contextual policy evaluation and for contributing to the theoretical literature.

The overall approach of our research included three main phases: the qualitative study of welfare practices through interviews with PCSWs' staff members, the administration of a complementary online survey to chief social workers of PCSWs, and the interviews with immigrant beneficiaries. In this chapter, we will provide details on how the data have been collected, processed, and analysed within this methodological framework.

1.   A QUALITATIVE STUDY OF WELFARE POLICIES AND PRACTICES ON THE GROUND

The first phase of the research consisted of identifying relevant case studies for the qualitative approach, that is, a series of municipalities from which to study the functioning of the PCSWs from the point of view of staff members (presidents, directors and other managers, social workers, and other profiles of field workers). The objective of this phase of the research was to study welfare policies and practices as they manifest themselves on the ground through the decisions and actions of the institutions' representatives and agents. With the aim of setting a panel of diverse but comparable cases whose study would allow us to have a comprehensive overview of the functioning of welfare system toward newcomers in Belgium, we considered a set of criteria that reflect 'the nature of the case, historical background, physical setting, and other institutional and political contextual factors' (Stake, 1998; Stake, 1995; cited in Hyett et al., 2014, p. 2) that may influence social assistance practices and the access to them. Indeed, four main factors may have a relevant impact on the implementation of welfare policies targeting immigrants, that are: (1) the level of pressure on social welfare agencies; (2) the presence of immigrant populations and newcomer beneficiaries of welfare service in particular in the concerned municipality; (3) the political orientation of the local government; (4) the demographic and environmental characteristics of the context. As already mentioned in Chapter 1, these contextual and organisational elements also influence the ways in which SLB and agents' discretion operate (Hupe & Buffat, 2014; Maynard-Moody & Portillo, 2010; Berman, 1978). Taking this framework into account, we considered the following data (reference year 2019) to choose our case studies: number of inhabitants, population density and environment (rural, semi-rural, urban); political orientation (main governing party or coalition); number of social incomes per 1,000 inhabitants delivered to refugees or holders of subsidiary protection status;[1] overall number of social incomes delivered per 1,000 inhabitants; and overall number of ISIP (Individualised Social Integration Project) set per 1,000 inhabitants.[2] These criteria were identified as substantive – that is, possibly leading to variations (Swanbord, 2010) with regard to our object of study.

Through a comparison of the collected figures and with the aim of studying the practices of PCSWs in contexts with distinct characteristics, we have selected a set of municipalities across the three regions whose names will not be mentioned for confidentiality reasons.[3] Once completed the case studies selection, we prepared topic lists and interview grids adapted to different profiles of PCSWs' staff members. Overall, in the interviews with presidents, directors, managers, and members of the local social council/committee (see Chapter 7) we focused on the domains of service delivery to newly arrived immigrants, the organisation of service delivery, the legal framework, the conditions of access to rights and social activation, the monitoring of the social services, the functioning of the decision-making process, and additional information concerning the context. These themes were also addressed in the interviews with the social workers in order to explore their own perspective on the issues involved, as well as additional questions about their day-to-day experience, degree of autonomy, and the exercise of discretionary power. Exploring these issues was functional to address our research aims, namely – as mentioned in the introduction of this volume – mapping practices regarding the granting of rights and social activation interventions targeting newly arrived immigrants; shedding light on the factors influencing social workers' choices and decisions regarding social benefits and social activation targeting newcomers; analysing the accessibility of social welfare for newcomers and of their experience with a European welfare state administration.

In this phase of the research, we faced two main challenges. First, the access to PCSWs was in some cases particularly problematic, due to the work overload of the agencies as well as to the additional difficulties brought by the COVID-19 crisis and the changes in working arrangements that this has brought about.[4] However, all selected PCSWs were eventually involved in the study, and a total number of 197 staff members across the three regions have been interviewed, including 81 social workers, 57 managers and directors, 38 presidents and committee members, and 21 other staff members (educators, reception agents, project coordinators, lawyers, and so forth).[5] The second main difficulty we encountered in the fieldwork with PCSW staff members is that very often our research participants – unless they only work with immigrant beneficiaries, that is, in the case of social workers engaged in specialised services –[6] emphasised that the functioning of the PCSWs and their work within these was not aimed at immigrants in particular, but operated on an equal basis with all beneficiaries. While the practical and conceptual rationale and scope of this approach will be discussed later in this book (Chapters 4 and 8), it is worth mentioning that this issue has been managed throughout the fieldwork activities through a set of research strategies. First, during interviews with all staff members, we paid attention to keeping the focus on immigrant beneficiaries, by specifying our questions and follow-up questions. Second, in the analysis of the collected material, we took this issue into account and distinguished between data concerning all beneficiary profiles, *including* immigrant and newcomer beneficiaries, and data concerning *only* immigrant and newcomer beneficiaries. The articulation of these two sets of data allowed us to analyse the functioning of the PCSWs under study and the work of their staff members with regard to all beneficiaries and the beneficiaries targeted by our study more particularly.

Throughout our fieldwork activity we considered research interviews as interactions and encounters between individuals – the researchers and the other research participants, discussing in more or less formal ways on a given topic. The use of an interview guide enabled the researchers to remind themselves of the main themes of the object of study, without, however, 'closing' the possibility of interactions outside pre-programmed standards and without putting at risk the discussion dynamic (Delaleu *et al.*, 1983). Indeed, the interviews also allowed the researchers to get more familiar with the 'local culture' of PCSWs, their internal functioning, and communication rules. The 'recursive' aspect of the interviews (Olivier de Sardan, 1995) consisted of formulating new questions based on what had been said in order to go deeper into the subject.

The qualitative approach to the study of PCSWs' practices towards immigrant beneficiaries adopted in our research also included some initiative of ethnographic observation. As highlighted by Brodkin (2017, p. 131):

> [E]thnographic approaches to political research treat human behaviour and thought not as phenomena that develop in a vacuum, but as phenomena that develop in real world settings. [...] ethnographic methods offer strategies for studying people as fully-constituted human beings interacting with the institutions and organisations in which they are embedded.

This methodological tool applied to public services and officials gives the opportunity to observe power relations, as well as 'the rules of the game' (Mascia & Odasso, 2015) performing concretely on the ground. Situational practices are observed (Dubois, 2010), revealing aspects on how the records are managed empirically, in relation with the institutional environment and the law framework. This allows a realistic ground-level view of policies (Dubois, 2009). Indeed, in the founding literature on SLB itself, public policy is the result of the combination of decision-making rules and practices and individuals' attitudes on the ground. Observation also allows attention to be paid to the way in which the relationship between agents and beneficiaries develops, in terms of mutual care and empathy, the tone used, body language, the way the setting is arranged, and so on. During the observation activities, it was also possible to gather 'paper' (Andreetta, 2019) relevant for the analysis, more particularly canvas and guidelines concerning the social enquiry carried out by social workers and the conditions to access the rights (see Chapter 8), which PCSWs' staff would not necessarily transmit in other ways.

In the light of these elements, observations allowed the researchers to gather data to complement those collected through interviews. Indeed, because of the impact of the measures to deal with the COVID-19 health crisis as well as the agents' workload, it was not possible to conduct systematic observations in all PCSWs and in all regions. Therefore, interviews remained the main source of data, that could be enriched by material gathered through observations in some social services among the selected case studies.

The study of the qualitative data was carried out through adopting an inductive grounded theory methodology (Glaser & Strauss, 1967; Bryant & Charmaz, 2011). The coding and analysis of the collected data was developed based on analytical units emerging from the field, put into perspective with the topic lists developed before the fieldwork activity and built on the literature review. Moreover, regional data were compared to highlight – when possible – convergences and divergences, and to describe the overall functioning of PCSWs with regard to immigrant beneficiaries as well as the role of social workers and other staff members within it. The main analytical issues raised by the fieldwork are reflected in the structure of this book.

2.   A QUANTITATIVE APPROACH TO WELFARE SERVICE DELIVERY

The preliminary results of the qualitative research targeting the PCSWs were also helpful to elaborate the survey aimed at collecting quantitative data – the second phase of our research. More particularly, this survey was administrated online to chief social workers of all Belgian PCSWs. In order to ensure comparability across the PCSWs under analysis, the core questionnaire included mainly closed-ended questions along with a few open-ended answer categories to capture the wide variety of possible responses. The questions – parallel to the topic list of the qualitative interviews – concerned the organisation of service delivery with regard to immigrant beneficiaries, the management of agency human resources, the implementation of labour market activation policies and practices, the decision-making process on immigrant beneficiaries' demands, language policies, and cooperation activities. The questions were aimed at getting a broader overview of the functioning of PCSWs in the three regions with regard to these topics – complementing the qualitative findings (see above).

Concerning the finer grains of the survey design, the sample selection consisted of the whole population the project targeted (Hibberts *et al.*, 2012), mainly the chief social workers of all PCSWs in Belgium. We opted for an online survey and not another survey media (such as face-to-face interviews, written interviews) not only due to the significantly lower costs (in terms of administration, personnel, and the usage of paper questionnaires) that online tools entail but also for avoiding bias caused by the interviewers to the responders to give 'socially desirable' answers (Neuman, 2012). Furthermore, the online survey mode gives the participants a safe space to reply honestly, at their own pace, and its accessible online modality facilitates the participation of the respondents.

In this context, the ethical aspects of the survey should also be taken into account. To increase the response rate of the survey, the survey contained a well-knitted framework of Survey Research Ethics (SRE) (Glasgow, 2005; Oldendick, 2012). The SRE included a pre-form to participate in the survey, the latter not only including the project aims and description to familiarise the participants with the project, but also a detailed explanation on the anonymisation and data treatment. Furthermore, the SRE included clauses of confidentiality, and a space to declare the consent to participate (Oldendick, 2012). In addition, the SRE included a clause that the respondents had the option to 'drop' from the survey should they have wished. While the survey was designed in English, in order to make it accessible to all survey participants, it has been translated into two of the official languages of Belgium (French and Dutch). The survey has also been adapted to the different Belgian regions (Brussels, Flanders, Wallonia, and also to the German-speaking community). Lastly, in order to ensure the completion of the surveys, the respondents' progress has been followed up via the online platform in an anonymous manner and reminders have been sent two weeks and seven weeks after the survey has been launched to those who had not yet started or completed the survey.

The survey has been programmed with LimeSurvey. It was launched on 22 March 2022 and a first reminder was sent on 5 April 2022. Due to a low response rate – in part related to the high work pressure in the PCSWs following the war in Ukraine and subsequent influx of Ukrainian refugees – one month after the initial launch of the survey the two Belgian organisations connecting all municipalities (for Wallonia the Union des Villes et Communes de Wallonie and for Flanders the Vereniging van Vlaamse Steden en Gemeenten) and the Public Planning Service for Social Integration (POD MI/SPP IS) have been contacted in order to make an additional call among the PCSWs to participate by addressing the survey in their respective newsletters.

In light of these extra calls, a second reminder has been sent on 9 May 2022. The survey was closed on 4 July 2022. The survey was sent to 542 PCSWs and was filled out completely by 99 chief social workers, thus giving us a response rate of 18%.

Due to the relatively low response rate, a short response analysis was carried out in order to obtain a better view of which PCSWs participated and to verify their representativeness in light of the entire population. As for the regions, the percentage of participants from Flanders and Wallonia reflected well the population distribution. Brussels, however, was slightly underrepresented. The analysis further showed that relatively more PCSWs in municipalities with a higher number of beneficiaries with a non-EU-background or refugee status have participated than could have been expected based on the overall population numbers. This could be explained by the relevance the topic of the survey has for those PCSWs. Indeed, a few PCSWs informed the researchers they would not participate in the survey as they simply did not have any newcomer beneficiaries in their PCSW the past years. Also, PCSWs in municipalities with a high median income and in small municipalities in terms of the number of inhabitants are underrepresented. This last finding is not surprising, as many immigrants tend to reside in larger cities.[7]

The data has been analysed using the statistical software package SPSS. The data gathered through the quantitative research activity were considered in the overall analysis and are reported in this book where they complement the findings of the qualitative fieldwork. While the survey results cannot confirm the qualitative research findings, they may 'contribute to greater confidence in the generalisability of results' (Jick, 1979, p. 604).

3.   IN-DEPTH INTERVIEWS OF IMMIGRANT BENEFICIARIES OF PCSWS

Another crucial element of the overall research approach adopted, which partly overlapped – temporally speaking – with the other two phases of the research (the qualitative interviews of PCSWs' staff members and the quantitative survey), was to conduct semi-structured in-depth interviews with newcomer beneficiaries. As outlined in the theoretical chapter of this book, extensive research has been conducted on welfare policies and their implementation on the ground by studying bureaucracy at street level; however, this should require taking into account the perspective of immigrant beneficiaries themselves (Raeymaeckers & Dierckx, 2013) – who are not seen as passive targets of social programmes. In our research, we interviewed a total number of 87 newly arrived immigrants,[8] beneficiaries of PCSWs. More particularly: 32 respondents in Wallonia, 21 respondents in Flanders, 34 respondents in Brussels, 32 women, 54 men, 1 family, aged from 21 to about 50 years old, and from diverse origins including Palestine, Syria, Brazil, Salvador, Turkey, Guinea, Eritrea, Burundi, Somalia, Afghanistan, Vietnam, Morocco, Lebanon, Yemen, Cameroon, Guinea Conakry, and Soudan. We sought to collect data from different profiles of people in terms of their migration trajectory, personal characteristics, employment status, and level of education and command of one of the Belgian national languages. The heterogeneity of our sample responds to our objective of exemplarity rather than statistical representativeness (Pischerit *et al.*, 2019), that is, our wish to reflect the variety of profiles of immigrant beneficiaries of Belgian PCSWs, the experiences they may have with social services and their representations and expectations concerning welfare assistance (Albertini & Semprebon, 2018). Moreover, through diversifying our sample, we aimed at avoiding overemphasising ethnicity and overlooking that 'empirical phenomena might be evoked by other boundaries, such as class or gender, which often intersect with ethnicity' (Barglowski, 2018, p. 152; also see Amelina & Faist, 2012).

The sample was also diversified in terms of the geographical location of the newcomers. In each region, three main locations were chosen – from the case studies of the research phase with the PCSWs – to gather the beneficiaries participating in the research.[9] The rationale behind this selection was to consider the experience of beneficiaries in relation with certain types of PCSWs, that is, smaller/bigger, located in rural/urban environment, managing a big/small number of social welfare demands, working with big/small numbers of newcomer beneficiaries – which were the criteria also used to identify the main case studies of the research, as explained above. We applied these criteria to identify relevant locations among our case studies where to contact newcomer beneficiaries, too. It is important to note that this rational selection effort on the part of the research team does not necessarily reflect the complexity and diversity of respondents' life experiences. Indeed, many of the respondents who were associated with a location in our selection have been involved with services in different places since their arrival in Belgium. This characteristic of our sample informs our analysis as (1) the diversity of experiences with different PCSWs (from LRIs to the city of residence) characterises the trajectory of many respondents and (2) it impacts the way newcomers make sense of their experience of the PCSW by allowing them to compare between different institutions and settings.

With regard to the access to the field, two main entry points were used. First, respondents have been recruited through regional centres for integration and (local) associations working with immigrants. We tried to avoid as much as possible the recruitment of respondents directly through PCSWs' services because of the bias regarding the possible selection of specific beneficiary profiles by the officers, and to avoid the risk that they would perceive our research activity as an evaluation of their own work by interviewing the beneficiaries they were in contact with.[10] Moreover, going through institutions not related to the PCSW appeared as a way not to be identified by the respondents as 'working with the PCSW' and to make them more comfortable to share their experience without perceiving the fear of impact on their situation as beneficiaries. Once in contact with the institution, the selection of respondents was generally done by the institution itself on the basis of the criteria communicated by the researcher. Typically, a worker of the institution would introduce the research to some of the institution's beneficiaries and ask them if they would agree to be contacted by the researcher. A list of possible contacts would then be communicated to the researcher. This procedure had some advantages. First, the respondents were introduced to the research in a context and by a person that they knew, which would tend to reassure them about the seriousness of the project. Second, as the project had been presented to the beneficiaries beforehand, contact with the researcher was facilitated. However, this procedure also had potential limitations. For example, as the selection of potential contacts was often carried out by employees of the institution, the researcher had limited control over the contacts provided and limited means to check that the selection criteria were in line with the research objectives. On some occasions, the interview revealed that the interlocutor selected by the institution was not fitting with the criteria of selection of the sample. Another element was that regional centres for integration or non-governmental organisations (NGOs) are not neutral actors. They operate within their own institutional logic and their workers are caught in a relation of mutual obligation with their public. Thus, the access to contacts often required to be negotiated with the institutions. For example, some institutions requested payment for the respondents (which could not be implemented). In another case, the researcher had to clarify and negotiate interview protocols after the staff of one institution expressed concerns that some interviews were being conducted outside their premises. Finally, not all of the potential participants selected by the institutions were responsive to the researchers' attempt to establish contact. The potential contacts were usually reached by email, telephone, WhatsApp message, or posts[11] on other social networks, either in a common language or – when deemed necessary – in the contact's native language.

Complementary strategies to enter the field included the use of the researcher's social network to identify possible respondents. This was particularly relevant in Brussels, where the researchers had already been in contact with groups of newcomers or volunteers and host families who were therefore contacted directly. This strategy had the advantage of finding contacts through already established relationships of trust, as well as of being put in touch with newcomer beneficiaries who had already developed some resources to understand and cope with the procedures and requirements of the PCSW. We also tried to identify some respondents through snow-ball sampling (Parker et al., 2019), although this was rarely fruitful. Indeed, potential respondents were sometimes reluctant to participate, fearing that the interview would negatively affect their future relationship with the PCSW. For those who agreed to participate, it was because their reluctance was alleviated by talking to other beneficiaries who had already been interviewed, and who reassured them that confidentiality would be respected throughout the process.

We conducted in-depth semi-directive interviews using a topic list prepared on the basis of our thematic focuses as well as the preliminary results of the research phase with PCSWs' staff members. The topic list included the life history and migration trajectory of the interviewee, the access to and use of welfare service delivery, a set of specific dimensions of accessibility (availability, timeliness, acceptability, and so forth), and in some cases the access to and use of other organisations, and some contextual factors (including the perception of the socio-cultural and political environment). One of the challenges met during the interviews was that the categories and terminology used by PCSWs' social workers to describe their institution – and that we included in our topic list – were not necessarily used by newcomer beneficiaries who developed their own understanding and vocabulary. While sometimes making it difficult for the researcher to identify exactly the type of services or the type of procedures that the respondent was referring to, this also gave precious information about how newcomer beneficiaries made sense of their experience of PCSW.

As some of the respondents did not have sufficient knowledge or did not feel comfortable enough in speaking a common language, interpreters have been used. In most cases, these were formal interpreters requested by the researcher (and thus no relation was present between the respondent and the interpreter), while in some other cases the research participants arranged their own interpreter. As for the latter, even though it could not be /.have been avoided that the interpreters (albeit in a very minimal number of interviews) intervened in the interview, in the case of a misunderstanding or unclarity they could also bring some clarification to the conversation as they were aware of the situation the respondent was in at the time or had been in in the past.

Concerning the analysis of the data gathered through the interviews with newcomer beneficiaries, it has been developed – as for the content of the qualitative research within the PCSWs – based on the pre-identified topics as well as on empirically grounded categories of analysis. We have paid particular attention to aspects related to the specificity of our target group and the thematic focus of this research – besides the elements of the experience of newcomer beneficiaries with welfare institutions in Belgium that are similar to those of other beneficiaries, according to the literature. The analysis of this material is included in the third part of this book, while in the conclusion we bring together all the data collected in order to elaborate a transversal reasoning on the complexity of the process studied.

NOTES

1. This figure allowed us to identify PCSWs that work 'at least' with this profile of newcomers.
2. All these figures were retrieved from institutional statistics databases.
3. This also applies to all research participants, who were informed about the content and objectives of our study and were granted anonymity. Their consent to participate in the research was obtained orally and recorded at the beginning of the interviews. Throughout the book, they are referenced by codes including region, city, interviewee's role, and date of interview.
4. The main fieldwork activities of the research project were conducted from November 2020 to January 2022.
5. While we selected the categories of respondents we wished to interview (presidents, directors, managers, social workers – more particularly those working with immigrants – and agents involved in the implementation of activation policies), we did not necessarily select the respondents themselves, that is, we interviewed those – for example, among social workers, the most numerous category – who were available to meet us.
6. However, the procedures and decision-making process for the granting of social benefit are described as operating in specialised services in the same way as in other general social services.
7. See https://www.myria.be/files/2020_JVMIG_-_Migratie_in_Belgi%C3%AB.pdf, accessed on 8 August 2022.
8. We considered people from third countries whose residence permit was five years old or less (in most cases, these were in fact people living in Belgium for less than five years).
9. Due to challenges in finding research participants in Flanders, the initial three main locations have been expanded to six. All of the new locations were part of the case studies at the PCSWs.
10. Despite this initial strategy, going through the PCSWs' services was necessary in a limited number of locations where local NGOs or organisations were not responsive to our demand of contacts.
11. This strategy allowed participants to contact the researcher directly without necessarily going through third parties or feeling 'obliged' to participate to please local friends or associations/institutions.

REFERENCES

Albertini, M., & Semprebon, M. (2018). A burden to the welfare state? Expectations of non-EU migrants on welfare support. *Journal of European Social Policy, 28*(5), 501–516.

Amelina, A., & Faist, T. (2012). De-naturalizing the national in research methodologies: Key concepts of transnational studies in migration. *Ethnic and Racial Studies, 35*(10), 1707–1724.

Andreetta, S. (2019). Writing for different audiences: Social workers, irregular migrants and fragmented statehood in Belgian welfare bureaucracies. *Journal of Legal Anthropology, 3*(2), 91–110.

Barglowski, K. (2018). Where, what and whom to study? Principles, guidelines and empirical examples of case selection and sampling in migration research. In R. Zapata-Barrero, & E. Yalaz (Eds.), *Qualitative research in European migration studies* (pp. 151–181). Springer, Cham.

Beiser, M., & Stewart, M. (2005). Reducing health disparities: A priority for Canada. *Canadian Journal of Public Health, 96*(2), S4–S7.

Bierman, P. (1978). *The study of macro and micro implementation of social policy.* RAND Corporation.

Brodkin, E. Z. (2017). The ethnographic turn in political science: Reflections on the state of the art. *Political Science & Politics, 50*(1), 131–134. http://dx.doi.org/10.1017/S1049096516002298

Bryant, A., & Charmaz, K. (Eds.) (2011). *The SAGE handbook of grounded theory* (Paperback edition). Sage Publications.

Creswell, J. W. (2003). *Research design: Qualitative, quantitative, and mixed methods approaches.* Sage Publications.

Delaleu, D., Jacob, J. P., & Sabelli, F. (1983). *Eléments d'enquête anthropologique: l'enquête-sondage en milieu rural.* Institut d'Ethnologie.

Dubois, V. (2009). Towards a critical policy ethnography: Lessons from fieldwork on welfare control in France. *Critical Policy Studies, 3*(2), 221–239.

Dubois, V. (2010). Politiques au guichet, politiques du guichet. In O. Borraz, & V. Guiraudon (Eds.), *Politiques publiques 2. Des politiques pour changer la société ?* (pp. 265–268). Presses de Sciences-po.

Fielding, N. (1993). Qualitative interviewing. In N. Gilbert (Ed.), *Researching social life* (pp. 135–136). Sage.

Glaser, B. G. & Strauss, A. L. (1967). *The discovery of grounded theory: Strategies for qualitative research.* Aldine.

Glasgow, P. A. (2005). *Fundamentals of survey research.* Virginia, Washington.

Greene, J. C., Caracelli, V. J., & Graham, W. F. (1989). Toward a conceptual framework for mixed-method evaluation designs. *Educational Evaluation and Policy Analysis, 11*(3), 255–274.

Hibberts, M., Burke Johnson, R., & Hudson, K. (2012). Common survey sampling techniques. In G. Lior (Ed.), *Handbook of survey methodology for the social sciences* (pp. 53–54). Springer.

Hupe, P., & Buffat, A. (2014). A public service gap: Capturing contexts in a comparative approach of street-level bureaucracy. *Public Management Review, 16*(4), 548–569.

Hyett, N., Kenny, A., & Dickson-Swift, V. (2014). Methodology or method? A critical review of qualitative case study reports. *International Journal of Qualitative Studies on Health and Well-being, 9*(1), 23606.

Jick, T. D. (1979). Mixing qualitative and quantitative methods: Triangulation in action. *Administrative Science Quarterly, 24*(4), 602–611.

Mascia, C., & Odasso, L. (2015). Le contrôle du mariage binational en Belgique: Les règles du jeu. *Revue de l'Institut de Sociologie, 85*, 41–68.

Maynard-Moody, S., & Portillo, S. (2010). Street-level bureaucracy theory. In R. F. Durant (Ed.), *The Oxford handbook of American bureaucracy* (pp. 252–277). Oxford University Press.

Neuman, W. L. (2012). Designing face-to-face survey. In G. Lior (Ed.), *Handbook of survey methodology for the social sciences* (pp. 227–248). Springer.

Oldendick, R. W. (2012). Survey research ethics. In G. Lior (Ed.), *Handbook of survey methodology for the social sciences* (pp. 23–36). Springer.

PART I

SOCIAL ASSISTANCE FOR NEWLY ARRIVED IMMIGRANTS

CHAPTER 4
EXPLAINING VARIATIONS IN FORMS OF SERVICE DELIVERY FOR NEWCOMERS

ELSA MESCOLI, HANNE VANDERMEERSCHEN, ADRIANA COSTA SANTOS AND CARLA MASCIA

This chapter aims at gaining a better understanding of the functioning on the ground of welfare policies in terms of service delivery for newly arrived immigrants, and of the rationales lying behind existing variations. It also endeavours to study whether PCSWs perceive specific needs of migrant beneficiaries and how they respond to them. To do so, the chapter first analyses the organisation of the PCSWs under study with regard to service delivery for newcomers. Despite common missions of the PCSW in Belgium, diversity is present in terms of organisational cultures and choices, political orientations, and concrete services developed in each agency (see Chapter 2). PCSWs are a 'general' welfare institution (rather than a migration-specific service), yet they can decide at the local level how to organise the aid to migrants, and whether or not to develop devoted services and/or to have social workers specialised in addressing their specific needs. Second, the chapter also reveals what social aids are delivered to newcomers, and what conditions of access are set. Third, the question is addressed to what extent there are differences in service delivery to newly arrived immigrants as compared to other beneficiaries. Fourth, it is examined whether/to what extent PCSWs rely on other institutions and organisations for the service provision to newly arrived immigrants, who are their main partners, and what factors might hamper effective cooperation. The chapter mainly relies on the qualitative findings from the interviews with professional actors at the PCSWs. However, when possible, the qualitative findings are complemented with results from the complementary BBOX survey.

1.   THE ORGANISATION OF SERVICE DELIVERY TO NEWCOMER
BENEFICIARIES: SPECIALISATION VERSUS GENERALIST APPROACH

In this section, we will analyse the ways in which service delivery is organised in the PCSWs under study with regard to newcomer beneficiaries. Indeed, as described in the second chapter of this book, despite common missions of the PCSWs in Belgium, diversity is present in terms of concrete services developed in each agency. Such diversity also concerns the ways in which each PCSW manages the applications submitted by the target group of our study, as well as any other action focused on them. Describing it is relevant to have an overview of the functioning in the field of the welfare social service delivery to newcomers, as well as to unpack and question the different approaches of PCSWs in Belgium.

We observed that PCSWs have two main ways of organising their services towards newcomers. One way is dealing with newcomers' demands and the related files directly at general social services; another way is to manage these records first at specialised social services, before being transferred to general social services.

The distinction between having or not a specialised service is significant for at least two reasons. First, it translates the approach and 'philosophy' of the PCSW, whether the agency in question considers it appropriate to distinguish its beneficiaries based on their profiles and adapt the management of their demands – thus focusing on specific needs and issues that would have to be addressed separately, rather than (or before) adopting a 'generalist' approach. Second, and connected to this, choosing to set a separate service to target newcomers often implies that the social workers working into it have developed particular expertise – either through training or through practice – to meet the above-mentioned specificities. This choice may also be linked to the presence of high numbers of newcomer beneficiaries, for example in big cities, but not necessarily, since we also observed devoted services being put in place in the PCSW of small municipalities.[1] The most frequent argument brought to explain this, however, is that the management of records of newcomer beneficiaries requires specific knowledge, as mentioned in the quote below:

> At the beginning, there was no [foreigners] service within the PCSW [...]. So [...] all the foreigners went to the traditional offices and there was a worker who was [...] more or less dedicated to these people. But the legislation is so specific, [...] we really created the specific foreigners' service, precisely to be able to train the workers, to be able to meet the needs

of foreigners as well as possible. [...] the legislation is quite complex, and if we don't have training on a daily basis, [...] we won't be able to [...] help them as we do now. (Wallonia, A, social worker, 17/2/2021)

This rationale resonates with the conceptualisation of accessibility reported in the first chapter of this book and describing it as a 'degree of fit' between beneficiaries and services (Penchansky & Thomas, 1981). The idea is then to make the service more accessible and effective with regard to specific profiles of beneficiaries and to their needs. The access of newly arrived immigrants to social aids is strictly connected to their legal status. This means that the social workers need to consider and monitor the rules governing the residence of foreigners on the Belgian territory and their implication in welfare rules, in order to verify the rights of newcomer beneficiaries. Those PCSWs that have set a devoted service to deal with the files of newcomers estimate that specialised social workers are necessary to meet this need. However, the will of the management is often to transfer these files to the general social services – whose social workers may not be trained to deal with immigration laws – as soon as this is considered appropriate and possible.

In our fieldwork, we encountered both approaches, having a specialised service or sticking to an overall generalist approach, as well as some configurations keeping the middle.

In the fieldwork in Wallonia, six out of eight of the Walloon municipalities of the qualitative research have a specialised service, usually named *'service étrangers'*, three of which also have a local reception initiative (LRI), while one has a LRI but not a specialised service and one none of the two. We observed that in most cases the transfer of the files concerning newcomers from specialised social services to general social services happens when the residence permit of the beneficiaries becomes permanent, and is no more – or to a lesser extent – dependent on the legislation targeting foreigners. However, it is interesting to mention that in one of the case studies, the specialised service is in charge of the records of foreign beneficiaries until they acquire the Belgian nationality, a fact that greatly extends the duration of the permanence at the specialised service. It also implies that newly arrived immigrants and beneficiaries with foreign nationality but with longer residence in Belgium are both targeted by a specific service and do not have access to general social services attended by Belgian citizens. Besides responding to the rationale of the need of specific knowledge in the field of foreigners' laws, setting these rules may also respond to the need of redistributing files and workload.

In the PCSWs under study in Flanders, a generalist approach was most prevalent, particularly in small and medium-sized municipalities. Indeed, all five small and medium-sized municipalities under study had a so-called local reception initiative (LRI), but apart from that, there was no special service devoted to newcomers. Instead, a generalist approach was taken, with a random assignment of newcomers to social workers. Only in one of these municipalities, all newcomers were referred to the same social worker who was also in charge of the local reception initiative. In the cities, on the other hand, the choice of generalist versus specific appeared more blurred. In one city, there was a specialised service for newcomers (without age restrictions, which was the case in the other Flemish cities), but only for a limited duration, after which the beneficiary is transferred to a 'general' social service. In a second city, overall, a generalist approach was taken, with a random distribution of newcomer files to the social workers. However, a specialised service was recently launched for the youngest newcomers (up to the age of 35) within the framework of an integrated initiative, housing various services. In a third city, an opposite shift was observed: at the time of research, a transition towards less 'categorisation' was taking place, opting for an 'inclusive' policy, which implies a move towards a more general approach, with however some extra policy measures to ensure a good service delivery to newcomers. While there was a centralised special service for foreigners in the past, the 'front office' is now the same for all beneficiaries. However, there is still a 'back office' with additional support foreseen.[2]

The generalist approach is widespread in the Brussels region, too, where none of the studied PCSWs has a specialised service or specific policies for newcomers, and where the files of newcomers are managed at the general social service and are distributed within each PCSW based on the geographical location (residence) of the beneficiary. Indeed, every social worker works on a precise number of streets within the territory of the concerned PCSW. In one case, the PCSW shifted from a territorial organisation to a centralised organisation during the COVID-19 pandemics: local offices were closed, and services were gathered in the same location, distributing the files – newly submitted demands or follow-up – randomly among social workers available on the spot. PCSWs can develop measures to facilitate social integration through 'internal partnerships' with devoted services. Therefore, some services, albeit not targeting newcomers at the outset, may end up being attended mainly by them:

> [I]n the early days when we thought up the project, we didn't have a public with an immigrant background as a target audience at all[;] we thought we were mainly addressing a demobilised French-speaking Belgian public. And it was precisely when I recruited the first group that the social workers

redirected the public with an immigrant background [...] we said to ourselves that we couldn't stay with our ready-made formula and drop this whole public, which I had nevertheless met, and that's how, barely six months after the opening of the service, we proposed to open a second target group and we readapted the contents to this [target group's] difficulties, then. (Brussels, G, manager, 12/04/2021)

As appears from the above, in our case studies, we encountered specialised services more often in Wallonia than in the other regions. However, based on the findings of the online survey, regional differences or 'trends' in the choice of a generalist versus specific approach could not be confirmed. Based on the survey, the generalist approach is dominant both in Flanders and Wallonia,[3] with more than 8 out of 10 participating municipalities stating they did not have a separate service for newcomer beneficiaries (regardless of the LRI, which exists in the majority of municipalities). Yet, rather than related to region, the choice for having (or not) a specialised service did seem to be related to the size of the municipality with small municipalities reporting a specialised service less often compared to PCSWs in larger municipalities. While overall, only a minority (16%) of PCSWs in our online survey reported having a specialised service, the majority of PCSW services (6 out of 10) reported having one or several social workers specialised in newcomer beneficiaries.

Based on the findings of our fieldwork, the generalist approach translates a discourse on promoting equity and inclusion of all beneficiaries and on avoiding stigmatisation:

It decompartmentalises [...] it avoids stigmatisation, it also creates solidarity between different groups of people who ultimately find common ground and develop strategies for solidarity between them. (Brussels, G, president, 15/04/2021)

However, the generalist approach may leave some 'blind spots' in identifying and responding to specific needs and difficulties encountered by newcomer beneficiaries and by the social workers managing their files. On the other hand, specialisation may lead social workers to become 'over-focused on a particular approach' (Trevithick, 2011, p. 142) at the expense of a broader perspective on the overall social situation and rights of the beneficiary (also see Minahan & Pincus, 1977).

To analyse further these distinct approaches, it is worth mentioning that the debate over the generalist versus the specialist approach in social work is vast, and takes different forms depending on the national and professional contexts concerned. Moreover, it not only concerns whether it is more useful and effective to have specialised skills or general ones within social work in order to best meet the problems presented and the needs of beneficiaries – indeed, there is little research on which approach has better outcomes (Parsloe, 2000, p. 145, cited in Trevithick, 2011). This debate also highlights the importance of identifying commonalities in casework and fostering professional cohesion and coherence – a 'content core' on which to ground all subsequent specialisations, with the will of establishing a common base for education and practice (Leighninger, 1980). The generalist approach corresponds to:

> the acquisition and application of a broad spectrum of knowledge and skills that can be used to address the range of different situations regularly encountered in social work. As such generalist knowledge and skill embody a 'foundation upon which specialisations that have professional and intellectual coherence can be built' (Stevenson, 2005, p. 81). This foundation has the advantage of being more transferable than the more in-depth knowledge and skills that are central to specialist practice. Indeed, even as a specialist, it is very likely that a practitioner will use a number of generalist skills because of their *transferability*. (Trevithick, 2011, p. 141)

Conversely, specialist practice concerns 'either a division of labour or superior knowledge and skill about a client group, problem area, methods or settings' (Parsloe, 2000, p. 145). Such specialisation is acquired through extensive practice experience and through specific training, and it is connected with the opportunities of local authorities to provide specialist services and post-qualifying programmes. However, the generalist and the specialist approach can overlap to some extent and complement each other in the concrete interventions of social workers – deploying generalist and specialist knowledge and skills along a continuum (*idem*).[4] Therefore, the issue may be which are the more effective ways to integrate and balance generic and specific elements and methods in practice (Leighninger, 1980), and more particularly with regard to welfare intervention targeting immigrants, as we will see later in this book.

2. SOCIAL AND FINANCIAL BENEFITS DELIVERED TO NEWCOMERS AND CONDITIONS OF ACCESS

PCSWs in Belgium are the main institutions of the country's 'residual non-contributory system of social assistance', which:

> is based on solidarity and financed through general taxation. It aims to provide a minimum social protection to those who are involuntarily without income and cannot benefit from the work-based social insurance system. This non-contributory system includes the minimum guaranteed income (also called integration income [...]), the guaranteed income for the elderly, [...] the minimum family benefits, [...] and disabled persons' benefits. (Melin, 2020, p. 50)

Indeed, our research participants mentioned many different social benefits, beside the integration income, such as: housing insurance (rental guarantee), first month rent, installation grant, house furniture, healthcare costs (including trauma counselling and psychotherapy), food aids, aids for children (education, socio-cultural activities, health, and so forth), assistance for water, electricity, gas, telephone charges, certification for social rates, aids for mobility and transportation costs, reimbursement for computers (during the COVID-19 health crisis), books, and expenses for a driving licence, and so on. Besides financial aids, assistance that may be given by PCSWs also includes support in administrative tasks – for example, to explore and 'open' any other right that the beneficiary may have (that is, family allowances and disability benefits) – housing search, including introducing a demand for a shelter or for social houses, job search, management of family issues (including child care, children enrolment in schools or other activities), socialisation activities, budget management counselling, debt mediation, support for seniors, and so forth. Specific support concerns applicants for international protection and can comprise in-kind support, including housing in LRI, administrative support, legal support, integration activities and courses, support on the asylum procedure, housing issues, health issues, and voluntary return procedure. This financial and non-financial assistance can be given either directly by the social worker in charge of the record of the concerned beneficiary, or through orienting towards specific (external or internal) services. These social aids and support projects are funded through multiple resources, including internal (municipal) funding, federal funding, special funding (energy, COVID-19), and other institutions' funding (regional funding, EU funding). Newcomers with a residence permit and in need of residual social assistance potentially have access to all other social aids than social integration income, too. However, as for any other beneficiary, their demands need to be approved. That is why all these social benefits and the effective opportunities to access them vary considerably depending on the internal policy of each PCSW – the procedure and the decision-making process will be analysed later in this book.

However, the starting point is that newcomers' access to social and financial benefits strictly depends on their legal status. Having a residence permit enables newcomers to access, in principle, all rights as any other beneficiary of PCSWs, provided that the other conditions established by the law are also met – and *albeit*, as described above, each PCSW can have its own approach in the organisation of the services where the demands of these aids are managed:

> As soon as they leave the LRI, they are considered to be inhabitants, ordinary citizens, so they benefit from all the services that the PCSW can offer to its entire population. And so, all the social services are part of it, it's social aid but it can be mediation, it can be family aid from the family aid service as well, from the socio-professional integration (SPI) service, all the services that the PCSW offers, can be guaranteed to them.[5] (Wallonia, D, president, 25/11/2020)

According to the law,[6] there are six conditions to access social welfare benefits in Belgium: (1) having the Belgian citizenship or any other European citizenship (with a right of residence of more than three months), or having a regular residence permit (the refugee status and the subsidiary protection allow access to 'regular' social income, while other residence permits give access to 'equivalent' social income); (2) living in the concerned municipality (territorial jurisdiction); (3) being of age; (4) not having other financial resources; (5) being ready and available to work (or bringing recognised justification for the impossibility of it); (6) not benefiting from any other social rights (since social welfare is a residual right).

Beyond this common discourse on the equivalence between the social rights of newcomers with a regular residence status and those of any other Belgian citizen, some considerations need to be highlighted. First, for beneficiaries with a precarious residence status, receiving social assistance exposes them to the risk of losing their residence permit.[7] Newcomers are generally informed about this risk by the Immigration Office, as well as by PCSW social workers themselves:

> [G]iven that when they apply for a residence card, they prove that they have the means to support themselves, they must not become a burden on the state. Because if they become a burden on the state, [...] they jeopardise their right of residence. [...] it is our duty to inform them of this risk. [...] when they come for family reunification, one of the members has vouched for them, so has proved that he has the means to support [...] his family, so if he is no longer able to support them ... [...] they are made to sign a document stating that they have been informed of this risk and [...] they decide either to continue with the application or to cancel it. [...] and often, when we discuss it, most of them tell me straight away 'Oh no, I'm not going to take that risk, I'm going to try and manage in another way.' (Wallonia, D, social worker, 10/12/2020)[8]

Family reunification may also be compromised – not possible – for newcomers working on an Art. 60 contract, leading them to rule out this possibility and seek other forms of employment instead. These examples show that some newcomers may decide not to ask for social benefits. The access to these rights is then compromised; the non-take up of social rights appears here as a constrained choice that only newcomers face – we will develop these issues further in Chapter 11. As Lafleur and Vintila write:

> Even when foreigners are entitled to claim benefits on equal grounds with their national counterparts, their access to welfare may still be indirectly constrained by the potential negative consequences that the take-up of such benefits could have for other migration-related entitlements. [...] reliance on social assistance is often considered as a burden on public funds. In turn, this can negatively affect the renewal of migrants' residence permits, their applications for family reunification, or even their citizenship applications, as the latter generally depend on conditions of social integration and proving one's stable income and self-sufficiency. This creates an extra layer of conditionality that could affect foreigners' practical access to welfare. (Lafleur & Vintila, 2020, pp. 27–28; also see Lafleur & Mescoli, 2018)

Moreover, since the conditions of access to social aids for newcomers depend on their residence status, the social aids to which they are entitled change over time, differently from other beneficiaries. In addition, the access to social integration income seems more difficult in recent times, when the possibilities of obtaining a residence permit are (further) restricted.

3.   DIFFERENCES IN SERVICE DELIVERY?

In our study, we also investigated whether there are differences in terms of service delivery to newly arrived migrants, as compared to other beneficiaries (Belgian natives or others). Clearly, there are different sides to this reality, as we need to distinguish between what is done willingly and consciously by social workers and the management level, possible hidden effects or unintended consequences, and the way the service delivery is perceived by migrants themselves. In this section, we discuss the approach taken by social workers and their team managers, based on their perspective. In the discussion, we stick to how the social workers and managers *describe* the service delivery to newly arrived immigrants. The *challenges* it can entail, on the other hand – especially in view of an accessible service – will be discussed at length in Chapter 5.

3.1.   The discourse of 'tailor-made for all'

When asked whether there are any differences in support, in measures or in approach for newcomers (compared to other beneficiaries), a share of respondents – mainly among those working in general social services – actually respond negatively at first. When digging deeper, they often mention some differences, not in the sense of different rules nor additional grants, but in the concrete approach taken (the trajectory being more intensive, taking more time to explain, and so forth, as discussed in what follows). Yet, overall, some respondents – and especially in the Brussels region – stress first and foremost that all support is tailor-made for all. In other words, it is not the fact of being a 'newcomer' that is essential, but rather the specific needs of the person, influenced by their personal context and profile (educational profile, language knowledge, family situation, social contacts, and so forth).

> That is also the interest of the ISIP, it's individualised. So, it really depends on the person. There is no specificity. There's no label. […] except for the Roma population department. Because there is a Roma department.[9] But there's no label of 'You were born in Belgium.', 'You're a newcomer from five months ago or three years ago.', 'You're a newcomer who's a bit older.', 'You're a European who works as a salaried employee.', 'You're a child, …' We don't put any labels on it. We individualise and I think that's really what we have to be cautious about. (Brussels, A, manager, 30/04/2021)

The idea of individualised, tailor-made support for all beneficiaries is a key principle in the daily functioning of the PCSWs. It can be witnessed through the very same definition and use of the Individualised Social Integration Project (ISIP),[10] but it is reflected in many other aspects of service delivery and local decision making as well (see Chapter 8) (for example, decisions on whether or not to support an investment in education and to support getting a driver's licence). It should be noted that asking about service delivery to 'newcomers' was 'our' categorisation as researchers; not all respondents necessarily reflected about it in the same way nor saw it as a particular target group prior to the interview.[11] Along the same line, the idea of equality was underlined, that is, the concern of giving the same opportunities to all (from the perspective of the social workers). In that context, the diversity among beneficiaries was also stressed.

> For all clients, the functioning is the same. Of course, the way I work depends on the questions or problems that the client has. Someone who already has possibilities of employment will receive different conditions or guidance from me than someone who is just starting out and still has to learn Dutch and get his/her administration in order. So that makes a difference. But in the sense of treating differently, no. (Flanders, A, social worker, 15/04/2021)

> We really do try to treat everyone equally. I think that tailored work, I think it is important, yes. That is the most important thing. (Flanders, E, social worker, 16/03/2021)

This is in line with the generalist approach taken in an important share of the cases in terms of organisation as well, as described earlier, with the underlying rationale being not to make any predefined difference between beneficiaries and deliver the same 'regular-but-tailor-made' service to all.

3.2. Existing differences in guidance and support

While the need for financial support is a common thread for most users – newcomers and other beneficiaries alike – most social workers and team managers do mention differences at some point in the interviews, both in terms of newcomers' needs, and in terms of the support that is given in reply.

First, respondents indicated the trajectory (that is, the steps to be taken during guidance and support) will be more 'standard' with newcomer beneficiaries, at least in the beginning. A number of financial, practical, and administrative issues need to be taken care of, and these are often the same for all newcomers, as most of them start 'from scratch'. In contrast with other beneficiaries, newcomers' files are more like a blank page at the start, with similar steps to be taken for all, such as arranging the integration income, organising housing, an installation grant, and so forth.

> At the end of the day these are the files which are, I would say, the easiest to deal with. Because they're fresh, landing here in Belgium. The story is the story that brought them to Belgium, but the path is much more quickly traced. [...] So the analysis of his requests is not at all the most complex matter [...] The guidelines, the way we conduct the interviews, we have a clear view, we don't get lost ... [imitating the reasoning with other beneficiaries:] 'so he has worked, so he may be entitled to unemployment, uh, but then he was there, so maybe we should see the mutual insurance company ...?' [...] No, we start from scratch, pretty much, and so it's much easier to initiate this kind of request and to directly put an objective, an accompaniment in place. (Brussels, A, manager, 30/04/2021)

> Newcomers very often come to the PCSW from a reception centre because they have been recognised [as a refugee/granted protection], are actually referred to us automatically. So the question is always about integration income, installation grants, bridging the gap to the first payment of integration income, help with rent guarantees, so I think these questions are very important in the first instance. (Flanders, A, manager, 22/04/2021)

However, this 'blank page' that newcomers arrive with (in comparison to many other beneficiaries), also implies they need more information and broader counselling, in different areas.

> The newcomers start from scratch, of course, so they need help in all areas of life, or they have questions about all areas of life. For example, they don't understand the post they receive every day, they don't understand their invoices, even advertising packages are things they don't understand at first, so they have a lot of administrative questions. [...] A lot of familiarisation with health care, so referral to a health insurance, joining a health insurance, giving the address of the health insurance, explaining how the stickers work, things like that. These are things that Belgian clients are familiar with, they know the system. (Flanders, A, social worker, 23/04/2021)

The civic orientation course embedded in the 'integration path' is found to be helpful in this respect, as it familiarises newly arrived immigrants with institutions in Belgian society, but when they arrive at the PCSW, they have not followed the course yet, nor will it solve the problem entirely (on this topic, see also Gossiaux *et al.*, 2019 for Wallonia).

Second, the fact that newcomers are not familiar with the complex Belgian (or regional) system and its institutions, with no prior knowledge of 'how things work' and having to make a new beginning very often also not knowing the language, causes them to need help and guidance with aspects of daily life otherwise often considered as 'normal' or taken for granted. In terms of service delivery, it results in more intensive and time-consuming trajectories.

> The difference is, of course, the time you put in. Uhm, so the time with my newcomers and, and, well, you, you have to spend much more time with them than actually, uhm, with the, yes, the Belgians. Uhm, I think that maybe it's also a bit of the language and the fact that they ask a lot more than the others. (Flanders, H, social worker, 14/06/2021)

> With newcomers, often there are questions in all areas of life, things they just don't know yet, they are not familiar with the jargon, with how things work in Belgium, not familiar with bank transactions, with bank applications, invoices. So we really help in all areas of life and these are topics that I always raise myself, whereas with the Belgian customers it is really demand-oriented: they ask a question, I answer it. With the newcomers, I touch on all the life domains to see what they know, where they need help. So these are more extensive and more complex conversations. (Flanders, A, social worker, 23/04/2021)

Yet, the need for more intensive guidance and support can be demanding for the social workers and cause pressure, particularly in a context of a high case load and time pressure (see Chapter 5 for a more ample discussion of how this is dealt with in the field), and depending on the municipality, in a context of general (that is, non-migration specific) service organisation.

> Even the class journals [from school], they bring it to me. And then it starts. The mail. At the beginning I even had mail, 'I got this' and everything by internet. No, but at some point I feel like my job is becoming the job of a secretary or an administrator. (Brussels, G, social worker, 04/03/2021)

> That makes it very, um, fascinating, but also very heavy. And the PCSW is not really adapted to that [...] I find it very pleasant that I see so many different people. But when I think of the clients themselves, I have the feeling that they would benefit more from a group that, or a group of social

workers who have a lot more, well, time and space. We have a lot of files. Yes, my refugees, whether they are getting lonely here, or whether they are doing really well all the time, I wouldn't dare put my hand in the fire for that. (Flanders, C, social worker, 04/06/2021)

The struggle to unravel and address psychosocial needs of newcomers, which is described by the last respondents, is a recurring element throughout the interviews, and will be discussed more in depth in Chapter 5).

A third difference that was regularly brought up is that social workers were sometimes more lenient towards newly arrived immigrants. More particularly, newcomer beneficiaries tend to be accorded more time by some social workers before making the transition towards employment. They are given time (and being encouraged) to learn the language first, for example. It is considered normal that their trajectory takes time, whereas other beneficiaries might be expected to (prove to) search for employment sooner. However, though it is a 'different treatment' compared to other beneficiaries, in the perspective of the respondents it is in line with the idea of an individualised approach, adapting expectations to the perceived abilities of the beneficiary. Put differently, they are accorded more time, not because they are newcomers as such, but because of the difficulties and challenges that life after migration entails.

Maybe we, or I personally have just a bit more patience with newcomers. Because you say, they still have to settle in. They still have to learn the language first, then after the language, we say a certain level of language, usually they want to work themselves. So that is also a, a difference with, uh, the Belgians that I have in my guidance, that you sometimes have to pull and push a bit more. Uhm, that may well be a difference in that the patience with the newcomers is a bit greater than when you say with the Belgians 'you already know the system, you already know'. (Flanders, H, social worker, 14/06/2021)

Researcher: You first said 'We lower our thresholds.' What do you mean by that?
Manager: The time aspect in particular. People get time to study Dutch, to find out 'What do they want now?' Do they want to get an education? Do they want to start working soon? What kind of things do they see themselves doing? They get much more time to go through those processes. Not with all assistants, but most of them. Maybe that's why people get more opportunities from their assistant to go through a longer process, than if you would let someone who has been here for a long time and who knows everything and ... (Flanders, C, manager, 23/02/2021)

Overall, there seems to be a lot of emphasis on learning the language, and sometimes less emphasis – or rather: later – on finding employment, though this observation does not apply everywhere (see Chapter 6).

Moreover, some social workers or managers also mentioned a difference in this respect between their position as social worker – seeing a number of pitfalls in going (too) straight to work, assuming it is better to take the time needed – and the position of the committee, which in some municipalities might insist more on timely entrance to work. In addition, in some cases, social workers and managers also reported on committee members being more strict or harsh with newcomers (see Chapter 8).

Fourth, a specificity for newcomers in some PCSWs is also the work of bridging figures, such as intercultural mediators, translators, or other personnel engaged as 'facilitators', who can be asked by the social workers to translate, but also to accompany newcomers to appointments in certain cases. Sometimes, they also give information sessions on specific topics (cf. supra). Yet, these bridging figures cannot be found in every PCSW. Overall, based on our case studies relying on such bridging figures seemed more common in larger municipalities, even though it also occurred in smaller municipalities.

Last, there can be often some additional, complementary initiatives that social workers can refer to. These are not to be considered as a categorical, 'specific' approach per se, but rather as additional options for referral and/or support. A typical example are conversation tables, but also buddy projects, psychological support, and mind spring (that is, a programme aiming to improve and protect mental health). These can be organised by the PCSW or the municipality, but often also by other organisations (such as Centrum Algemeen Welzijnswerk or the Centre for General Welfare in Flanders and Brussels, and local integration initiatives in Wallonia) and/or by volunteers.

In the complementary online survey, PCSWs were asked whether there were any projects targeting newcomers that are organised by the PCSW and/or to which the PCSW refers. This was the case in more than 8 out of 10 municipalities in our survey (83%). The most commonly reported (non-exclusive answers) were activities with regard to language (such as conversation tables) (56%), language courses (53%), buddy projects (26%), and social group activities (such as excursions or workshops) (25%), but also courses of social integration (24%), other individual social activities (such as volunteering) (21%), and information-providing activities (for example, welcome sessions) (18%) were reported. The PCSW not only refers to existing activities, but often organised this type of activities themselves. This was often the case for buddy projects, but also other activities such as informational activities or individual activities can be provided by the PCSW.

The organisation of, and referral to, activities brings us to the broader question of partnerships in the service delivery to migrants. In the remainder of this chapter, we will discuss in more detail the cooperation of the PCSWs with different partners when it comes to service provision, assistance, and support to newcomer beneficiaries.

4.   PARTNERSHIPS AND COOPERATION IN THE SERVICE DELIVERY TO NEWLY ARRIVED IMMIGRANTS

Clearly, welfare institutions do not work in a social vacuum, and the transnational shift from a central organisation towards 'governing with and through networks' (Rhodes, 2007, p. 1246) is apparent in Belgium as well. PCSW do not stand alone, but are actors in a network, and this also holds for service delivery to newly arrived immigrants. Looking at this from a different perspective, various local actors have a task and responsibility related to the assistance and support of newly arrived immigrants, and these actors need to work together. Although social workers and managers at the PCSW stress the importance of working in a network in the follow up of newly arrived immigrants and other beneficiaries, the practices of cooperation are nevertheless complex. While some collaborations are organised or even institutionalised (with partners such as regional integration centres, public employment services, or schools for language training), many other cooperations – with NGOs, for example – often depend on personal initiatives, preferences, or connections of social workers. In either case, effective and successful cooperation cannot be taken for granted. In this section, we start by identifying different fields where partnerships are present in the support of newly arrived immigrants, and explore what role is taken by the PCSW and partners respectively. In a final section, potential pitfalls in cooperation on social assistance to immigrants in practice are discussed.

4.1.   Identifying partners for service delivery to newly arrived immigrants

Social workers, managers, and directors were asked who they considered as important partners with regard to the guidance, assistance, and support to newly arrived immigrants. The resulting list of organisations was rather extensive. Yet, as key partners, we should first mention the regional centres for integration and local integration initiatives (dealing with integration courses, equivalence of diploma, specific support services – ex. housing search), other municipal services (for example, focusing on diversity or integration), institutions and organisations for language learning and employment services. In what follows, we take a closer look at these key partners, even though it needs to be mentioned that what are considered as important partners differ between cases; an organisation that is a partner 'on the margin' for one PCSW might be a key partner elsewhere. Moreover, the aforementioned organisations are institutionalised partners, and some level of partnership is to be expected given the broader legal framework on integration and activation (cf. infra), which is why we consider them as important partners, but as we will see in what follows, the cooperation with these organisations is not necessarily intensive in practice.

The first partners mentioned above are the regional centres for integration, alongside other local integration initiatives. In our complementary online survey, 7 out of 10 PCSWs (72%) stated to work together with the regional centre for integration. The participating PCSWs were also asked about the motives for this cooperation (if they did report a cooperation), with the provided options being (1) the follow up of the steps of the newcomers' civic integration process, (2) monitoring the administrative situation of the newcomers, (3) cooperating in social integration initiatives apart from the civic integration programme (housing, preparation for entering the labour market, and so forth), and (4) getting in touch with other local associations (with several answers being possible simultaneously). All answer options about reasons for cooperation were chosen – respectively by 36% (administrative situation), 39% (other integration initiatives), and 24% (other local associations) of the PCSWs who stated to cooperate with the PCSW – but the most recurrent answer was by far the follow up of the steps of the civic integration process. Indeed, 88% of the PCSWs who reported having a cooperation with the regional centre for integration stated to work together in the follow up of the civic integration process. The latter corresponds to our prior expectations, given the mandatory nature of integration courses, both in Flanders and Wallonia. Indeed, specific policies have been dedicated to the integration of newcomers since 2004 in Flanders (and Flemish-speaking Brussels) with the 'inburgeringstraject', and since 2014 in Wallonia with the 'parcours d'integration pour primo-arrivants'.[12] These reception and integration policies – which have specificities and differences according to the regions – may overlap or interfere with the policies and practices of the PCSWs targeting newcomers. This is the case, for example, of the interaction between the ISIP (Individualised Social Integration Project), managed by the PCSW, and the integration programmes mentioned above managed by the regional integration centres.

Second, the partnership with language institutions can also be explained by the mandatory integration process, as language courses are part of it. But also more generally, in addition to the obligation as defined by the regional legal framework in terms of integration, many social workers, managers, and committee members attach a large importance to learning the language (see Chapter 6 and 7). Learning the language (and taking classes) is often included in the ISIP as well, and the PCSW will verify the fulfilment of this condition.

A third partnership is the cooperation with other municipal services. The nature of this cooperation – and the specific services involved – is rather diverse. Local governments can organise themselves and divide responsibilities, competences, and service offer as they see necessary and fit, resulting in differences in organisation in our case studies. The availability of funding and related specific programmes is also essential to define the opportunities of collaboration. Yet, an interesting element in the cooperation is the referral to initiatives specifically designed for newcomers. Such activities can be organised by the PCSW, a local non-profit organisation or other organisation, but also by the local government. Based on the survey, overall, both the PCSW and non-profit organisations are more frequently mentioned as lead organiser, but also local governments are found to organise information activities (28% of the cases in which information activities were provided), 'other' individual social activities (29%), buddy projects (23%), social orientation courses (21%)[13], language activities (20%), social activities in a group setting (16%), or language courses (12%).

A fourth partner are public employment services. Cooperation here is to be expected as well, given the central task of 'social activation' of PCSWs, of which socio-professional integration is an important part (and a final goal when possible). In light of this, cooperation with the public employment service was not as elaborate and extensive in our case studies as one might expect, with many social workers (both in general services and socio-professional integration services) expressing that they (as PCSW) were the lead actor in terms of guidance towards the labour market of their beneficiaries rather than the public employment service, or that they preferred to council the beneficiaries themselves. The latter was confirmed by the results of the online survey, as only in 19% of the cases the public employment service was considered the lead actor in terms of labour market activation for newcomer beneficiaries (compared to 57% the service of socio-integration at the PCSW and 12% the 'general' social worker). In our fieldwork, and depending on the region, collaboration with the PES was occasionally even limited to the obligation of social welfare beneficiaries to register as job seekers. Such a step is often included in the beneficiary's ISIP and it's a means of social activation towards employment. The cooperation with the public employment service – and more particularly, the role distribution – will be discussed in more detail in Chapter 6 on labour market activation.

In Flanders, also the 'general welfare centres' (CAW – Centra voor Algemeen Welzijnswerk) certainly are an important partner, for example in terms of support in the search for housing or in administration.

Also frequently mentioned throughout the interviews as partners – across all regions – were schools and other educational institutions, local associations (work, housing, basic needs, socialisation, legal support, support of specific publics – young people, specific origins, trafficked persons), health centres (both physical and mental health), health insurance, centres providing support to pupils, interpreting services, Fedasil (the federal agency in charge of the reception of applicants of international protection), child care, the governmental agency for youth care and family support, and so forth.

4.2. When do partners come into play in supporting beneficiaries?

Partnerships are considered essential, not only with the institutionalised partners mentioned in more detail above, but also with local organisations, ranging from schools and health centres to small NGOs. The exact 'patchwork' of partnerships is different in every municipality, and the same holds for the intensity of collaborations, but in all cases, social workers make referrals to other organisations and services, both internally and externally. In terms of *internal* services, examples are services for socio-professional integration or budget management. In what follows, we focus exclusively on the referral to *external* organisations.

A first situation in which social workers often refer to external organisations is when a need arises in the contacts with the beneficiaries, and input of a more specialised partner is needed. For example, social workers can decide to refer to a mental health centre if it becomes clear that the beneficiary needs psychological support or has mental health issues. Similarly, a social worker can refer to the CAW in Flanders, or to other organisations, if it becomes apparent that a beneficiary is striving for family reunification and needs information about the law and legal possibilities. The same holds for other legal information with regard to the right to stay.

> For everything that concerns the procedures really linked to residency [*séjour* in French], we [the PCSW] are clearly not the best in the sense that we are not the most qualified, so for all the questions concerning the residency, we are really more of a relay between the person and the contact person they will need, depending on their situation, So I would say that once we have made the link between the person and the organisation that can help them, we no longer need to act as an intermediary and the person should be able to rely on the organisation in question. (Brussels, D, director, 12/03/2021)

These are just a few examples; similar referrals are made to other organisations, in other domains as well, such as health insurance, schools, and so on. In addition to emerging needs, other reasons for referral are possible as well, based on the situation of a beneficiary and the legal framework (for example, enrolment in health insurance and taking up other benefits one is entitled to). Yet, a precondition to make the suitable referrals is to be able to attribute enough time to clients in order to identify additional needs. In practice, this is not always the case, because of time pressure and high caseloads, as we will see in the next chapter. Yet, partners can also contact the PCSW.

> Then you just don't have the possibility to go and see everyone week after week and say 'And how are things now, and how are you doing?' […] The child level for example is something we almost always have to ignore or can't do anything else but ignore, because you just don't have the time. If you have a family with 14 children, you cannot go and do 14 parent contacts or so on, to look for 'Ah yes, maybe there are problems.' It can still be relevant in your guidance, because it can, it can appear for example that they need homework support or that it is best to appoint a speech therapist, for which a PCSW can help cover the costs and so on. That's all possible. But those are things that, at the moment that's not going to happen. So you have to expect, or hope, that a 'CLB' [centre providing support to pupils] or a school or such like will contact us to pass on such information so that we can get to work on these questions. (Flanders, C, manager, 23/02/2021)

While time shortage can affect the adequate referrals negatively, inversely, it can also be a motivation to refer to other services. Indeed, social workers can choose to refer to other services in case they estimate that another organisation can take up a part of the support that needs to be provided, or when they expect that a social worker or volunteer in another organisation will be able to take more time to help out the beneficiary (for example, in terms of support with administration and search for housing).

> These [associations, the local community] are real relays that we can rely on to support people where we are not able to do so. In the end, what they want us to say is that we are a relay and that our job to help people is to direct them to where they can get help because we aren't able anymore to give them the help they ask for. […] for example, help in finding housing, help with training, so there are people who will grit their teeth in the Directorate, because we have services that deal specifically with that, but the services are full. (Wallonia, B, social worker, 11/1/2021b)

Social workers, managers, and directors seem to hold diverging opinions in terms of what a social worker should do him/herself, and when to refer – or put differently, where the responsibility and expertise of an PCSW should stop or how intense the counselling and support should be. However, respondents tended to agree that they should at least detect the needs and ensure follow-up. Yet, as we have seen, and as will be discussed in more detail in the next chapters, time shortage does not always allow to do this adequately.

Apart from having enough time, as noted by a director of a PCSW, the expectation to refer beneficiaries implies that the staff of the PCSW needs to know the (local) 'social map' as well:

> You don't live on an island with your PCSW. A PCSW has to build many bridges with other agencies. We also have many – though luckily not that many – families who fall under juvenile court jurisdiction. Yes, you also need to have good contacts with them, with those supervisors. Or electronic surveillance, for example. You are dependent on many different partners. That makes it very interesting, because as a PCSW employee you cannot know everything, but you do need to know your social map very well. (Flanders, E, director, 02/03/2021)

Institutional collaborations may be set in the framework of specific funding, projects, and agreements (think of projects in the framework of AMIF – the European Asylum, Migration and Integration Fund, or ESF – the European Social Fund). Alongside more institutionalised forms of cooperation, collaborations are often established by social workers themselves through informal channels and tools. Social workers develop their own 'address book', while a high staff turnover in some municipalities can challenge the awareness of the local associative network.

> Once I started as a social assistant, because I knew that networking was very important, my priority was to build up an address book, because sometimes you call, it is sad to say it, but if you have a direct contact in [local association], it is better than staying on hold for 15 or 30 minutes on a line with the number of files we have to deal with. (Brussels, G, social worker, 10/03/2021)

According to some social workers, more collaboration is needed in some of the studied locations, where there may be a lack of knowledge about the tasks of all associations and institutions on the territory. In addition, the possibility of establishing collaborations depends also on the existence and availability of services/associations, which are less present in rural contexts.

> Who we are working with, so with the regional agency for integration as I said, basic education, VDAB [the public employment service] also has a specific department for non-native speakers, learning how to apply for a job, learning how to use computers and so on. But for the rest, it's a matter of looking for the right people according to their needs. We have no organisations in [name of the municipality] to fall back on. There is no volunteer work, there are no associations or organisations that deal with non-native speakers or refugees. Of course schools are also important partners, how do we communicate with the families and the teachers, we often accompany them, we go to parents' meetings or we help with the registration of the children. Especially if they do not know any other language than, for example, Arabic, then we go with them to the school. So that collaboration is also very good. But for the rest, it's a tailor-made search starting from what we need here and who can offer us that. (Flanders, F, director, 07/05/2021)

At the same time, there may be less need of passing the tasks to partners in smaller municipalities/rural context if social workers have less workload and have the possibility to take in charge these tasks themselves. Where there is a 'thick' associative network, there are multiple potential collaborations, but also a wider amount of workload and information it seems, which can hinder the capacity of networking of the social workers. The latter seemed to be the case in Brussels' municipalities under study.

4.3. Pitfalls in cooperation

Although the PCSW relies on and refers some beneficiaries to the associative network, the relationship between partners – and their dependence on workers' strategies and practices (Eule, 2014; Franssen, 2014) – is not always easy or continuous. Garnier and Piva (2019) observed dynamics of institutional innovation and complementarity for labour market insertion of refugees in Brussels. Through the analysis of partnerships, the authors show how the complementarity is put forward by actors mainly due to the pressure of demands and the lack of available resources to respond to them, while they regret the difficulties of collaboration. If the main reason evoked by the authors are the lack of institutional coherence and political obstacles (namely in terms of distribution of funding and mandates among different actors), they also contend that these same obstacles do not prevent the sector providing responses to the needs through innovation and complementarity. In our fieldwork, we find the same discourses on the need of collaboration, followed by a set of constraints that are identified by the PCSWs' staff.

> I think what we need to do is to be more efficient, especially in our relations with our external partners. Because the external partners don't like us, don't like the institution and we don't like the external partners, so it's a *happy* situation [*c'est joyeux*]. Whereas social action is about rights and connections, the PCSW opens up rights but it is not good at connections, and the associations, the external partners, are good at connections but they don't know how to open up rights, so we have to form an alliance. (Brussels, A, director, 09/03/2021)

PCSWs and associations might have varying interpretations regarding what social work means. Moreover, the approach of the social workers of the PCSWs and of the institution itself may be the object of critics. Some actors defend different definitions of social work, perceiving negatively the PCSW's strictness about the legal and political framework, and denouncing opacity on their procedures.

> The [local] environment is full of all kinds of associations that are real support and real relays for this type of population, with people who often take us for inhuman beings. And sometimes we get into a tizzy with the associations because they don't understand, we've already had altercations with social workers who tell us that we've had the same training [as social workers], 'How can you be so inhuman and cruel?' (Wallonia, B, social worker, 11/1/2021b)

The practices and the professional identities of the workers seem to play an important role on facilitating or impeding networking (Franssen, 2014), yet also the institutional culture is likely to have an impact. In some cases, respondents believe that the associations are 'activists' and constantly asking for more rights and services, despite the policies, whereas the PCSW must operate within the established legal framework, without necessarily questioning it.

> Sometimes there are tensions that arise from the different philosophies of work. For example, someone from the associative sector who has a lot of time to accompany a beneficiary doesn't understand my work [...]. I've already seen that, I was clearly told, it made me cry. They told me in an email, basically it was 'because of the botched social work of Mrs [...]'.

Because he had the time, he had been accompanying this person for months and when the person arrived here, we have five days in internal policy, to make an appointment, I contacted him the next day, for him it wasn't fast enough. So I left him a message saying that I would contact you again two days later because there was a holiday and I had taken time off, which is my right. He didn't appreciate it [...]. (Brussels, G, social worker, 25/05/2021)

I'm sorry, this is going to be mean what I say, but sometimes they [name of NGO] encourage this, these unrealistic expectations. A fridge from the charity shop is not good enough at that moment. No, it really has to be an energy-efficient fridge. Yes, and then we are also like, well, do we have to do this now? Does it have to be the best of the best, the fanciest? [...] Yes, but sometimes they dare to cross the line [in terms of respecting the choices of the public welfare centre], I will say. To really stand up for human rights, but to go a bit too far. Sometimes it goes a bit too far, I would say. (Flanders, F, social worker, 25/05/2021)

Moreover, local associations/contacts may end up being overloaded by the demands of the social workers of the PCSWs, who in their turn undergo extreme administrative workload, so that the collaboration finally comes to an end. Local associations may blame the PCSWs of offloading their responsibilities, and to be overloaded of work because of this.

Conflictual relations may arise, namely when associations perceive a delegation of responsibilities on basic needs of vulnerable populations (for example, the case of undocumented immigrants), or when there is a risk of saturation of other social services if the information is not balanced or concerted. All these aspects are perceived as obstacles for the interaction of the social workers with other actors, to build an assessment or in-depth support.

Caritas helped them with that too, well, they also helped them with all the procedures with the CPAS, they acted as intermediaries and they were also ... In everything practical. [...] And that was fantastic. [...] There were results. [...] but that no longer exists. [...] They told me 'Listen, we can no longer ... In any case we no longer offer our ... our help to refugees, well to people who come from Fedasil or from the centre, we only concentrate on people who come from our network.' [...] in fact there were too many? ... They had too much work. So I thought it was a pity that there wasn't [...] an agreement or a broader agreement to hire more people or to find more volunteers. (Wallonia, H, social worker, 22/12/2020)

To conclude, even though the literature stresses the role of networks of different actors in policy-implementation (Laws & Hajer, 2006) and social workers support the need of collaborating and sharing expertise in the follow-up of beneficiaries, our results indicate that effective and positive cooperation presents challenges and some PCSWs struggle to take the most of their networks.

Moreover, even when there is a will of structuring partnerships at the local level, there are organisational or systematic obstacles making cooperation not always easy. An example is the cooperation with the regional centres for integration. Previous research has shown that integration policies have not been elaborated – nor are they always implemented – in concertation among the different political levels and actors involved, which, according to Gossiaux *et al.* (2019), may lead to malfunctioning, and this seems to be reflected in our findings as well, with regional centres for integration and PCSWs sometimes struggling to develop well established forms of cooperation.

> When I see the mediocrity of the relationship we have with [the regional centre for integration], and there's no real collaboration, I can't say exactly what they can do and what they can't do. We don't have any follow-up, we asked for it because it was interesting to know the integration procedures for us, everything related to naturalisation, driving licences, all that is what the majority of our people ask for, and we don't have any follow-up, we don't have anything at all, there is no collaboration, nothing. (Wallonia, B, social worker, 15/1/2021)

As with regard to the organisational and systemic difficulties mentioned above, we observed that in many cases the ISIP contract established with newcomers (that is, the actions they have to carry out in order to achieve their individual project, demonstrating activation and deservingness of the social aid) includes following the courses of the regional integration path. When this is the case, the regional integration centres can be mentioned but not integrated as partners in the monitoring of the tasks. Instead, the beneficiaries are asked to bring certificates of participation during ISIP formal evaluation moments. In parallel, the regional centres also develop internal evaluation procedures with participants, potentially originating a double use of integration tools (and a double process of evaluation and control) and multiplying the formal steps that newly arrived immigrants must attend.

As proposed by Garnier and Piva (2019, p. 10), social innovation on tackling integration of newcomers (in Brussels in the case of this article) does not necessarily mean that the concerned actors will be able to articulate their action within the 'Belgian institutional puzzle'. In general, but even more so when structured agreements are absent, the conditions of work and the (un) availability of time to set, maintain and improve partnerships are bound to weaken the collaborations between PCSWs and external partners.

NOTES

1. However, the results of the complementary survey do indicate that specialised services are less common in PCSWs in smaller municipalities (cf. infra).
2. To be more specific, there is a helpdesk for social workers to get information on legal matters, and there are so-called 'soft specialists', that is, social workers spread over the different teams who are experts in working with beneficiaries of foreign origin/newcomers, who can give support to, and sensitise their colleagues when dealing with newcomers.
3. Due to the limited participation of PCSWs in the region of Brussels, we do not have any information about the prevalence of a generalist versus specific approach in Brussels based on the survey.
4. Indeed, we observed that in some cases, PCSWs, whether or not they have a specialised service for newcomers, may mobilise intermediating figures ('consultants', or 'educators' in the French-speaking regions) to facilitate the interactions between newcomers and the institution, as well as to support newcomers in some of the steps they take.
5. In the case mentioned here, newcomers have access to regular social service as soon as they acquire a residence status, be it temporary or not.
6. References and additional details are included in Chapters 2 and 7.
7. This concerns, for example, foreigners who have a recent residence status for family reunification, as stated in the immigration law of 15 December 1980.
8. The authors and editors of this book are aware of the male bias in certain phrasings of this respondent and others (for instance, speaking of 'he' and 'him' only, whereas it could also concern female beneficiaries as well). The decision was taken to keep the quotes as they were expressed by the interlocutors, even though they were not always thinking and speaking in terms of gender, but rather in terms of a non-gendered beneficiary. This holds for quotes in other chapters and parts of this book as well.
9. Although we understood the relevance of this statement, we did not go further into the analysis of this practice as it was beyond the scope of our research.
10. GPMI (Geindividualiseed Project voor Maatschappelijke Integratie) or PIIS (Projet Individualisé d'Intégration Sociale) in Dutch and French respectively.
11. The methodological challenges of this situation are discussed in Chapter 3.
12. In Brussels the BAPA (Bureau d'Accueil pour Primo-Arrivants, or Reception Office for newly arrived immigrants), a French-speaking reception programme for newcomers, has been operationalised since 2016 (Xhardez, 2016).
13. This percentage might be an underestimation, due to a mistranslation of this term in the French version of the survey.

REFERENCES

Eule, T. G. (2014). *Inside immigration law: Migration management and policy application in Germany.* Routledge.

Franssen, A. (2014). CPAS et Services publics de l'emploi: une coopération conflictuelle dans l'accompagnement des jeunes entre enseignement et emploi. In I. Pannecoucke, W. Lahaye, J. Vranken, & R. Van Rossem (Eds.), *Pauvreté en Belgique* (pp. 297–321). Academia Press.

Garnier, A., & Piva, A. (2019). Participation au marché du travail des réfugiés et demandeurs d'asile à Bruxelles: Innovation et complémentarité institutionnelle. *Brussels Studies, Collection générale,* n° 135, http://journals.openedition.org/brussels/2707.

Gossiaux, A., Mescoli, E., Rivière, M., Petit Jean, M., Bousetta, H., Fallon, C., & Fonder, M. (2019). *Évaluation du parcours d'intégration et du dispositif ISP dédiés aux primo-arrivants en Wallonie* (No. 33). IWEPS.

Lafleur, J.-M., & Mescoli, E. (2018). Creating undocumented EU migrants through welfare: A conceptualization of undeserving and precarious citizenship. *Sociology, 52*(3), 480–496.

Lafleur, J.-M., & Vintila, D. (2020). *Migration and social protection in Europe and beyond (volume 1): Comparing access to welfare entitlements.* Springer Nature.

Laws, D., & Hajer, M. (2006). Policy in practice. In M. Moran, M. Rein, & R. E. Goodin (Eds.), *The Oxford handbook of public policy* (pp. 409–424). Oxford University Press.

Leighninger, L. (1980). The generalist-specialist debate in social work. *Social Service Review, 54*(1), 1–12.

Melin, P. (2020). Migrants' access to social protection in Belgium. In J. M. Lafleur, & D. Vintila (Eds.), *Migration and social protection in Europe and beyond (volume 1)* (pp. 49–63). Springer Nature.

Minahan, A., & Pincus, A. (1977). Conceptual framework for social work practice. *Social Work, 22*(5), 347–352.

Parsloe, P. (2000). Generic and specialist practice. In M. Davies (Ed.), *Blackwell encyclopaedia of social work* (pp. 133–153). Oxford University Press.

Penchansky, R., & Thomas, J. W. (1981). The concept of access: Definition and relationship to consumer satisfaction. *Medical Care, 19*(2), 127–140.

Rhodes, R. (2007). Understanding governance: Ten years on. *Organization Studies, 28*(8), 1243–1264.

Stevenson, O. (2005). Genericism and specialization: The story since 1970. *British Journal of Social Work, 35,* 569–586.

Trevithick, P. (2011). The generalist versus specialist debate in social work education in the UK. In J. Lishman (Ed.), *Research highlights: Volume on social work education* (pp. 233–254). Jessica Kingsley.

Xhardez, C. (2016). L'intégration des nouveaux arrivants à Bruxelles: Un puzzle institutionnel et politique. *Brussels Studies, Collection générale,* n° 105, http://journals.openedition.org/brussels/1429.

CHAPTER 5
UNDERSTANDING CHALLENGES AND PITFALLS IN THE SERVICE DELIVERY TO NEWLY ARRIVED IMMIGRANTS

ADRIANA COSTA SANTOS, HANNE VANDERMEERSCHEN AND ELSA MESCOLI

INTRODUCTION

While Chapter 4 gives a clear view on how service delivery to newcomer beneficiaries at the Public Centres of Social Welfare is organised, it is important to reflect on some specific challenges and pitfalls of providing services to this specific population. In a first paragraph, a number of general challenges of service provision within the PCSWs are considered. The willingness and ability of street-level bureaucrats to act in a certain way towards newcomers is partly determined by the general context in which they operate, a context that is characterised by a high workload, time pressure, and institutional requirements and constraints. In the second and subsequent sections, we shift the focus to newcomers and the specific challenges in terms of welfare provision for this group. A first aspect that is discussed here is the difficulty of providing sufficient support at the social level (such as psychosocial support and guidance). A second challenge – which is intrinsically linked with the accessibility of the PCSW to newly arrived immigrants – lies in the understandability of the system and its procedures, and the resulting awareness of entitlement to rights and benefits. Indeed, knowledge is found to be essential for the take up of rights, and existing knowledge (and power) asymmetries in PCSW services between staff and beneficiaries seem accrued for newly arrived immigrants. Third, and related to the previous point, language problems are a major stumbling block in the communication, while communication is essential in the aid relationship. We therefore examine the strategies that are used by PCSWs' staff members/social workers to circumvent these issues. In addition, we consider the impact of language problems (and the approach to them) on the accessibility and quality of services. It should be noted that most of these challenges – perhaps with the exception of language problems in some cases – also exist for other beneficiaries, or at least to some extent. However, dealing with newly arrived immigrants, these difficulties tend to be exacerbated for various reasons, which will be shown in this chapter.

1. THE CHALLENGING CONTEXT OF SERVICE DELIVERY AT PCSW: DISCERNING WORKING CONDITIONS AND THEIR IMPLICATIONS

As mentioned in earlier chapters, research on street-level bureaucracy (Lipsky, 1980) confirmed the importance of considering organisational routines as a factor impacting the behaviour of social workers (Jewell & Glaser, 2006; Hawkins, 2001). These features are also present when we consider the increased pressures weighing on the PCSWs. The PCSWs, and therefore primarily their staff, have experienced a strong intensification of work over the past 20 years, leading to a scarcity of time and resources, among other things.

Among the challenging features of social work in PCSWs to consider in this context are first and foremost the time pressure and workload (with a large regional and local variety),[1] as well as the difficulties to respect the deadlines, in particular in large agencies. There are variations depending on the PCSW service where the social worker works, and on the size of the municipalities[2] and associated number of beneficiaries, but overall, the time pressure and workload are stressed by a considerable number of respondents.

> It is not even about what I want to offer, but about what would be necessary. What you want to offer is, of course, much more, but what is minimally necessary, even for that there is not enough time. (Flanders, G, social worker, 20/04/2021)

Other structural factors that challenge social workers concern the very same functioning of PCSWs, described as 'archaic' and 'slow' institutions (Wallonia, B, social worker, 11/1/2021b). At the same time, structural welfare changes occurring over time (for example, concerning the access and duration of unemployment benefits) made the number of beneficiaries of PCSWs increase, affecting the provided service, and increasing workload. In addition, a limited budget is allocated to PCSWs: only 60% of this budget is refunded by the federal state, and social funding may not be a priority of all municipalities. The limited budget of PCSWs has an impact on the staff management as well. All of these structural, institutional, and organisational features together make for a challenging work context for social workers.

In addition – and as a result – many social workers perceive an imbalance between the time spent on administrative tasks (complying with procedures, filling in reports, and using management tools) and the time spent on social support. The latter also means that there is often not enough time for problem detection.

> We have an oppressive workload. If, on top of that, you have to put yourself back in the picture for two weeks to be able to understand the person completely … I know it's a bit violent to say it like that, but … […] I was talking about how the work is changing, [becoming] more and more as a bank. We do payment work, the social work part is becoming more and more residual and so the relationship I have with people depends on how far I have progressed in the cases. (Wallonia, B, social worker, 11/1/2021b)

> I think if you have a bit more time to see people and have a bit more of a conversation without it being about 'What question and what problems do you have?', but more about 'How are you doing?' and not just 'Well oh I have a headache!', but really going deeper into 'How are things for you?', that we can mean a lot more. We sometimes make ourselves believe we do, and we do try to. I think I speak for my colleagues here or for most of them: everyone is interested and really wants to do that, but it doesn't always work out. And certainly, with people who you have been counselling for less time, I think that is far too little. (Flanders, A, social worker, 27/04/2021)

As showed in many local studies on the evolution of PCSWs' policy into practice, many social workers describe the change of social work itself, the transformation of the missions and tasks carried out – also depending on a changed political approach of the institutions itself (Degraef & Franssen, 2013). The main tension that social workers put forward in our fieldwork is the gap between financial-related tasks and 'actual social work' and support.

> It is constraining, because we are not social workers to pay people, to be in control. At one point, we felt very strongly that the PCSW was looking for fraud and so I wasn't a social worker for that. I was there for helping, mutual aid, social support, and in the end here, yes, it's part of our mission, but it's not what we do the most and at times we are even frustrated at not being able to do it, […] we are in a payment role. […] they talk to us about performance […] we have to account for what we have done. (Wallonia, B, social worker, 15/1/2021)

As mentioned in Chapter 4, in some cases social work is partially taken in charge by 'educators' or 'consultants', at least in the PCSWs where this profile of workers exists. Thus, delegating part of the social work with beneficiaries who need more intensive counselling to other departments and agents, in order to diminish the workload of generalist social workers, can be perceived as a double-edged solution. If it actually relieves the charge, it can also increase the imbalance between administrative and 'actual social work' and contributes to emptying their function of 'sense' and social interactions.

> It's really administrative overload, [...] spending your time filling in papers, things like that, I find that we don't even have time to do in-depth social work. That's why we have to hand over a lot to the educators, etc. Because ... We don't even have time to do social work anymore, really. Except, fortunately [...] when we make home visits, we can still take the time to ... there, to do social interactions with the person, but otherwise, well ... I'm not going to say that it's an assembly line job [*travail à la chaîne*, in French], but ... (Wallonia, A, social worker, 17/2/2021)

Accordingly, other research in the Belgian context (Zara, 2019), showed how the creation of departments and new functions within the PCSW participated to a segmentation of work and to a loss of sense and substance on the work of frontline agents (see also Astier, 2007).

The academic literature on street-level bureaucracies explains how 'an implicit tension between resource constraints and the inexorable demands for public service' (Lipsky 1980, p. 172) characterises street-level work, meaning that there is an inherent gap between policy goals to be achieved and the resources allocated to do so: while citizens' demand for public services is unlimited, in fact, bureaucratic resources of time, information, and staff are necessarily constrained. As a consequence, when constraints are increasing and/or resources are diminishing, 'bureaucrats do not do just what they want or just what they are told to want. They do what they can' (Brodkin, 1997, p. 24). Similarly, the conditions of work often lead to the development of practices, in some cases redefining the initial objectives of public policies (Brodkin, 2012), or to create precedents in the processing of tasks, thus establishing ways of doing things that are no longer questioned (Lempert, 2001). These statements correspond to what was observed in our study as well. While some social workers complain about doing 'incomplete' social work and the lack of decision-making power outside the strict law framework (being impossible to 'go any further', Wallonia, B, social worker, 11/1/2021b), of having no time for problem detection and detailed information, some other respondents perceive not engaging with broader support (or even not informing users about social aids) as a strategy to avoid extra work. In other words, strictly following the legal/internal framework is both denounced as limiting the chances to respond to a beneficiary's needs, and as a way of coping with the conditions of work.

> Unfortunately, or fortunately, I don't know, for me it's unfortunately, some of the social workers have become accustomed to dealing with their files solely in an administrative manner, which respects the legal requirements and that's it. As soon as you apply the law to the letter without questioning it, legally it's correct. Does it meet the user's needs? Probably not. (Brussels, D, manager, 02/04/2021)

> There are two types of social workers, those who do administrative work and they will never be late, because they limit themselves to administrative work, and those who are more into human relations and global social aid. [...] The administrative work [...] is too much and [the social support] doesn't fit anymore with what is asked by the institution, they ask that the payments be made. Once they are done, we can start to discuss, but to make the payments, there are so many papers, so many procedures, it takes a long time. You have to write down the same information several times in different places, it's full of little things that slow down everything. (Wallonia, B, social worker, 11/1/2021b)

Among the organisational constraints that are reported in the PCSWs, we also find turnover being often mentioned by managers and directors. Turnover is often due to the impact of workload on the health of social workers – their absence causing in its turn the increase of caseworks to manage, which creates an endless vicious circle.

> At one point, I had a 6-month burnout. After that, I had a workload of 180 files. With the same requirement to respect in all the files. [...] we have endless work, it never stops, really, when I go on holiday I try to get ahead, and until recently, it was impossible to get ahead, so I knew that going on holiday meant accumulating backlogs for the new school year. When you're ill, it's the same thing. (Wallonia, B, social worker, 11/1/2021b)

Moreover, the renewal of the staff due to the arduousness of the work impacts the lack of proficiency of the teams. Last but not least, in the case of the PCSW, timing difficulties add to the pressure of social workers. Examples are the need of providing urgent help, even if not covering all needs (for example, food aid), to cope with status changes during the procedure (which obliges the social worker to build the record again with the elements brought by the new situation), to cope with delays in giving income supplement (*complément de revenu*) because the social workers need to wait for payslips that the beneficiary receives at the end of the month, and so forth. Indeed, social workers identify a set of challenges related to the temporality of the response to the beneficiaries' demands. These challenges are of two types: on the one hand, they concern the need for the institution to respect the deadlines established by the legal framework (see also Chapter 7); on the other hand, they concern the provision of a timely response in relation to the moment when the beneficiaries' needs emerge.

> You then have the deadlines of the intakes coming in so you have 30 days to conduct the social investigation, make your report and submit it to the committee. And then you have your monthly deadlines of integration income files. Which makes every month particularly 'heavy'. Because, yes, right now our deadline for the end of March is tomorrow afternoon, so next Tuesday is the last committee. But this is also something that always plays on your mind: you definitely want people to receive their living wage on time. Because if we don't make the deadline, it also means that people will receive their living wage a week later, which means they won't pay their rent on time and they will be in financial difficulties. So that actually causes you quite a lot of stress, also emotionally, because you know, if they don't make it right, our beneficiaries are stuck. Well, we are screwing ourselves but we are also screwing our people. (Flanders, C, social worker, 16/03/2021)

About the respect of the deadlines, most PCSWs take a decision on the applications within the 30-days delay, although the responsible and staff of some large PCSWs declare always being late.

> We are bound by deadlines, we know that we normally have one month legally to give a response, which is completely unfeasible. (Wallonia, B, social worker, 15/1/2021)

Apparently, such delays are not sanctioned nor have specific consequences on the functioning of PCSWs,[3] while they do have a direct impact on beneficiaries' life, as is also apparent from the findings based on newcomers' perspective in Chapter 11. Moreover, it should be noted that the delay in the allocation of social income or other social aids has an impact in particular for recognised refugees once they leave the reception centre. This is mainly related to the fact that their registration at the PCSW is conditioned by having an address in the municipality. Hence, once they found a place to rent and the demand for financial aid is addressed, they will often be in need to pay the first month and a deposit in order to keep this place.

> We always pay in arrears, […] so people already have no money, the only thing they have is their installation bonus, so we give it to them as a matter of urgency, but then they also have to choose between buying a bed and eating, because you have to sleep for a month on a blanket. […] I've already found myself with people who hadn't received their social assistance for three months, and that too, on the phone or in front of people, you have to have the argument and at some point, it's a mental burden that's exhausting and destructive, because you don't know what to say. At first, the person is late, then I'm late […], then when I've finally done my file, it's the others who are late, my boss, then the encoding [service], then … And we find ourselves in the past three years with people who bring us a letter [from the landlord] that says, 'I'm kicking [the person] out', and there we are completely against the wall saying what am I going to do, and we break a box. [*on pète une case*, in French] (Wallonia, B, social worker, 15/1/2021)

Indeed, the length and complexity of the PCSW's procedures can have consequences on the newcomers' relationship with the institution. Non-take-up of rights by non-demand, as theorised by Warn (2016, p. 4) can be a consequence of the difficulty to cope with the procedures, as is also discussed in Chapter 11 from the newcomers' perspective. This occurs, for example, when newcomers decide not to demand for certain types of support they are aware of and entitled to, to avoid engaging in lengthy and complex procedures (see Chapter 11).

In sum, the challenging context as described above impacts the actions, behaviour, and everyday choices of social workers and thereby affects service delivery to all beneficiaries. Therefore, it inevitably affects welfare provision to our group of focus as well, that is, newly arrived immigrants. As will become apparent, the issues related to high workload and associated time pressure, as discussed above, are intertwined with other major, more 'migrant-specific' challenges and pitfalls encountered in the service delivery to newly arrived immigrants, more particularly the difficulties to provide adequate social guidance, the (overly neglected) struggle to ensure an understandable system of service delivery for newly arrived immigrants, and the challenge to deal with language issues.

2. DIFFICULTIES TO PROVIDE ADEQUATE SOCIAL GUIDANCE AND SUPPORT TO NEWCOMERS

As mentioned above, the time pressure and workload have a negative impact on the social guidance and support provided to beneficiaries, with social workers stating that too much time is spent on administration, and too little on beneficiaries' needs, and what could be considered as the 'core task' of a social worker. In what concerns newly arrived immigrants, high workloads are told to be exacerbated, since these beneficiaries are in need for more intensive counselling, explaining, and additional support compared to other beneficiaries (see Chapter 4), while there is a lot of administrative work to be dealt with. As a result, the amount of financial and administrative issues to tackle in the beginning can make it difficult to detect other issues. While the start of the support at PCSW to newly arrived immigrants is generally characterised by the many financial and administrative issues, later, more complex issues might arise. Indeed, other, more psycho-social issues often only become visible at a later stage (that is, after a longer period of time), as it takes time before there is room – as well as trust and good communication conditions – to discuss them. Surfacing traumas are mentioned in this respect, but also the confrontation with the sometimes-harsh reality of life as a migrant. Social workers also mention the frequent problem of loneliness and social isolation. The social workers can do their best and invest some more time in the relation with newcomer beneficiaries if they know the person has few contacts, but at the same time, due to time constraints, there is often not enough room to discuss the person's needs in detail.

> In the first instance, that is exactly, well, or seems to be quite straightforward, those practical things that have to be put in order. But if you then look further into the project, you often notice that the situations are very complex, or that the problems are also very complex. And I'm thinking of loneliness, for example, which these people [newly arrived immigrants] have to deal with, or they come here with certain expectations. And then they have to conclude that those expectations cannot be met in the way they would like it to be, in their minds. Or they have studied in their home country, for example, and then they find out here, that they cannot actually do what they did in their home country, or that their diploma does not serve them here. And that causes a lot of frustration and, yes, a lot of difficulties. (Flanders, C, social worker, 16/03/2021)

> The basis is often what you need to spend some time on. This is often the start of the assistance process, which means that you do not focus on a

number of other areas. Someone who has been here for a long time, or a Flemish person for example, will just have his intake, and then they will check whether or not his or her papers are in order. But after that, you can start focusing on other domains in your assistance, while here [with newcomers] more attention has to be paid to other aspects. (Flanders, C, manager, 23/02/2021)

A concrete example of consequences of time shortage and workload is also that social workers will be more inclined to (or feel obliged to) simply refer to other organisations, instead of accompanying the beneficiaries or helping out themselves (see also Chapter 4 on cooperation and referrals), and especially for newcomers, it can affect the quality of the service delivery, as is apparent from the quote below. In this aspect, some social workers assume that, even if their aim is to promote and build-up autonomy, for newcomers' first steps in a completely new system, they would prefer to propose more intensive guidance (and even physical accompaniment) not to get lost in the meanders of the administration. Nevertheless, they regret that doing so would be in detriment of their mission with other beneficiaries.

> We noticed that sometimes things go wrong with these referrals. For example, people who didn't understand it properly, which is why it didn't work out in the end. Uhm, which is why we sometimes think that an individual thorough approach for non-native newcomers, such an intensive approach, is better to get them on their way than all the referrals. But of course, you have to be able to do everything. (Flanders, D, social worker, 19/03/2021)

According to some of the social workers, this is particularly evident at present, whereas in the past, the social work with beneficiaries and in particular with newly arrived immigrants in PCSWs was different, in the sense that they could adapt the time spent on accompanying them when the need was detected.

> I can guide them by saying you can go there or there but I can't take them by the hand, I did that at the beginning when I started working, I went as far as accompanying people to the bank to show how it worked, […] standing orders, direct debits and help them put in place practices that facilitate budget management, schools … I had regular contact with the [school social workers] to see how the children were doing, we are talking about children who don't speak French so there are things that are put in place. (Wallonia, B, social worker, 11/1/2021b)

Recently, and at the moment of our fieldwork, the pandemics of COVID-19 also affected social workers' support to newly arrived immigrants in particular, with, for example, changed modes of communication having a particularly strong impact on (some) newly arrived immigrants (for example, increased use of phone contacts and e-mail, while dealing with difficulties in language learning and cutting face-to-face communication with people at higher risk of social isolation). The health crisis challenged the accessibility of the PCSWs and of the social support itself, for all the beneficiaries, yet, according to some, with a stronger impact for those in need of understanding a whole new system, country, and language.

> [W]ith the sanitary conditions, we're a bit stuck with it. And we get a lot of requests from people who ask me when I'm coming, because it's important for them to have contact, because these are often people who are isolated, their family is still in the country, and with the language barrier they don't dare to go towards others. And the French school, for example, is now at distance, so they no longer see the friends and acquaintances they have at the French course and are therefore even more socially isolated. So, it's important to maintain contact even at a distance, to have video conferences with them, to check up on them. (Wallonia, F, social worker, 3/12/2020b)

> Especially since the lockdown, or at least the health situation, I have the impression that we are really only in the administrative side. I miss [...] a little bit the interview side for things, even to discuss, it was good, it changed the work in any case and it can be seen in them too. Some of them [...] are more stressed because there is no visual and when there is only the telephone or email, they don't know how to ask questions or answer properly than if I was face to face with them. It changes a lot in some people that. And they want an interview but unfortunately, we can't do it at the moment. (Wallonia, B, social worker, 12/1/2021)

More generally, also regardless of the COVID-19 health crisis, the possibility to provide ample support is said to vary and evolve over time as well, depending on the broader societal and migratory context. Among these factors, we can find, for instance, migratory flows, changes in the management of the reception of applicants for international protection, or in political approach at the immigration office.

> It depends on the periods, [...] in 2015 there was the big wave of migrants, [...] in 2017 all these migrants who had arrived in 2015 started to leave the

asylum centres. [...] we went through a period of one year where it was really very difficult because we had the impression that we had become machines for new applications, we were conducting interviews and we had to try to close them as quickly as possible because other people were arriving. (Wallonia, C, social worker, 15/3/2021)

Belgium's migration policies have changed a lot and, as a result, when I started there were still many asylum seekers who came to ask for financial aid [...] the places of registration were not especially the reception centres because there was saturation and the PCSWs took over. [...] There were also precarious residency statuses related to the application for regularisation for health problems, and for a long time the simple fact of submitting the application for regularisation, once it was recorded by the Foreigners' Office, the person received a residency permit that allowed them [...] to have access to financial aid. (Wallonia, B, social worker, 11/1/2021b)

Another challenge related to service delivery to newly arrived migrants concerns the struggle to correctly inform newcomer beneficiaries about their rights, and to provide insight in the goals and functioning of the PCSW as an institution, which also affects the accessibility of care and support for this group. In the coming paragraphs, this issue is discussed in detail.

3.   FROM ENTITLEMENT TO THE TAKE UP OF SUPPORT

Another challenge PCSWs are confronted with, and a fortiori with newcomers, is to ensure the take up of social rights. In what follows, it is explained how social workers have a crucial role to fulfil to help ensure the take up of rights by newcomers, for example by clear and ample communication. In general, but more strongly with the target group of newly arrived immigrants, the take up can be threatened by a lack of knowledge and information about the system and the specific aids available, and by the opacity of the procedures at the PCSW. The lack of information is discussed in the final part of this book as well, from the perspective of the newcomers. Here, we focus on the challenges and pitfalls as mentioned by the social workers and their managers, and what they (can/need to) do to help protect the rights of newly arrived beneficiaries. However, as discussed at the end of this section, it implies an awareness of the specific challenges for newcomers, which cannot be taken for granted.

3.1. Understanding the system

A first challenge in service delivery at PCSW, and a fortiori to newly arrived immigrants, regards the understandability of the system of aid, and of the PCSW as an institution. Put differently, it is challenging to make sure the beneficiaries understand what PCSW stands for, what help they can get, what the goals are, and so forth. This knowledge cannot be taken for granted, and even less with newcomer beneficiaries, as was also observed by Ratzmann and Heindlmaier (2021), studying knowledge asymmetries between (EU) migrants and welfare administrators. As discussed in Chapter 1, this relates to the accessibility of the service as well, and more particularly to the dimensions of approachability (transparency, outreach, information, and so forth, see Levesque *et al.*, 2013) and accommodation (organising the service in such a way that it suits the context from which the beneficiary comes; see Russell *et al.*, 2013), but also the awareness of beneficiaries, for example of which services and rights are available to them.

Concretely, the fact that many newcomers do not know the system (as discussed in Chapter 4), implies they do not know what to expect and to ask. Moreover, to some, it can be difficult to explain, if they have not been familiarised with a comparable institution in their home country.

> Newcomers are not familiar with our system either and do not know what to expect or not to expect, or what to ask or not to ask. This also makes it a bit difficult for us sometimes, that we have to explain things so that they have an idea or get a grasp. And that is something that is not always easy. (Flanders, C, social worker, 16/03/2021)

It should be noted that other studies addressing newcomers and other beneficiaries arrived at similar conclusions as what we have observed here: the complexity of the procedures and formularies, the juridical language, and the fact of not clearly knowing what to ask are obstacles to the access to rights (Caldarini, 2018). Moreover, the complexity of the system of social support can prevent beneficiaries asking for extra aids. Some social workers contend that newly arrived immigrants do not always know the difference between federal asylum centres, the PCSW, or the municipality. The difficulty to ask is also related to shyness or the embarrassment of being perceived as a 'beggar', a feature found on the PCSW's beneficiaries in general (Bomblet, 2021) and supported by the literature of non-take up as well (Warin, 2014, p. 18). These aspects will be discussed from the perspective of newcomers in Part III of this book.

3.2.   A lack of systematic information provision on social aids

Throughout the fieldwork, we found a large variation between PCSWs and social workers, in terms of systematic (or not) communication about social aids. Even if many actors mentioned the 'duty of information' as it is defined by law, in practice either the beneficiary formulates the request in a specific way, or the social worker identifies a need and proposes additional aid (see also Chapter 7). The quote below also illustrates the strong dependence of the beneficiaries on their social worker.

> One of the missions of the social workers in the PCSW is the duty to inform people of their rights, their general rights and also at the PCSW level, 'Ah no, no, you have the right to ask for help to buy a new fridge.' Some people know and really come with their lists. We do social work, we do a bit of psychology, we do mediation, we do a bit of parenting, we do a bit of lawyering, we do a bit of everything, so it's really rich and it also depends on the investment of the social worker obviously, the amount of work. It's obvious that if you have a lot of work, you might not want to give yourself more work. Well, if I propose it, it means that I know that [it will bring extra work] …; etc. And that's a bit of everyone's professional identity. The workload of each person. His/her personality. (Brussels, A, social worker, 30/04/2021)

Thus, information is mainly given by social workers during social enquiry and face-to-face meetings, on an individual basis. Although social workers have guidelines for their work, these do not include a text for beneficiaries that brings together the available information on all the potential support to which an individual may be entitled. In order to avoid disparities on information provision about the beneficiaries' rights, internal debates were raised in some PCSWs under study about having or not a document or a list of the basic social aids that people can ask for, but in most cases the dominant opinion was that it would skew the individual-tailored logic of treating beneficiaries. According to some, the risk incurred by this tool would also be that the beneficiaries ask abusively and would not be sufficiently accountable about the aids they receive.

> It's up to each social worker, that's sad, we discussed it once in a meeting, my bosses wanted to make a little document saying all the aids they could claim, it's a bit limited, some social workers said 'Yeah, afterwards it's like a self-service and they're going to start asking for everything and anything.' (Brussels, G, social worker, 25/05/2021)

The quantity and quality of the information given to beneficiaries is subject to contradictions and dilemmas that emerge in the narrative of fieldworkers describing their practice (and as we will see in Chapter 10, it echoes the experiences of the newcomer beneficiaries as well). Some of them recognise that informing beneficiaries depends 'on the goodwill of their colleagues' to do a thorough analysis of the needs and the social aids provided for by law and by internal guidelines. The latter implies equal treatment cannot be taken for granted. It is often envisaged as a question of work overload, which would lead social workers to discharge a maximum of tasks towards external partnerships or internal services. In some of the cases under study (particularly in the region of Brussels), social workers regret that beneficiaries are not fully informed about their rights, due to lack of time of treating the subsequent demands:

> I've already replaced some colleagues and the people didn't even know that they were entitled to diapers for their children, so it's less work for the social assistant, yes it's true, but people are not concretely informed of their rights. (Brussels, G, social worker, 25/05/2021)

In some cases, the failure to inform about rights would also be independent of the availability of time, and due to other – not explicit – factors:

> Normally the medical card, yes, there are some who don't come to get it because they don't know. But this is usually done automatically because as soon as the social integration income is proposed, the medical card is automatically encoded. So it's not extra work and there's a counter down here at the reception where they come to print their medical card, they don't really go through the social worker, so you can imagine that it's generally an aid that the social workers don't forget to offer because it's not extra work. (Brussels, G, social worker, 25/05/2021)

The fact that newcomer beneficiaries do not know the system nor what to expect and to ask for complexifies the task of the social workers, since – as explained by some fieldworkers – they need to try to explain what it entails, but they also need to be more proactive in the provision of social guidance and support, for example, in terms of problem detection, actively checking what newcomers know and/or need, and so on. As newly arrived immigrants are often unaware of their rights, this can also have repercussions on the effective possibility to address their needs.

We normally see them once a month, but that's not much. So yes, that does mean that we miss a lot anyway. But asking questions for people is difficult if one doesn't know what's out there. (Flanders, A, social worker, 27/04/2021)

The problem is exacerbated by the fact that these challenges increase the newcomer's dependence on social workers. Moreover, it can lead to unequal treatment, hampering service delivery, as well as the non-take-up of social rights.

Even though the discussion about proposing a list of social aids does not seem to have been taken forward, in some PCSWs we found internal measures taken at the level of the committee through guidelines that are adopted in order to standardise social aids and limit discretion, as will be discussed in Part II of this book. Among these measures, we find, for example, systematically giving medical cards, diapers, free transports formulary, and so forth.

3.3. Opaque procedures

In addition to the understandability of the system of aid, of the PCSW as an institution, and of the particular social aids available, also the understandability of the procedures at the PCSW should be considered. Our findings indicated that these pose particular challenges in the work with newly arrived immigrants as well.

Overall, a considerable share of the social workers and coordinators estimate that the procedures concerning the application for social assistance and related measures such as the ISIP are sufficiently understood by beneficiaries, when they are carefully explained. This means that understandability is not really brought forward as a 'big issue' in most of the interviews. Some state, for example, that immigrant beneficiaries might not understand in the beginning, but it gradually becomes clearer to them. For instance, they might not know what is an ISIP but they understand that there are steps to follow and that these are compulsory to keep receiving financial aid. In other cases, respondents argue that having a written support, such as in the case of the ISIP, can help newly arrived immigrants, even if they do not fully understand in the moment of signing, to have it translated later out of the PCSW.

It is compulsory and certainly for these families [newcomers], [...] as strange as it may seem, the fact of having something on paper [the ISIP contract] also allows the person to have things explained later to them in their own language, that they would not have been able to understand during the interview in terms of the subtitlies [...] that say this is what we are going to ask you to do and this is what the PCSW will do for you. [...]

the fact that it is written down brings a lot of benefits, in the sense that if the user has not necessarily understood everything, he can go and have someone explain it to him. (Brussels, D, manager, 02/04/2021)[4]

Yet, some others stressed the administrative burden and the difficulty to grasp and to follow the ISIP tool for newly arrived immigrants, as for other beneficiaries. Others stated that it hampers the relationship with the beneficiaries: the tool needs to be introduced from the start, whereas doing so does not fit well with building a relationship of trust. Studies in the Belgian context highlight the diversity of practices and representations concerning the ISIP from one PCSW to another, and even from one social worker to another within the same institution (Franssen, 2016). According to other studies, the most part of social workers support the ISIP as a support tool on the basis of a contractual form, but there is also a generalised demand to reduce the administrative burden of using this tool (Caldarini, 2018).

In our fieldwork, it is to note that the very nature of the ISIP, as an individual-tailored project that is meant to be 'negotiated' between the social worker and the beneficiary, and engaging the latter on a series of duties and rights, is barely questioned – though there are certainly exceptions – when social workers assume that newcomers are not always aware of what they are signing. In other words, a tool for 'problem detection' and 'project determination' seems to be predominantly envisaged as an imposition or simply a procedural formality,[5] as soon as some of the interlocutors assume that 'they will understand it later', eventually at the moment of evaluation of ISIP where they may find out that they did not comply with the requests of the institution, and risk to be sanctioned. This question will be further developed from the perspective of newly arrived immigrants in Chapter 10.

3.4.   A lack of awareness by social workers

Not only are there differences in terms of what is *explained* by social workers (cf. supra): there is also a huge variation in the extent to which social workers are *aware* of the problems mentioned above (that is, newcomers not understanding the system, not knowing what they can ask for, and so forth), the consequences it entails, and how they deal with it, and in that sense, we consider it as a pitfall in the service delivery to newly arrived immigrants.

I also have the idea that social workers are not trained to work with newcomers. The idea that our Western assistance is not known to newcomers, that's something, that's something hard to get into. I've noticed that since

I started telling them about it at training sessions or, they do stop to think about it. Explaining that the way of providing help, of looking for help, is also different in other countries, often they don't realise that. (Flanders, B, specialist in newcomers, 01/06/2021)

More generally, we noted that there was little reflection upon the accessibility for immigrants, and little questioning of the 'system' and common practices in that sense. Yet, as explained by Ratzmann (2022), discrimination can arise from a systematic lack of awareness for certain beneficiaries' needs, which are so-called organisational blind spots (Bach & Wegrich, 2018). Put differently, the lack of awareness of the difficulties of newcomers to understand the system and make the best use of it is likely to have real consequences in the service delivery they receive, leading to implicit discriminatory treatment in practice. Some aspects will be further discussed in Chapter 8.

4. LANGUAGE ISSUES HAMPERING COMMUNICATION

Among the specific difficulties faced in service delivery to newly arrived immigrants, the most mentioned concern language issues, as also Van Robaeys and Driessens (2011) highlight. The access to, and use of services and benefits is greatly influenced by language, as on it depends the possibility of reciprocal understanding between social workers and beneficiaries. Language-related inequity experiences have been stressed in the literature, and language has been shown to contribute to the social stratification of access (see, for example, Brubaker, 2015; Cederberg, 2014; Holzinger, 2020; Ratzmann, 2021).

In our study as well, some respondents acknowledge that the lack of common language also has an impact on (the extent to) which newcomers' needs are addressed. Language problems affect mutual understanding and can make it difficult to touch upon 'deeper' issues (involving issues related to psychosocial wellbeing, for example), hence impacting the support given to newcomers.

Language is of course a very important factor. Because of the language, some counselling sessions can remain very 'basic', I'll put it this way, whereas if you can talk to each other in plain Dutch, then there are a lot of differences in nuance, there are a lot of …, yes, you can go further, and you can understand each other better in certain details of the counselling. Yes, I don't know how to put it, but if you use 'basic' language, then you do the bare essentials, and you try to explain, but … (Flanders, E, social worker, 16/03/2021)

But when I look at my own role in it, I go and answer a certain question or look for an answer. At that point, I am partly an anchor. But if they don't understand the language, people are not so inclined. That is something that I do feel very strongly about, to go deeper into certain problems, there is a kind of inhibition there, the language (Flanders, G, social worker, 20/04/2021).

Failing to understand one another in a detailed way affects the content and nuances of communication, and hence the quality of the service delivery. Yet, the strategies put in place at the general social service are mainly individual and the actual solutions are generally described as being not always adapted to enhance comprehension between newcomer beneficiaries and social workers. It is worth noting that, despite the fact that many respondents pinpoint the issue of language, generally there is no systematic or structural solution offered to it.

One possibility in the toolbox of social workers to deal with language problems is the reliance on external professional translation services, such as a regional (or sometimes more local) services of social interpreting. The decision whether or not to make use of these services is often an individual decision rather than the result of a consistent policy. Moreover, social workers declare that resorting to these services is hard to put into practice due to complicated procedures and unavailable languages or dialects, representing additional work and time to them without a necessarily positive outcome. The costs are a refraining element as well, in some cases.

The access to interpreters is complicated. We worked systematically with them and then we were forbidden to do so, and we were told that you were never forbidden to do so, and then we were told that now you can do it again, but there is a particular procedure and when we asked for the procedure, no one knew about it. It's the administration, that's all. (Wallonia, B, social worker, 11/01/2021b)

I try to arrange an interpreter as often as possible. That's just desperate. That's, I think on two out of ten times when I have an interpreter it's a lot. So that's super hard, you know. […] And then I ask the agency 'Yes, can you get me an interpreter by then, that hour? Yeah, no, we don't have an interpreter'. Yes, then you are stuck. (Flanders, F, social worker, 25/05/2021)

Many social workers explain that very often they end up coping with language barriers through gestures, drawings, and using Google translate.

> There are many who don't speak French, and so, with my colleagues, we try, as much as possible, to get by, and so sometimes, during the interviews, we even make drawings to try to make ourselves understood … (Wallonia, A, social worker, 17/02/2021)

Other internal dynamics can be put in place, such as the participation of *agents d'accueil* or *toeleiders/taalhulpen*, often engaged by Art. 60[6] contracts and whose role can be to mediate or translate at the reception, in the conversations between social workers and beneficiaries or in specific activities. Social assistants generally mentioned many advantages of working with such 'internal translators', in the sense that it is easier in practice (for example, more flexible). However, concerns were also raised related to the quality of the service delivery. For example, internal translators may not be sufficiently trained, may lack the context, and give an own interpretation instead of sticking to translation.

> I rely mostly on a language assistant [*taalhulp*]. I rarely use interpreters from the professional service. So that plays a role as well [in having misunderstandings]. They really do their best, but of course, they are not always fully informed about our service. And they sometimes fill in things which are not entirely correct, with the best intentions. This way, there can be noise in the communication. Usually it goes well, but these things do happen. (Flanders, A, social worker, 27/04/2021)

Moreover, internal translators working under Art. 60 contracts only have this function for a limited period (one or two years maximum), which implies they cannot build up experience for a long time. In addition, some also mentioned that even internal translators became less available, due to the limited (and decreased) availability of formal interpreters (which causes the internal translators to be overly demanded as well).

Another recurrent strategy to deal with language issues is to ask the beneficiary to come with a family member, friend, or acquaintance who can help translating. The fact that newcomers rely on relatives or even on their children raises questions within certain teams – beyond doubting the quality of the translation when done by other citizens, ethical questions have been raised in supervision around the role of exiled children in the integration of parents in the host country.

What bothers me a bit with newcomers, what is complicated is that children in general, I'm disturbed when it's a child translating, when I call a parent and it's the child who has to answer and it makes me very uncomfortable that it's the child who has to go and do the work. Sometimes they come with the parents directly to the interview and I'm a bit uncomfortable with that because I have the impression that the child is taking all the responsibility […] it's a bit heavy on their shoulders. (Brussels, B, social worker, 27/05/2021)

It is worth mentioning that recent literature addresses the issue of children as language brokers in the immigration process involving them and their families, and the dynamics of family role redefinition and 'parentification' to which they are subjected. However, this literature highlights the potential negative and positive outcomes of this practice (see, for instance, Bauer, 2016; Bossuroy & Jouve, 2021; Weisskirch, 2010).

Other strategies are also present or being considered, more particularly in some PCSWs where language skills within the teams (also due to the presence of social workers with immigrant background, as we will see in Chapter 8) make it possible to identify 'volunteer' translators who are available to translate to their colleagues. However, the multicultural character of the teams does not necessarily imply a willingness to make use of the potential benefits of multilingualism, and tensions and dilemmas may arise. Moreover, some social workers stated that they made the choice not to speak their mother tongue (when different from one of the national languages), because they consider that this can lead to relations of favouritism, or to unmet expectations, when beneficiaries pretend that someone from the same cultural community shall not refuse to grant them the rights they reclaim (we will study this issue further in Chapter 8).

To conclude, across the interviews it became clear that there is a large variation in how social workers deal with language issues. Language comes forward as an important aspect and barrier in the communication, but the way it is dealt with differs largely, not only between situations (short practical communication might require different strategies from sensitive discussions, for example), but also between services and social workers, while a number of respondents stress how the lack of (using a) common language affects the accessibility and quality of service delivery.

Social workers develop their own strategies, informally counting on colleagues, on relatives of the beneficiary, and even on their children. Apart from 'practical concerns' (such as the availability of interpreters, costs, and time-consuming organisation), ideology also clearly plays a role in determining how to deal with language problems. Many case workers stress the importance that beneficiaries learn the regional language as an issue of integration, therefore they mostly rely on the exclusive use of the regional language. On the other hand, others go further in organising translation, stressing the importance of good and nuanced communication. Overall, social workers usually do not have a professional framework at hand to deal with this question. The fact of not having a professional framework was severely criticised by one of the respondents, specialised in working with newcomers:

> [interviewee:] What that I also notice is when it comes to working with newcomers, we find it justified that we go by our opinion and no longer by our professional framework.
> [interviewer:] In what sense?
> [interviewee:] You can always fall back on that. For example, uhm, should I give an example. Ah yes. We're allowed by our organisation to ask for an interpreter to, we're actually allowed to ask for an interpreter at any time. There's also, uh, we can request that from a program. But there are social workers who say 'Ah. I think, sir, you already had to know Dutch, so I'm not going to request an interpreter.' But actually professionally we are just expected, if our client doesn't speak enough Dutch, we have to inform people. That's our duty. So then we request an interpreter. (Flanders, B, specialist in newcomers, 01/06/2021)

The large diversity in terms of approach with regard to language echoes earlier findings from Scheibelhofer, Holzinger, and Draxl (2021), in a study of street-level bureaucrats' strategies to deal with linguistic diversity among the Austrian Public Employment Service. Similar to our findings, these authors describe the approach to linguistic diversity among beneficiaries as a continuum, '[r]anging from a reflective, critical approach towards linguistic diversity that is at least partly based on ideas promoting the value of multilingualism to frequently encountered notions of the need for monolingualism' (p. 24). The authors report that monolingualism (and thereby the expectation towards service users to speak German) remains dominant, while at the same time, multiple multilingual practices could be identified in the everyday work of employees of the public employment service. Nevertheless, and in line with the findings of our study, these multilingual practices and strategies 'reflect a disorganised mix of side strategies rather than a coherent institutional strategy' (Scheibelhofer *et al.*, 2021, p. 31). Yet, as demonstrated by Ratzmann (2021), selective and incidental implementation of language policies can result in unequal treatment, producing differences in terms of the receipt of support in practice. Ratzmann concludes that beneficiaries' ability to speak the national language becomes 'an instrument of strategic exclusion from de facto benefit receipt, whether intended or not' (p. 9). The lack of consistent policy, and the discretion to deal with language issues as observed in the Belgian PCSWs under study, is likely to have a similar effect.

Moreover, as pointed out by Ratzmann and Heindlmaier (2021), the vulnerability caused by not knowing the language, in the case of many newcomer beneficiaries, comes on top of the vulnerability caused by not knowing the system and understanding the formal entitlements and procedures, exacerbating existing power asymmetries. The issue of power asymmetries will be discussed further in Chapter 10.

NOTES

1. In the online survey, the average caseload reported per social worker was 50, with a median value of 45. The highest reported caseload per social worker in the survey was 120 (based on the answers in Flanders and Wallonia). In the fieldwork, some social workers reported an even higher caseload in the Brussels region. In the survey, the average caseload reported was higher in Wallonia (average 54, median 50) than in Flanders (average 46, median 40).

2. The online survey confirmed this finding from the fieldwork, as it showed a much larger caseload in large municipalities (average 91, median 90), compared to small municipalities (average 39, median 40), with medium-sized municipalities occupying an intermediate position in terms of reported caseload (average 56, median 50).

3. The beneficiary has the right to introduce a complaint and be auditioned by the committee, but the very access to these tools depends on the information obtained from the institution. Non-take-up of rights will be further discussed in Chapter 11, from the perspective of newly arrived immigrant beneficiaries.

4. The authors and editors of this book are aware of the male bias in certain phrasings of this respondent and others (for instance, speaking of 'he' and 'him' only, whereas it could also concern female beneficiaries as well). The decision was taken to keep the quotes as they were expressed by the interlocutors, even though they were not always thinking and speaking in terms of gender, but rather in terms of a non-gendered beneficiary. This holds for quotes in other chapters and parts of this book as well.

5. It is to note that the funding of the social income allocated to the PCSWs by the ministry is also determined by the compliance with compulsory procedures, for instance being dependent on the obligation of signing an ISIP for the target population, that is a reason that is sometimes put forward by social workers – 'it is a financial thing' (Brussels, G, social worker, 10/03/2022) – when asked about the use of the tool with newcomers.

6. The Art. 60§ 7 of the Organic Law of the PCSW established a mechanism of employment engaged by the PCSW to beneficiaries of social integration income to 'prove a period of work in order to obtain the full benefit of certain social benefits [namely, unemployment benefits] or in order to promote work experience' (Castaigne, 2020:4) (see Chapter 6).

REFERENCES

Astier, I. (2007). *Les nouvelles règles du social*. Presses Universitaires de France.

Bach, T., & Wegrich, K. (2018). Blind spots, biased attention, and the politics of non-coordination. In T. Bach, & K. Wegrich (Eds.), *The blind spots of public bureaucracy and the politics of non-coordination* (pp. 3–28). Palgrave Macmillan.

Bauer, E. (2016). Practising kinship care: Children as language brokers in migrant families. *Childhood, 23*(1), 22–36.

Bomblet, P. (2021). *Dans quelle mesure le travailleur social joue-t-il un rôle dans le phénomène du non-recours ?* [Master thesis, Université catholique de Louvain].

Bossuroy, M., & Jouve, P. (2021). Les enfants qui jouent le rôle d'interprète pour leurs parents: De la parentification à la parentalisation. *Dialogue, 233*, 175–193.

Brodkin, E. Z. (1997). Inside the welfare contract: Discretion and accountability in state welfare administration. *Social Service Review, 71*(1), 1–33.

Brodkin, E. Z. (2012). Reflections on street-level bureaucracy: Past, present, and future. *Public Administration Review, 72*(6), 940-949.

Brubaker, R. (2015). Linguistic and religious pluralism: Between difference and inequality. *Journal of Ethnic and Migration Studies, 41*(1), 3–32.

Caldarini, C. (2018). *Projet Individualisé d'Intégration Sociale: vers un accompagnement de meilleure qualité* [Rapport des groupes focus avec un échantillon de citoyens bénéficiaires]. CPAS Schaerbeek.

Castaigne, M. (2020). Le point sur l'article 60 § 7. Namur: Fédération des CPAS;

Cederberg, M. (2014). Public discourses and migrant stories of integration and inequality: Language and power in biographical narratives. *Sociology, 48*(1), 133–149.

Degraef, V., & Franssen, A. (2013). *Recherche-action sur l'accompagnement des personnes dans les CPAS Bruxellois* [Rapport de recherche]. Université Saint-Louis.

Franssen, A. (2016). To PIIS or not to PIIS? Les injections paradoxales à l'autonomie. *l'Observatoire, 88*(1), 51–56.

Hawkins, K. (2001). The uses of legal discretion: Perspectives from law and social science. In K. Hawkins (Ed.), *The uses of discretion* (pp. 1–46). Oxford University Press.

Holzinger, C. (2020). 'We don't worry that much about language': Street level bureaucracy in the context of linguistic diversity. *Journal of Ethnic and Migration Studies, 46*(9), 1792–1808.

Jewell, C. J., & Glaser, B. E. (2006). Toward a general analytic framework: Organizational settings, policy goals, and street-level behavior. *Administration & Society, 38*(3), 335–364.

Lempert, R. (2001). Discretion and behavioral perspective: The case of a public housing eviction board. In K. Hawkins (Ed.), *The uses of discretion* (pp. 185–230). Oxford University Press.

Levesque, J.-F., Harris, M. F., & Russell, G. (2013). Patient-centred access to health care: Conceptualizing access at the interface of health systems and populations. *International Journal for Equity in Health, 12*, 1–10.

Lipksy, M. (2010). *Street-level bureaucracy: Dilemmas of the individual in public services* (30th anniversary expanded edition). Russel Sage Foundation. (Original work published 1980)

Ratzmann, N. (2021). Deserving of social support? Street-level bureaucrats' decisions on EU migrants' benefit claims in Germany. *Social Policy & Society, 20*(3), 1–12.

Ratzmann, N., & Heindlmaier, A. (2021). Welfare mediators as game changers? Deconstructing power asymmetries between EU migrants and welfare administrators. *Social Inclusion, 10*(1), 205–216.

Russell, D. J., Humphreys, J. S., Ward, B., Chisholm, M., Buykx, P., McGrail, M., & Wakerman, J. (2013). Helping policy-makers address rural health access problems. *Australian Journal of Rural Health, 21*(2), 61–71.

Scheibelhofer, E., Holzinger, C., & Draxl, A-K. (2021). Linguistic diversity as a challenge for street-level bureaucrats in a monolingually-oriented organisation. *Social Inclusion, 9*(1), 24–34.

Van Robaeys, B. & Driessens, K. (2011). *Gekleurde armoede en hulpverlening: Sociaal werkers en cliënten aan het woord* [Coloured poverty and care. Social workers and clients speaking]. Lannoo.

Warin, P. (2014). Le non-recours aux prestations sociales: quelle critique du ciblage? *Les Politiques Sociales, 2*(2), 12-23.

Warin, P. (2016). The analysis of non-take-up: Going beyond the service relationship model. *Vie Sociale, 14*(2), 49–64.

Weisskirch, R. S. (2010). Child language brokers in immigrant families: An overview of family dynamics. *MediAzioni, 10*, 68–87.

Zara, N. (2019). *D'un sentiment d'ambivalence à la souffrance au travail: le rôle de la relation d'aide et des stratégies identitaires chez les travailleurs sociaux en CPAS* [Master thesis, Université Catholique de Louvain].

CHAPTER 6
LABOUR MARKET ACTIVATION AND NEWLY ARRIVED IMMIGRANTS

HANNE VANDERMEERSCHEN, ADRIANA COSTA SANTOS AND ELSA MESCOLI

INTRODUCTION

The idea of an 'active welfare state' has led to the expectation that welfare institutions such as the PCSW not merely offer a 'passive' form of social assistance, but also invest in citizens and promote social integration, and more particularly through employment whenever possible (Carpentier, 2016; Dumont, 2012; Hermans, 2005). Beneficiaries of a social integration income are expected to make the necessary efforts to take steps in this direction. Put differently, 'disposition to work' (being ready and available to work) is a condition to access – and keep – social benefits (see Chapter 4; see also Hermans, 2005; Van Parys, 2016). In this chapter, we focus on labour market activation of newly arrived immigrant beneficiaries, as part of the guidance and service provision towards this target group.

In a first section, we dwell on the perspective on 'socio-professional integration'[1] – the emic term that reflects labour market activation policies in our case studies and in Belgium more generally – in PCSW services, exploring how they interpret this term and, by consequence, which goals are set by the social workers. To do so, we rely both on the results of the online survey, presented first, and on the data collected during the fieldwork. Next, in a second section, we discuss the role of the PCSW and its social workers in terms of guidance towards socio-professional integration. We also consider that the PCSWs are not the only actors involved in this process, as there are also public employment services for example, as well as other organisations, whose mission is labour market activation. Yet, as we will see, PCSWs mostly stay in charge when it concerns the socio-professional integration of their beneficiaries, including newly arrived immigrants. This chapter provides a deeper insight in current practices and the rationales behind.

Even though the expectation of disposition to work holds for all beneficiaries, newly arrived immigrants, and others alike, our fieldwork revealed that newcomer beneficiaries were often considered 'not ready' for the labour market by the social workers and the entrance to the labour market is often postponed. Therefore, in a third section of this chapter, the central topic is the assessment of 'readiness to work' (employability). We explore the factors that may hold newcomers back, and more particularly the conditions set by social workers in order to be considered 'ready' to enter the labour market. Put differently, the third section provides a better understanding of the steps preceding (or preventing) the actual entrance to the labour market.

1.   THE AIM OF SOCIO-PROFESSIONAL INTEGRATION

Previous studies have shown that an 'activation turn' has been taken in Belgian PCSWs since approximately the beginning of the 21st century (Carpentier, 2005; Dumont, 2012; Hermans, 2005). However, it has also been shown that concepts such as 'activation' can cover different perspectives, and have varying underlying ideologies (Hermans, 2005), potentially leading to different choices in terms of policy practice and implementation (see also De Greef, 2018; Franssen, 2016). Therefore, in particular in the complementary online survey (see Chapter 3), we sought to clarify the current perspective in PCSW services on this matter. More specifically, respondents were asked how they would describe the vision on *socio-professional integration* in their PCSW service. Respondents were asked to rank a set of descriptions according to the priorities set by their PCSW service, starting with the description that best suited the perspective in their PCSW and ending with the description that was least accurate. Table 6.1 provides an overview of description given and their mean scores (with scores closer to 1 being the best fit, and closer to 6 the worst fit).

Table 6.1 Mean scores on the descriptions of socio-professional integration (based on ranking from 1 (worst fit) to 6 (best fit))

Description	Mean score
Guidance to work for those who can, socio-cultural participation for others	5.2
Preparing for entry into the labour market	4.7
Having paid work as soon as possible	3.4
First socio-cultural participation, then [taking] the step into the labour market	3.3
Receiving benefits as soon as possible	2.6
Mainly socio-cultural participation, guidance to work is less our concern as PCSW	1.7

The results confirm the focus on employment in PCSWs as described in the introduction. Indeed, with 'guidance to work for those who can, sociocultural participation for others' (5.2) and 'preparing for entry into the labour market' (4.7) being chosen as the most suitable descriptions of the vision on socio-professional integration in their PCSW, and the item containing 'guidance to work is less our concern' obtaining the lowest score, it is clear that (guidance towards) labour market entry is a central concern for PCSWs. This point echoes our findings from the fieldwork as well, with social workers and managers, but certainly also committee members emphasising the expectation of disposition to work, and the requirement to prove it (for example, by demanding a certain number of job applications, but also by providing proof of attendance in language courses, sharing results of education, and so forth; cf. infra, see also Chapter 8).

Overall, the results on this survey question were similar for Flanders and Wallonia, with the exception of the item 'Preparing for entry into the labour market', which had a mean score of 4.5 in Wallonia and 4.9 in Flanders, indicating a somewhat stronger emphasis on (preparing for) labour market entry in Flanders. This finding 'sets the scene' and is illustrative for what we observed throughout our fieldwork and report in this chapter: a general focus on (the preparation of) entry to work of newcomer beneficiaries within PCSW services, with, however, some regional differences, with a more conditional or stricter approach in Flanders compared to Wallonia.

In a study on activation policies for newly arrived immigrants in Norway, and addressing the tension between aims of employment and social inclusion and participation in a wider sense, Hagelund and Kavli (2009) distinguish two frameworks of interpretation among case workers, namely an activation perspective and a citizenship perspective. In the activation discourse, a clear emphasis is put on labour market inclusion, with paid employment being the primary goal, while the citizenship discourse broadens the goals to include other forms of social participation. The authors explain that in the activation discourse, all actions taking place in a programme should have the improvement of labour market prospects as a goal, whereas the citizenship discourse takes a broader focus, broadening the goal to include wider forms of social participation. In the citizenship discourse, while acknowledging the importance of employment, work requirements are softened by extending the time frame in which this is expected to be accomplished (Hagelund & Kavli, 2009). Based on our findings from the fieldwork, and complemented with the online survey, the employment discourse seems dominant in Belgian PCSWs, and particularly so in Flanders. This means that social assistance recipients are generally expected to make every effort to find a job and thus to get out of the welfare system ('the system of aid' in the words of many among our research participants) as quickly as possible. However, as already mentioned and as we will see in more detail later, when it comes to newcomer beneficiaries, this discourse and the related expectations take specific forms.

2.   THE ROLE OF THE PCSW IN TERMS OF LABOUR MARKET ACTIVATION FOR NEWCOMERS

The socio-professional integration of the PCSW beneficiaries is often challenging (De Wilde *et al.*, 2016). The limits and difficulties in socio-professional integration of their beneficiaries have led many PCSWs to develop a wide variety of organisational forms and professional practices, such as 'socio-professional insertion services', measures and tools for the employment of beneficiaries. Our fieldwork revealed that most PCSWs had a socio-professional insertion service. This was confirmed by the results of the online survey as well: among the participating PCSW services, 9 out of 10 (89.6%) had a specialised service for socio-professional integration. Put differently, even though there is a specialised institution for labour market activation (that is, the public employment service), most PCSWs have installed their own specialised service.[2]

In the online survey, participating PCSW services were also asked who they considered as being the main actor in terms of the labour market activation of newcomers. Based on the findings, we observe that more than half of the participating PCSW services (56%) considered the PCSW's socio-professional integration service as the main actor. The public employment service follows at large distance (less than one in five considered the PES as the main actor in terms of labour market of newcomer beneficiaries, or 19%). The same holds for the general social worker (case worker) (13%), local associations and organisations (6%) or other (6%). A follow-up question brought insight in the reasons why most did not consider the public employment service as being the main actor in terms of the labour market activation of newcomer beneficiaries (the answer options were based on the findings from the fieldwork). Table 6.2 gives an overview of the results (respondents could choose multiple options).

Table 6.2 Reasons for not considering PES as the main actor in terms of labour market integration (multiple answers possible)

The offer of the PES does not always provide sufficient opportunities for newcomers	59%
The offer of the PES does not always provide sufficient options for clients with a weaker profile	53%
By guiding clients in the PCSW itself, we feel more certain that there is sufficient follow-up	45%
In our PCSW we want to follow the progress of our clients, but this is not easy when a client is referred to the PES	35%
It requires specific expertise to deal with our clients: we believe that the social workers of the PCSW have more experience with this than the PES counsellors	33%

The findings from the survey, which are in line with the image that emerged from our case studies, indicate that different reasons coexist. Providing a suitable offer (containing sufficient and suitable/adapted opportunities) is definitely considered as a weak point in terms of the possibilities of support by the public employment service. Also, the provided follow-up, and expertise in dealing with the target group were regularly marked as reasons for not considering the public employment service as the main actor (and, by consequence, keeping the lead in terms of labour market activation within the PCSW for their own beneficiaries). The following quote illustrates the same point based on our fieldwork. While the stronger tone of this quote cannot necessarily be generalised for most other respondents, the underlying feeling it was better 'to do it himself/herself' was shared by many.

> Plus, the people who do the follow up from the PES ('VDAB') do not do that intensively at all. […] Yes, I actually think, I'll say 5%, but I actually don't think I've had a single client who ended up finding work that way, so for me that's a bit of a waste of time. (Flanders, A, social worker, 19/04/2021)

Moreover, it is also the general case worker and/or the social worker from the service for socio-professional integration who will determine when a beneficiary is ready for labour market activation, rather than the PES. This was observed in our fieldwork, and later confirmed by the online survey as well. Indeed, in the survey, when asked who decided when a beneficiary was ready for labour market activation, 80% stated that it was the service for socio-professional integration deciding and 60% stated it was the 'general' case worker deciding, compared to 'only' 5% the public employment service or no-one (1%).[3]

Furthermore, as we will see in the next paragraph, it takes time before social workers consider newcomer beneficiaries as 'ready for work' (or from the perspective of general case workers, ready to be transferred to the service for socio-professional integration); and they also decide on the path to follow before entry to work (whether or not in consultation with the beneficiary). Social workers and managers assert the PCSW's expertise on determining the profile of beneficiaries in terms of 'employability'.

> We take a look at their career path, where they are at, and according to this we establish a series of actions to be implemented with them. And so, either we consider that they are not yet ready for a whole series of reasons, and we work on the obstacles linked to finding a job. Or we find that they are indeed ready for employment, and so we propose an Art.60 or, for more specific cases, we propose support in a job search in the private sector […]. There are situations where we realise that the person still has too many obstacles and that, in the end, having put them into employment too quickly puts them in difficulty. […] And we have to go and work on the social skills upstream to be able to eventually re-propose a job, or in any case re-start the integration trajectory. (Wallonia, B, manager, 18/12/2020)

The social workers keep the role of determining the beneficiary's project, for instance by focusing on strengthening skills and competences before directly orienting to the PES or elsewhere. Therefore, we conclude social workers at the PCSW are to be considered as important gatekeepers for newcomer beneficiaries in terms of entry to the labour market.

Article 60 (or Art. 60),[4] which is referred in the quote above, is an activation measure in the form of a temporary work contract (one or two years). Individuals benefiting from this measure can be working in the PCSWs own services or at third-party services or companies. By working under an Art. 60 contract, the beneficiary can acquire professional experience as well as recover the right or have access to unemployment allocations. The duration of the contract corresponds in fact to the necessary duration which the beneficiary needs to be entitled to unemployment allocations at the end of the contract. Art. 60 is considered as a learning phase and a steppingstone towards obtaining a 'regular' job, also because this work experience is followed up by the social workers of the PCSWs throughout its duration.

However, while the PCSW stays in charge of the process and determines the steps to be taken, the PES can still come into play for particular steps in the process. A first and obvious example is that beneficiaries will enrol to the PES (as a step to be fulfilled in their ISIP; on the ISIP see also Chapter 2), but the PES can also provide support in making a CV or applying for jobs for example, or in job search. PES are also privileged partners on delivering training to newcomer beneficiaries, and the PES will take over follow-up after completion of an Art. 60 contract. Overall, throughout our fieldwork, the PES was a partner of reference who was regularly 'somehow' involved, but to highly varying degrees, and rather for specific requests, that is, for particular beneficiaries (for example, beneficiaries with a stronger profile, considered easily employable by the PCSW) and/or for particular needs (for example, job search and learning how to build a CV), rather than to the 'overall' follow-up of newcomer beneficiaries.[5]

3. ASSESSING READINESS TO WORK FOR NEWCOMERS

When addressing the specificities of labour market activation with newly arrived immigrant beneficiaries, 'readiness' for employment (employability) is told to generally depend on one's background, education level, family constraints, social skills, administrative situation, housing conditions, health, gender, and culture. The diversity among newly arrived beneficiaries is stressed by the respondents in our fieldwork, even though social workers and managers also identified some specific difficulties and needs of newly arrived immigrants. The latter is not surprising, as these difficulties are emphasised in the literature on labour market integration of newly arrived immigrants as well (see, for example, Chiswick & Miller, 2009; De Vroome & Van Tubergen, 2010; Sultana, 2022, among many others). Examples are administrative constraints (among which the precariousness of legal status), the perceived obstacles of language learning, the need for additional training, and cultural differences. As a result, while the transition to work of beneficiaries of an integration income in PCSWs is generally considered as difficult (De Wilde *et al.*, 2016), the labour market integration of *newcomer* beneficiaries is often considered as particularly challenging, though varying with the specific profile of the newcomers concerned.

> So we do try [to integrate newcomer beneficiaries professionally], but the language is really a big problem. For some people at least, because I have to say, with the new stream of refugees, especially the Syrians, it is less now. But the ones we really get now, the Turks too, they are highly educated people, they have a plan and yes, they often succeed. But if they are mothers, yes,

they have had very little education in their homeland and yes, there are really illiterate people and that is a very big problem to be able to activate them. (Flanders, E, director, 2/03/2021)

Beneficiaries do not only have to be 'willing' to work, but also 'ready' to work (in the sense of employable), so the term 'disposition to work' actually covers two dimensions. In our interviews, focusing on newcomer beneficiaries, it is mostly the 'readiness'/'aptness' to work which is questioned. Being disposed to work then also implies being willing to take steps to become a more attractive candidate on the labour market. While newly arrived beneficiaries are said to be often eager to be quickly employed, social workers declare that they have to dampen their determination to let them reach a satisfactory level of language and to improve social and professional skills.

Indeed, overall, social workers and their managers declare that the referral of newly arrived beneficiaries towards labour market activation policies and measures is often done later than for the other beneficiaries. These findings are in line with the results of Carpentier, Neels and Van den Bosch (2017). Comparing the duration of stay in social assistance for migrants and natives (Belgians), these authors found that migrants have lower exit rates than natives. A longer duration of residence in Belgium was associated with shorter periods of benefits, or put differently, recent migrants stayed in social assistance for longer periods of time.

As mentioned above, social workers function as gatekeepers in terms of access of labour market activation. Yet, in addition to having a decisive role in terms of assessing readiness, evaluating employability, and deciding on the course of action, social workers reported they also temper the expectations of newcomer beneficiaries. Indeed, social workers estimate the path to take before employment as lengthier compared to newcomer beneficiaries themselves.

There are all those situations where people come to us saying I want an Art.60 and then we know very well that the person is not at all, at all ready to return to work, so it requires a lot of work. (Wallonia, D, manager, 29/01/2021)

There are people who are shy or who don't know how to explain what they had to do or why they had to come, or who haven't yet come to terms with what they had to give up on [...] there can be a pressure in certain situations from people who say 'I don't want this, it has to go faster, this is not how I imagined things, this is not what I was told, I was promised that I could have a job straight away.' (Brussels, D, manager, 02/04/2021)

In addition to the time it takes to be ready for work, downward social mobility is mentioned by social workers; also in this sense, they report they (need to) temper expectations of newcomer beneficiaries.

> At some point, you have to make people understand. I know it's complicated [...] some people come to us with a university education [...], we are aware [...] of the difficulty of this change of life [...], of the social status they had at home and no longer have. [...] we are aware of this, now we have an operating system that we explain to them and that we ask them to respect. (Wallonia, D, manager, 29/01/2021)

In what follows, the concrete conditions to be considered ready for work, and the reasons behind the long trajectories are discussed, from the perspective of the social workers. These regard the general living conditions (a stable life context), the development of language skills, the investment in professional training, sustainable employment, and cultural skills.

3.1. Evaluating the general life context

Even though socio-professional integration is considered as a priority, social workers estimate readiness to work presupposes having a stable life context (or peripherical conditions); the latter needs to be fulfilled before one can start looking for a job. Examples are having childcare, sufficient mental health, and acceptable conditions of housing. Actions and activities may be put into practice by beneficiaries, in some cases with the support of social workers, pursuing the aim of building autonomy, for instance through learning to manage individual/family costs, understanding that rights come with duties and the role and constraints of social aids, learning to deal with administrative tasks and to respect schedules, or to show to be proactive in searching for solutions.

In line with the fieldwork, the online survey confirms the presence of other 'conditions' in terms of stability of life context before activation in terms of employment will be considered by the PCSW. In the survey, particularly psychosocial stability (66% of participating PCSW services), stable and/or adequate housing (60%) and childcare (56%) came forward as items that are frequently set as conditions. Remarkably, the share of PCSWs mentioning childcare was much higher in Flanders (75%) compared to Wallonia (34%). A possible explanation could be a potentially stronger focus on the activation of migrant women in Flanders, though this could not be empirically verified.

3.2.   Learning the language

Second, when questioned about formal internal criteria to assess readiness to work, a large share of respondents evoked the need of learning one of the national languages. This is indeed a practice – and sometimes a condition – largely impacting newly arrived immigrants' access to socio-professional integration measures, and more broadly their integration path.

> We have a service called the integration service [*service d'insertion* in French] which follows these people, […] effectively for newcomers, especially for those who don't speak French, […] it's not a pure job search, […] the readiness to work will also involve learning French […]. So, we would say that the person is willing to work because he or she is taking French classes and, given that he or she is taking French classes, […] he or she is part of an integration scheme. (Wallonia, C, social worker, 15/03/2021)

> The thing is, for blue collar jobs, then your Dutch needs to be really good, then they really need to have a certificate of a reasonably high level of Dutch, so that is often difficult. Those people almost always want to work as fast as possible; they are the exceptions who want to focus on Dutch first. So those people want to work as quickly as possible, and if that is what they want and if that is OK for them in a job like [name of a company known for low level executive jobs], then I am not going to stop them. But if they want to focus on improving their Dutch first in order to increase their job opportunities, then that is also allowed, if it is feasible. (Flanders, A, social worker, 23/04/2021)

Moreover, language learning is considered part of the socio-professional integration path of newly arrived immigrants. Some social workers consider this approach too demanding or defend the idea of proposing to improve language *through* employment, rather than keeping newcomers on classes before getting access to a job – notwithstanding the type of job concerned.

> During our Art.60 employment, I also give newcomers who do not yet have a full command of the language the opportunity to go to school for two half-days during their employment. That counts as hours worked, so that's something we developed especially for them of 'Do that and in the meantime keep up your Dutch', but they are obliged by us to talk to colleagues in Dutch. They also have to talk Dutch on the shop floor with their colleagues during breaks. Which they don't always do, of course, but that's the incentive we try to give them and if they do their best, who knows,

a contract might come out of it, which it sometimes does, and sometimes not. (Flanders, E, social worker, 16/03/2021)

The results of the online survey indicate that there are regional differences in the extent to which PCSWs consider knowledge of the local language as a precondition to labour market mediation. The share of PCSWs stating that there is no 'minimum language level' set as a precondition and that a beneficiary will be helped in their quest for employment regardless of their language level, is lower in Flanders (23%) than in Wallonia (38%). Given the small sample size, we cannot consider these percentages as showing the 'exact' difference between the regions, but they do signal a tendency. Reversely, in Flanders, two out of three PCSWs state to have a 'minimum language level' (although most declare to make exceptions when a beneficiary speaks another language). In Wallonia, this holds for less than one in three PCSWs.

As mentioned in Chapter 4, language lessons are often included in newcomers' Individualised Social Integration Projects (ISIPs), and class attendance will be verified; this is considered as an equivalent of proving the disposition to work. However, according to Wikstrom and Ahnlund (2018) in their study on individualised work strategies in the context of a Swedish refugee settlement programme, the controlling and reporting on presence and absence in activities conditionalising support might put pressure on the individual to remain active but can also have a negative impact by worsening experiences of stress and incapability. In a different but relevant context, more precisely a study on the activation of youngsters, Van Parys (2016) warns for the potentially negative effect of controlling functions on the interaction styles used by counsellors. In any case, in PCSWs, and especially in Flanders, a strong emphasis is put on language learning. It is considered as important (or necessary) in terms of job prospects (and therefore considered as a 'normal' condition when receiving benefits), and by extension sometimes also as a proof of willingness to integrate. While we have not empirically verified the effects of the exertion of control, the fieldwork has indicated that proof is expected and followed up, leading to warnings and possibly (but rarely) to sanctions if not respected (see Chapter 8).

3.3. Education and vocational training

Third, newcomers can be advised to follow additional training in order to improve their chances on the labour market, for example to learn specific skills, or to learn the techniques and/or vocabulary common in the local (Belgian) labour market of a specific profession.

The need for training is often linked with another factor impacting access to socio-professional integration: the recognition of equivalences and diplomas. As suggested by previous studies, obtaining the formal equivalence of diploma is a major issue for newcomers (Brücker *et al.*, 2021). They face linguistic, economic, and procedural barriers that deter many of them, and impact labour market outcomes. We consider, for instance, the financial and bureaucratic cost of the procedure, the struggle to gather the required documents from the institutions of their country of origin, and to see certain trainings recognised in the EU framework (Gossiaux *et al.*, 2019). Consequently, newcomers often end up reorienting their careers and choosing training and jobs that do not necessarily fit with their original education and professional experience. Based on our findings, information about the required formalities in terms of diploma recognition is done at the general social service, or in few cases there may be 'educators' in charge of these tasks, but generally beneficiaries are redirected to specialised external partners in order to be supported in the procedure of recognition of equivalences and diplomas.

In the case of partial recognition or non-recognition of their degree/professional experience, some respondents have stressed that a share of newcomers are eager to restart university studies, generally considered to be at an 'unusual' age (older than 25 years old) to be students at the PCSW. This opportunity is not always well received by the committee and depending on the PCSW and the local committee, the beneficiaries might be encouraged to opt for vocational training instead, allowing for a quicker integration in the labour market. Trainings that were frequently mentioned in our fieldwork were, for example, ICT, electrician, and caregiver (mainly for women).

Even though complementary studies are legally accepted as steps and actions in favour of social activation, some social workers stressed the need not to postpone too much the entrance of the beneficiaries into a work-oriented path, despite the risk of downward occupational mobility.

Internal guidelines with regard to following training are often that it is decided on a case-per-case basis (with the committee having the final say). Yet, social workers propose as main criteria: the odds of success, the necessity (for example, if one has a bachelor diploma that is enough to find work, one will be expected to start working), and the expected 'employability' after completion of the proposed educational track.

Now, someone who tells me at the age of 40 that they want to go back to school because they want to become a physicist … I'm going to say to him 'That's nice but it's not going to be possible with the PCSW.' (Brussels, A, social worker, 30/04/2021)

In the online survey, when asked about the criteria that are used in practice to determine whether or not a beneficiary can enrol in a training or educational track (with multiple answers possible), the most commonly reported criteria were the language level of the beneficiary (77%), their alleged motivation (62%), followed at a distance by the chances on the labour market with the chosen studies (41%), and the chances on the labour market with the current diploma (37%), and the likelihood of success (apart from the language level) (33%). Age comes in sixth position, with 23% of participating PCSW services reporting this as a criterion in the decision whether or not to approve the enrolment in a training/educational track. Considered as less important were the agenda of the beneficiary/the training being full-time or part-time or in the evening (13%), obtained qualifications in the country of origin (12%), and the budgetary space of the PCSW (2%). Yet, also in this regard, we noted considerable differences between the regions, with Flemish PCSWs reporting more criteria overall, indicating a 'stricter' approach in Flanders. In terms of the specific criteria, the largest difference were to be found in the importance attached to the chances on the labour market with the current diploma (51% reported this criterion in Flanders, compared to 16% of the participating PCSW services in Wallonia), the chances on the labour market with the chosen studies (53% in Flanders versus 21% in Wallonia), and the likelihood of success (apart from the language level, 45% in Flanders compared to 14% in Wallonia). Yet, in line with the findings on regional differences concerning the emphasis on language learning, here, too, we observed that the language level of the beneficiary was mentioned more frequently as a criterion in Flanders (82%) compared to Wallonia (70%).

3.4. Sustainable employment?

A fourth reason evoked for delaying newcomers' access to labour market activation measures is that social workers feel the need to better prepare the beneficiaries for sustainable insertion, it is to say, to avoid that the beneficiaries 'return' to social benefits. Social workers contend that, most likely, by going too quickly towards employment, beneficiaries find themselves back on social security, moving from integration income to an Art. 60 contract and then to unemployment benefits, and eventually returning to integration income. This is in line with earlier findings in other studies in the Belgian context (for example, Denis, 2020; Huens, 2013).

> If it's to have another failure, because we don't get the job we started or the
> Art.60 we can offer, it's no use either. It's not the aim of the game to have

another failure [...] So integration [...] is not just getting people back to work because often we confuse socio-professional integration with getting back to work, it's a small part of their work. (Wallonia, D, manager, 29/01/2021)

Once you're in the job, it's quite different. It's respecting obligations, regular hours, and that's sometimes more difficult for the person. [...] the idea is really to prepare them to enter the job market in the long term and not to say 'Well, once I've finished my Art.60 contract, I'm entitled to unemployment, I stop [working/looking for job], and life is good.' (Wallonia, B, manager, 18/12/2020)

Moreover, although the priority of social activation measures is to promote integration through employment, some respondents assume in general that newcomers are 'not ready' to such a project, and even evoke the need of 'protecting' them from a harsh labour market. It is not just about being 'willing' to work, but also about having realistic options on the labour market, an issue that presents a struggle for the PCSW as well.

The horizon of social work is to get people into employment, the horizon of the active welfare state in which we are, is to get people to contribute, to put them back into the solidarity mechanism. [...] Then we have to recognise that there is a very big barrier on the ability to do this, the first brake is not the will of the people to be put into employment, because people want to be put into employment, want to contribute. The big barrier for a PCSW in achieving the objectives of the active welfare state is its capacity to put people into employment, it is our internal capacity. (Brussels, A, director, 09/03/2021)

Following the same logic, delaying the access to activation measures is also justified by social workers regarding the internal resources of the PCSWs. Social workers claim that they do not want to 'drown' the socio-professional integration departments with candidates that they consider not to be able to enter the labour market, nor to be 'employable'.

In the same line of reasoning, based on a study on active labour market policies for refugees and asylum seekers in the UK, Calon, Montgomery and Baglioni (2022) demonstrate that the discourse of deservingness (see Chapter 8) and the emphasis on individual responsibility to improve employability develop in a context where structural barriers hinder the access to good quality employment, and the support to newcomers is fragmented (for example, difficult access to vocational training, problems in terms of diploma recognition, barriers to work during the asylum application causing large gaps in their CV, and/or outdated skills). Moreover, studying employment assistance provided to refugees in the UK, Shutes (2011) describes how refugees are pressured to achieve short-term job outcomes. More than 19 years later, Calon *et al.* (2022) reach the same conclusion, arguing that, in practice, newcomers are deterred from meaningful, sustainable, and long-term plans for integration through employment. Overall, as appears from the above, our findings in Belgian PCSWs are not fully in line with these conclusions. While the contradiction between emphasising individual responsibility and the presence of structural and institutional barriers as mentioned by Calon *et al.* (2022) seems to be true in the Belgian context as well, the pressure to achieve short job outcomes is not comparable, or at least not on a general scale, and as mentioned above, a 'lengthier' path is often proposed by social workers in Belgian PCSWs. However, newcomer beneficiaries must demonstrate that they are active during this journey as well.

More generally, a distinction is made in the literature between the 'work first' model, prioritising quick employment under the premise that any job is better than none, and the 'human capital' model, prioritising the development of attitudes and skills that will allow people to find and retain suitable jobs (Dean, 2003, p. 442). Our findings situate the approach of PCSWs rather in the human capital model. Nevertheless, the concern for the durability of employment does differ between PCSW services and between social workers, and the same holds for the 'ambition' reflected in the goals put forward and the strategies that are being chosen. More generally, social workers struggle to find a balance between (1) quick entry to the labour market, (2) sustainable insertion, and (3) jobs corresponding to newcomers' abilities and qualifications. The strategies they choose and the priorities they set in this balancing act differ between social workers and between PCSWs.

A concrete illustration of the variation in terms of strategies can be found in the use of Art. 60. Whereas in some PCSW services, social workers and managers stress that their beneficiaries will generally do a training before doing an Art. 60 job, in order to avoid the trap of being 'stuck' after it (that is, falling into unemployment benefits, and eventually ending up in social assistance again), whereas in other PCSW services, beneficiaries are sent to Art. 60 whenever possible. Similarly, in some municipalities, employment opportunities for Art. 60 are limited to more 'classic' tasks such as cleaning and gardening in municipal services, whereas in other municipalities, options in other services or with private employers are explored as well, based on the interests and profile of the beneficiary. Put differently, whereas in some PCSW services Art. 60 is used as a 'quick exit' to some type of employment only (without a long-term plan), in others the use of Art. 60 reflects a search for the best possible match between a person's interests and skills on the one hand, and the job placement on the other, and is part of a broader strategy of maximising learning opportunities and facilitating a transition to regular employment in the future.

As a second example of the varying emphasis on sustainable employment, we observed that the extent to which social workers let beneficiaries (co) decide on their path towards socio-professional integration also varies. While some social workers and services will respect beneficiaries' wish for quick entry, even though it is not the best option in the long term with regard to qualitative job prospects, others will strongly encourage or expect newcomer beneficiaries to invest in additional learning first. A third example are the decisions about granting or refusing a demand to invest in education: as we have seen above, decisions are taken on a case-per-case basis and criteria differ between PCSWs. Here too, we can say the importance given to advantages in the long term varies between services (and even between beneficiaries, as decisions are taken on an individual basis).

In sum, there seems to be no universal approach in the guidance of newcomers in terms of socio-professional integration, and the same holds for the concern for (and awareness of) the durability of employment. The differences in strategies and approach are both related to the use of discretionary space as well as to a difference in policy lines, as safeguarded by managers and/or directors and the committee, which will be discussed in Chapters 7 and 8.

3.5. Broader integration and adapting to the local culture

When social workers assess 'readiness' to work of newly arrived immigrant beneficiaries, the concept of social activation is often coupled with a discourse on integration, based on concrete language learning and training, but also on the assimilation of local values and culture, to 'acculturate to Belgium'. (Wallonia, B, manager, 18/12/2020)

Everything is done in such a way that this person can integrate, can acquire, let's say, the possibilities to function like any other person here in Belgium. (Brussels, A, manager, 27/05/2021)

It's a socio-professional integration, it's not a professional integration. So that means that the more strings the person has to pull, the easier it will be in everyday life to manage administrative procedures, to dare to make decisions, to take a stand, to meet people, to start a family, etc. That's what it's all about too, isn't it? It's not just about getting people into jobs and work and the country's economy. (Brussels, A, social worker, 30/04/2021)

[Learning language] should be an obligation for two years, we learn French intensively in good programmes, to avoid that people [...] stay at the PCSW for a whole life. [Through only providing financial assistance] we [the PCSWs] are not aiming for integration, we're [...] aiming to [make people] stay in the pockets of a society [*aux crochets d'une société* in French] and that's a shame because everyone has something to contribute to society. (Wallonia, B, social worker, 15/01/2021)

In terms of how social workers address newly arrived immigrants' access to the labour market, we also find some cultural and gender-based representations that influence social workers' perception and implementation of social and labour market activation. For instance, while social workers find that male beneficiaries want to enter the labour market (too) soon, female beneficiaries are often represented as reluctant to work or to do training, with cultural values being often presented as obstacles.

Because in their country it's not in the mentality of many to work, the first thing is to take care of the children and so we can't do that and so it's a job that we also do with them by saying here it is for your autonomy. (Brussels, D, social worker, 11/05/2021)

In other words, the social workers report perceiving a contrast between their own goals (and those of their institution) with the wishes and ambitions of the beneficiaries, an observation that corresponds with earlier findings from Van Robaeys and Driessens (2011) in the context of their research with social workers in 'general welfare centres' (CAW – Centra voor Algemeen Welzijnswerk) and PCSWs in Antwerp.

Therefore, specific programmes may target the social activation of women beneficiaries, focusing in particular on acquiring skills on how to manage family and training/work needs. These programmes also target the empowerment of women as they are conceived under a gendered lens – based on what is socially expected from a woman, and intersected with cultural representations (Holmes & Jones, 2013; Abbasian & Bildt, 2009).

You can't imagine the metamorphosis it makes in some [women] beneficiaries who can't afford to go to the hairdresser, or who don't want to take care of themselves anymore. They get out [of such an initiative of social integration] with a new hairstyle and they've learned to make products from yoghurt, everyday things that don't cost much, they've had a great morning. It wasn't a theoretical thing, but it did them more good than if

> we had given them four hours of [theory]. And we have some successes, we have a lady thanks to this who has resumed her studies, who has felt better, and others who really leave feeling better. [...] So sometimes it's things as simple as that, that will lead to improvements and well-being for some of the beneficiaries. [...] by restructuring positively [...], rebuilding herself and not being seen again [at the PCSW] and evolving in her life. (Wallonia, D, manager, 29/01/2021)

Indeed, social workers may also see behaviours associated with the beneficiaries' culture of origin and related alleged habits as needing to be changed, before they can enter the labour market.

> It's a learning process, a mechanism, because it's a truth, it's not a matter of being slow or not, it's a matter of lifestyle, we don't live here like we do over there, there aren't the same pressures, it's not the same active life. (Wallonia, B, social worker, 15/1/2021)

> We used to say, the big prejudices, generally, people of African origin are often late. And then when you dig a little deeper, you say to yourself that maybe they don't have the same notion of time as we do, it's not that they're late, it's maybe that in their country of origin, the notion of time was different. Therefore, the idea of [...] participating in social integration workshops is also to get back into a rhythm, to understand that finally, there are schedules, you have to respect, because if you don't respect the schedules, there are implications for the group. [...] there's a whole range of things that we could work on in social integration to allow them to have all the social skills to be able to start a training course leading to a qualification. Someone who always arrives late, who is going to register for training, it's clear that he won't last long. [...] It's not like repairing a car, repairing a human being, it's very complex. (Wallonia, B, manager, 18/12/2020)[6]

In the above quote, the 'pedagogical' aim mentioned is seen as a real work on the social or even cultural skills of the person, otherwise risking to be deviant in relation to local norms. This corresponds to earlier findings of Van Robaeys and Driessens (2011) as well, who describe the struggle of social workers in dealing with clients of foreign origin who have another frame of reference. In Chapter 8, we will analyse in more detail how discrimination and stereotypes affect, more generally, the relation between social workers and beneficiaries and its outcomes in terms of allocation of rights.

To conclude, in this chapter we have focused on how labour market activation works in the Belgian PCSWs, which we studied based on the data collected through the online survey and the fieldwork. Beyond an overall attempt to find convergences on how socio-professional integration is signified among our case studies (and considered regions) when dealing with newcomer beneficiaries and how this translates into practices, we have highlighted the difference in approach and concrete actions on the ground.

NOTES

1. This translates the French term *insertion socio-professionnelle*, where 'insertion' is often used as synonym of 'integration' and the two are considered very similar notions. Therefore, without neglecting the scientific debate on these terms, we use them interchangeably in this chapter.
2. In one of the case studies (a small municipality), a collaboration (and formal agreement) was mentioned with a neighbouring city. The PCSW in that municipality did not have a service focusing on socioprofessional integration, but along with other small municipalities in the area, they referred to the service of the neighbouring city.
3. Multiple answers were possible; and as is also reflected by the findings in the fieldwork, the general case worker and the service of socio-professional integration can exchange internally about a beneficiary and co-decide.
4. Art. 60§ 7 of the Organic Law of the PCSW established a mechanism of employment engaged by the PCSW to beneficiaries of social integration income to 'prove a period of work in order to obtain the full benefit of certain social benefits [namely, unemployment benefits] or in order to promote work experience' (Castaigne, 2020).
5. It is worth mentioning that some PES agencies also have specific services dedicated to (or professionals dealing with) newcomers/migrants. However, we rarely found any information on this subject during our fieldwork, and very little mention of specific collaborations with these services (and professionals).
6. The authors and editors of this book are aware of the male bias in certain phrasings of this respondent and others (for instance, speaking of 'he' and 'him' only, whereas it could also concern female beneficiaries as well). The decision was taken to keep the quotes as they were expressed by the interlocutors, even though they were not always thinking and speaking in terms of gender, but rather in terms of a non-gendered beneficiary. This holds for quotes in other chapters and parts of this book as well.

REFERENCES

Abbasian, S., & Bildt, C. (2009). *Empowerment through entrepreneurship: A tool for integration among immigrant women?* (CISEG Working paper Nr. 6 (s.l.)).

Brücker, H., Glitz, A., Lerche, A., & Romiti, A. (2021). Occupational recognition and immigrant labor market outcomes. *Journal of Labor Economics, 39*(2), 497–525.

Calo, F., Montgomery, T., & Baglioni, S. (2022). You have to work … but you can't!: Contradictions of the active labour market policies for refugees and asylum seekers in the UK. *Journal of Social Policy* (in press).

Carpentier, S. (2016). *Lost in transition? Essays on the socio-economic trajectories of social assistance beneficiaries in Belgium* [PhD thesis, University of Antwerp].

Carpentier, S., Neels, K., & Van den Bosch, K. (2017). Do first- and second-generation migrants stay longer in social assistance than natives in Belgium? *International Journal of Migration and Integration, 18*, 1167–1190.

Castaigne, M. (2020). *Le point sur l'article 60 § 7.* Fédération des CPAS.

Chiswick, B., & Miller, P. (2009). The international transferability of immigrants' human capital. *Economics of Education Review, 28*, 162–169.

De Greef, V. (2018). The varied and changing forms of activation in Belgium. *Revue de droit compare du travail et de la sécurité sociale, 4*, 1–11.

De Vroome, T., & Van Tubergen, F. (2010). The employment experience of refugees in the Netherlands. *International Migration Review, 44*(2), 376–403.

De Wilde, M., Cantillon, B., Vandenbroucke, F., & De Bie, M. (Eds.) (2016). *40 jaar OCMW en bijstand [40 years of PCSW and assistance].* Acco.

Dean, H. (2003). Re-conceptualising welfare-to-work for people with multiple problems and needs. *Journal of Social Policy, 32*(3), 441–459.

Denis, F. (2020). *Assistance sociale. Aide à l'emploi et l'insertion socio-professionnelle: évaluation de l'article 60 § 7 en CPAS* [Master thesis, Université de Liège].

Dumont, D. (2012). *La Responsabilisation des Personnes Sans Emploi en Questio:. Une étude Critique de la Contractualisation des Prestations Sociales en Droit Belge de l'Assurance Chômage et de l'Aide Sociale.* La Charte.

Franssen, A. (2016). To PIIS or not to PIIS? Les injections paradoxales à l'autonomie. *l'Observatoire, 88*(1), 51–56.

Gossiaux, A., Mescoli, E., Rivière, M., Petit Jean, M., Bousetta, H., Fallon, C., & Fonder, M. (2019). *Évaluation du parcours d'intégration et du dispositif ISP dédiés aux primo-arrivants en Wallonie* (No. 33). IWEPS.

Hagelund, A., & Kavli, H. (2009). If work is out of sight: Activation and citizenship for new refugees. *Journal of European Social Policy, 19*(3), 259–270.

Hermans, K. (2005). *De Actieve Welvaartstaat in werking: Een Sociologische Studie naar de Implementatie van het Activeringsbeleid op de Werkvloer van de Vlaamse OCMW's [The active welfare state in functioning. A sociological study into the implementation of the activation policy on the workplace of the Flemish PCSW's].* KU Leuven.

Holmes, R., & Jones, N. (2013). *Gender and social protection in the developing world: Beyond mothers and safety nets.* Bloomsbury.

Huens V. (2013), *Article 60 § 7. Derrière le mécanisme administratif: des travailleurs, des réalités et des enjeux.* SAW-B.

Shutes, I. (2011). Welfare-to-work and the responsiveness of employment providers to the needs of refugees. *Journal of Social Policy, 40*(3), 557–574.

Sultana, R. (2022). The labour market integration of migrants and refugees: Career guidance and the newly arrived. *International Journal for Educational and Vocational Guidance, 22*, 491–510.

Van Parys, L. (2016). *On the street-level implementation of ambiguous activation policy: How casewokers reconcile responsibility and autonomy and affect their clients' motivation* [PhD thesis, KU Leuven].

Van Robaeys, B., & Driessens, K. (2011). *Gekleurde armoede en hulpverlening: Sociaal werkers en cliënten aan het woord [Coloured poverty and care. Social workers and clients speaking].* Lannoo.

Wikstrom, E., & Ahnlund, P. (2018). Making refugees work? Individualized work strategies in the Swedish refugee settlement program. *Nordic Journal of Working Life Studies, 54*(8), 47–65.

CONCLUSION PART I

HANNE VANDERMEERSCHEN

In the first part of this book we focused on service provision towards newly arrived immigrants from the perspective of the PCSW and its staff. In Chapter 4, we explored how service delivery to this population group is organised in practice. We observed a rather large diversity between local PCSWs in terms of how service delivery is handled, with some PCSWs choosing a specialised approach, having designated services for the guidance and support of migrants only, whereas others (the majority) opting for a general approach or having a mix of both approaches. The choice for a generalist approach is motivated by a discourse on promoting equity and inclusion of all beneficiaries and avoiding stigmatisation. On the other hand, however, the choice for a generalist approach can leave some blind spots in identifying and responding to specific needs and difficulties encountered by newly arrived immigrants, as will be apparent in Part III of this book.

Along the same lines, while a discourse of 'tailor-made support for all' was identified among social workers, managers, and committee members, differences in service delivery to newcomers (compared to other beneficiaries) were also apparent. One of the key issues mentioned by social workers in this regard was the need for more intensive guidance and support (or at least on average, since newcomer beneficiaries are a heterogeneous group with different needs and abilities, as social workers rightfully emphasise).

In Chapter 5, we went deeper into the challenges of providing support to newcomer beneficiaries. In sum, based on the accounts of social workers, the main challenges in working with newly arrived immigrants in the setting of the PCSW are time and language, and to a lesser extent (or more precisely, mentioned by fewer respondents), new migrants' unfamiliarity with the system. Looking back at the concept of accessibility, as introduced in Chapter 1, accessibility was described as the degree of fit between the system (and multiple actors involved at different levels), and its users. Logically, we need the account of the beneficiaries, provided in Part III, to have a full view, but at this stage, already some conclusions are apparent, in the sense that several dimensions of accessibility seem to be problematic. First, there is a problem of *availability* of service provision – with social workers and managers stating that the vast number of administrative tasks take up the time at the expense of discussing and providing support for other issues, related to psychosocial well-being. Related to that is also the question of language, with services being provided in a language the beneficiary often does not understand, and without structural solution to this, at the expense of the quality of service delivery, and with beneficiaries' problems remaining undetected or unanswered, which is a problem of *accommodation* and of *appropriateness* of service delivery. In addition, there is an issue of *awareness,* as some experienced social workers indicate that it is difficult for newly arrived migrants to understand the PCSW service and what it entails, and what they can ask for or expect. Reversely, social workers are not always aware of this difficulty. Furthermore, based on the account of social workers, it became apparent there is no systematic information provision (in terms of what aids are available and under which condition, and so forth). The latter contributes to the dependency of migrant beneficiaries to their social worker, an issue that was strongly brought forward by newcomers as well, as will be discussed in Part III.

A key aspect in the service provision to newcomer beneficiaries is labour market activation, which we dwelled upon in Chapter 6. On the one hand, both our fieldwork as well as the survey showed the central importance attached to preparing the entry to work, which is linked to the key principle of disposition to work. On the other hand, however, labour market entrance often seemed a long-term goal, with many steps to manage beforehand. Our analysis of labour market activation of newcomer beneficiaries revealed the large role that is played by the PCSW services and its social workers, with the latter acting as gatekeepers in the access towards employment (for example, judging when a person is ready for labour market activation programmes – such as the Art. 60 – or labour market entry). Moreover, while public employment services are by definition a key player in the field of employment and labour market activation, it is generally social workers at the PCSW who stay in charge of the overall choices and general follow-up.

While Part I has provided many insights into the organisation and management of social assistance for newly arrived immigrants, and the challenges and pitfalls that come with it, concrete policy practices still depend on the translation of policy lines into a multitude of decisions for individual beneficiaries. Therefore, Part II of this book presents an analysis of the decision-making process in PCSW services.

PART II

POLICY IN PRACTICE: THE DECISION-MAKING PROCESS

INTRODUCTION

ELSA MESCOLI

In the following chapters, we analyse the decision-making process operating in the PCSWs under study as well as the role of different social actors within it. The aim is to understand how welfare policies work in practice with regard to newly arrived immigrants. More particularly, we will focus on the levels and ways in which discretion operates when institutions and their agents decide whether to allocate or not any social benefits to newcomers – and under which conditions. This analysis reveals relevant aspects of the immigration–welfare policy link (Bommes & Geddes, 2000; Slaven *et al.*, 2021) as it functions on the ground. It explores the overall structural approach of the social protection system towards immigrants and its more or less developed inclusiveness (Geddes, 2003; Vintila & Lafleur, 2020), as well as its implementation through local agencies and individuals' practices (Maynard-Moody & Portillo, 2010; Berman, 1978). After a short reminder of the law and policy framework that governs the functioning of PCSWs in Belgium and that constitutes the main context of the decision-making process, this section highlights the possible room for manoeuvre and interpretation that institutions have, that is, the differences in the overall approach towards the demands of beneficiaries. Indeed, each PCSW may adopt a different positioning towards this framework and translate it into specific internal guidelines. Chapter 7 discusses the functioning of the decision-making process itself in terms of hierarchised procedure, in which the role of different actors of PCSWs – including managers and committee members – emerges. Chapter 8 studies the discretion of social workers and analyses which factors influence the actions and decisions they take. Throughout this section, we will refer to and expand the theoretical framework presented in Chapter 1.

LAWS AND GUIDELINES

The legal framework that structures the decision-making process as well as
the very same functioning of PCSWs in Belgium is composed of three main
laws, which are the Law of 2 April 1965 on the assumption of responsibility
for assistance granted by the PCSWs and stating the territorial competence
of the institutions; the organic Law of 8 July 1976 on PCSWs; and the Law of
26 May 2002 on the right to social integration. Additional amendments and
state, regional, and local measures are also mentioned to complement this
law framework, that is described as strictly established, leaving small room
for manoeuvre on the ground. Indeed, the main contents of these policies
are gathered into a book that social workers often call 'the Bible of PCSW',
to highlight the normative and prescriptive nature of the laws regulating the
access to welfare entitlements. As a result, the conditions to access social
benefits, already studied in Chapter 4, are described as hardly negotiable
in principle.

However, and paradoxically in a way, most research participants also state
that interpretations of the law framework are indeed possible, and that room
for manoeuvre and variations exist with regard to the translation in practice
of PCSWs' definition of social benefits (as we will see later in further details),
therefore leading to different forms of implementation on the ground. These
interpretations and variations mainly concern the fact that two notions on
which this framework are based are highly subjective (Soumoy, 2010): the
concept of 'state of need' and that of 'human dignity'. The law framework
states that each individual has the right to live in dignity and that if their state
of need with this regard is attested, he/she is entitled of social benefits. The
assessment of these factors goes through objective calculations – the balance
between revenues and expenses of the individual – and subjective evaluation,
mainly made by the social workers that are in charge of the social enquiry
and of building the beneficiary's file, as we will see later in depth. Different
interpretations of these notions are then possible:

> We have all the [law] articles that tell us how to act, under what conditions,
> this is really our reference. [...] it's always a bit of an interpretation for
> the state of need. [...] we have to see the state of need, but there is no real
> definition in the law, so it's up to each person to interpret it. (Wallonia, H,
> social worker, 28/01/2021)

A first level[1] where discretion with regard to the rules operates is the institutional level, because each PCSW can take own positionings and decisions with

regard of what the concepts of 'state of need' and 'human dignity' correspond to concretely, and communicate them to managers and social workers through internal guidelines that frame their work:

> The guideline is [...] the translation of a political decision and a law, and to say that this is how it is interpreted, it is validated by the legal services, by the general policy project of the municipality, by the general policy project of the PCSW, and so we apply it and there is no question about it. (Brussels, D, manager, 02/04/2021)

In principle, guidelines enable social workers to know how to act in specific situations, and to take decisions on the allocation of social benefits that are coherent with the law and the approach of the agency, although some cases may need additional evaluation:

> In other words, [guidelines say] in such and such a circumstance, what type of aid is granted, up to what amount, etc. Afterwards, there are always situations that are a bit outside the framework, that go beyond the established frameworks, and each time a report is submitted and a discussion takes place between the services that present the situation, that give us a report, and the representatives. (Brussels, G, president, 15/04/2021)

The translation of laws into internal procedures and guidelines is a response to the PCSWs desire to standardise practices, and this often goes together with a higher bureaucratisation and digitalisation[2] of the staff tasks, and with lesser space for autonomy and discretion at the level of caseworkers. Although variations exist in our case studies and not all PCSWs have the same number and types of directives, usually through setting guidelines, PCSWs' management and political representatives try to avoid the creation of discretionary routines on the ground by street-level bureaucrats, therefore setting top-down rules that control their work. In principle, internal guidelines ensure equal answers to similar demands and therefore facilitate the decision-making process itself – also relieving some social workers who may not be at ease with working in a less structured framework and with greater autonomy. They also prevent allocating social benefits that are not generally granted by the PCSW concerned, so not to create a pull-effect or rather to set 'precedents', to mention a word frequently used on the ground:

> The funds of the PCSWs are not bottomless, unfortunately. There are obviously limits to the use of these funds. [...] Therefore, the problem is

twofold: it is financial on the one hand, […] it is a question of priority. Is [the demand] a priority compared to other emergency situations? […] and on the other hand, there is the question of creating a precedent. […] because if we intervene for [this demand], why wouldn't we intervene for a similar situation later on? (Wallonia, G, director, 12/01/2021)

Indeed, while each PCSW could decide to allocate whatever social benefit to whatever beneficiary who ask it by drawing on its own funding, this would mean not receiving the reimbursement of the concerned benefit from the state. The following quote describes this process and the consequent director's dilemma in relation with the demand of a family in which only one member has a regular residence status:[3]

One of the children is of age and has been recognised as a refugee. Therefore, she is followed-up […] with the integration income. However, the parents and the other sister are not recognised. And we can't intervene for anything. Except for urgent medical assistance […]. So that's obviously very difficult, […] the young adult […] was struggling to manage the family a little. But here we found ourselves faced with problems […] bills to pay, that sort of things. And that put us […] in a bind because it's very complicated to be able to intervene without creating a precedent, and so […] it was more external groups[4] that intervened, than us as a public organisation. (Wallonia, G, director, 12/01/2021)

We observed that the larger the municipality, the more important the framework (internal rules and guidelines) seem to be, while a more informal framework operates in smaller PCSWs.

That is knowledge that is in the heads most of the time. That is something we know we fall short a bit. That is a disadvantage of being a small PCSW. There is a lot of knowledge in the heads, you can always ask someone, but actually it is not really recorded somewhere or not always stored somewhere. We are now trying to do this more systematically. (Flanders, H, director, 4/03/2021)

The existence of a formally structured framework also brings about a more systematic follow-up of the suitability of such framework and of the adaptations needed to respond to new challenges or to changes in political orientation. Indeed, the political orientation of the municipality can influence the choices of PCSWs, first because of funding issues – the budget allocated to social affairs may change depending on the political programmes of the municipal government – and then because of ideological priorities. The promptness of changes that may occur also depends on how much a political ideology is rooted in the local context, creating a sort of path-dependency.

> Our presidents have always been presidents of the socialist party. Therefore, [...] we have always developed a social policy [...], which was intended to be as favourable as possible for the underprivileged, whoever they are. (Brussels, A, director, 07/05/2021).

Scholarly literature confirms that the political orientation influences welfare attitudes and opinions on redistribution more in the regional context rather than at the national level (Eger & Breznau, 2017, p. 449–450).[5] However, we see in our case studies that different attitudes develop in terms of how social matters are dealt with in the municipality, rather than in terms of the specific approach to newcomer beneficiaries of social welfare.

> It's a commune [...] bourgeois, it's right-wing, so they still have trouble with the foreign public, I think. So they also have trouble with poverty, it's still a taboo subject, although there's already been an evolution compared to 20 years ago, but I think that [...] there's still this mentality that's there, we still have trouble with poverty. (Brussels, F, social worker, 31/05/2021)

Because of its political ideology, a municipality may take a strict approach to the allocation of funds to the management of social issues, reducing social assistance to its minimum (that is, what is mandatory). Also in the specific case of a municipality deciding to open a local reception initiative (LRI), the reasons to do it may range (and combine both factors) from an effective will of engaging in the reception of asylum seekers and refugees determined by a politically oriented positive attitude towards immigrants, to economic and financial interests.

> The PCSW over the years has made [...] savings with the LRI subsidies, but this was planned, Fedasil was not contrary, and we were able to invest in buildings. [...] the local reception initiative has allowed us to work on social issues and to develop employment in the two municipalities [...], four and a half full time jobs thanks to the LRI. For small communes, well, it's quite interesting [...] it has allowed the PCSW to create a heritage as well, so that now the housing belongs to the PCSW. And it's true that if in three, four, five years we are told that now the system is changing, there

is no more LRI, all the newcomers go to a centre and stay in a centre, well
the PCSW still has social housing to provide people with. [...] I go to the
consultation table at the commune, so we have to defend the project too.
(Wallonia, H, director, 15/01/2021)

Indeed, the funding received from Fedasil can function as a positive argument
to 'convince' committee members to accept to open a LRI, since this additional
budget can help de facto with the overall management of the agency, as well as
with expanding its housing property and capacity of the PCSW. In addition,
receiving funding from Fedasil makes it possible to cover the social welfare
claims of LRI residents without affecting the agency's structural budget.

PCSWs' internal guidelines are applied through a set of pre-established
forms that social workers need to fill when preparing the record of the
beneficiary, checking standard elements regarding their situation. This way
of functioning, according to the interviewees, allows additional 'gain in
objectivity' and prevents differences in treatment depending on the 'sensitivity' of the social worker (Wallonia, C, social worker, 15/03/2021). Moreover,
these standards permit keeping track of the social and administrative history
of the beneficiary, that is, their demands and the ways in which they have
been answered, as well as their engagements and actions. The literature
shows that the paperwork that social workers have to comply with in assessing migrants' entitlement to social benefits may limit the possibility of
accessing migrants' rights (Andreetta, 2019). However, as we will also see
below, documentary practices[6] can equally be crucial for social workers to
influence the positive decision to grant benefits or to create opportunities
to reverse negative decisions.

In general, these different positionings and decisions among PCSWs do
not concern the social income itself, since it seems that no arbitrariness is
possible: either the beneficiary complies with the conditions of access to it,
or not. However, we gathered some examples of exceptions to this rule. First,
the situation of a minor living with parents and asking for social income is
subject to interpretations, since the law stipulates that the revenues of the
parents can be taken into account *or not* when deciding whether the minor
is entitled to social income. More particularly with regard to newcomers,
another example concerns undocumented migrants: while they are not
entitled to social income, this can be allocated to their children in case the
latter are Belgian. This situation is recurrent in the case of an individual
who has started a regularisation procedure through family reunification
with their child whom he/she had from a Belgian partner. However, the
allocation of social income through the child is not systematic. Another

issue that can be interpreted differently among PCSWs is the 'disposition to work' as condition to access social income. As we saw in Chapters 2 and 6, this concept is crucial in labour market activation policies and practices, in particular when dealing with newly arrived immigrants. Each PCSW can be more or less strict on what 'being available for employment' means with regard to newcomer beneficiaries, and therefore demanding different kinds of actions from them in order to prove their engagement – a condition to get (and deserve)[7] the social aid. For some PCSWs, being registered at the regional job agency is enough to testify the disposition to work, also because the beneficiary will then respond to the obligations set by this institution. For other PCSWs, the beneficiaries also have to bring to the social workers and the committee proofs of their active search for a job, or of their regular participation to training and social activities aimed at preparing them to enter the job market. In rural contexts, PCSWs may be less demanding when they take into account the greater difficulties that beneficiaries can face compared to an urban context:

> Here in [rural municipality], eight job [search] proofs when it's a person who doesn't have a driving licence, who has children, he's quickly blocked, so finding eight here, it's always the same thing: the two bakeries, the Delhaize, it's always the same ones that come back. And we know that in these places, people are not looking for work, so it's a bit of a problem. (Wallonia, H, social worker, 28/01/2021)

Besides these possible interpretations of the conditions to access social income, a variety of different decisions is present among PCSWs concerning the demands of other social aids. First, each PCSW can assess if certain types of demands are relevant or not – again in relation with the principle of human dignity and the assessment of the state of need – and whether they generally take them in charge – and to what extent – or refuse them. This can concern, for example. transportation costs, funding for study, and house rental guarantee. Different decisions occur because of mathematical calculations depending on a figure that varies from one agency to the other. Generally, each PCSW establishes the minimum budget needed for one adult (depending also on if they have children or not) to live. Then, the actual resources of the beneficiary are calculated subtracting their expenses from their revenues. The comparison of these figures (checking if the actual resources are or not higher than the minimum needed budget) should allow for deciding whether the beneficiary is able or not to cover the expenses for which he/she asks social assistance. Moreover, we observed that changes in these calculations occurred in some of the studied PCSWs during the COVID-19 health crisis, because of both new needs and specific funding, and this is again a local decision:

> The balance available in the 'resources and expenses' […] is specific to each PCSW. The 'resources and expenses' have been adapted [additionally during Covid times] in our PCSW […]. […] We don't have to have the agreement from above, I mean it's internal. (Wallonia, A, social worker, 17/02/2021)

PCSWs are autonomous in adopting different approaches to the implementation of the law, a fact that determines concrete variations in social assistance delivery. Moreover, this can affect the very same experience that beneficiaries have with different welfare agencies. In the next chapter we will study the functioning of the decision-making process within the framework described above and in relation with the overall approaches adopted by PCSWs.

NOTES

1. Discretion also operates in different forms at the social workers level and at the committee level, as we will see later.
2. This process also develops through the implementation of internal and external centralised computerised databases. The impact of digitalisation on the work of street-level bureaucrats and on the possibility of performing discretion has been studied (Bovens & Zouridis, 2002; Hansen et al., 2018; Busch & Henriksen, 2018), leading to the statement that the introduction of digitalised systems in public services is definitely not to be neglected while analysing their functioning (Pollitt, 2011).
3. On this subject, see the section on 'interacting with local welfare offices' in Andreetta (2022, p. 8).
4. The reference is to voluntary associations.
5. The authors show, '[T]here is a positive relationship between the percentage of the regional population that voted for a left party and support for the welfare state' (Eger & Breznau, 2017: 450). Similarly, they state, 'Left-wing parties are likely to favour integration policies that grant labour, welfare and citizenship rights to settled migrants, while right-wing parties may oppose such policies to maintain a more malleable, flexible and "returnable" immigrant workforce' (Natter et al., 2020, p. 5).
6. In Chapter 11 we will also look at how 'collecting papers' plays a role for the newcomer beneficiaries themselves.
7. The analysis of the concept of welfare deservingness and the study of its development in street-level bureaucrats' practices will be the object of Chapter 8.

REFERENCES

Andreetta, S. (2019). Writing for different audiences: Social workers, irregular migrants and fragmented statehood in Belgian welfare bureaucracies. *Journal of Legal Anthropology, 3*(2), 91–110.

Andreetta, S. (2022). Engaging with the State: Illegalized migrants, welfare institutions and the law in French-Speaking Belgium. *Migration Politics, 1*(1), 1–20.

Berman, P. (1978). *The study of macro and micro implementation of social policy.* The Rand Corporation.

Bommes, M., & Geddes, A. (2000). *Immigration and welfare: Challenging the borders of the welfare state.* Routledge.

Bovens, M., & Zouridis, S. (2002). From street-level to system-level bureaucracies: How information and communication technology is transforming administrative discretion and constitutional control. *Public Administration Review, 62*(2), 174–184.

Busch, A. P., & Henriksen, H. Z. (2018). Digital discretion: A systematic literature review of ICT and street-level discretion. *Information Polity, 23*, 3–28. https://doi.org/10.3233/IP-170050

Eger, M. A., & Breznau, N. (2017). Immigration and the welfare state: A cross-regional analysis of European welfare attitudes. *International Journal of Comparative Sociology, 58*(5), 440–463.

Geddes, A. (2003). Migration and the welfare state in Europe. *The Political Quarterly, 74*(s1), 150–162.

Hansen, H. T., Lundberg, K., & Syltevik, L. J. (2018). Digitalization, street-level bureaucracy and welfare users' experiences. *Social Policy & Administration, 52*(1), 67–90.

Maynard-Moody, S., & Portillo, S. (2010). Street-level bureaucracy theory. In R. Durant (Ed.), *Oxford Handbook of American Bureaucracy* (pp. 252–277). Oxford University Press.

Natter, K., Czaika, M., & De Haas, H. (2020). Political party ideology and immigration policy reform: An empirical enquiry. *Political Research Exchange, 2*(1). https://doi.org/10.1080/2474736X.2020.1735255

Pollitt, C. (2011). Technological change: A central yet neglected feature of public Administration. *Journal of Public Administration and Policy, 3*(2), 31–52. https://doi.org/10.2478/v10110-010-0003-z

Slaven, M., Casella Colombeau, S., & Badenhoop, E. (2021). What drives the immigration-welfare policy link? Comparing Germany, France and the United Kingdom. *Comparative Political Studies, 54*(5), 855–888.

Soumoy, H. (2010). Loi organique des CPAS et loi accueil: quels enjeux pour les CPAS?. *Pensee plurielle, 3*, 37–61.

Vintila D., & Lafleur J.-M. (2020). Migration and access to welfare benefits in the EU: The interplay between residence and nationality. In J. M. Lafleur, & D. Vintila (Eds.), *Migration and social protection in Europe and beyond (volume 1).* IMISCOE Research Series. Springer, Cham. https://doi.org/10.1007/978-3-030-51241-5_1

CHAPTER 7
THE ALLOCATION OF SOCIAL ASSISTANCE AS A HIERARCHISED DECISION-MAKING PROCESS

ELSA MESCOLI AND HANNE VANDERMEERSCHEN

Despite varying approaches to policy implementation of PCSWs, we observed a high standardisation of the decision-making process concerning the allocation of social assistance and reflecting the law framework described above. Eventual differences in the decision-making process only concern internal organisation, that is, how and by whom decisions are actually taken,[1] while the process itself is the same across the agencies. Indeed, the correct management of the records is also the object of regular verification by the Ministry (Social Integration). In this chapter, we will analyse this process as well as the role of each actor involved, arguing that decision making is highly hierarchised in Belgian PCSWs. It takes the form of a 'decision horizon', which means a decision-making process composed of different professional figures and procedural steps and influenced by contextual organisational factors – including previous knowledge, experiences, and protocols (Emerson & Paley, 2001).

1. FROM THE DEMAND TO THE DECISION

The graph below represents the decision-making process from the demand introduced by a (potential) beneficiary to the decision of the committee and a possible appeal. The detailed description of this process, visually summarised in figure 7.1, is necessary to understand – at a later stage of this analysis – the role of each social actor involved and how and when discretion operates on the ground.

Figure 7.1 The decision-making process, author's diagram

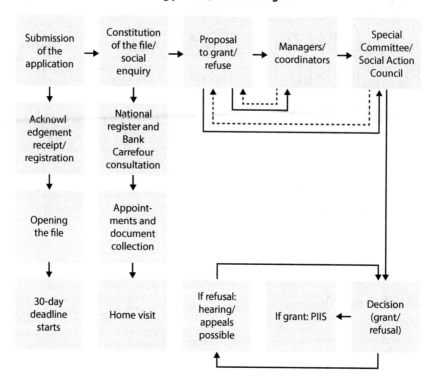

The applicant submits their demand to the PCSW, generally at the reception desk, where he/she receives an acknowledgement of receipt and the demand is registered. Commonly a reception agent, who may be a social worker himself/herself, or not, manages this step. In many – but not all – cases, we observed that this function is fulfilled by workers engaged through Art. 60, who are often people speaking foreign languages (newcomers themselves in some cases, or people of foreign origins). At this stage, the file of the potential beneficiary is opened, and 'dispatched' to social workers who will take in charge the next steps of the procedure – be this in a specialised social service or in the general social service. The 30-day deadline established by the law to answer the demand starts at its registration. Once the newly opened file arrives to the social worker, he/she completes it with all the information needed for the social enquiry. Moreover, if the reception agent has not yet done this, the social worker in charge of the file gets administrative details concerning the potential beneficiary through the national register and the Crossroads Bank for Social Security (CBSS).[2] It is checked, first and in particular related to immigrants, the residence status, and the pending procedures,[3] and then the financial resources of the person (other social benefits and professional occupation). The social enquiry also includes the collection of documents needed to analyse the financial situation of the potential beneficiary, that is, attesting resources and expenses. These documents are gathered through communication and appointments with the applicant, as well as through home visits. The aim is also to identify the beneficiary's concrete integration projects and opportunities.

> First of all, we consult the CBSS to see a bit of the person's life history. Then we interview them and we look at the family composition, if the person has children, if they live with other people, then the financial situation, do they have any income, do they have a savings account, [...] the current account for which we need bank statements to prove it. Then the family allowances, the person even if he has a small income like the family allowances we note it. The health situation too, if the person has a mutual insurance company, if they are in order to be reimbursed, if they have any health problems, if there is any psychological follow-up that needs to be put in place on the side or something else [...]. Otherwise, we look at the person's professional background, whether they have already worked, whether they have studied, whether they are interested in studying again, having a job, following a training course, whether they are willing to work and, in general, we will put together an individual social integration project [...]. We also look at the social and family situation, where the person has lived, what their background is, whether there is still contact or little contact with the family. So it's a bit like the whole life of the person, it's quite complete. (Wallonia, H, social worker, 28/01/2021)

As many social workers themselves state, these tasks may be perceived by beneficiaries as control measures aimed at verifying whether they are *really* in a situation of need and if they actively comply with their obligations. Indeed, social enquiries are aimed at gathering 'proofs' concerning the situation of the beneficiary, as well as at confirming or contradicting 'suspicions' (Wallonia, C, social worker, 15/03/2021) that social workers may have concerning the beneficiary's truthfulness.

> There are people who do not tell us the whole truth, who lie to us [...], there are also things they can hide, [...] I'm not going to say that we control when we make home visits, but there is also this little notion of control that is there ... we mustn't hide it. [...] And when I see that there's a problem, that I have a doubt, I call the person in, really, to clarify things. [...] if I

find out [the lie] in another way, [...] afterwards, I'll have a complicated relationship with the beneficiary. [...] There is still a percentage of people who lie and try to take advantage. (Wallonia, A, social worker, 17/02/2021)

As we will see later, the relation established between the beneficiary and the social worker and the assessment of deservingness are crucial in the delivery of social benefits, and these factors also influence social workers' use of discretionary power. Once the social enquiry and the file is complete with the needed information, the social worker proposes a decision on the demand of the applicant and forwards the file to the manager or service coordinator, who will analyse it and either confirm or ask for modifications or additional enquiry.[4] Each PCSW, most often depending on its size, can have one general manager and/or one or more managers for each service, which frequently implies additional steps of analysis of the files, for example all managers together in some of our case studies. After this, the files go to the Social Action council of the PCSW. Depending on the size of the agency, the number of councillors varies, as well as the number of councillors delegated to decide on the benefits applications.[5] Also in this case, the committee can ask social workers to modify their file, for example if information is missing or if the suggested decision is poorly motivated. When the file is complete, the committee decides whether to approve the social worker's proposal, or to take a different decision. Usually at least one manager or social worker participates in the committee, and both may also have the opportunity to 'defend' their proposal at the meeting if they feel that the committee's decision is inappropriate. The decision over a demand for social benefits is communicated to the applicant by a formal letter and through further communication by the social workers. It is worth mentioning, in relation to the previous analysis on the accessibility of PCSWs' practices and rules by migrants, that this letter may be difficult to understand by migrants due to the legal terminology used (in the regional language concerned) – a fact that would also make the applicant neglect the possibility of an appeal. The opacity of this letter translates the lack of transparency of the decision-making process itself (Schafer, 2013) and hides the possibility of contradicting it, which affects the efficiency and fairness of the service provided from the perspective of its beneficiaries. In case the demand concerns the social income, and it is accepted, the PIIS is opened. If the demand is refused, be it for social income or any other social aids, the applicant can ask for a hearing at the committee assembly and/or submit an appeal to the Labour court.

2.   SOCIAL WORKERS AND MANAGERS

Within this structured functioning, a set of social actors play relevant roles. First, the reception agent, who first receives the beneficiary's demand, marking the beginning of the process of allocation (or refusal) of social benefits. This professional figure functions as a filter, although not in terms of discretion over the demands of the beneficiaries, since all applications submitted to the PCSW must be registered. The presence of reception agents means instead that the beneficiaries generally do not have direct access to the social workers, except for small PCSWs. The social workers contact the beneficiaries afterwards, depending on the urgency they consider. Reception agents also have the task to provide documents requested by beneficiaries, for example for medical expenses, or certificates for social tariffs.

As for social workers, their role is then to gather all relevant information that would enable to decide whether to allocate social benefits or not, to propose a positive or a negative response (we will analyse further their role and the factors influencing their choices and decisions in Chapter 8), and to follow up on the case. Concerning managers, they examine the records built by the social workers, in order to validate them before their submission to the committee. It is worth analysing the functions of this member of the PCSW hierarchy further.

As mentioned above, depending on the organisation of the agency, on its size (including internal divisions), and on the number of caseworks, managers can be more or less numerous and fulfil different functions – beyond the general supervision of social workers' everyday work.

> In principle, that is the basic task of you as a coordinator. That is making your team work, and making sure that your team does what it is supposed to do and that each individual in the team does what they are supposed to do. (Flanders, C, manager, 23/02/2021)

In our case studies, we found a large range of professional profiles of managers, including managers responsible for one local antenna, others in charge of each whole service (whether or not it is divided into different branches), and directors (of different grades, with general, specialised, or financial functions). As for the presidents of the PCSWs under study, we consider their role as operating in-between managers and the committee,[6] with more or less proximity to the social workers themselves depending on the size of the agency. Therefore, the structure of each PCSW can be characterised by different levels of complexity, and imply a varying number of verification steps of the records and proposals submitted by the social workers. Indeed, independently of their specific functions, each manager has the authority to ask social workers to review the file if he/she estimates that it is lacking information or that it presents mistakes or incorrect assessments.

> There is always an intermediate passage, which is the ratification of the head of department. [...]. Therefore, there is an internal control that is put in place for everything related to the management of legality, document management [...]. Once the file is ready at the social worker's, there is then a passive verification by the administrative department. (Wallonia, G, director, 12/1/2021)

> I am an assistant in the social action department [...], the final decision is ours in relation to a series of actions [the social workers] can carry out. [...] they all work very, very well, but the decision making power for the next stage, which is at committee level, decisions and approvals by the committee, or if they have questions about a situation that is perhaps a bit more complex, well, we help to decide on that. [...] in any case the verification is our responsibility. (Wallonia, D, manager, 29/01/2021)

As mentioned in Chapter 1, managerial control (Brodkin, 2011a, 2011b) is an integral element of the decision-making process, and it orients street-level practices (Riccucci *et al.*, 2004; Ellis, 2011; Brodkin, 2011a). Managers are responsible for translating the guidelines into concrete task templates, ensuring that they are implemented, and that the decisions proposed over the allocation of social benefits are appropriate and coherent with both the law and the specific approach of the concerned PCSW to the policy implementation. Although not all managers in our case studies perform this control, many among them regularly assess the work of social workers – also in relation with organisational goals and 'regimes of performance measurement and inspections' (Harris & White, 2009; cited in Jessen & Tufte, 2014, p. 270) – and this can result in informal or formal sanctions. We have gathered examples of these situations especially in Brussels:

> We come across cases where the behaviour of the social worker was obviously a problem, and so at that point [...], depending on the seriousness, it's either a supervision procedure, and we try to correct it and see if there's an improvement, or if it was too serious, we terminate the contract. This has happened. But it's still exceptional. (Brussels, D, manager, 02/04/2021)

[Managers] check the number of reports that are made, the interview sheets that are made. [...] it's the only way to control us, but I find that this control is becoming an obsession, schizophrenic, unhealthy, [...] they're only concentrating on that! [...] to control and to reduce us to simply carrying out a task. (Brussels, F, social worker, 31/05/2021)

The following quote suggests that control measures are seen by managers as part of the formal aspects for which they are responsible:

But you know your colleagues in the long run. I know very well, with that person I have to keep questioning this or checking this person has done that. Our computer systems are made in such a way that if you follow how it should be done, you can very well inquire for all your clients. But of course you also have to follow it up as a manager that it happens. (Flanders, E, director, 2/03/2021)

These control measures may also target the duration of the interviews with beneficiaries, which have to be limited – affecting the possibility of needs detection, which we will discuss later. These measures transform the aim of social work from responding to social needs to satisfying procedural and quantitative requirements – the politics of performance and numbers (Brodkin, 2012; Gabarro, 2012).[7]

Some managers also indicated that they could suggest training to social workers to improve or update their knowledge and skills. Interestingly, managers also have an important role in supporting the social workers when they propose a decision that falls outside the established framework. Indeed, social workers consult managers in case of doubt, uncertainty, or disagreement between colleagues.

I have to say, I've been in the profession for 13 years now, I think, if I may say so about myself, I don't need much advice. I am now in a phase where I need less advice. I sometimes go and check certain ideas or thoughts, now especially with my manager because our team has been rather rejuvenated lately, people have left and people come in with a little less experience. (Flanders, G, social worker, 20/04/2021)

During the week, they call me for client discussions. A discussion of 'That's the situation, how are we going to handle it best.' I can say 'That colleague has experience with this, check again how he did it'. Or, yes, that really depends, 'Perhaps inform that or that authority.' (Flanders, E, director, 2/03/2021)

Actually, people mainly come to me with problem files, or an exception. Or also when, after consulting a colleague, they are not sure what to do about it, for example. (Flanders, H, director, 4/03/2021)

Asking for exceptions to the rules by the social workers is also part of the decision-making process, as we will see later. However, in most cases, this needs the approval of managers first, before the committee is called upon, also because it is often managers who present the records and discuss them at the councils.[8]

I don't submit a file as it is if I know it's going to get stuck [...], it'll be refused. If I know it's going to get stuck, I'll already discuss it and I'll give my opinion, etc. Depending on that, either she [supervisor/head of department] will say yeah, it's fine like that, you can do it and so it'll be positive anyway, or she'll say it's problematic, we need to make a pool,[9] we need to explain it, we need to make a decision at a higher level. [...] and so it comes back to me with what they've decided, and I'll resubmit it. (Wallonia, B, social worker, 15/01/2021)

[Social workers] submit their proposal, then we defend it before the committee, so obviously we read all these proposals before they are presented and if necessary we discuss them again with the social worker, and if we don't agree we discuss it with the social worker, we try to find a solution. We're never in opposition, it's the same principle as the committee has. [...] we think differently about the most appropriate assistance to offer the beneficiary. (Wallonia, D, manager, 29/01/2021)

Therefore, managers can be both limiting and supporting the work of social workers, and their decisions do not necessarily imply the refusal of allocating the requested social benefits. While preparing their proposal, social workers take into account not only the elements that they have at their disposal concerning the beneficiary's situation, but also the expected reactions of the managers (and the committee), which translates the functioning of the described decision-making process as a decision horizon (Emerson & Paley, 2001), as mentioned above. Variations also depend on managers' own approach, but in any case, they challenge the discretionary power of street-level bureaucrats (Jessen & Tufte, 2014).

[I]t all depends on how [the case] is presented, but it also depends on who you have in front of you, sometimes you have bosses who don't want to hear anything, the rules are the rules. Just as I had a situation with my former boss, where for me it was necessary to make a withdrawal [of the social income] […] and she thought not to, so I had to grant it. (Wallonia, B, social worker, 15/01/2021)

Indeed, managers would ensure that the decisions taken over a beneficiary's demand are 'objective' rather than 'subjective', complying to the rules rather than to the personal opinions of social workers – although, as we have seen, subjective interpretations are embedded in the very same law framework regulating the functioning of PCSWs – and with the aim to avoid 'biases'. This can be done by proofreading and checking files and reports before they are submitted to the committee, or by organising group meetings.

Experienced forces are going to dare to bring their own story in there much more strongly and make it clear 'What is it exactly here?' Uhm, but yes, I think that one of my roles is to make sure that this does not translate too strongly into a difference in how decisions are made. That in itself is also something specific to being a social worker: you have to find your own style […], but I think that for me my role there is of course to be able to take a step back again and to objectify a bit: 'Apart from that aspect, are we sufficiently proportionate in our judgments in different files? Are we taking similar decisions in similar situations?' (Flanders, A, manager, 13/04/2021)

[I]t's always a joint advice that goes to the […] committee. I then kind of monitor the vision, how did that approach go, did [the social workers] take into account the possibilities and the expectations of the client, are they not being too strict or should they not be more strict on this. When you interact with someone [a beneficiary], you always have that personal aspect, in case you have a click with one and you don't have a good connection with the other and you're going to make different decision in it, that's why we look at it as a group, to take away that personal interpretation a little bit. […] I try to play a neutralising role somewhere. And by that I mean: we also organise team meetings in which certain things actually have to be supported by everyone as much as possible before they are granted or not. (Flanders, F, director, 7/05/2021)

So we have case discussions at my service where social workers have the opportunity to discuss grey zones, as I call them, with the team and then see: 'What are the different opinions here?' I think that's important too, I think it's important that they enter into a dialogue with each other about such things. (Flanders, C, 23/02/2021)

Managers act as a 'buffer' between the social workers and the committee, which would help to ensure that the social workers' proposals are accepted.

> We are not immune to bias, [...] when I come across it, I have the social worker correct it, and we try to avoid the bias being discovered by the committee because that is more painful. (Brussels, D, manager, 02/04/2021)

But above all, it is an issue of guaranteeing, in principle, equal treatment of the beneficiaries and their demands, despite the case-by-case and tailor-made approach generally adopted (discussed in Chapter 4) and the variations that this can actually imply.

3.   THE COMMITTEE

Going back to the decision-making procedure, after the validation of the records and proposals by the managers, the committee of the concerned PCSW comes into play.

The committee plays a crucial role in the decision making at the PCSW, as committee members have the final say in particular when it comes to requests for financial support. This can be the decision to grant a social integration income, but also to grant other types of complementary financial support (installation grant, support for energy bills, and so forth), or the agreement to cover other expenses (medical bills, glasses, driving lessons, and so forth). When a beneficiary wants to follow an educational programme (for example, a bachelor's or master's degree), this needs to be discussed by the committee as well. Other examples include the approval of the start of an Art. 60 (see Chapter 6), or the non-compliance with conditions set in the Individualised Social Integration Project (ISIP) (see Chapter 2), in which case the committee will decide upon sanctions. These decisions are taken in regular meetings by the committee.

As mentioned above, the basis for the decisions of the committee are the files prepared by the social workers, and the suggestions they make. The proposals of the social workers can be approved exactly as they are, but alternatively the committee can also ask for clarifications or for further information, make suggestions, choose to take a different decision. In all municipalities under study, the suggestion of the social workers was followed in a large majority of the situations. In situations where the committee did not follow the suggestion of the social worker, reasons can, for example, be that the social workers are considered too generous/not generous enough in their proposal, decisions can be judged incoherent with regard to decisions taken in the past in similar situations, or reasons of human dignity can be invoked. In other situations, a suggestion might not be followed because the information is incomplete, as mentioned above, or for more administrative reasons, such as a mistake in the interpretation of the law or a miscalculation.

The committee already exerts an influence on the proposals made by social workers as well: social workers and their managers adapt their files and actions based on the expectations of the committee, as we will see in more detail later, which the social workers and managers learn through experience.[10] For example, in some municipalities there is a stronger focus on activation and on providing proof of the willingness to work, for instance by complying with the role of submitting five job applications per week. In that case, the social workers will advise their beneficiaries accordingly. Also in their files, social workers will emphasise the elements they know the committee wants to hear, depending on the priorities of their committee (for example, emphasising the efforts for learning the language), or might adapt their file on what they estimate most realistic to be approved by the committee. In other words, the influence and power of the committee resides in the final decision, but also in the process that precedes it as well, as their past actions and decisions shape the actions and proposals by social workers (and the approval or remarks of their managers). This process, as we have seen, demonstrates the decision-making process in PCSWs as a 'decision horizon' (Emerson & Paley, 2001).

There are important variations in the way the committees operate and in the organisation of decision making. For example, in some cases, particularly (but not exclusively) in small-sized municipalities, the committee will actively consider and discuss the files of all beneficiaries where a decision needs to be taken. In other cases, different streams of files are being created, with, for example, 'a-files' and 'b-files',[11] with 'a-files' being actively discussed, and b-files passing without much further debate. In these cases, the so-called b-files are files for which the rules and guidelines are clear and well set, whereas the 'a-files' refer to situations for which the guidelines are less well defined or where an exception might need to be granted. In larger cities, some decision-making power can be granted to the team managers (followed by an automatic ratification by the committee), in which case there are strict guidelines about what managers can decide and what not. This delegation of power takes place because of the high number of files (or, as some respondents have highlighted, the increased number of beneficiaries): the committee would otherwise be unable to check all files in time.

So, as we are a large PCSW, we have the possibility to do this. In fact, the committee has placed a certain amount of trust in the people in charge of the agency [the team managers], so if we judge that the situation is clear and according to the criteria defined by the committee, we can grant [...] the aid, but which is ratified by the committee afterwards. It is to go faster in a sense, because you need to know that per week – and it is only my agency – I send between 30 and 50 files to the committee but there is all the rest [the other files that can be ratified without debate]. (Brussels, A, manager, 11/05/2021)

Moreover, there are also considerable differences in the extent of involvement and interference of the committee. In some of the cases under study, the committee asked a lot of questions, giving suggestions, requesting more information, and so forth – sometimes leading to frustrations by social workers because of the additional workload and the perceived lack of trust – whereas in others, social workers were surprised by the little (or lack of) involvement of their committees. The quotes below demonstrate the large diversity in approaches, by mentioning one of the most pronounced examples in both directions. Other committees kept the middle between those more extreme situations.

For example, someone who is undergoing counselling with a psychiatrist. Then the question can be asked, for example, 'What is the further course that has been agreed with the psychiatrist?' Such things can be asked. So, they actually go into more detail about a number of things that we follow up with our people [beneficiaries]. But this often leads to frustrations among colleagues, because we have an enormous workload and because we are not always able, due to lack of time and the high caseload, to deal with these things. Or equally, the committee asks us questions and we think, well, 'What kind of questions are they asking us? Do they really think that we are not engaged with our people?' So that does lead to some frustration sometimes. (Flanders, C, social worker, 16/03/2021)

We get incredibly few questions. We get an incredible amount of trust, I think, from our committee members. I have a few friends who work at other PCSWs. There, the committee often lasts three hours. With us it ends within half an hour. That's very funny [...] Very easy. Yes, in this sense we have it very easy, um, but I have to say that these are very big differences with other PCSWs, apparently. So, euh, I know social workers in [name neighbouring municipality] and in [name neighbouring municipality], and there the meetings last for hours. And they have to plead their cases and then with us it's often, yes, we read our report, everyone agrees, yes okay. That's it. Very occasionally those of the opposition who say 'no' or ask a question, but very few, very few. [...] We're surprised that they don't have more comments than that. And then we think, yes, okay, that's a sign that we're doing it right, yes. That's our conclusion then. But well, we do think it's weird, though. But anyway, it does make us feel like they trust us in our work, though, so that's how we look at it then. (Flanders, E, social worker, 16/03/2021)

In our study, we have also explored how the committee reached their decisions. There is a discourse on the fact that the committee is always working and taking its decisions within the framework of law (*travailler dans la légalité*) (Wallonia, H, councillor, 3/02/2021). Clearly, this is an essential starting point. However, the committee does have freedom and autonomy and it makes practices of discretion.

> There is a legal framework, all employees of the PCSW must absolutely fol-low the legal framework that exists. Of course, there can be interpretations of the legal framework too. And also case law, and even case law specific to each PCSW, that also exists. But the role of the committee is to analyse the files individually and to take an individual decision, a decision specific to the file. And sometimes there are certain situations that require a decision [...] where the interpretation of the law is so great that it leaves the committee a freedom that the social worker does not have. And the situation can be resolved by the committee more to the benefit of the person, whereas this case, if it had been managed strictly by the administration according to its obligations [...], is sometimes not necessarily to the advantage of the person and to the advantage of the general interest. [...] [at the level of the committee] there is this autonomy, this freedom, and above all there is the legitimacy that the social worker could not have if he does not respect the legal framework in the strict sense, whereas the committee has the legitimacy. (Wallonia, B, councillor, 06/01/2021)[12]

Examples of this are that the committee can establish the rate of an aid (when not all the amount of a demand is taken in charge, but only a percent – this concerns one-off aids, not the social integration income), or the scope and the duration of a sanction. The committee also has the possibility of intervening with own means (*fonds propres* in French) in whatever terms, however, there is a discourse on the risk of creating a precedent (giving in one case, will mean to give in all similar cases, as mentioned above). In sum, overall, in addition to the framework of the law, there is a discretionary space to make decisions and shape daily policy and practice. In this discretionary space, the idea of adapting decisions to individual needs and deciding on a case-by-case basis is also very present in the discourses of respondents, including presidents and managers, who also stress the 'public' nature of the allocated benefits.

> It's case by case and [...], and the committee's reflection is obviously to say also, the money that is distributed is everyone's money. Is it the wisest way to help the person to pay this? [...] If we help him at this point, is this really the right solution? [...] You don't leave the person without help. But it's a different kind of help. (Wallonia, D, manager, 29/01/2021)

A similar conclusion arises with regard to the hearings, which are another part of the task of the committee. Indeed, as described earlier, beneficiaries have the right to be heard when they disagree with a decision. It is a legal obligation to provide this possibility to beneficiaries. However, in practice, the (frequency of the) use differs between municipalities. Hearings were not only said to have an impact on final decisions, but it was also acknowledged that they are often the cause of a deviant decision, and – in the words of one of the respondents – often 'creativity is applied' (examples given relate to beneficiaries following an educational track):

> We then hear the client and if indeed that image and that motivation of that client also appears from that hearing, then we very often also work out a rather creative alternative proposal. For example, that could be of 'Look, we stop here now, we stop giving you a social integration income, but if you now continue with your exams and you pass everything, come back and we will give you support again', that could be an example. Or it can be 'Okay, listen, basically that doesn't work out, but if you pass so many credits it can continue.' You see, so in that way we deal with that fairly creatively. It also happens sometimes that we pronounce certain sanctions, for example, partially [effectively] and also partially conditional. (Flanders, B, president, 9/03/2021)

Committee discussions about less straightforward files are also an arena in which priorities are rendered explicit, and rules of conduct for this and future cases are set.

> There is, of course, an impact in terms of content [*een inhoudelijke stempel*]. That makes sense in a way, given the way that PCSWs are organised. There is an authoritative committee. I think if you were to look at it in percentage terms, it would be the majority of reports that are followed [...] And there is a residual percentage that fluctuates a bit with periods, for which there is

still discussion. Sometimes discussions can be quite technical in nature, such as, 'Are we going to grant something on loan or are we just going to grant it?' It stems rather from that angle. Yet, sometimes it's about more principled issues of course, 'Are we going to go along with this at all in a particular story or are we not going to go along with it at all?' (Flanders, A, manager, 13/04/2021)

Committee members are political representatives. A question that arises in this context is to what extent politics are involved in the decision making of committee members, especially since – as we have seen – not all decisions are straightforward nor always captured in clear guidelines, decrees, or laws. Here too, based on our findings, we conclude there is considerable variation across municipalities in terms of the influence of politics on the functioning of the committee, and ultimately on the decisions taken. A discourse that was held by a considerable number of respondents, is that because the committee meetings happen at '*huis clos*', away from media and public, they are of a very different nature compared to political debates occurring under the spotlight, for example in municipal councils. Nevertheless, the ideological positioning of the members may be visible to some extent also in the committee. However, overall, it was generally said that the political affiliation did not dominate the debates, particularly in the sense that it did not turn into 'politics'. In a considerable number of cases, respondents indicated that in their municipality, the committee was able to operate as a 'team', though with team members who might have different perspectives at times.

We are all on the same wavelength, we may not have convergent opinions, we each have our sensitivities, our ways of seeing things, our political opinions, but, in any case, from what I have experienced here at the PCSW, I have never known any tensions […] I have always obtained almost unanimity in the files that I present. (Wallonia, D, president, 25/11/2020)

This is absolutely not the case in the committee [engaging in opposition]. It wasn't like that in the past either, there was the occasional discussion about general policy, but certainly in the individual records it is noticeable that we are actually one entity. It makes a difference that there is no press and there would be no press attention. So, we are actually a very good group. That's important, I think, it's about people, not about policy choices, that's done in the municipal council. But when it comes to support, we're actually all on the same page. (Flanders, H, president, 18/02/2021)

Yes we do have different political groups [parties] of course. But we do insist on that, that politics doesn't play. This is about individual files, it's not about projects, not about building or 'How are you going to do this or that?' Roads that need to be built or the like more. This is about a problem situation of an individual or a family. And that's a different angle than dossiers that end up on a municipal council, for example. Then politics actually plays a lot less, not to say not at all (Flanders, F, president, 23/06/2021)

Nevertheless, social workers did report receiving biased questions from certain committee members, and also managers stated they had to deal with politically coloured or tendentious questions (cf. infra). However, in many cases, this was attributed to personality rather than political stripe. It was also mentioned that, when there were problems with certain 'deviant' individuals (for example, showing a racist bias or questioning elements that are actually defined by law), they would tend to get outvoted in the committee (hence not being able to affect the final decision for an individual).

Overall, rather than politics or political,[13] personal sensitivity and individual appreciation are predominant, since the members of the committee state to be 'working with the human', that is, dealing with very personal and delicate situations and life experiences of individuals.

I find that the human aspect is really at the heart of the decisions made by the board. And we always try to defend the interests of the person as much as possible. If a negative decision is taken with regard to the person, it is either because we don't have enough elements to determine if he or she is indeed in the right conditions, or there is abuse. (Wallonia, G, director, 12/01/2021)

Yet, the latter accentuates the room for *manoeuvre* – rather than the strict application of a set of rules – in the committee decisions as well. Committee members often describe their role as 'helping people', and 'having the heart in the right place', and so forth, while also being firm to what is considered abuse.

Somewhat along the same line, committee members (and social workers) revealed on several occasions and in different regions that 'personal' background information was used as well, in addition to the files of the social workers. Indeed, some members of the committee may know the beneficiary's personal situation, in particular in smaller municipalities. Committee members use this information in the discussion when a decision needs to be taken, and/or rely on it in their feedback to social workers. Some indicated it was unavoidable in a small municipality.

[T]those are the profiteers if I may use a heavy word. This is someone who has stood in a café waving his mother's bank card at me: 'Look, whether I get money from you or not, I'm going to keep going to the café.' […] We, as members of the committee, we all live in the municipality, of course, so a lot of people we also know from seeing or from this or that. Sometimes we have a bit more information than a social worker and then we can say 'Keep this or that in mind', it's not forbidden. (Flanders, H, president, 18/02/2021)

If a request is made, some have already been refused because, for example, the PCSW councillors were aware that the person was sending money to Africa and they said, 'We will not accept the request because this person is sending we don't know how much money to Africa, he or she has made this choice, so we will not help him or her if he or she decides to send money.' It's a bit tricky, and as we are a small PCSW in a small village, sometimes the councillors know things that we don't know. (Wallonia, H, social worker, 28/01/2021)

So there are files that are very well known and when we say 'Aaah him again!' […] obviously there may be an a priori, we may not be able to be completely neutral because we know the whole life of the beneficiary so that's inevitable anyway. When there are preconceived ideas, we can't … but we try to be as neutral as possible in any case. (Wallonia, C, manager, 24/03/2021)

While the objectivity of this 'background information' that is being used seems questionable to us as researchers, and the professionalism of this approach as well, it is in line with the personal, and sometimes paternalistic approach (see later), which is reflected in the discourse of a number of presidents or committee members.

More generally, notwithstanding the many good intentions emphasised in the accounts of presidents or other committee members, the way the committee is organised and operates led to many criticisms in the field by social workers and managers. A first criticism, made especially by social workers, relates to the unpredictability of decisions, with similar situations potentially resulting in different decisions.

Well, there was one time, and I didn't really agree with the decision that was taken, but well, unfortunately sometimes you can't do otherwise, it was a man with a child […] he had asked me to take charge of a washing machine. And so, well, I don't usually have too many problems, the 'resources and expenses' were good, well … For me, he was completely within the conditions, and I was refused the file, so they refused to take charge of the aid because he could go to the laundry. I found that a bit … I mean it's more personal, because my other files go through that way, and why this time it didn't go through … And the only answer I got was, 'Well, he doesn't fit the conditions, he can go to the laundry because he only has one child.' And that's a little bit … Because he has two, he can have a washing machine, I mean, I found that it was not very coherent. Unfortunately, sometimes things aren't always consistent either. (Wallonia, A, social worker, 17/02/2021)

You can't estimate the council in advance what they're going to decide, but it can also be very dependent: this week they might have made a different decision than the same file next week. (Flanders, A, social worker, 27/04/2021)

[interviewer] You mentioned earlier that sometimes there are different judgements even though the request is pretty similar. How do you deal with that? [interviewee] Yes, that is very difficult, because it is purely on the basis of the past in a particular case or a type of person that does not suit them at that moment and then it is just very personal from the council of the PCSW. But that's it, you can't do anything about it. They have the final decision and there are times when I really don't agree with a decision and that's, yes, that's very frustrating, because you then have to 'sell' something to someone that you don't support at all. (Flanders, A, social worker, 19/04/2021)

Yet, social workers complain about other elements as well, which – brought together – seem to question the professionality of (some of) the committee members. For example, social workers complained about the impertinence of questions they get (for example, 'Have you discussed contraception?'), with some committee members questioning suggestions that are (according to the social worker) a mere application of the law. One social worker mentioned that committee members were checking social media profiles to obtain background information about beneficiaries, and then asking questions about it.

I notice very often that they are quite focused on social media at the council and they often find things on Facebook profiles for example. An advertisement for someone offering to work as a painter, unofficially, and a council member has then seen that on the Facebook page of the client for whom the proposal was made. Then I get the question to check that out too and discuss it with my client and then share the reaction. (Flanders, A, social worker, 23/04/2021)

Other members outstep what concerns them (for example, asking more question when one knows the person, while the questions are not all relevant for the request being made) (Flanders, G, social worker, 20/04/2021), or ask tendentious questions (for example, 'Is he still not working?'; 'How is it possible he still doesn't speak Dutch?'). It was also mentioned that committee members are prejudiced, asking more questions when it concerns someone of foreign origin, or making distinctions between 'deserving' refugees, who fled war (also see below), and other migrants, taking a more critical stance towards claims for support from the latter.

> [interviewee] If I have to be completely honest about it: what some members of our committee find difficult is that the newcomers who come to Belgium from a non-war zone, so to speak, and who immediately open up rights to social security. We certainly try to do that, it's not that they don't have the right to do so, but sometimes there can be discussions about that, 'Yes they came here and, *allez*, they are the golddiggers.'
> [interviewer] But is it then about family reunifications for example, or …?
> [interviewee] Or the marriages of convenience, they are also quick to say if it is a marriage with a Belgian that it could be a marriage of convenience, while I think that, that certainly shouldn't be said. But they do dare to say that. The fact is that we still have a predominantly social board. So, we can put it into perspective, but I notice that sometimes the social workers sigh a little, 'Oh dear, it won't be the case again that they say it's a marriage of convenience.' (Flanders, D, director, 01/02/2021)

One president complained himself about the functioning of his committee, stating that it was a kind of 'expo of prejudices', instigated by time constraints and the speed at which decisions had to be made.

> I find that a weekly theatre of … and finally, not a theatre, a kind of exhibition of prejudices, and then the whole series of xenophobia about bodyism, about genism, everything, so I find that actually an aberration. I want to say that first, because that in itself has nothing to do with newcomers, that holds for others as well. But of course, having said that, for newcomers, it means that that you feel it very strongly, it also has to do with the amount of files, the speed with which of course you're supposed to decide. So you only get a fragment, a time fragment and you then judge people very quickly, where actually all the prejudices, the clichéd viewing of people the prejudiced viewing of people, that is only reinforced for newcomers. That you then …, there are those classic questions of '*Allez*, he has been here a

long time and he still doesn't speak Dutch, how can that be?', 'Allez, what level of Dutch do you have, *allez* 1.2.', as if we then know what that means in concrete terms. 'You should speak a bit of Dutch.' This only reinforces my idea and I'm not talking about the staff of the PCSW (Flanders, president).

His opinion (of which this quote is only an excerpt) about the committee is not representative for the perspective of other presidents, as others expressed themselves in a more nuanced way, underlining also the perceived value of the committee. However, his statement does add to the 'evidence', as voiced by social workers and managers, of bias and prejudice in decision making targeting foreigners.

A recurring criticism on (some of the) committee members is also a lack of empathy (for example, not understanding that not everyone can 'just work'), and a lack of knowledge about reality, which creates frustrations. On a more general level, it is apparent throughout the interviews that committee members lack basic knowledge about the functioning of a PCSW and need a lot of explanation, especially at the beginning, in order for them to appreciate what is at stake, or to understand the files of social workers and the decision that needs to be made (for example, they need to be familiarised with an ISIP contract).

It should be noted that, overall, social workers and managers did not oppose the existence of a committee as such, and different arguments are given in favour of a committee. A first argument is that the committee would be a more neutral organ (not so 'close to the beneficiary') and that it might be beneficial in terms of equal treatment.

Sometimes also […] social workers […] often find it difficult to say no sometimes. And to sometimes take a little distance from situations […] which are very difficult to live with, we are well aware of that. And sometimes grant the coverage of certain invoices which, for the council and for me beforehand […] fall outside the scope of the PCSW's tasks. […] (Wallonia, G, director, 12/01/2021)

There is a large majority of cases where it is followed up by the councillors, now we work with human beings so there is not always the right solution. So, the proposal that is made, well, we hope to find the best solution in the least bad, we'll say, depending on the situation. And this feeling is not necessarily always the same at the level of a committee, which is perhaps more neutral, which does not know the beneficiaries and which does not have this relational and human side which means that we will perhaps defend situations and they have a more neutral view and sometimes the reflection is carried, is it the most judicious? (Wallonia, D, manager, 29/01/2021)

Second, the fact that the responsibility over a decision lies elsewhere, is mentioned as an advantage as well (see Chapter 8). A third argument that was often heard – and voiced in particular by presidents – is that the PCSW uses taxpayers' money – meaning 'public' money, as mentioned above, and it involves a political responsibility, which calls for an organ like the committee.

I think, it's a very good thing, we have really reached a point of balance in [name of the municipality] [...]. [Social workers] build the files and reports based on guidelines to facilitate decision making. But in the end, it's still the representatives [committee members] who make the decision, which ultimately obliges us politicians to measure the impact of any decision, positive or negative. Because underneath, the person can intervene, interfere by saying 'Listen, you've taken this decision, but do you realise what it means for my situation.' At the same time, it allows us, the representatives, and in any case, on a personal level, it has allowed me to better perceive, to better feel the situations and realities of each person. So yes, we set out 'generic' frameworks, but afterwards each story is unique, each situation is particular, and we have to be able to arbitrate at a given moment between ... a budgetary issue but above all a human issue. That's because, as political representatives, we are not social workers, so we don't necessarily always have a vision or an understanding of the situation from a social work point of view. We are on a political point of view and therefore we are on budgetary issues [...], so if we let our heart speak too much, we have an expression which is well known: the heart bleeds if we let ourselves go too much to listen to our heart, well, at some point it's not good from a budgetary point of view either, so we have to find a certain coherence and above all to avoid differentiated treatment and arbitrariness. Because I think that would be the worst thing, it would block everything and create a lot of resentment in the beneficiaries and then in the social workers, it's incomprehensible, it's clearly preventing them from doing their job properly. (Brussels, G, president, 15/04/2021)

However, social workers and managers do indicate that a team of experts, that is, people working in a relevant sector, would be better.[14] It is not the existence of committee as such, but rather the lack of expertise or fruitful support that is criticised. Already at present, when members have a relevant background in the committee, they are perceived as a huge asset. Examples given were a doctor, a headmaster of a school for special education, and a psychologist.

To conclude regarding the committee, the findings indicate that the committee has considerable discretion in terms of decision making, while their professionalism – or at least the professionalism of some members, not the entire committee per se – is questioned. The organisation of service delivery – and particularly the hierarchy with a committee of political representatives on top – can therefore have an impact on the equity of service delivery to newcomers and others, even though the committee is often said to be able to take a more neutral and distant stance. The committee can level out differences between social workers, but its own objectivity – or even fairness? – is questionable to some extent as well. On the positive side, the fact that the committee operates as a group (deciding in unanimity or by vote if needed) helps to level out the most extreme positions, as they get outvoted in the final decision, even though we can assume such prejudiced statements still influence the tone of the discussions.

NOTES

1. We refer, for example, to the possible different levels of delegation of responsibilities to managers (in particular due to increased numbers of caseworks to assess and the obligation to comply with formal deadlines), as well as to the presence of more or less intermediaries between the social workers and the committee/president of the concerned PCSW.
2. National database that centralises the information concerning the social security benefits perceived by each citizen, as well as their professional situation.
3. This is an example of what Andreetta and Borrelli point out, namely, 'How digital practices support increasing control of non-citizens and how migration policies continue to affect their access to welfare' (2022, p. 2).
4. However, not in all our case studies do managers check the files submitted by social workers, unless specifically requested by the social worker, and so this step can only be formal in these cases.
5. Sub-groups may exist within the committee for this specific task, while the whole group discusses broader political and organisational issues. The composition of the committee reflects that of the municipal government in terms of parties and proportions, but differently from the municipal council, the members are designated and not elected.
6. Indeed, while the presidents of PCSW may take autonomous decisions in emergency situations, their opinion on caseworks is assimilated to that of the committee members.
7. Interestingly, according to these authors, the managerial approach to social work would also have an impact on where social workers' discretion operates – moving it 'out of sight' (Brodzin, 2016, p. 448).
8. As mentioned earlier, in some cases a social worker may be responsible for presenting all cases to the committee, and/or for "defending" a specific case. However, this possibility is increasingly rare in many of our case studies and was even more limited during the COVID-19 health crisis, due to the internal reorganisation of the public service to comply with government measures.

9.   Regular meeting among managers of different antennas and services, to discuss problematic cases.
10. This can also be translated into concrete guidelines, renewed at each election period, as was the case in some of the Brussels case studies.
11. The terminology varies between cases (another example is 'regular' versus 'problematic' cases), but the same logic holds.
12. The authors and editors of this book are aware of the male bias in certain phrasings of this respondent and others (for instance, speaking of 'he' and 'him' only, whereas it could also concern female beneficiaries as well). The decision was taken to keep the quotes as they were expressed by the interlocutors, even though they were not always thinking and speaking in terms of gender, but rather in terms of a non-gendered beneficiary. This holds for quotes in other chapters and parts of this book as well.
13. We have seen above that the political orientation of the municipality influences more the global approach to social issues (and related funding) than the decisions taken over the allocation of social benefits to newcomer beneficiaries.
14. While it can happen that members of the committee also have a professional training/occupation in social domain on personal engagement of social issues, this is not the rule.

REFERENCES

Andreetta, S. (2022). Engaging with the State: Illegalized migrants, welfare institutions and the law in French-Speaking Belgium. *Migration Politics, 1*(1), 1–20.

Andreetta, S., & Borrelli, L. M. (2022). Digital practices of negotiation: Social workers at the intersection of migration and social policies in Switzerland and Belgium. *Journal of Social Policy*, 1–19.

Brodkin, E. Z. (2011a). Putting street-level organizations first: New directions for social policy and management research. *Journal of Public Administration Research and Theory, 21*(2), 1199–1201.

Brodkin, E. Z. (2011b). Policy work: Street-level organizations under new managerialism. *Journal of Public Administration Research and Theory, 21*(2), 1253–1277.

Brodkin, E. Z. (2012). Reflections on street-level bureaucracy: Past, present, and future. *Public Administration Review, 72*, 940–949.

Ellis, K. (2011). Street-level bureaucracy revisited: The changing face of frontline discretion in adult social care in England. *Social Policy and Administration, 45*(3), 221–244.

Emerson, R. M., & Paley, B. (2001). Organizational horizons and complaint-filling. In K. Hawkins (Ed.), *The Uses of Discretion* (pp. 231–247). Clarendon Press.

Gabarro, C. (2012). Les demandeurs de l'aide médicale d'État pris entre productivisme et gestion spécifique. *Revue européenne des migrations internationales, 28*(2), 35–56.

Harris, J., & White, V. (Eds.). (2009). *Modernising social work: Critical considerations*. Policy Press.

Jessen, J. T., & Tufte, P. A. (2014). Discretionary decision-making in a changing context of activation policies and welfare reforms. *Journal of Social Policy, 43*(2), 269–288.

Riccucci, N. L., Meyers, M. K., & Jun Seop Han, I. L. (2004). The implementation of welfare reform policy: The role of public managers in front-line practices. *Public Administration Review, 64*(4), 438–448.

Schafer, J. A. (2013). The role of trust and transparency in the pursuit of procedural and organizational justice. *Journal of Policing, Intelligence and Counter Terrorism, 8*(2), 131–143.

CHAPTER 8
THE DISCRETION OF SOCIAL WORKERS TOWARDS NEWLY ARRIVED MIGRANTS

ELSA MESCOLI

In the introduction and in the previous chapter of this section, we described the legal framework structuring the functioning of PCSWs and outlining the decision-making process as a hierarchical model. These elements have the consequence of limiting the room for manoeuvre of social workers. This may confirm the works on street-level bureaucracy which point at the alleged 'death' of discretion (for a critical review see Evans & Harris, 2004), and that also brings a rich – and unsolved – debate on the curtailment versus the continuation of social workers' discretionary power and practices within a process of high standardisation and control of welfare policy implementation. Indeed, in this chapter we will analyse the practices of social workers on the ground, with the aim of studying whether discretion operates, in which forms and with which results.

1. ACKNOWLEDGING DISCRETION

As discussed in Chapter 1, discretion is multi-dimensional, corresponding to the autonomy of social workers in their professional activity, the room for manoeuvre they have within policy implementation, and their ability to subvert the rules. Therefore, discretionary practices take different forms on the ground and their outcomes are equally varied – indeed, as the literature shows, discretionary practices can result in the inclusion or exclusion of immigrant beneficiaries. In this chapter, we will study the forms of discretion encountered in our fieldwork.

Social workers generally have a discourse on being impartial, on strictly adhering to the law, and not deciding themselves, since the decisions of allocating a social benefit or not are taken by the committee:

> The social workers have no decision making power. They can only pro-
> pose […], it is the […] committee of the social service, which will decide

according to the reading of the social report whether it agrees or not with the proposals of the social worker, or even possibly modify them. (Wallonia, C, social worker, 15/3/2021)

This discourse also allows them to offload their responsibility in the overall process. Indeed, guidelines, predefined procedures, and documentary practices imply a deresponsibilisation and disempowerment of the social workers, who by following the procedures may no longer feel responsible for a refusal, in particular of the social income (since the reason of it would only be that the applicant does not comply with the institutional requirements).

'Disempowerment' is understood as the worker losing the sense of agency or control she or he once had in performing her or his job responsibilities (Holmes & Saleebey, 1993; Rappaport, 1987, in Riffe & Kondrat, 1997, p. 42)

The legal and theoretical framework referred to above resonates in the words of the social workers who we met in the field, most of whom asserted firmly during interviews that they do not have any power of decision over the allocation of social benefits, since they only apply the law and respond to its rules. Therefore, our fieldwork in many cases took the form as a 'search for discretion', scrutinising the discourses and practices of our interlocutors to look for spaces of autonomy and for an active role in designing the possible effects of welfare policies. Indeed, we found these elements showing that

[g]radations of power [...] exist in the relationship between managers and professional workers within public services. [...] discretion is not an 'all-or-nothing' phenomenon. Rather, it operates along a gradient, allowing different degrees of professional freedom within a complex set of principles and rules. (Evans & Harris, 2004, p. 881)

Indeed, social workers also seem to have the choice, that is, the discretionary power, between strictly adhering to the rules – which may lead to allocate lower aid – and engaging more with the rule – finding spaces of interpretation to increase the social aid.

When I look at the situation, I can simply say to myself that we are going to grant the man the aid from the date of his new application[1] [...], and so we don't care about the past [...], it's not my problem. [While if] I analyse it more and I see all that I can try to give to the man [more], [...] I have the impression that it's still my responsibility, whether I want to or not. [...] I feel that my responsibility is to give him as much as possible. (Wallonia, B, social worker, 15/1/2021)[2]

That's a lot of decisions you still have to make yourself. […] There is a lot of difference around. […] you start looking up from 'Okay, what, what do I think about this?' And, and depending on whether you're looking very hard or less hard, you're going to find, you're going to find things that you can use as an argument. (Flanders, A, social worker, 19/04/2021)

As described above, as part of the overall process of implementing social assistance policy and allocating social benefits, social workers are responsible for carrying out the social enquiry to build up the file of the potential beneficiary and for monitoring it. This enquiry targets a set of information: residence status and procedures, the access to other rights, the place of residence, the situation of the beneficiary from a financial, health, professional, social, and family point of view. The social enquiry is aimed at assessing and proving the state of need, so to propose and justify an appropriate response to the beneficiaries' demands as well as to assess the rights they are entitled to. Social workers are also in charge of the follow-up of the ISIP established once the social benefits are allocated. Social workers have relative autonomy in the preparation of the files and in the ways they implement the guidelines – as we will see later, this concerns their attitude and relation with the beneficiaries – before they are submitted to the managers/committee. Moreover, they do not need to discuss with their hierarchical supervisor to validate the extension of the social income once it has been allocated – until new evaluation and in case there are no changes in the beneficiary situation. The committee generally automatically validates these caseworks:

I am autonomous for my extensions etc. […] [we] are not autonomous for the granting, withdrawal and refusal. (Wallonia, B, social worker, 12/1/2021)

All the files that are under review, […] these are files that will not be presented to the committee, that will be presented to them but only in the form of a list, where they will know that we are continuing an integration income for such and such a person, but, without having a social report […]. All the new caseworks go to the committee, and then effectively all the problematic files. (Wallonia, C, social worker, 15/3/2021)

Indeed, when a new decision has to be taken, the proposal of the social workers needs to go through the hierarchised decision-making process, which limits the autonomy and the possibility of discretion of the agent. However, and paradoxically, a discourse widely disseminated on the ground is that the committee as well as managers generally 'trust' the social workers and that in most cases their suggestions are accepted.

> [Social workers] have *carte blanche*, they are the ones who have the relationship of trust with their public, they are the professionals in the field, the professionals who listen, so generally when they bring me a file, well I tend to trust them. (Brussels, D, director, 12/03/2021)

This factor could stimulate social workers' discretion, although their proposals should not deviate too much from the standards.

> General aid [social income], yes, that is in terms of the legislation, we have to follow it. But for specific aid, it's really the social worker who grants or does not grant the aid that is given according to his or her report and analysis. […] we still have to comply with the legislation at least, otherwise, it will cause problems for the hierarchy, but we still have… a lot of leeway […] to motivate our decisions to do what we want to do. Most of the time, what the social worker proposes will be granted by the committee. […] we are the masters of making decisions, […] afterwards it's up to you to motivate […]. We still have the freedom, I would say, to go a little bit beyond what the legislation requires of us. Now, you have to be consistent. Because we can't just propose anything. (Wallonia, A, social worker, 17/2/2021)

In our research, we found that social workers have different level of awareness of their discretionary power and of the possible effects of it. However, they seem to know that applying it would most probably mean to give beneficiaries the chance of receiving increased social benefits. Therefore, it is also a matter of finding a balance between working in a tailor-made way (on a case-by-case basis) and keeping policy lines to ensure equity. Analysing deeper the rules and the situation of the beneficiary to increase social benefits is not the habit of all social workers, and asking for exceptions to the guidelines is also discretionary. Although asking for exceptions is an integral part of the system – also because legal rules and guidelines may not cover (and not exactly) all the possible situations encountered in the field – it needs the engagement and motivation of the social workers. This means that they acknowledge their discretionary power and they take responsibility in performing it.

If you motivate something very well, you often succeed in obtaining it. But for some requests you need to dig deeper than for other requests. And sometimes, especially now that there's so much work, you don't actually have the time to find all those elements, all that social research, to be able to write that motivation. The freedom is there, but the time to use it is not always there. (Flanders, A, social worker, 27/04/2021)

The framework I think is quite clear, afterwards there are always ways of getting around things. [...] you can always get around it and explain why yes, why no, it all depends on your arguments [...]. The guidelines are there to give you a line, but all guidelines can be deviated from [...], so it all depends on how you see the guideline and how you try to counter this guideline. [...] there are the conditions: if Mr. or Mrs. so-and-so meets the conditions, [...] [he/]she doesn't meet the conditions, but I know that the beneficiary citizen needs this thing, so I'm going to derogate. (Brussels, B, social worker, 27/05/2021)

As Giladi recalls (2021, p. 8), it has been shown that working conditions marked by the limitation of temporal, material, and financial resources, as well as by the amplification of performance imperatives and managerial pressure, affect the use of social workers' room for manoeuvre – de facto 'favouring efficiency at the cost of responsiveness, quality, and even efficacy' (Brodkin, 2012, p. 944). Not asking for exceptions – even when it happens because of work overload and managerial control – means not using the possible room for manoeuvre by social workers; in other terms, strictly complying with the norms is also a discretionary practice (Mascia & Santos, 2021). Asking for exceptions depends on the social worker, their personal characteristics and approach, the available time, the inclination to follow the rules versus taking the needs of a person as a starting point, the will to engage in a more complicated process, their human sensitivity, and the assessment of the deservingness of the beneficiary (discussed later). Experience is also a factor influencing the possibility of arguing for exception:

There is a lot of vagueness, and in the beginning I found that very difficult when I started at the PCSW, because you have to make proposals and everything is just blurred. I find that a bit tricky, too. But I also understand it because social situations are not black and white. (Flanders, C, social worker, 04/06/2021)

Differences between social workers are considered evident and inevitable, although this may lead to different experiences lived by beneficiaries.

> I like social workers to seek out that discretionary power, but you also feel that this is a tension field of 'How far can I go?' And that social workers also like to have the grip/certainty [*houvast*] of the rules. Some are very rule-oriented, others look for possibilities in a very creative way. Therefore, that's very individual. And that leads indeed to differences between the trajectories. (Flanders, C, president, 11/1/2021)

> Within our team we have colleagues who, […] as I do, [take] a lot of time for our people and look at the big picture. And on the other hand, I also have colleagues who are more like, 'OK, the file for the integration income must be in order and it must be administratively in order.' And that's it. […] if those clients of the social worker who actually sees it in a demarcated way and who is then on leave or who falls ill or who is absent and the clients then come to you with their question, then you find yourself in a bit of a conflict of, yes, I would approach this differently. And that remains a difficult one, because it is not your client. […] the guidance and help that the client can get is very dependent on the social worker, the one you end up with, and we dare say that if I were a client and ended up with a social worker, I would either be very happy or not so happy. (Flanders, C, social worker, 16/03/2021)

Recognising to have discretionary power could also be problematic for some social workers, who state that in particular when working with newly arrived immigrants, prejudices of different kinds could have an impact on the decisions taken at all levels – from social workers to presidents. In the next section, we will analyse in more detail the discretionary practices of social workers – the implementation of which indeed depends on the aforementioned level of awareness of their discretionary power.

2.   A VARIETY OF PRACTICES

As announced already, the discretionary practices of social workers observed in the field are diverse. They operate at two main levels: that of the relation established with the beneficiary, and that of the building of the casework. The approach of social workers to beneficiaries may differ, for example, with regard to whether they strictly respond to the received demands within the framework of the rules, and delegate social tasks to external partners, or they engage in a broader need detection (listening more to the beneficiary and analysing their situation).

> When you look at your colleagues, where do you think the biggest differences are? I am thinking of how the regulations are applied. There are colleagues who are very strict in that respect: these are the rules and this is how we are going to do it, and exceptions are exceptional. While other people are more inclined to look at 'What does this family need and how does that fit in with the rules.' Yes, the reverse order. (Flanders, A, 27/04/2021)

> I think everyone works differently anyway. I think maybe also by strictness that can also differ. I think one also offers more opportunities to the person. Yes, I think that also has to do with how is someone and how are their own experiences, personal experiences of social workers. But in general, I still think our approach is pretty much tailor-made. (Flanders, D, social worker, 19/03/2021)

This difference in approach is crucial also because social workers have a central role in the assessment of what aid is needed – beyond what may be claimed by migrants themselves. In addition, each social worker can make more or less effort to reach the beneficiary, which could also mean to decide more or less quickly to apply a sanction. Some social workers may also show more or less empathy – therefore being more or less accommodating – towards immigrant beneficiaries. The approach is influenced by personal characteristics but also by time pressure and workload that compromise individual follow-up (see Chapter 5). These elements affect the relation and the interactions between social workers and beneficiaries, which in turn influence possible choices of action (the level and type of 'engagement' in the management of the case – addressed later in this section), although they do not automatically lead to discretionary decisions concerning the allocation of aids itself.

In contrast, when social workers build the record of the beneficiaries, that is, they gather all information and documents needed to take a decision on the allocation of social aids, they put in place micro-practices of discretion that can change the course of the application. More particularly, they can adopt a style of writing that 'touches' the committee – although some members may be more sensitive than others (Wallonia, C, social worker, 15/3/2021) – meaning that they describe the beneficiary's situation with empathy and through emphasising the state of need.

[D]epending on the way we write something, it will tend more towards one side or the other. If we talk about 50% dead or 50% surviving, we say the same thing, but the person who receives the information does not experience it in the same way. (Wallonia, B, social worker, 11/1/2021b)

Social workers can submit records that are more or less complete, 'fiddling around a bit' (Wallonia, A, social worker, 17/2/2021) depending on the effect they want to reach: whether they want to prove the need of a higher aid, they would gather all possible documents attesting the expenses of the beneficiary, for example. While when they estimate that there is no need for the committee to be informed of an aspect of the situation of the beneficiary, they can just leave this information out of the record – for example, in case the beneficiary has a temporary or occasional informal job, not much increasing their own financial resources.

You don't write everything down. We have to, but sometimes there are things that we omit to put. We try, depending on the situation, from time to time, depending on what we put down, we'll help more or less, we have this capacity to influence a little bit, but that's inherent to all reports. (Wallonia, B, social worker, 11/1/2021b)

However, as we saw above, social workers can also decide not to search for additional information on the beneficiary's needs. We also observed discretion concerning the information given to beneficiaries about their rights and in particular the possibility of appealing against the decision of the PCSW. While all social workers are obliged to give this information by their professional framework and ethics, and therefore they do it, the degree of commitment can vary.

Sometimes we are at odds, not with our direct hierarchy but with […] the authorities, because we feel that what they are doing to others is not human and we are in the middle of the road. Sometimes we give advice that we should not give but we do it anyway. It also allows us to manage this state of feeling human in the face of humans. Not being robot machines there to apply rules. (Wallonia, F, social worker, 3/12/2020a)

In particular concerning the possibility of appealing against the refusal of social benefits, social workers can either just present it, or explicitly suggest the beneficiary to undertake the procedure. With the recorder switched off at his demand, we collected the experience of a social worker, who identified a mistake in the management of a demand of social aid submitted by a beneficiary, that was refused. This mistake concerned the application of the rules in the treatment of the demand, and it was not remarked by managers nor by the committee. Appealing this decision would most likely have meant that the Labour Court would have overturned the judgement of the PCSW and indulged it to pay the aid claimed – which is what happened. Therefore, the social worker firmly suggested the beneficiary to appeal to finally receive the aid. An appeal can also lead the Labour court to order the PCSW to grant social income to a person whose residence permit does not, in principle, allow access to it. The right to social benefits is proved against the initial refusal by the PCSW and against the refusal of the residence status by the Immigration Office.

> These people found themselves illegally resident from one day to the next, they lodged an appeal with the court and that's when we intervened by saying, you have the possibility of lodging [an appeal] if you don't agree. And officially at the level of the institution we can't, but as a social worker, my role is to advise them, and I advised them [...] to go and lodge an appeal in order to be able to maintain the right to social assistance. (Wallonia, B, social worker, 11/1/2021b)

Social workers also practice discretion when establishing priorities in the management of the records of which they are in charge. While the time, obligation, and related deadlines structure their work and imposes them to deal with the demands in a chronological way – the first arrived, the first dealt with – in some circumstances, they estimate that some requests may be more urgent and need quicker management. This is the case, for example, for newly recognised refugees, who have to leave the reception centres where they were living during their asylum application within a short time, and therefore not only find an accommodation but also provide themselves with basic necessities. Their record will then be managed as soon as possible, and most probably before others that prove less urgency.

Another way of applying discretion in the building of a casework and in its follow-up is to help outside the framework (that is, the welfare system responsibilities), through supporting the beneficiary with additional aids to face their needs, although this may also be sanctioned by managers:

> There is a lot of demands and there are many things that we are no longer able to do, or that we are no longer authorised to do. [...] we were reminded by the management that it wasn't our job, that we were supposed to be working with the PCSW laws and not informing about the laws on access to the territory. (Wallonia, B, social worker, 11/1/2021b)

As a further example, the 'listening' role of social workers towards newly arrived beneficiaries that are experiencing discomfort is stressed in the following quote:

> Sometimes I have people who come just for me to listen to them [...]. These are people who have no family here, so they are also looking for a link to hold on to. (Wallonia, B, social worker, 12/1/2021)

In this case, as in others, the cultural proximity between the beneficiary and the social worker – of immigrant origins herself – seems to favour this exchange.[3] Other examples may concern the engagement of the social worker in helping the beneficiary with the house search, the management of the relation with the school or other institutions, the contact with external services, and so forth. These tasks do not necessarily fit within the PCSWs social workers' mission, or at least they would not be blamed for not doing it, especially in contemporary times – work overload and other constraints having undermined a broader social approach to beneficiaries, as described in Chapter 5.

The data analysed in this section and the examples brought allow us to state that social workers act with discretion towards immigrant beneficiaries and their demands in the PCSWs under study, despite the strict law framework and hierarchised decision-making process in which their work is embedded. Such discretion operates in different forms, which leads us stating that street-level bureaucracy itself needs to be apprehended in its situated meaning and scope, as well as through considering its specific effects.

> Discretion is understood as power – a discretionary power – to act or decide within a certain normative context, meaning within the parameters of certain formal and informal rules (legal constraints) and within certain social and organisational constraints. (Miaz, 2017, p. 377)

In our case studies, social workers' use – or non-use – of their discretionary power makes street-level bureaucracy appear as a field where agents can challenge restrictive policies concerning migrant welfare beneficiaries. In these terms, social work functions as a social justice practice (Lundy, 2004; Reisch, 2008) that social workers may or may not choose to engage in, to face migrants' disadvantages as welfare clients (Boccagni, 2015). We have mentioned already in Chapter 1 the relevance of social workers' agreement with policy content in affecting decisions (May & Winter, 2009; Tummers, 2013). Moreover, the debate on 'professional work' versus 'bureaucracy' – mere application of rules – has been studied (Evans & Harris, 2004; Ellis,

2011). Looking at our data, we can extend this analysis and argue that spaces and opportunities to challenge such policy content are left to social workers, and that street-level discretion therefore operates in deciding whether or not to seize them, engaging with moral and value commitment related to social work. Social workers' professional identity may be underpinned at different degrees by an ethic of human rights, social justice, and solidarity (Voélin *et al.*, 2017, p. 23; Giladi, 2021, p. 9). Besides influencing the decision on the eligibility of immigrants to social entitlements, social workers can have an active role in increasing the opportunities of immigrants to access rights (also refer to Marrow, 2009; van der Leun, 2006), instead of only applying – restrictive – rules.[4] This process is reflected in the experience of beneficiaries, as we will see in Part III of this book, although beneficiaries' perception of this process may be different. In the next section of this chapter, we will study the factors influencing the different approaches adopted by social workers in the implementation of their work more deeply.

3.   FACTORS INFLUENCING CHOICES AND DECISIONS

As analysed above, social workers perform a variety of discretionary practices and adopt different approaches to guidelines and welfare policy implementation towards immigrant beneficiaries, and this depend on a set of factors that intervene in the process of the assessment of the beneficiaries' needs. These factors fall into two main categories: institutional aspects (the process of professional socialisation of social workers in the services frequented by immigrant beneficiaries) and the personal characteristics of social workers. This chapter studies these factors, therefore approaching street-level bureaucracy from a micro-level perspective. Indeed, the literature shows that individual determinants as well as institutional guidelines operate in public services and influence bureaucrats' decisions. These determinants include personal views and representations of social workers concerning the beneficiaries of social allowances, as well as their moral judgement on fairness and unfairness, and on deserving or not the aid (Maynard-Moody & Musheno, 2000). Moreover, personal characteristics such as gender and related social status and life experience (Saidel & Loscocco, 2005; Wilkins, 2007), as well as racial and ethnic background (Pitts, 2005; Wilkins & Williams, 2009; Hindera, 1993) also influence – in varied ways – the interactions between social workers and beneficiaries as well as the course of the case.

The data collected through fieldwork reveals that among the factors influencing the approach of social workers is, first, the way in which they evaluate the attitude of the beneficiary, that is, how he/she is viewed and perceived, based on personal moral positionings as well as institutional expectations. Such assessment may reflect some prejudices of the social workers and reveal unbalanced power dynamics, in which beneficiaries are at the mercy of the judgements produced on them. We observed that beneficiaries' attitudes are positively assessed – which possibly leads to most favourable decisions, because of increased engagement of the social workers in supporting their demands and 'defending their case' – when they 'collaborate' and demonstrate 'willingness', motivation, and commitment.

> And you also have to have a, yes, with that person you also have to have a bit of a feeling of 'Okay this, this succeeds or this doesn't succeed. That one is motivated or that one is not motivated.'. And I think it just depends from colleague to colleague. And that one may be less inclined to, to make all that effort because he feels that, that he or she is not motivated, I know, *allez*, I think everyone does to the extent possible do what he can. But yes, everyone has his own feelings and has his own experiences from which that he departs. (Flanders, A, social worker, 19/04/2021)

> I think the basics are always going to be the same, but everyone has their own character and, and, yes, dealing with people can also be different. With one client you have a good connection, the other can be annoying. Yes, haha, that's when we might start being a bit annoying too. (Flanders, E, social worker, 16/03/2021)

The principle of 'reciprocity' described in Chapter 1 emerges not only in relation to the active contribution to society by the potential beneficiary of social benefits as a condition to deserve the aid (Petersen *et al.*, 2011), but also in terms of 'giving back' – in a logic of gift/counter-gift – the welfare allowance through appropriate behaviour. Connected to some extent with that of reciprocity, the notion of welfare deservingness (van Oorschot *et al.*, 2017) describes the conditionality of the support given by the PCSWs. Welfare deservingness is assessed by social workers not only through applying the guidelines and through verifying that the beneficiary complies with the conditions of access to the social benefits. It is also valued on a personal moral basis. Indeed, social workers consider that when the state of need is objective and the demands are appropriate (for example, the cost for the driving licence if it is to use to work and basic furniture if any are present in the house), there is no reason for refusing the aid. Social workers also take into account the situation of precariousness and the difficult life history of immigrant beneficiaries, as well as the contextual factors that may hinder their socio-professional integration (for example, the lack of appropriate work opportunities in rural contexts, as mentioned before, and other elements of 'background knowledge', or the impossibility for the beneficiary to work or to enrol in education or training for health or family reasons). Moreover, 'active' beneficiaries who make efforts to exit the situation of financial dependence on the welfare system are positively assessed, which proves 'behavioural conditions for eligibility (Clasen & Clegg, 2007; Standing, 2005; Van Kersbergen & Hemerijck, 2012)' (De Wilde, 2018, p. 166). In these cases, social workers estimate that the beneficiaries not only have the right to social security, they also deserve the assistance. The following quote, from a committee member, explains this process:

> [PCSWs'] generosity is very paternalistic. The beneficiaries are often seen in a positive light, but if they are deserving. They have to be kind, full of gratitude towards the PCSW [...], so generous. [...] so you have to deserve the generosity of the Belgian society. (Wallonia, D, councillor, 12/4/2021)

The perceived welfare deservingness of beneficiaries (also see Laenen, 2018; Laenen et al., 2019; Ford, 2016)[5] is connected to their attitude. Responding to the convocations, bringing the needed documents, being honest, understanding what is being asked and why the aid is or is not granted, accepting and following the advice of the social workers, engaging in socio-professional integration initiatives, including the willingness to learn the national language concerned, and so forth are perceived as appropriate attitudes for social assistance recipients, and therefore function as prerequisites for accessing and maintaining the social right. Moreover, social workers expect that the beneficiaries do not overreact on the decisions communicated to them, and that they do not act as welfare abusers. They also assess whether beneficiaries respect the temporality of the procedures and judge negatively if they put pressure on it because of their own objectives.

> I have a hard time especially with people who come across as so demanding, but that's, yes, also something very personal. People who already come with a certain objective and know perfectly what and how, uhm, and have no patience or respect for the procedure that is there. I do have a hard time with that. (Flanders, D, social worker, 19/03/2021)

Indeed, as Lafleur and Mescoli (2018) show, social workers may express judgements on the legitimacy of asking social rights and promote 'welfare chauvinism' (Mewes & Mau, 2013; Freeman, 2009), that is, excluding de facto foreign citizens from the access to rights. The expected attitude from the beneficiary also implies that he/she trusts the work of the social workers and that he/she is not reluctant in sharing information about their private life, in asking aid and in detailing how he/she uses it.

> But then you see on bank account statements that there is money going to, to family and money going to …, that there are cash withdrawals that they don't want or can't account for, yes then of course it stops. Because if you don't want to say where your money goes, then I'm not going to give you anything extra. Yes, because yes, if you just spend your money differently, then you would have had the money. (Flanders, A, social worker, 19/04/2021)

Cultural prejudices also operate in the relation between social workers and beneficiaries, in which the first expect that the latter comply with local cultural norms (and do not put cultural barriers to the relation itself)[6] and are not influenced by their community,[7] which may spread fake information and suggest inappropriate attitudes.

> Once the community is there […] often they will come and say, 'My friend told me that.' And he will stick to what his friend told him. But what his friend told him is not correct at all and so […] [this] makes the work much, much, much, more difficult. It's exhausting […], I tell them that if you listen to me, things will go more easily. (Wallonia, B, social worker, 12/1/2021)

This process reveals '[t]he influence of family-, community- or religion-based ties, obligations and mutual expectations' (Boccagni, 2015, p. 614). Social workers' prejudices make them observing or supposing specific culturally oriented attitudes from immigrant beneficiaries, which highlights a process of categorisation and generalisation.

> There are people with certain ideas or convictions. If you have a client who you like less or who is more difficult or with whom you have more problems, then yes, your attitude is different. […] There are social workers who find it very unpleasant if someone doesn't want to shake hands. Others don't take offence at all. There are also social workers who resent it if the woman is almost out of the picture. […] Let's be honest, if you live in a house that is too small and often not in order, and you have 14 children, go ahead to start a labour market trajectory, good luck. (Flanders, C, manager, 23/02/2021)

> We are all a bit racist […] we have prejudices, we categorise certain popula-
> tions. […] People have already made remarks to me, but I think they are
> unfounded because I don't give more to one person than to another, I give
> what I can give […], people who feel racism very strongly, also use it very
> strongly as soon as they feel attacked to defend themselves, […] it's not
> always objective but it's human. (Wallonia, B, social worker, 15/1/2021)

Such process depends not only on the social workers but also on service's
routines. It may happen that in certain services all the social workers have
similar discourses about one or another nationality, which highlights a common internal socialisation (Miaz, 2017).

Explicit discriminating or stereotyped statements can be present in the
discourse of social workers, concerning the cultural background intersected
with the social background and the gender of the beneficiaries. As research has
shown (Maynard-Moody & Musheno, 2012; Raaphorst & Groeneveld, 2018;
Thomann & Rapp, 2018), stereotypes influence the judgements of social workers.

> We have quite a few isolated men who come, […] they are the most difficult
> to deal with, whether in terms of the maintenance of the accommodation
> or even in terms of their requests, because […] they think they are entitled
> to everything, immediately. (Wallonia, H, social worker, 17/12/2020)

> For example, Guinean women, who are veiled, who are Muslim, who have
> children, they don't want to do anything, they don't want to work, they don't
> want to do any training, they don't want to learn French, they want to look
> after their children. They are respectful, I have nothing to say, but I mean
> their aim is not to integrate indeed, because they tell me clearly 'No, you want
> to take my values away from me.' (Brussels, G, social worker, 04/03/2021)

> I had to explain it because culturally, why doesn't she ask for a dining room,
> because culturally they eat on the floor. […] when you come from the
> same culture or you understand the culture of the other, it's much easier
> to argue, to understand, to justify […]. I have already accompanied social
> workers on home visits when the beneficiary citizen has made requests
> for furniture, […] they were shocked as to why the lady or gentleman was
> asking for mattresses and not beds. (Brussels, B, social worker, 27/05/2021)

However, social workers may not consider these kinds of statements as
prejudices or discriminations negatively influencing their decisions; they
rather present them as ways of demonstrating their understanding of the

specific cultural characteristics and habits of the immigrant beneficiaries, a fact that may lead to developing stronger arguments to defend their demands in some cases. In some others, identifying the cultural characteristics and alleged consequent habits and priorities of some beneficiaries is not enough to justify attitudes deviating from the expectations of the social workers and the institution that they represent.

> The young Afghans I have at the moment, well, they're not too interested in learning to speak French, I think. They absolutely want to work. Well, that's very good, the car washes and everything, they often have work contracts there. But I have some, they've been here for five years and they don't speak a word of French. [...] They always tell me 'Yes, yes, I'm looking for French lessons', but they never bring any proof, nothing. So, at some point, [...] you have to tell them. (Wallonia, A, social worker, 17/2/2021)

This reflects the theoretical debate on the 'culturally competent approach' developed within social work with ethnic minorities and immigrants, which may result in diverse practices and outcomes, showing that such an approach has limitations and ambiguities, and it is anyway confronted with organisational and system constraints (Harrison & Turner, 2011; Robinson, 2014). In fact, we can suppose that cultural knowledge/prejudices may also affect negatively the decisions, through the influence on the reasoning and the assessment process of the social worker. As Boccagni highlights, also alerting about the 'traps of culturalisation' (of which we will see examples below),

> [c]ulture, or for that matter ethnicity, can easily be employed by social workers as a cognitive schema and overarching explanatory category, helpful for making cursory sense of psychosocial needs and problems with more varied and subtle roots (van der Haar 2009). (Boccagni, 2015, p. 614)

Our fieldwork findings are in line with Van Robaeys and Driessens (2011) as well, who studied the ways in which social workers perceive their interactions with clients with a migration background and concluded that social workers often refer to 'culture' to describe and explain problems encountered in the relation with clients. Social workers use culture as a way to give meaning to people from a different ethnic background. Yet, it risks being used as a 'catch-all explanation', and impeding social workers to dig deeper and look at other relevant aspects in the context of beneficiaries (Van Robaeys & Driessens, 2011). Moreover, as other literature has shown, even when the decisions are not 'biased' – culturally based assessments and discrimination do not lead to either penalising or advantaging immigrants – the tone and attitude with which they are communicated can be unpleasant, reveal a negative moral judgement, and act as a deterrent to recipients applying for social assistance (Einstein & Glick, 2017 Hemker & Rink, 2017).

We also encountered positive stereotypes on immigrant beneficiaries, whose attitude is described as more appropriate than Belgian ones, who can be more aggressive towards social workers. Immigrant beneficiaries can be described as more grateful to the social workers in the relation established, and this fact positively influence social workers' assessment of the efforts made by immigrants to overcome communication barriers.

> I find that they are very kind, very welcoming, I almost never have a problem with them. They always respect everything they are asked to do, [...] they rarely have a higher word than the other, even if from time to time they get angry. But it's very rarely towards me, it's more towards the legislation and the laws, which I can understand. They are extremely nice. It's really a public ... I mean, I love it. [...] when they don't speak French, always finding ways to understand each other, well I love it. That's a bit of a challenge too, and I love all that side of it. (Wallonia, A, social worker, 17/2/2021)

Therefore, social workers developing such representation – which often goes together with increased empathy with regard to people who are estimated living a *real* situation of need – may be less demanding throughout the assessment of the beneficiaries' eligibility to social rights. This attitude is particularly common towards recognised refugees, since more empathy and understanding seem to develop concerning people escaping from a war or other 'objectively dangerous' situations than towards other migrant profiles.[8] Indeed, different legal categorisations not only 'result in more or less constrained structures of opportunities for professional action (regarding clients' authorised length of stay, eligibility for social welfare provisions, etc.)' (Boccagni & Righard, 2020, p. 378), they also interact with social workers' assessment of beneficiaries' vulnerabilities and related different degrees of deservingness for social aid.

Other factors intervene in the relation between the social workers and the beneficiaries, influencing the decisions taken, and these factors concern the personal characteristics of social workers. The profiles of the social workers met during the research are diverse. However, we can identify some recurrent characteristics that are described as influencing the work with newcomers to a certain extent. Among these aspects is social workers' humanistic approach towards beneficiaries and their demands: being 'passionate about others, about humanity' (Wallonia, F, social worker, 3/12/2020a) is seen as crucial in working with migrants. The 'human aspect' lying behind the records favours social workers' understanding of the beneficiaries' situations as well as their commitment in ensuring the access to social rights. However, this aspect is also described as possibly leading to too subjective interpretations, as well as to ethical dilemmas between the social worker's moral priorities and those of the institution that he/she represents.

> [A]t the structural level, in relation to the decisions that are taken at the PCSW level, [...] it's black or white, there are no more grey areas. Now, on a human level, it's horrible, because we're dealing with people, it's their life, we're dealing with migrants. [...] My humanist side will say that [refusing residence permit and consequently the social assistance] is wrong because the Earth belongs to everyone and those we have [at the PCSW] didn't specifically choose to come here, there are circumstances [...] in terms of being exposed to extreme poverty, linked to difficult living situations. It's not easy either, we're not faced with papers, we're faced with people who are in their daily lives and who explain to us that at a certain point when you're illegally resident, you don't have any money, and when you don't have any money you don't know how to feed the children. And so, on that basis, having been in contact with these people, is it good [to refuse the social benefit]? No. It prevents the children from eating. (Wallonia, B, social worker, 11/01/2021b)

The humanistic approach of the social workers makes it more difficult for them to accept the strict framework in which they operate and that constrains their work as well as their 'will to give':

> Working in a PCSW, the most difficult thing is the framework. [...] It took me a number of years to integrate it because at the beginning we disagree a lot, because we want to give to people, we are in the saviour side of things, [...] and so we are often frustrated. Whereas now, I am no longer frustrated, I know what I can give the person, what I can't, I try to do my best, I discuss it with my manager, [...] and I say to myself, well, never mind, at some point you have to succeed in putting the responsibility on everyone's shoulders. [...] at the beginning of my career, [...] I was very strongly reproached for, [...] because I had been in reception centres, etc., so I was used to trying to do a lot of things for people and it wasn't the same thing. Here we don't do anything for the people, here we work for the PCSW, it's sad to say. (Wallonia, B, social worker, 15/01/2021)

Having worked in the domain of asylum reception or in other migration-related services leads to the development of specific expertise, knowledge, and attitudes that may be in contrast with the PCSW approach. Connected to this, having foreign language skills can be useful to facilitate the communication with the beneficiaries. However, the institution – relying on the law – can limit the possibility to use foreign languages with beneficiaries. In some cases, social workers may speak the same language of the foreign beneficiaries, because they have foreign origin themselves, for example. Interestingly, this is the case for many agents – *albeit* certainly not all – working in specialised services among the case studies targeted by our research, a fact that brings us to elaborate at least two questionings: whether the migration background of social workers is seen by welfare institutions as a condition to work with immigrant beneficiaries; and whether social workers with foreign origins are 'relegated; in a way to specialised services targeting migrants, revealing an ethno-stratification operating within the domain of social work itself, or at least 'the significance of ethnocultural diversity in the self-representations of social work institutions and in their organisational arrangements' (Boccagni, 2015, p. 609). However, the migration background of the social workers can have a positive impact on the development of empathy towards the difficulties encountered by newly arrived beneficiaries and of the commitment to support them.

> I'm a foreigner myself, so [...] I also have a background as a newcomer, learning the language, etc., so I think that you need someone to hold your hand to be able to progress. For me, to think that these people could manage on their own is not possible, or in any case, it's not within everyone's reach. So I say to myself that, depending on their experiences etc., there are people who find it more difficult to do things on their own [...] and yes, for me, we must help them. (Wallonia, C, social worker, 15/03/2021)

Cultural diversity is also present among social workers working in PCSWs located in multicultural municipalities such as Brussels, as a reflection of the local demographic composition and most probably revealing the 'ethnocultural diversification of staff recruitment and of service providers' (Boccagni, 2015, p. 615). The cultural, racial, and ethnic proximity between social workers and beneficiaries can have different outcomes in the relation established. According to some respondents, newcomers have representations about the (assumed) ethnicity of social workers and on how this might influence the follow-up of the cases. For example, some social workers reported that newcomers refuse the social worker assigned to them out of mistrust of his or her background or, on the contrary, ask for someone of the same ethnicity in the belief that this will lead to preferential treatment. An example is the case of a social worker (responsible for labour market activation) stating that her immigrant background was an asset in building a positive relation:

[Interviewer] Do you think that plays into it? That you have that background yourself?

[Interviewee] Yes, I do think that. If I'm honest, my clients have a very good relationship with me. Some, when I send them letters or email and I say, I found work for you, doesn't matter if they're interim or are Art.60, they're grateful to me. 'Thank you, you did that well, [first name] thank you, I feel good with you, I trust you.'

[Interviewer] Is that then linked to the fact, what is the link to your other background then?

[Interviewee] For some people it's a bit difficult to, yes how should I put it. When they see that I also for example, I don't really want to introduce myself directly, I don't want to say 'I'm [name] and I'm from Iran.' But some, they see of ah okay, here's another social worker. So I don't mean they don't want a social worker who is Belgian. But for example some who are from Iran say, yes [first name], that's kind of the same culture. (Flanders, C, social worker in charge of socioprofessional integration, 12/02/2021)

From the institutional perspective, it is worth mentioning that literature exists on 'ethnic sensitive social work practice' (Schlesinger & Devore, 1995; Balgopal, 2000; Potocky & Naseh, 2020; Sowers et al., 2008) and 'cultural responsiveness' (Chow & Austin, 2008), as well as specific intercultural training sessions developed on the ground, which testifies that 'the need to take diversity into account is increasingly recognised, rhetorically at least, within welfare institutions and organisations in Europe (Faist 2009) – including social service agencies' (Boccagni, 2015, p. 615). This also means that 'while dealing with superdiversity calls for a flexible, open-ended and personalised approach to immigrant clients, it also requires organisational and professional resources – in terms of training, supervision and workload allocation – that should not go unnoticed' (Boccagni, 2015, p. 618). However, specific policies and training are not systematically implemented, nor do they target all social workers working with immigrants, although intercultural sensitivity is indeed described as needed. To be more precise, we refer to the absence of critical self-awareness about the implications of one's own cultural background, social locations, preconceived notions, ideological values, and inevitable biases, to use the words of Azzopardi and McNeill (2016, p. 294). Moreover, a multidimensional approach to the factors that intervene in the relation between social workers and beneficiaries, shifting the view from *only* ethnic and cultural aspects to intersectional elements, may be beneficial for both research and practice. Linked to this, it is worth mentioning that accounting for gender was not easy throughout our research, since most of our respondents are women, in particular at the level of social workers. This factor on the one hand reflects the well-known dynamics of gender stratification of the labour market and related educational paths (Collins, 1971; Murgatroyd, 1982; Stevanovic & Mosconi, 2007), also affecting the domain of social work and connected representations (Fiore & Facchini, 2013). On the other hand, it makes more difficult to compare social workers' approaches on a gender basis – alone or intersected with other identity markers.

As mentioned already in Chapter 4, specialised expertise is often considered necessary when working with newcomer beneficiaries. An aspect that is stressed in this sense is the knowledge of migration-related legislation and how it affects the access to welfare rights. Indeed, this characteristic is common to social workers working specifically with migrant beneficiaries (although it may be absent in the case of general social workers), whether the expertise has been developed in the field or through specific training. In addition, social workers gain knowledge about integration policies targeting newcomers and, as mentioned above, contacts and cooperation with associations implementing integration programmes are likely to be developed. In general, we also found a positive discourse on the impact that social benefits and social income in particular may have on the integration process of migrants. Indeed, social workers recognise the financial difficulties that newcomers face, and the barriers to employment that can hinder their labour market activation. Therefore, they believe that the financial support that the state can provide will help newcomers to prepare to work – becoming economically autonomous at that point.

> [The social income] is important because a person who leaves a reception centre, if he doesn't have the PCSW, he is not entitled to anything. Therefore, he is not entitled to unemployment … I mean, we are really a residual aid. I mean, after us there is nothing […] financially. […] I think that this is the first thing we should do for people. When a person no longer has the financial constraint, they can start to take steps towards other objectives that they have. (Wallonia, A, social worker, 17/02/2021)

We rarely met on the ground an explicit discourse on migrants as 'welfare abusers', although some social workers have highlighted that among welfare beneficiaries there are some who do not make any efforts to 'get out' of the social assistance, finding it convenient or not seeing advantages in finding a job – from both an economic and social point of view.

> People who find the right place [*la bonne planque*, in French], [...] people who come and settle down and say 'Oh I live well with the PCSW', there are also some. But [...] these people we are behind. We're behind them, breaking their backs, telling them to do something. (Wallonia, C, social worker, 15/03/2021)

Social workers may develop this judgement more quickly and more often about those they identify as 'economic migrants', that is, who have not left their country for – according to them – objective reasons of danger (whereas, as seen above, refugees are subject to greater empathy). Social workers can decide to sanction those beneficiaries who demonstrate not taking active steps toward their socio-professional integration and more particularly their labour market activation. We will analyse further in the next section the use of sanctions by social workers and the function and effects of this instrument, which is embedded in the Belgian social security policy itself.

4.   SANCTIONING THE BENEFICIARIES

Beneficiaries of PCSWs in Belgium can be the object of sanctions – meaning the suspension (for a varied period) or the interruption of the social income – and these are handled differently depending on the PCSW concerned and the social workers. Indeed, the degree of 'tolerance' towards non-compliance or frauds with the rules and engagements can be established at the institutional level (through formal or informal agreements), but also be differently applied on the ground.

In some cases, our respondents associated the PCSW institutional approach on sanctions (more or less applied) to the political orientation of the municipality:

> Clearly, on issues like socio-professional integration, there are PCSWs that are fully into social activation because they have a very liberal colour. There are PCSWs that are almost never in the sanctioning business, that extend the rights to social assistance to a whole part of the population that has more than the integration income because they are of a rather left-wing political colour. (Brussels, D, director, 12/03/2021)

As far as the application of sanctions on the ground is concerned, it is highly discretionary and depends on the individual assessment of the social worker.[9] Indeed, the social income can be suspended for administrative reasons – lack of documents, availability of other resources (work, other), and in general no (more) compliance with the conditions of access. In other cases, social workers may estimate that the beneficiary needs to be sanctioned for other reasons, for example when he/she does not respect the engagements taken through the ISIP, and more generally the steps established towards socio-professional integration and labour market activation. Indeed, the sanction is conceived as leverage for activation of the 'non-collaborating' beneficiary, since in the opinion and experience of social workers, once the social income is interrupted, the beneficiary changes their attitude and engages with their responsibilities. The sanction targets the 'unwillingness' of the beneficiary and enables the social worker to 'wake (him/her) up' (Flanders, E, social worker, 16/03/2021) when, according to the social worker, he/she is not doing the effort he/she should. Retaining the payment will have an immediate effect: 'If they need the money they will react quickly' (Flanders, E, social worker, 16/03/2021).

> In some cases, we may have to withdraw for lack of cooperation. And so if the person readjusts after that, we can also review our decision. Because sometimes people need this sanction to say to themselves, 'Oh well, I'm going to go, I agree, I'm going to collaborate and I'm going to mobilise so that my situation changes.' And then, at that point, we can give the help again and review our positions. (Brussels, A, director, 07/05/2021)

> [W]hat weighs through? […] I think that's the person himself, if he, if we find that there's no point to… to consult or to make proposals and, yes, if there's no cooperation, if there's especially no cooperation, then we're going to say more quickly 'Okay, if you really don't want to cooperate, then it's time to give a signal that this is not acceptable.' (Flanders, D, president, 04/03/2021)

The sanction is also described as way to re-establish the communication with the beneficiary, which is the condition for the social support.

> So we're really in situations where we can't get in touch with the beneficiaries, […] and the only way, it's unfortunate to say […], after they apply for the income support, the only way we have found to get them to come back to us and for us to resume social support, is to cut off the integration income […]. (Wallonia, D, manager, 29/01/2021)

Although, as we will develop later, the possibility of sanctioning the beneficiary is most often used by social workers as a 'threat' and quite rarely applied, according to our research participants, many social workers stress that sanctioning can be used to reactivate the relationship with the beneficiary, to identify the difficulties he/she is facing, and to adjust social support:

> If you don't keep your appointments regarding employment, you will receive a warning because you are not prepared to work. But then your integration income is not stopped. Or, if one of the conditions for receiving the integration income is that you have to attend language lessons and you don't go or you are unlawfully absent several times, then you can also receive a warning. But then again, I think it is important to know why you are absent so much. What is the problem, because often there are also peripheral problems that prevent them from attending classes? (Flanders, C, social worker, 16/03/2021)

We have previously described that the attitude of the beneficiary is assessed by social workers as condition of an appropriate relation, which leads to a facilitated process of access and maintenance of social rights but that also reveals unbalanced power dynamics. Indeed, social workers can also apply sanctions when they estimate that beneficiaries have 'taken it too far'.

> [Interviewer] Does it often come to sanctions in practice?
> [Interviewee] It does happen sometimes, yes. That does happen sometimes. Uhm, if, for example, they don't go to Dutch classes and, uh, are unlawfully absent, don't keep appointments. Then it may well be that sanctions follow. Now, we're fairly lenient about that, because we're always like, 'Oh, would we sanction now? Yes, he did this and this and this.' But then it usually has to get out of hand before a sanction actually follows. Then they really have to be rattling our feet already. But we do give a lot of chances, I must say. Actually, sometimes we come across as very strict, but in the end we give so many chances. (Flanders, F, social worker, 25/05/2021)

> Sanctions are used but, alright, it must be quite extreme before a sanction is given, I think. Uhm, it's not at the first time or the first, uhm, three appointments that someone hasn't come, that a sanction is given immediately. There's really going to be some, some other path followed before a sanction is given, for example, by going on a home visit, uhm, by actually trying to contact them intensively one more time. It's not that that immediately, baf, file for, and hup, we're off. That you don't help people with that. (Flanders, D, social worker, 19/03/21).

As said, according to social workers, the sanction is rarely used as activation means for newcomers, since they would tend to respect their engagements, and sometimes there may be misunderstandings justifying the lack of 'collaboration'. Moreover, the possibilities and the situation of the beneficiary are often taken into account. Therefore, in many cases, social workers seem to focus on finding the reasons why beneficiaries do not comply with the requirements and giving them additional opportunities to do so instead of sanctioning them directly.[10] As Gschwind *et al.* have pointed out (2021), disciplinary measures intended to punish illegitimate receivers of welfare services – who do not demonstrate sufficient compliance with the job search obligation – are applied to a lower rate to newly arrived immigrants, since they are considered to have limited control over their labour market position. The authors stress that this finding leads to a complexification of deservingness judgements in relation with immigrants' entitlement to welfare benefits. Yet, we saw in our research that some sanctions may be given, for example if newcomers do not follow language or other courses that they are supposed to attend. As mentioned in the following quote, young people not respecting the rules[11] may also be the object of sanctions.

> Normally we can do sanctions, but I think we never do sanctions. It's very rare. I have never had to impose sanctions. I don't know if it's because the people I follow are very motivated and respect what they are asked to do, but I've never had any problems. I mean, sometimes there are small reminders, especially for young people, etc. Sometimes you have to give them a bit of a warning. Sometimes you have to put them back on the right track. (Wallonia, A, social worker, 17/02/2021)

Indeed, the sanction is seen as the last resource to reprimand the beneficiaries, once all other attempts to make them follow the rules have failed, and functions as a warning to remind the beneficiary of their obligations.

> A termination will only happen if there is really no cooperation and totally no willingness to work eh. So that doesn't happen very often either. A suspension could occur sooner, but also based on very important agreements in the ISIP. I would like to say that not following Dutch courses and stubbornly postponing or refusing them can be a reason for suspending an integration income. If there is no valid reason for that eh. If someone has been sick for a whole period of time or childcare has been cut and they can't go. That's a different story. Then there are equity reasons. But if it's really because of unwillingness or refusal or no motivation, then that's e.g.

a reason to suspend. But someone who, for example, does not participate in the discussion group, an extra learning opportunity, we're not going to suspend an integration income for that if that person does follow Dutch lessons on other days. So yes it is, it depends on what conditions in the ISIP that they don't comply with. It does have to be one with enough weighting and severity. (Flanders, G, director, 26/02/2021)

The introduction of the ISIP as condition to maintain the social income for some categories of beneficiaries, including newcomers with certain residence status, has led to the formal possibility of applying sanctions. The ISIP is seen by some social workers as a tool to 'legitimate' the sanctions and to apply formal and standardised rules. Following the ISIP, sanctions can be applied when the beneficiary has not reached the planned objectives or has not respected the deadlines (and he/she is not able to objectively justify why), and only after an established number of formal warnings.

We generally have to carry out one review [of the case] per year, [...] then a follow-up at the level of the individualised social integration project, [...] with three evaluations per year on the person's project [...]. This allows us to impose sanctions, if we see that at the second evaluation the person has still not looked for a job despite having been offered one, and that they say they are looking for one but there is no proof, we can impose sanctions on the social income [...]. And that allows us to put the tick in the box [*mettre le coche* in French] because it's not always easy to get people back to work and if there are no sanctions they don't necessarily understand. (Wallonia, H, social worker, 28/01/2021)

However, some other social workers reject the idea of control and sanctioning that would be implicit in this tool. In addition, from the government point of view, the ISIP would not have been introduced to legitimate the sanctions – is this only a collateral effect of it? – but rather to better accompany the beneficiary in their activation.

The PCSW must therefore use this tool [ISIP] to optimise its support and not as a tool to sanction a user (even if in extreme cases of non-compliance with the objectives, sanctioning is possible). Therefore, in inspections, when it is found that a PCSW regularly uses this tool as a sanctioning tool, the PCSWs are reminded of the philosophy of the law; for example, if the user has not achieved the objectives set out in the ISIP, the PCSW is asked to analyse why these objectives were not achieved (perhaps they were poorly defined or too ambitious for the user) and to adapt them rather than automatically sanctioning. I recall that the GPMI is not part of the conditions of granting that the social income applicant has to fulfil in order to be entitled to his social income. According to Art.13 of the law of 26/05/2002, the ISIP is a right that the PCSW must grant to the user and that must be adapted to his/her situation (and not be established on the basis of additional granting conditions imposed by the PCSW via this contract). In particular for newcomers, the ISIP should not be confused with the obligatory Flemish *inburgering* contract. (Extract from email communication with the SPP Social Integration, inspection service, 10 February 2021)

Indeed, PCSWs can receive comments by the government to adjust their use of sanctions, if found out to be too severe.

It is also worth mentioning that specific sanctions can be given to residents in LRI, who do not benefit from social income. For example, they may be asked to pay for extra charges they made in their house – concerning energy, for example – or for lack of respect of internal rules, lack of property, and so forth. Also in case of conflicts, they could be sanctioned up to the transfer to another municipality by Fedasil (disciplinary transfers) or even to the exclusion from Fedasil network.[12]

When you go to the accommodation you realise… […] the concern for cleanliness in particular. […] there are different sanctions, if […] it goes really badly, from a report to an oral order, it can go through the mail, and the extreme is the exclusion from the Fedasil network. Now it's not because it's not swept away that we're going to exclude them. But there is a graduation of sanctions imposed by Fedasil, and once again, it's not us who created them. […] and that, again, is in the rules they signed on the first day, so they know it too. (Wallonia, H, social worker, 17/12/2020)

Taking into account the elements described in this section, we can argue that sanctions are applied to beneficiaries when social workers consider that they do not deserve the social assistance, because they believe that they do not particularly need it – they have other resources – and that they do not meet the expectations regarding their integration and activation process (De Wilde, 2017). According to social workers, deserving the social aid also means respecting the duties established for beneficiaries. Therefore, the sanction becomes an instrument to make (foreign) beneficiaries understanding the functioning of the Belgian welfare system and complying with its rules – based on redistribution.

It's the PCSW, but who is the PCSW? It's the community and at some point… I mean you can be social as much as you want, but when you touch the [collective] money […]. The thing that I'm going to put in place now is that you don't take your steps with the social laws, we'll withdraw the aid, that's the best way for them to understand how it works. Because I think, it's better for people to work more, to learn French, to do a good training leading to a qualification […]. At some point we say stop, because why them and not the others? […] this is even supposed to be the approach of the PCSW, […] the PCSW asks us to do this. (Wallonia, B, social worker, 15/01/2021)

The institutional approach concerning welfare allowances, as described in Chapters 2 and 6, requires the activation – social and professional – of the beneficiaries as the main condition but also the main aim of the social intervention. 'Getting out' the system of help is a process embedded in the welfare system itself and developed under different forms on the ground.

NOTES

1.   The mentioned example concerns the possibility of not or allocating social welfare arrears.
2.   The authors and editors of this book are aware of the male bias in certain phrasings of this respondent and others (for instance, speaking of 'he' and 'him' only, whereas it could also concern female beneficiaries as well). The decision was taken to keep the quotes as they were expressed by the interlocutors, even though they were not always thinking and speaking in terms of gender, but rather in terms of a non-gendered beneficiary. This holds for quotes in other chapters and parts of this book as well.
3.   We will discuss further this aspect in the next section.
4.   This reasoning does not mean that those who have a more 'bureaucratic' approach are not doing their job properly or fully. It is a question of approach and degree of commitment, also resulting, as Giladi highlights, speaking of 'organisational determinism' (2021, p. 9, 11), from adaptive strategies to the working conditions framing the action of frontline workers (Lipsky, 2010; Brodkin, 2012; Brodkin & Majmundar, 2010; Hupe & Hill, 2015).
5.   On the specific impact of employment in welfare deservingness, see Chauvin et al., 2013.
6.   Obstacles to the relationship may depend on gender-related factors, for example when beneficiaries mistrust social workers because of their gender, or on racial or ethnic factors, when mistrust is directed at social workers from black and/or ethnic immigrant backgrounds.
7.   Conversely, we will see in the third part of this book how networks function as forms of social and cultural capital for the beneficiaries themselves.
8.   The reference is often to migrants arrived in Belgium within the framework of a family reunification, where social workers may suspect 'fake marriages'.
9.   Generally, as mentioned above, the sanctions proposed by social workers also need to be validated by the committee.

10. As we will see in Chapter 10, this is partly reflected in the experiences of beneficiaries, although their perceptions of sanctions are varied.
11. As seen before, this concerns having a paid informal job, instead of attending courses and training.
12. These rules are established by Fedasil itself.

REFERENCES

Azzopardi, C., & McNeill, T. (2016). From cultural competence to cultural consciousness: Transitioning to a critical approach to working across differences in social work. *Journal of Ethnic & Cultural Diversity in Social Work, 25*(4), 282–299.

Balgopal, P. R. (Ed.). (2000). *Social work practice with immigrants and refugees.* Columbia University Press.

Boccagni, P. (2015). (Super) diversity and the migration–social work nexus: A new lens on the field of access and inclusion? *Ethnic and Racial Studies, 38*(4), 608–620.

Boccagni, P., & Righard, E. (2020). Social work with refugee and displaced populations in Europe: (Dis) continuities, dilemmas, developments. *European Journal of Social Work, 23*(3), 375–383.

Brodkin, E. Z. (2012). Reflections on street-level bureaucracy: Past, present, and future. *Public Administration Review, 72*, 940–949.

Brodkin, E. Z., & Majmundar, M. (2010). Administrative exclusion: Organizations and the hidden costs of welfare claiming. *Journal of Public Administration Research and Theory, 20*(4), 827–848.

Chauvin, S., Garcés-Mascareñas, B., & Kraler, A. (2013). Employment and migrant deservingness. *International Migration, 51*(6), 80–85.

Chow, J., & Austin, M. (2008). The culturally responsive social service agency. *Administration in Social Work, 32*(4), 39–64. https://doi.org/10.1080 /03643100802293832

Clasen, J., & Clegg, D. (2007). Levels and levers of conditionality: Measuring change within welfare states. In J. Clasen, & A. Nico Siegel (Eds.), *Investigating welfare state change: The 'dependent variable problem' in comparative analysis* (pp. 166–197). Edward Elgar Publishing.

Collins, R. (1971). A conflict theory of sexual stratification. *Social Problems, 19*(1), 3–21.

De Wilde, M. (2017). Deservingness in social assistance administrative practice: A factorial survey approach. In W. van Oorschot, F. Roosma, B. Meuleman, & T. Reeskens (Eds.), *The social legitimacy of targeted welfare* (pp. 225–240). Edward Elgar Publishing.

De Wilde, M. (2018). *Between legislation and realisation comes implementation: The effect of the multi-layered implementation process on social policy outcomes* [Doctoral dissertation, University of Antwerp].

Einstein, K. L., & Glick, D. M. (2017). Does race affect access to government services? An experiment exploring street-level bureaucrats and access to public housing. *American Journal of Political Science, 61*, 100–116.

Ellis, K. (2011). Street-level bureaucracy revisited: The changing face of frontline discretion in adult social care in England. *Social Policy and Administration, 45*(3), 221–244.

Evans, T., & Harris, J. (2004). Street-level bureaucracy, social work and the (exaggerated) death of discretion. *British Journal of Social Work, 34*(6), 871–895.

Faist, T. (2009). Diversity: A new mode of incorporation? *Ethnic and Racial Studies, 32*(1), 171– 190. https://doi.org/10.1080/01419870802483650

Fiore, B., & Facchini, C. (2013). Social work as gendered issue from a generational point of view. *International Review of Sociology, 23*(2), 310–325.

Ford, R. (2016). Who should we help? An experimental test of discrimination in the British Welfare State. *Political Studies, 64*(3), 630–650.

Freeman, G. P. (2009). Immigration, diversity, and welfare chauvinism. *The Forum, 7*(3), 1–16.

Giladi, M. (2021). Travail social et pratiques discrétionnaires: Introduction. *Les Politiques Sociales, 34*(3), 4–14.

Gschwind, L., Ratzmann, N., & Beste, J. (2021). Protected against all odds? A mixed-methods study on the risk of welfare sanctions for immigrants in Germany. *Social Policy & Administration, 56*(3), 502–517.

Harrison, G., & Turner, R. (2011). Being a 'culturally competent' social worker: Making sense of a murky concept in practice. *British Journal of Social Work, 41*(2), 333–350. https://doi.org/10.1093/bjsw/bcq101

Hemker, J., & Rink, A. (2017). Multiple dimensions of bureaucratic discrimination: Evidence from German welfare offices. *American Journal of Political Science, 61*, 786–803.

Hindera, J. J. (1993). Representative bureaucracy: Imprimis evidence of active representation in the EEOC district office. *Social Science Quarterly, 74*, 95–108.

Holmes, G. E., & Saleebey, D. (1993). Empowerment, the medical model, and the politics of clienthood. *Journal of Progressive Human Services, 4*(1), 61–78.

Hupe, P., & Hill, M. (Eds.). (2015). *Understanding street-level bureaucracy.* Policy Press.

Laenen, T. (2018). Do institutions matter? The interplay between income benefit design, popular perceptions, and the social legitimacy of targeted welfare. *Journal of European Social Policy, 28*(1), 4–17.

Laenen, T., Rossetti, F., & van Oorschot, W. (2019). Why deservingness theory needs qualitative research: Comparing focus group discussions on social welfare in three welfare regimes. *International Journal of Comparative Sociology, 60*(3), 190–216.

Lafleur, J.-M., & Mescoli, E. (2018). Creating undocumented EU migrants through welfare: A conceptualization of undeserving and precarious citizenship. *Sociology, 52*(3), 480–496.

Lundy, C. (2004). *Social work and social justice: A structural approach to practice.* University of Toronto Press.

Marrow, H. B. (2009). Immigrant bureaucratic incorporation: The dual roles of professional missions and government policies. *American Sociological Review, 74*, 756–776.

Mascia, C., & Santos, A. C. (2021). « Suivre la règle », ou le (non)-usage du pouvoir discrétionnaire. *Les Politiques Sociales, 34*(3), 93–104.

May, P. J., & Winter, S. C. (2009). Politicians, managers, and street-level bureaucrats: Influences on policy implementation. *Journal of Public Administration Research and Theory, 19*(3), 453–476.

Maynard-Moody, S., & Musheno, M. (2000). State agent or citizen agent: Two narratives of discretion. *Journal of Public Administration Research and Theory, 10*(2), 329–358.

Maynard-Moody, S., & Portillo, S. (2010). Street-level bureaucracy theory. In R. Durant (Ed.). *Oxford Handbook of American Bureaucracy* (pp. 252–277). Oxford University Press.

Mewes, J., & Mau, S. (2013). Globalization, socio-economic status and welfare chauvinism: European perspectives on attitudes toward the exclusion of immigrants. *International Journal of Comparative Sociology, 54*(3), 228–245.

Miaz, J. (2017). From the law to the decision: The social and legal conditions of asylum adjudication in Switzerland. *European Policy Analysis 3*(2), 372–396.

Murgatroyd, L. (1982). Gender and occupational stratification. *The Sociological Review, 30*(4), 574–602.

Petersen, M. B., Slothuus, R., Stubager, R., & Togeby, L. (2011). Deservingness versus values in public opinion on welfare: The automaticity of the deservingness heuristic. *European Journal of Political Research, 50*, 24–52.

Pitts, D. W. (2005). Diversity, representation and performance: Evidence about race and ethnicity in public organizations. *Journal of Public Administration Research and Theory, 15*(4), 615–631.

Potocky, M., & Naseh, M. (2020). *Best practices for social work with refugees and immigrants.* Columbia University Press.

Raaphorst, N., & Groeneveld, S. (2018). Double standards in frontline decision making: A theoretical and empirical exploration. *Administration & Society, 50*(8), 1175–1201.

Rappaport, J. (1987). Terms of empowerment/exemplars of prevention: Toward a theory for community psychology. *American Journal of Community Psychology, 15*(2), 121–148.

Reisch, M. (2008). From melting pot to multiculturalism: The impact of racial and ethnic diversity on social work and social justice in the USA. *British Journal of Social Work, 38*(4), 788–804.

Riffe, H. A., & Kondrat, M. E. (1997). Social worker alienation and disempowerment in a managed care setting. *Journal of Progressive Human Services, 8*(1), 41–55.

Robinson, K. (2014). Voices from the front line: Social work with refugee and asylum seekers in Australia and the UK. *British Journal of Social work, 44*, 1602–1620.

Saidel, J. R., & Loscocco, K. (2005). Agency leaders, gendered institutions, and representative bureaucracy? *Public Administration Review, 65*(2), 158–170.

Schlesinger, E. G., & Devore, W. (1995). Ethnic sensitive social work practice: The state of the art. *J. Soc. & Soc. Welfare, 22*, 29–58.

Sowers, K. M., Dulmus, C. N., & White, B. W. (2008). *Comprehensive handbook of social work and social welfare: The profession of social work (vol. 1).* John Wiley & Sons.

Standing, G. (2005). *Promoting income security as a right: Europe and North America.* Anthem Press.

Stevanovic, B., & Mosconi, N. (2007). Les représentations des métiers des adolescent(es). *Revue française de pédagogie, 161*, 53–68.

Thomann, E., & Rapp, C. (2018). Who deserves solidarity? Unequal treatment of immigrants in Swiss welfare policy delivery. *Policy Studies Journal, 46*(3), 531–552.

Tummers, L. (2013). *Policy alienation and the power of professionals: Confronting new policies.* Edward Elgar.

Van Der Haar, M. (2009). Disentangling culture as explanatory factor. In S. Algashi, T. Hylland Eriksen, & H. Ghorashi (Eds.), *Paradoxes of cultural recognition* (pp. 145–158). Ashgate.

Van der Leun, J. (2006). Excluding illegal migrants in The Netherlands: Between national policies and local implementation. *West European Politics, 29*, 310–326.

Van Kersbergen, K., & Hemerijck, A. (2012). Two decades of change in Europe: The emergence of the social investment state. *Journal of Social Policy, 41*, 475–492.

van Oorschot, W., Roosma, F., Meuleman, B., & Reeskens, T. (2017). *The social legitimacy of targeted welfare: Attitudes to welfare deservingness.* Edward Elgar Publishing Limited.

Van Robaeys, B., & Driessens, K. (2011). *Gekleurde armoede en hulpverlening: Sociaal werkers en cliënten aan het woord.* Lannoo.

Voélin, S., Davolio, M. E., & Lindenau, M. (Eds.). (2017). *Le travail social entre résistance et innovation/Soziale Arbeit zwischen Widerstand und Innovation.* Éditions ies.

Wilkins, V. M. (2007). Exploring the causal story: Gender, active representation, and bureaucratic priorities. *Journal of Public Administration Research and Theory, 17*(1), 77–94.

Wilkins, V. M., & Williams, B. N. (2009). Representing blue: Representative bureaucracy and racial profiling in the Latino community. *Administration & Society, 40*(8), 775–798.

CONCLUSION PART II

ELSA MESCOLI

The second part of this book was devoted to the analysis of policy in practice, by studying the decision-making process concerning the granting of social benefits to newcomer beneficiaries. In particular, attention has been paid to the levels and ways in which discretion operates in this process, impacting on the decisions made.

We first presented the law and policy framework that governs the functioning of the PCSWs in Belgium and its decision-making process. Second, we have given examples of how institutions may interpret this framework differently, leading to different approaches to meeting the benefit claims of (immigrant) recipients. In Chapter 7, we then discussed the functioning of the decision-making process itself – from application to decision – highlighting the role of the different social actors of the PCSWs involved (including managers, committee members, and social workers). Chapter 8 looked specifically at the discretionary power of social workers, examining how it operates and what factors influence the actions and decisions that social workers take. This chapter also includes a section on the use of sanctions, that is, the reasons and motivations behind it and its expected effects.

Our main research results, derived from the analysis of the theoretical and empirical material mobilised in this section, concern both the functioning of the welfare delivery 'system' in Belgium – as manifested in our case studies – and the practices of the social actors involved.

At the level of the system, we found a very hierarchised decision-making process, involving first of all a set of normative rules that includes not only laws issued at different levels of government, but also internal guidelines translating these laws into local standards. While this framework is to some extent described as difficult to negotiate, these norms are in fact diverse in our case studies, demonstrating that despite the existence of an overarching state structure, the implementation of policies varies on the ground. Within this functioning, each social actor involved (presidents, committee members, managers, and social workers) has a specific role and intervenes at different temporal and decisional stages between the reception of the application for social benefits and the decision to grant it or not. Moreover, the role of each interacts with that of the others, both in terms of formal procedures and in terms of reciprocal influence and expectations. A complex matrix of interprofessional dynamics emerges as a key driver of the decision-making process.

Indeed, regarding the practices of the social actors involved in the decision-making process, our data show that there are no 'ideal types' that describe and normalise the concerned professionals' work. This means that, although everyone's role in the decision-making process is well defined, actual attitudes – and the outcomes that follow – change according to a range of contextual, organisational, and personal factors. Although in the discourses gathered in the field, it seems clearly defined who is in charge of which tasks, and how the responsibilities are distributed in the decision-making process, the ways of translating this functioning into concrete practices vary. Therefore, the impact of these various practices implemented in the field is not straightforward, in terms of the 'weight' of each professional in the decision-making process but also in terms of the concrete outcomes – positive or negative response to the demand – which result from it.

Most importantly, we realised that social workers have different levels of awareness of their discretionary power, which, in the case of low awareness, can lead them to rely strictly and solely on laws and guidelines to guide their work. The consequence is the risk to neglect the needs of the beneficiaries as well as the additional possibilities to meet them that can be found by further interpreting the law and based on a more thorough analysis of the beneficiaries' situations. This approach also results in a discharge of responsibility for the decisions taken. On the contrary, recognising and using discretion can lead to an increase in possible social benefits, through active – rather than passive – engagement with and questioning of the law. This approach thus makes it possible to challenge – often through micro-practices of discretion – the restrictive policy framework and to work towards greater social justice. It also seems to reveal, paradoxically, that the rules of the welfare state as such fail to ensure that human rights and needs are met and that the use of discretion is necessary to fill this gap.

In trying to understand what factors determine social workers' choice of one or the other approach (or gradients between the two), we have identified elements that fall into two main categories: institutional aspects (the laws and guidelines mentioned above) and the personal characteristics and approach of social workers. With particular reference to the latter category, we found that the assessment of the attitude of the beneficiaries in their relationship with the social workers is crucial to prove the deservingness of the social benefit. This assessment is based on moral and relational aspects, such as how newcomer beneficiaries comply with their 'duties' towards the institution and, more broadly, towards public funding in their host country. In this context, sanctions – although quite rarely used – can function to 'activate' the non-cooperating beneficiary and to remind him/her the 'rules of the game'. Finally, it should be recalled that cultural prejudices also intervene – among other factors, including the migratory background of social workers and their previous professional experience in the field of migration – in the relationship between social workers and beneficiaries in various ways, in terms of reciprocal representations and expectations that influence, explicitly or implicitly, the decisions taken.

By analysing the complex workings of welfare policy implementation on the ground, the main aim of this section has been to contribute to the literature on the immigration–welfare policy nexus by shedding light – anchored in field data – on the impact of street-level bureaucracy in particular on challenging restrictive policies and ensuring greater social justice towards newcomer welfare beneficiaries.

PART III

ACCESSING WELFARE SERVICES IN BELGIUM: THE PERSPECTIVE OF NEWLY ARRIVED IMMIGRANTS

CHAPTER 9
PATHWAYS OF ACCESS: ANALYSING NEWLY ARRIVED IMMIGRANTS' ACCESS TO WELFARE SERVICES

MARIJE REIDSMA AND MICHELLE CRIJNS

The central subject of this chapter is the accessibility of the PCSWs from the beneficiaries' perspective. Both the extent to which current service delivery is accessible to newly arrived immigrants and the elements that impact accessibility will be analysed. Following Levesque *et al.* (2013, p. 4), we understand access as '[enabling] people to make the steps that enable them to enter in contact and obtain' welfare benefits and support. We will use their model of access to health care as discussed in Chapter 1 as an inspiration for our analysis of access to welfare services. More specifically, we will follow their logic of understanding access as a sequence consisting of multiple steps, ranging from having needs (and the perception of them) to receiving the appropriate support or benefits. The chapter starts with a description of the needs newly arrived migrants have in order to become a beneficiary at the PCSW. Second, the 'pathways' through which newly arrived immigrants are informed about, oriented, and given access (or not) to services and rights are discussed. More specifically we will focus on how newly arrived immigrants learn about the PCSW and get referred to it, on how newly arrived immigrants learn about the services and rights the PCSWs offer and the types of services they use, and on enhancing and impeding factors that affect the newly arrived immigrants' capacity to access the welfare services (such as reachability, language policies, and internal staff changes). While in the first part of this book we studied those very same elements from the perspective of the social workers – highlighting how they depend on structural conditions and on the agents' approach – we will explore in this section how these impact the experience of beneficiaries and how beneficiaries deal with them. It should be noted that interviews have been conducted *only* with newly arrived immigrants that are or have been beneficiaries of one or several PCSWs and thus have had access to welfare services, although the extent of this access differed. Newly arrived immigrants with certain needs who did not reach the services of the PCSW, whether voluntarily (for example, unwillingness to go to the PCSW) or involuntarily (for example, unawareness of the PCSW and its services), were not included in this study.

1.   THE EMERGING NEED FOR SUPPORT: WHEN AND WHAT?

In order for anyone to seek help at or be referred to the PCSW, they must have certain needs. In our fieldwork we saw that needs might arise, for example, after the loss of a partner or a divorce. While this type of event can happen to anyone, the impact of it on newly arrived immigrants may differ from that on native residents who find themselves in the same situation, due to – among others – lower social and cultural capital related to the host country (Simich *et al.*, 2005). Usually newly arrived immigrants who experienced such an event have already lived in Belgium independently for a (short) while, and our fieldwork showed that they were mostly in need of financial support. In some instances, they were also in need of more general support, such as finding social housing or a job. Our fieldwork showed that most respondents, however, became a beneficiary at the PCSW after leaving the reception centre for applicants of international protection. Indeed, the majority of newly arrived immigrants in our fieldwork were refugees or persons granted subsidiary protection.[1] Many of them first moved to a Local Reception Initiative (LRI)[2] often organised by the PCSWs after receiving a positive answer and leaving the reception centre.[3] When we asked them directly which needs they had that led them to seek support from the PCSW, the majority could not mention any specific needs. This might be related to the fact that they spent several months or years in complex procedures and that the PCSW is perceived as a step in this continuum of procedures. Indeed, as we will see later, they usually were referred to the PCSW by an employee of the reception centre. They often did not know about the PCSW and its services, which led to them having no expectations before their first appointment and they thus did not think of any specific needs the PCSW could or could not answer (cf. infra). That is not to say they did not have any needs. In fact, in the interviews their needs became mostly apparent from the way they described their situation as well as from the benefits and support they eventually received from the PCSW (cf. infra). As the following quotes show, most refugees needed support in general – meaning not only financial support, but also some orientation in society – as they were new in Belgium, had no knowledge of where to go, and no resources:

It is hard to live without support, without the PCSW. We don't have family here. Maybe other people have more experience or have lived here before, but we don't have anyone. That's the problem, we don't have a social life here. (Flanders, D, beneficiary, 25/02/2022)

Then I came to [name of the city] and I had a little problem for the language, for the people, how to search for a house and how do you see what is 'for sale' and 'for rent'. We don't understand. (Flanders, A, beneficiary, 01/03/2022)

According to Levesque *et al.* (2013), the first two steps in getting access to health care (or in our case welfare services) are having needs and becoming aware of them (including the desire for support). While it became apparent from our interviews that newly arrived immigrants clearly had needs that could be answered by the PCSW, in particular refugees did not perceive their needs as such due to the fact that they were often following a referral to the PCSW and were not aware of the PCSW and its services. This also means that the third step of accessing welfare services, which consists of seeking welfare support, is not applicable in this case as well. The framework of Levesque *et al.* (2013) thus only seems to work for those newly arrived immigrants who are aware of their needs and have to actively search for support.

Generally, not everyone experiences the same needs to the same extent. Heidinger (2022) has shown in her study of refugees' service needs and utilisation in Germany that a need for help varies from service domain to service domain (for example, finances, job search, learning the language, medical care, and housing) and is also dependent on the level of human capital (understood as the skills and knowledge gained before migrating), social capital and socio-demographic characteristics (region of origin, gender, age, length of residency in host country, and so on). A differentiation in needs is also present in our fieldwork. We already saw that newly arrived immigrants who reached out for support after already having lived in Belgium independently for a (short) while often merely needed financial support. The needs of newly arrived immigrants who had just left the reception centre, however, were quite diverse and were to a large extent focused on settling in Belgium. The needs that newly arrived immigrants expressed during the interviews also often encompassed different temporalities. Indeed, while the need for immediate support (with the goal of being able to cover for basics such as shelter, food, and so forth) always emerged from the interview, this need was often expressed in relation with the broader aspiration of obtaining education and/or finding a job in order to become autonomous and contribute to society. This link between the need for immediate support and long-term goals is illustrated by the following fieldnotes taken during a discussion with a group of newcomer beneficiaries.

> [on the question what are the group's projects, their desires for the future]
> R1: Personally, I want to work to settle here. Work is mandatory. [...] When you work you can do a lot of things! [...]
> R2: For me the first thing is the house and then the job. Without a house, you cannot work. (Wallonia, A, group interview with beneficiaries, 08/02/2022)

Our fieldwork also showed that a few newly arrived immigrants experienced a recurring need for welfare service provision. One respondent, for example, worked in several short-term contracts the first years in Belgium, having to go back to the PCSW in between contracts:

> I have been in [the city] for two years now. Yes, I started with the PCSW of [this city]. I stayed a bit in this PCSW because the problem was that when I worked, it was not full time. I worked for two months, three months ... I can't have unemployment [benefits] after that. So I worked for two months, three months, and then I come back to the PCSW. (Wallonia, O, beneficiary, 05/06/2021)

The emergence of needs and subsequent support seeking is therefore not always a linear process with a starting and end point, but can also form a circular process. In the remainder of this chapter, we will mainly focus on the first time the newly arrived immigrants got into contact with the PCSW.

2.   FROM ACCESS TO THE PCSW TO THE USE OF PCSW SERVICES

After having distinguished the newly arrived immigrants' needs, even though they themselves did not always perceive them as such, this paragraph will focus first on how newly arrived immigrants actually seek support at or get into contact with the PCSW, and second on some enhancing and impeding factors that impact access to welfare services (following the framework of access by Levesque et al. (2013)). As discussed in Chapter 1, accessibility is a broad concept encompassing various elements: the 'degree of fit' between clients (that is, beneficiaries) and the system, the interplay between multiple actors at different levels, and the multidimensionality of the concept. This paragraph is written with those elements in mind, in particular the 'degree of fit' between the system or service on the one hand, and the beneficiaries on the other. Indeed, accessibility is not solely a characteristic of the service side, but is also impacted by the side of the users. Applied to our study, it means that even if some welfare service characteristics are the same for everyone, the resulting accessibility may differ between newly arrived immigrants and other groups in society. In other words, the fact that welfare services exist is not a guarantee that potential beneficiaries make (full) use of it. For example, in the study of Heidinger (2022) service utilisation is linked to a higher socioeconomic status and educational attainment, higher language proficiency, a smaller intra-ethnic social network, and a larger inter-ethnic social network. In what follows, we will analyse the accessibility of the PCSW with a specific focus on the particularities for newly arrived immigrants.

2.1. The path to the PCSW

Following the framework of Levesque *et al.* (2013), the next step in accessing welfare services after identifying the needs is to seek support. While most refugees were referred directly to the PCSW and as such did not need to seek support themselves, for other newly arrived immigrants this is not an easy task. Generally, we may assume that a lack of relevant knowledge, cultural capital,[4] and/or social capital[5] related to the host country may impede one's capacity to seek help, especially when it is the first time experiencing a need for welfare services (Heidinger, 2022; Ma & Chi, 2005; Simich *et al.*, 2005). Newly arrived immigrants need to learn 'where to go for what' (Simich *et al.*, 2005, p. 261) in a period that is perceived as stressful due to, for example, financial insecurity, family separation, and gender role changes. Awareness of social services is also often limited because of a lack of language skills, social isolation, and insufficient information supply from the welfare institutions or government. However, being informed about welfare services is of critical importance in having access to it (Choi *et al.*, 2013; Simich *et al.*, 2005). As for our fieldwork, similarly to what was reported in Chapter 5, a recurring finding is that the majority of respondents did not have any prior knowledge about the PCSW and the services it could offer before the first contact with the institution, whether they were new in Belgium or had already been staying in the country for some years. As such, they were not aware that the PCSW could support them with their overt or covert needs and had no prior expectations. Those who did know about the PCSW, were often informed by other sources than the PCSW itself and mostly knew about the financial support the PCSW offers (see below). Other services, such as assistance in finding education and a job, are less known and less seen as a primary task of the PCSW by the newly arrived immigrants:

> I heard from others [residents] in the reception centre that you get
> weekly money from the PCSW to live, that's it. (Flanders, D, beneficiary,
> 01/03/2022)

Another way in which newly arrived immigrants gained some knowledge
about the PCSW and its services upfront was by accompanying others to
the PCSW before becoming a beneficiary themselves. This occurred in a few
cases when the respondents were native speakers (in French-speaking regions)
or learned the language before or during the procedure for international
protection, and then volunteered to translate for others.

The different trajectories the newly arrived immigrants followed or certain
events that led them to become a beneficiary (for example, leaving the reception centre, family reunification, divorce, or loss of a partner) are reflected
in the way they came into contact with the PCSW. For those who left the
reception centre and moved to an LRI, the first contact they had with any
institution after leaving the reception centre was often with a social worker
from the PCSW:

> We were brought to the PCSW with all our stuff in a car from the reception
> centre, where they explained us everything: what we are entitled to, that
> we have to make an appointment if we need anything, waste separation …
> After that we got the key to our social housing. (Flanders, D, beneficiary,
> 06/03/2022)

It must be noted that, while many in our fieldwork resided in an LRI, it should
still be considered a special case as the first contact with the PCSW is not
with the 'regular' services, but with the specialised and temporary LRI. The
newly arrived immigrants' experience in the LRI might also shape their
ideas and opinions about the regular PCSW in case they receive a positive
answer and become a regular PCSW beneficiary. As mentioned earlier, before
moving to the LRI usually the employees in the reception centre made an
appointment for them and as such they perceived the PCSW as a mandatory
step, not knowing about the function of the PCSW. Sometimes newly arrived
immigrants leaving the reception centre were informed about the PCSW by
other residents, and as such the social network also plays a role in the path to
the PCSW. The importance of social capital in accessing welfare services will
be discussed further in this chapter. Information is sometimes also provided
by the social workers in the reception centre or LRI, or by the municipality
when the newly arrived immigrants go there to register themselves.[6]

Others who have been living independently in Belgium for some time when the need for support emerges, were often referred by friends or acquaintances or other (local) institutions. This was the case for example for one respondent after she had had to leave her husband in her country of origin because of domestic abuse:

> I stayed at a friend's house. Three months in her house. I waited. I was constantly saying that I would go back to Turkey. [My friend] said 'No!' [...] because she was angry at my husband. After three months, I was still waiting at her home. Then she told me: 'Come with me, come to the PCSW.' (Wallonia, A, beneficiary, 15/02/2022)

This underlines again the importance of having a social network in being able to reach the PCSW. Interestingly, this social network is often comprised of people with the same ethnic background, a factor that has been described in the literature as hindering access to services (see, for example, Heidinger (2022)). For many newly arrived immigrants such as the respondent quoted below, the social network can also compensate for the lack of skills in a common language and the lack of cultural capital (that is, local know-how) (Nawyn et al., 2012).

> It was information by people. I remember, through the internet, I was following all the groups of Syrians who are in the internet who sometimes ask questions. [...] I had seen that when there were people asking for the PCSWs, the social, the social aid things, at the same time my Belgian host family, my sister who had worked as a social worker at the PCSW. [...] She told me about all the information that all the people start like that. (Brussels, E, beneficiary, 27/09/2021)

Following the many ways in which respondents were made aware of and referred to the PCSW, we could also discern a great variation in how beneficiaries effectively got in contact with the PCSW for the first time. Sometimes a social worker from the reception centre or LRI would make an appointment, while in other cases the reception centre or LRI would, instead of making an appointment, tell the beneficiaries to go directly to the reception of the PCSW after signing a rental contract. In case the beneficiary was assisted by a local association, the latter also often made appointments. Persons in the beneficiaries' local network sometimes contacted the PCSW in order to make an appointment as well. It also happened that beneficiaries went to the PCSW themselves for making an appointment (often accompanied by a friend or relative) after they were informed of the institution's existence by their social network (for example, friends, family, by information of other newcomer beneficiaries, or by accompanying them for translating).

In conclusion, as many respondents were not aware of the PCSW and the services it could offer, they were dependent on others who would refer them to or tell them about the PCSW. In some cases the referral was made by institutions such as the social worker in the reception centre or the municipality, while in other cases beneficiaries depended on their social network for information on and getting in contact with the PCSW.

2.2. Gaining knowledge about PCSW services

After having established contact with the PCSW, the next step is to get access to benefits. How newly arrived immigrants perceive the accessibility of welfare benefits depends strongly on how they perceive the administrative burden, in particular the learning costs. The learning costs are defined as such: 'Citizens must learn about the program, whether they are eligible, the nature of benefits, and how to access services' (Moynihan et al., 2014, p. 46) (see Chapter 1). Here we could discern many differences between the newcomer beneficiaries, which also impacted to a great extent the access they had to certain benefits. As will become apparent in this paragraph some found themselves with easy access to benefits in terms of knowledge and eligibility, whereas others experienced considerably more difficulties.

It is important to note that part of our study took place in the COVID-19 pandemic, which had an impact on the modalities of the functioning of the PCSW. Some respondents mentioned they had never seen their social worker 'in person', which may also have had an influence on the service delivery. The impact these differences in access to information and benefits (or other types of aid) had with regard to both the relationship with the social worker and the issue of non-take-up of benefits will be further elaborated in respectively Chapter 10 and Chapter 11. Here we will exclusively focus on the description of the ways the newcomer beneficiaries gained knowledge of the PCSW services and their impact on the (perceived) service accessibility.

2.2.1. Four channels of information

In the interviews, four different channels came up as sources of knowledge about the opportunities and available services at the PCSW: the social worker who provides an overview and explains the available services, other professionals/organisations – such as the reception centre, the regional integration centres, or local non-governmental organisations (NGOs) and associations – the beneficiaries' own network (friends, family, other newly arrived immigrants) and gained knowledge through previous experiences with the PCSW in the same or other municipalities. We will first discuss the social worker as a possible channel of information. Considering many newly arrived immigrants did not know about the PCSW and its services upon their first contact, ideally the social workers would provide an in-depth explanation and overview of available services. Indeed, in some cases beneficiaries were directly informed by the social worker about the benefits and services they were entitled to. In the majority of cases, however, beneficiaries had to ask the social worker themselves for certain benefits:

> The assistant in [previous city] was very good and always told us what we were entitled to. But then when we were living in the social housing in [other city], we always had to hear it from friends and ask the assistants for it ourselves. (Flanders, D, beneficiary, 06/03/2022)

Hence, we observed many differences in the approachability of the PCSW, which refers to the extent to which welfare services make themselves known among the population (encompassing transparency, outreach activities, and information regarding available benefits and services (see Levesque *et al.*, 2013)). These differences strongly impact the beneficiaries' access to benefits, especially when their sociocultural capital is limited, and they are thus very dependent on their social worker. The following quote is an illustration of the general viewpoint among newly arrived immigrants regarding the provision of information by the PCSW on possible services and benefits:

> Everyone who is affiliated with the PCSW do so because they have no choice. The PCSW is supported by the government to help refugees and newly arrived immigrants. The PCSW thus gets that task. It would be good if they would communicate to everyone what they are entitled to. That way, everyone can know what services you can request at your PCSW and what you are entitled to. They don't need to communicate everything, but still be largely transparent. (Flanders, C, beneficiary, 20/01/2022)

A lack of information about PCSW services by the social worker can to a certain extent be bypassed by the three other channels: by gaining information from professionals from other organisations, by previous experiences in the same or another PCSW, and by communicating with other beneficiaries in the social network. As Ricketts and Goldsmith (2005) argue, accessibility is a dynamic concept: beneficiaries can learn from previous experiences or communication with others and adjust their behaviour to that acquired information. As such, access to benefits can be increased. The role of the beneficiaries' sociocultural capital with regard to the host country, for example in terms of the ability to look up information on services and procedures and having a social network, in accessing welfare benefits should therefore not be underestimated (Heidinger, 2022; Nawyn *et al.*, 2012; Simich *et al.*, 2005).

> Maybe we don't know all the rights we have, I don't know … Maybe there are some things that we could ask for but that we don't know about [laughing]. […] I think it also depends of the municipalities or the provinces. Some people say that there are tickets … How do you call that … I don't know how you call that but a ticket with which you can go to a store and have goods. But I don't know if they do this here. (Wallonia, C, beneficiary, 21/05/2021)

We may assume that especially for newly arrived immigrants who just arrived in Belgium their sociocultural capital related to the host country is rather limited. Besides, in some cases, even with the support of other institutions and the circulation of information, there was still a lack of complete information. We thus observe a degree of fit – referring to the degree in which the supply side of services and benefits (the PCSW) and the demand side (the beneficiaries) are adjusted to each other (see also Chapter 1) – between newly arrived immigrants and the PCSW that we expect to be lower than for the native population in this respect. The role that sociocultural capital plays in dealing with the discretionary space of social workers as street-level bureaucrats will be further discussed in Chapter 11.

2.2.2. Comparing experiences

Having previous experiences with the PCSW or communicating with others (whether with professionals or people from the newly arrived immigrants' social network) about their experiences also leads to comparing experiences with social workers and/or municipalities. This may increase the information on and access to benefits, but also lead to discontent. A first factor of dissatisfaction is the perception that the way services are offered to beneficiaries differs among social workers and/or municipalities, which might impact (or have impacted in the past) the beneficiaries' usage of benefits and ultimately their living conditions.

The assistant in [current city] tells us everything. For example, for ordering the study books for my brother she told us to tell her what he was studying and which year he was in. She works automatically, you understand? [...] In [previous city] it was not like that. For example, the assistant did not know anything about money for clothes. If my brother did not know anything about the money for clothes, he would not have said anything, you understand? (Flanders, D, beneficiary, 01/03/2022)

Second, beneficiaries also experienced differences in the actual service delivery between social workers and/or municipalities: some beneficiaries were, for example, entitled to certain services in one PCSW, but after moving to another municipality the new PCSW did not provide the same services (or vice versa). This can be confusing for beneficiaries, as the following quote illustrates:

Once I asked a superior [of the respondent's social worker at the PCSW] to please explain to me the way they work so I know what I can expect and what not, so that it's clear. Then the superior told me that in Belgium all PCSWs work in the same way and there's no difference. The reason I asked for more explanation is because in [current municipality] there is a certain rule that people who have families get extra support on top of their Social Integration Income. [...] That is something that not everybody gets and is dependent on the assistant you have. [...] That's something I saw that exists in [current municipality] and not in other municipalities. (Flanders, C, beneficiary, 24/01/2022)

Other beneficiaries noticed a difference in service delivery when they were comparing their local PCSW with PSCWs where friends went or with information from friends:

Some PCSWs are good, I have many friends here who get food from the PCSW when they arrive for the first time: macaroni, oil, milk, ... Something more. Where I stayed, this was not the case. Maybe there were too many people in this place [at the PCSW]. (Flanders, A, beneficiary, 01/03/2022)

Sometimes I ask and she [the social worker] says no directly, sometimes she says that she will have to ask her boss if it is possible [...]. My friend told me that as a student I had the right to apply for a computer. And when I asked her, she told me I don't because I learn French. (Brussels, B, beneficiary, 23/09/2021)

2.2.3. The perception of rights as favours

As the quotes above suggested, beneficiaries feel that the differentiation in services and aids is not always properly explained or addressed by social workers. While social workers have the feeling their discretionary space is limited as they have to work within a framework that to a large extent structures the functioning of the welfare institution (although discretionary practices are still recognised, see Chapters 7 and 8), the experiences that newly arrived immigrants have are very different. Some respondents also mentioned that there is no similar institution in their country, making it harder to understand why and how certain decisions are made. In Chapter 1 the interplay between multiple actors at different levels (the service providers, the system, society) was mentioned as an element that influences the accessibility of welfare services, but for the beneficiaries that we interviewed it is mostly the service provider (in this case the social worker) who is the deciding factor. While indeed social workers differ in the way they provide information, in certain cases this might lead to an overestimation of the social workers' discretionary power with respect to the decision-making process. All this can give beneficiaries the feeling of arbitrariness, whether correct or incorrect. Put differently, in the interpretation of beneficiaries, 'rights' are perceived as 'favours'. This idea is not new and not specific to newly arrived immigrants: Lipsky already wrote back in 1984 that rationing access to benefits and benefits themselves in times of high demand and limited resources '[r]einforces the view that aid from the welfare state depends on luck, "connections", persistence, or other factors over which people have little control' (Lipsky, 1984, p. 9). One respondent in our fieldwork analysed this issue as such:

> In general, the functioning of the PCSW differs from city to city, from village to village. We hear many stories of other people who are not getting support. Everyone has a different reason or argument. It is not always the same service that is being offered. [...] I just mean that everyone has their own experience with the PCSW. People talk to each other and so additional expectations come up. For example, if someone is helped well and gets extra benefits, he will pass this information on. Then another person will also apply for it even though they are not eligible for the same benefit. (Flanders, H, beneficiary, 08/02/2022)

The (perceived) differences in information and service provision also contribute to blur the full apprehension of the institution and beneficiaries' rights, which in its turn may lead to feelings of anxiety and insecurity regarding their rights as a beneficiary.

2.2.4. Use of benefits by the newly arrived immigrants

Following the above description of how newly arrived immigrants gain knowledge of PCSW services, we will now focus on the actual benefits they make use of. To start with, it is important to mention that this section only discusses the benefits and services that were mentioned by the respondents in our fieldwork, following the beneficiaries' perspective, and as such it does not form an exhaustive list of all possible forms of support and also does not display correctly the basis on which benefits or services are provided (that is, on the basis of the legal framework, internal guidelines, discretionary power of the social worker, and so forth).

The most common service or benefit that the respondents made use of was the Social Integration Income: a financial support measure to ensure a minimum financial means of existence. Other financial support measures mentioned were rent subsidies and loans for rental deposits, loans to buy furniture and household appliances, financial assistance for utility services (water, electricity, and so on), a driver's licence, and reimbursements of school expenses (such as a laptop, books, train or bus tickets, and a bicycle). These benefits seemed to be less systematically requested by and granted to newly arrived immigrants and mostly depended on the information provided by the social worker on those benefits. The PCSW can also provide general discounts for public transport and help with the application for a social tariff for the rent, water, electricity, and Internet. Some respondents were also provided with basic needs such as clothing and food packages. Finally, several beneficiaries mentioned that their social worker had taken on their general orientation upon their arrival and had supported the beneficiaries in accessing services not directly related to the PCSW. Beneficiaries reported getting assistance in finding and entering (language) schools, integration courses, and work (often Art. 60), and registering for health insurance, leisure, and other services. This type of support was mainly mentioned by those who were referred to the PCSW after leaving the reception centre or got in contact with the PCSW immediately after their arrival in Belgium. Interestingly, not all respondents could answer the question directly which services or benefits they made use of, as they seemed to be unaware of it or did not fully understand. Instead, the researchers had to give examples. In other cases, a few benefits or services were mentioned upon asking, but then it became clear over the course of the interview that the respondents made use of more services.

2.2.5. Enhancing and impeding factors impacting access to welfare services

In Levesque *et al.* (2013) several dimensions of access were discussed that can have an impact on the steps leading to access to health care (or welfare services).

Some of those also came up in our research: for example, the dimension of availability and accommodation on the side of the welfare service (geographic location, opening hours, appointments mechanisms) and ability to reach (living environments, availability of transport, mobility, social support) on the side of the welfare support seeker. These elements can impact the accessibility to welfare services and will be discussed in this section. In particular, the focus will be on the reachability of the PCSW, language issues, staff changes, and administrative barriers. Although not all of these factors are newcomer- or migrant-specific, the implications of these factors on access to welfare services might differ between newly arrived immigrants and others, as stated before.

Reachability
Reachability can be interpreted in two different ways: first, we understand reachability as the physical distance to the PCSW and the level of difficulty to overcome the distance. Second, reachability refers to the level of difficulty of entering the PCSW and being referred to or being able to get in contact with the right person within the PCSW. As for the physical distance, travelling time can impose a constraint on accessing welfare services (Hernandez & Rossel, 2015). In our fieldwork, however, the respondents were in general rather satisfied with the reachability of the PCSW in terms of the physical distance. The PCSW is usually within walking distance or at a manageable distance with a bicycle or public transport. In some cases, the distance was harder to overcome, but then another solution would be found – although this was not always to the liking of the beneficiary, for example when the social worker would propose to have contact by email instead of having a 'live' meeting. In a few cases, the respondents mentioned their social worker would pass by their house if needed or would arrange a dial-a-bus[7] and as such help to overcome the distance.

The reachability of the PCSW or social worker can also be assessed in terms of (the time investment of) making contact (Hernandez & Rossel, 2015). Rather large differences between the three regions could be observed in our case studies. In Flanders, most respondents mentioned that it is easy to contact their social worker if they have questions. In those cases, the contact is usually not face-to-face, but by e-mail, phone call, or instant messaging app. Quick replies are usually given. Face-to-face meetings generally only take place if the social worker has some documents for the beneficiary to fill out or sign (or vice versa). In that case, the social worker arranges the meeting. The low frequency of face-to-face meetings might be related to the COVID-19 pandemic, as generally face-to-face meetings should take place on a regular basis. However, not all experiences were positive. Some newly arrived immigrants who were a beneficiary several years ago (that is, before the COVID-19 pandemic), mentioned that their social worker only allowed contact through the PCSW reception. In one case, the reception staff would not speak any other language than the regional language, which made it more difficult for the newcomer to explain the reason for an appointment and to arrange a meeting with the social worker.

In our case studies in Brussels and Wallonia, having to go through the reception was more common than in Flanders. In some cases, the 'filtering' function of the reception staff translated in making access to the PCSW more challenging for newly arrived immigrants (see also Chapter 7), as the following quote illustrates:

> One day, I went [to the PCSW] for a meeting. The person from the reception, who gives the ticket … Well I was a bit late … Yes I was three minutes late or something like that. This person says that I have to come back the day after. So I was angry, I left. The day after, I came back. The man told me to wait. I waited until noon, until the afternoon and nothing! So I was late by three minutes and they told me to come back the day after. I come back the day after, all afternoon and [they say] busy, busy, busy! That's it […]. So for him three minutes but for me, I have to wait all the afternoon. (Wallonia, B, beneficiary, 21/10/2021)

This beneficiary experienced a high administrative burden with regard to the use of PCSW services, more specifically high psychological costs in the sense of 'stresses of dealing with administrative processes' (Moynihan *et al.*, 2014, p. 46). In general, many respondents in Brussels (and also to a lesser extent in Wallonia) faced issues when trying to get in contact with the PCSW or the social worker, which could have a discouraging effect as a result.

To start with the case studies in Brussels, social workers were in the majority of cases deemed hard or even impossible to reach. The respondents had to go through the reception instead of being able to contact their social worker directly (in case they tried, the social worker would not answer the phone), but were not welcomed at the reception. Many did not have any 'live' meetings for almost a year. This physical inaccessibility of the social workers and the unavailability on the phone are put forward by the majority of the respondents from Brussels as determining factors impeding their access to the PCSW.

> It's just that when you need to get in touch with them, I don't know if you know, but it's hard to reach them, actually, on the phone. You have to phone a thousand times so that, yeah, you get someone. (Brussels, E, beneficiary, 11/03/2021)

As mentioned before, the lockdown related to the COVID-19 pandemic has increased the barriers between the beneficiaries and the social workers, but when asked how it was before that, the respondents mostly replied that it was already very hard to get an appointment on the phone and that they had to go to the PCSW many times before getting to talk with their social assistant. Many episodes of misunderstanding at the reception desk arose:

> [W]hen I arrived [at the reception], I couldn't pronounce the lady's name, so the person I met at the reception desk was a little bit, I don't know, maybe the person got up on the wrong foot, so the person didn't know who I was talking about, who I was… And since I had never seen the person, I couldn't describe. (Brussels, G, beneficiary, 08/02/2022)

The lack of reachability is perceived by some of the respondents as a lack of respect for the beneficiary and/or a lack of willingness to open the access to their rights. Moreover, their struggle to receive support impacts the interpretation of rights as favours, what in turn can influence non-take-up of social rights (see also Chapter 11), even knowing that they could ask for it:

> Frankly, [at first] I didn't ask, because I didn't know. But on the one hand, because it's okay and on the other hand because I thought, when I was already in training I didn't know if I had the right to ask again. (Brussels, G, beneficiary, 08/02/2022)

In Wallonia, then, the data from the fieldwork suggest a variation in situations regarding the reachability of social workers. While many newly arrived immigrants describe the contact with their social worker as relatively easy, with a good responsivity of the social worker, some experienced difficulties in maintaining contact. For some respondents, the difficulty was caused by the type of the medium that was used by the social worker:

> After that, I called for a signature. I called three times but Madame [the social worker] did not [answer] […] No [she would just use] emails. Personally, I can't use emails because French is difficult for me. I am a foreigner. So talking face-to-face, for me, is easier. (Wallonia, B, beneficiary, 21/10/2021)

Also, in Wallonia a difference is regularly made between 'small' PCSWs where the contact with the social workers is experienced as relatively easy and the PCSWs of large cities where social workers appear less responsive and more difficult to meet in person. Some respondents were critical about social workers who would not actively try to maintain contact with them (by regularly calling to check up on them) and who would merely answer the newly arrived immigrants' questions. Here, too, we see an effect of the COVID-19 pandemic and of the related lockdown measures in the reachability of PCSW's services, as for some newly arrived immigrants meeting with social workers were cancelled and moved online or by phone. This represented an additional barrier for newly arrived immigrants who are not native nor at ease with the regional language.

In general, the availability of the social worker and the reception conditions at the front desk have a stronger influence on the accessibility of welfare services for our respondents than potential 'material' difficulties of access, such as the distance of the PCSW and the means of transport to get there. Especially in Brussels and Wallonia many beneficiaries experienced a high administrative burden (Moynihan *et al.*, 2014) when they tried to contact their PSCW or social worker, sometimes with a discouraging effect and ultimately also impacting their access to welfare services.

Language
As already observed in the precedent sections of the analysis (see Chapter 5) and also consistently mentioned in the literature, a deciding factor having a specific impact on the access of newly arrived immigrants to welfare services is language (Choi *et al.*, 2013; Heidinger, 2022; Nawyn *et al.*, 2012; Simich *et al.*, 2005). As Nawyn *et al.* (2012, p. 276) put it: 'the availability of and legal access to state resources [...] are irrelevant if immigrants cannot access those resources through an inability to communicate (directly or through an interpreter)'. The (in)ability to communicate can not only be traced back to the knowledge of common languages by *beneficiaries* and/or their access to ways to overcome language issues (such as by bringing an interpreter, the use of translation apps, or by using gestures). It is also influenced by the internal language policies of the PCSW (such as allowing social workers to speak other languages or providing formal interpreters) and the personal recourses (for example, not only the language skills, but also the motivation to deploy them) of the *social worker*.

Language issues form a determining factor in the relationship with the institution. Not understanding the language hampers first of all the access to complete information and the possibility of claiming aids by not being aware that they can be claimed. The beneficiaries we interviewed who were able and allowed by the social worker to speak a common language other than the official language of the region were usually better informed about services and benefits. Difficulties arise when beneficiaries do not speak a common language or are required by the social worker (or PCSW) to speak the official language of the PCSW's region: they often seem to struggle to understand the PCSW and its services. While a language policy consisting of the obligation to speak the official language of the PCSW's region stands for equal treatment, our data suggest it also means that certain groups of beneficiaries have less access to information than others and therefore less access to PCSW benefits and support (see also Chapter 5 on the impact of language issues). Put differently, 'formal equality does not necessarily guarantee social equality' (Koning & Banting, 2013, p. 584). To ensure proper information provision about the PCSW to all newly arrived immigrants regardless of language skills, one beneficiary that initially had trouble understanding the working of the PCSW suggested including the PCSW in the integration course, as this course is given in the immigrants' native language:

> If the integration teacher tells the people 'The PCSW does this, this and this', people can understand well. The first time [at first] I didn't understand it, really. […] Yeah, no, the first month you go to the integration school. And if in the integration school the teacher tells you what are the rules of the PCSW, what is this, … Every integration course is given in the people's mother tongue. This is not in English, [so] people can understand well. (Flanders, A, beneficiary, 01/03/2022)

Language also plays a role in the relation with the social worker – which is central in terms of trust and self-perception (see Chapter 10) – which can create misunderstanding and embarrassment: miscommunication with the social worker is common when the beneficiary and social worker do not have (or are willing to speak) a common language, leading in a few cases to conflictual situations, stress, and fear to ask for certain things. In case the beneficiary has to speak a certain language without being at ease, it thus impacts the relationship with the social worker and has an additional impact on service accessibility. Requiring a beneficiary to speak a certain language, then, can be seen by beneficiaries as an unwillingness of social workers to assist them, making it an instrument of power in the relationship and in the access to welfare benefits:

> It really went very, very bad. The social worker said 'After that, you have to come alone, you have to take care of yourself. You have to speak French.' But I said 'If I come [alone], I will not understand a word. How do you want me to come alone? And I don't know a word of French.' (Wallonia, A, beneficiary, 24/03/2022)

She [the social worker] said then that she did not understand me, but at that moment there was also someone who speaks my language and works at the PCSW. I asked if he could help us facilitate the communication. She said that was not possible and that if I wanted someone, I had to take care of it myself, and that she only wanted people who speak Dutch and not someone who speaks another language. At that moment I did not know anyone who spoke Dutch. I knew someone who spoke English and French, but she refused. (Flanders, C, beneficiary, 24/01/2022)

Several practices and strategies by both social workers and beneficiaries are deployed when it comes to overcoming language obstacles. As for the contact with the PCSW, respondents mentioned that many social workers are willing to speak a common language until their understanding of Dutch or French is at a sufficient level, as the following respondent explained:

In the beginning, in the first eight months, yes [the beneficiary and social worker spoke in English]. But now, we try to speak Dutch. And her [the social worker's] e-mails are in Dutch. [...] Because she wants me to read and to translate and to understand something. And I don't know, I hear a lot of stories from my friends about other assistants. They don't speak English, they speak only Dutch. But my assistant, she never speaks a language that I don't understand. (Flanders, C, beneficiary, 21/01/2022)

Also, some beneficiaries already gained knowledge about the PCSW before becoming a beneficiary, through looking up information online in a language the beneficiary understands and/or through information sessions in reception centres held in a common language. Another common strategy is the use of translation apps, though some information can still get lost. More sporadically mentioned is the use of (informal) interpreters. Indeed, earlier in this book it was already mentioned that there is no structural use of formal interpreters. Often help with interpretation needs to be arranged by the beneficiaries themselves, who therefore bring a family member or a friend to translate. In other cases, a local association provides an (unofficial) interpreter. However, as we have seen above, bringing someone who can help translating was not always allowed by the social worker. Moreover, the translation made by friends or local associations does not always brings clarity about services and rights. As in most cases the interpreter who was brought in was not a professional, the beneficiaries mentioned that his or her function was mostly supportive instead of providing a proper translation. In other words, while third parties make it easier to overcome the difficulties of access encountered at the outset of the newly arrived immigrants' relationship with the institution, their intervention does not always contribute to making the information clearer: according to some beneficiaries the communication is not always directed to the beneficiary and the facilitator may take certain decisions or not properly explain or share all of the information with the concerned beneficiary.

In conclusion, despite strategies such as bringing an informal interpreter or using translation apps, beneficiaries who do not speak a contact language or have to speak the official language of the PCSW's region often miss out on information about available services and rules that can then lead to non-take-up (see Chapter 11). Not all PCSWs thus seem to be prepared to receive immigrant beneficiaries who do not speak a common language and be able to ensure the same level of service delivery as for native speakers. Often the situation improves as the newly arrived immigrants learn the local language, but crucial information – such as information about rights and procedures – gets lost at the start of the relationship with the PCSW.

Staff changes
Another element that may impact the accessibility of welfare benefits are (temporary) staff changes at the PCSW that lead to files being transferred from one social worker to another. This turns out to occur quite frequently, and could have either positive or negative consequences according to the respondents. A negative consequence that was pointed out was that beneficiaries had to explain their situation over and over again. However, staff changes can also be perceived as something positive, as the following quote by a beneficiary who got a new social worker assigned every six months explains:

> If you have a negative assistant, for example, that says no to everything, it's nice to know that after a couple of months you get another assistant who is 50% positive and 50% negative. (Flanders, C, beneficiary, 20/01/2022)

This quote also makes a point on the centrality of the relation with the social worker, that is perceived by the beneficiaries to be a question of luck and that can change from one social worker to the other, without an institutional coherence on the follow-up of the beneficiaries. This is another example of how access to welfare benefits and services can be perceived as arbitrary, depending on the social worker instead of on fixed guidelines. The question of luck in relation with the social worker will be further developed in Chapter 10.

Also, one beneficiary can be assigned to several social workers spread over different services/departments. The fact of meeting different social workers is also a factor increasing confusion and misunderstanding about the functioning of the PCSW, as beneficiaries do not always fully understand who they have to contact for which aspect of their lives (one social worker for financial issues, one for studies, one for the job search) and why they present different ways of working, different attitudes, requests, and agendas.

Turnover (already briefly mentioned in Chapter 4 from the perspective of social workers) is also experienced by the beneficiaries. Many respondents explained that their social worker is said to be on sick leave or holidays very often when they try to contact the PCSW, which can bring important consequences to their lives: for example, when the Social Integration Income is cut for a certain reason, not meeting their social assistant and not being able to reach another assistant means that they will have to live without sufficient income for some time.

> When I started working I had to come every time with the pay slips, like this, they would do the calculations. […] I remember once I came with the pay slips and wait, next month, I didn't work, I had to come with the paper that said I didn't work, I didn't receive anything from last month, not now, and every time I asked to meet my assistant, there was nobody answering, the social worker she was […] absent. […] I remember, I had just lived with 50€ for three months. (Brussels, B, beneficiary, 23/09/2021)

While staff changes on the side of the PCSW have an impact on welfare accessibility for any beneficiary, possible language and/or cultural barriers might make it more complicated for newly arrived immigrants to explain their situation and build up a relationship with the new social worker if files are transferred. What is more, especially in the case of refugees – who often have to deal with damaged trust – time is needed to build up a relationship of trust with the social worker. Changing the social worker then undoes this relationship of trust and might even create a certain level of mistrust in the institution (see also Essex *et al.*, 2021).

So far we have discussed staff changes initiated by the PCSW. Several respondents mentioned, however, that it was them (or people they know) who requested to get another social worker assigned to their case due to a difficult relationship. Whereas staff changes at the PCSW were often casually announced and sometimes even happened unannounced, such requests by the side of the beneficiaries were often refused.

Administrative barriers

Finally, administrative barriers can have an impact on accessing welfare services and benefits. Many forms need to be filled out, which can be quite overwhelming, especially considering those forms are in a foreign language. Also, certain procedures that need to be followed are – as mentioned earlier – not always clear to the beneficiaries. Moreover, procedures are sometimes said to differ between municipalities:

> [when asked about specific difficulties for newcomers] The first thing is about the [need of] information, because we don't know Belgium and we don't know how things work, and it's different between cities. I was in other places and it's different how they work. So we don't know, we don't have information. (Brussels, I, beneficiary, 14/09/2021)

This leads to a combination of the three components of the administrative burden (Moynihan *et al.*, 2014): the learning costs (that is, learning about the requirements and procedures) and psychological costs (that is, the stress arising as result of these administrative requirements and procedures) as mentioned before, and also the compliance costs or 'burdens of following administrative rules and requirements' (Moynihan *et al.*, 2014, p. 46). Providing 'proof documents' in order to comply with the Individualised Social Integration Project (ISIP) they signed (often referred to as 'the contract') and thus receive a certain benefit can form a burden, for example, by not knowing exactly which documents to bring. The complexity of the procedure also makes some services more difficult to access with an important cost for the newcomer in terms of energy and time:

> First, I said that I needed a washing machine and [the social worker] told me to make a demand and to bring documents of information from two shops. [...] When I did that, they [the committee] chose the less expensive [...]. So [the social worker] tells me to go to the shop again to ask to buy the machine myself. I did not know how to do it, so I go, I explain and [the shop] gives me a document with information: price, telephone number, account number. I give this to the assistant but she tells me that it is not like that [...]. (Wallonia, C, beneficiary, 10/05/2021)

One small mistake, such as getting the paperwork wrong or missing a certain assessment appointment, can have large consequences on the newly arrived immigrants' lives, as it might lead to loss of income (while being in a situation of scarcity). As such, the level of understanding of the administrative requirements can impact to a large extent the access that beneficiaries have to certain benefits and services. How newly arrived immigrants deal with these administrative barriers will be further discussed in Chapter 10.

CONCLUSION

As seen in Chapter 1, access to welfare services encompasses various dimensions. In this chapter we focused on both access to the institution and access to the actual welfare benefits and services, taking several of those dimensions into account. It was observed that newly arrived immigrants can face various challenges in accessing the PCSW and social welfare benefits and services. As became apparent in this chapter, information, communication, and issues of understandability are central themes when assessing the accessibility of the PCSW in general and its services and benefits in particular. While beneficiaries barely addressed issues regarding the physical (in)accessibility of the PCSW, they often mentioned difficulties regarding the interactions in situ. The power relation in play between the institution, more specifically the social worker on the one hand and the beneficiary on the other, is one of the central themes of the next chapter.

In order to gain access to welfare benefits, help-seekers first need to be aware of the existence of the institution(s) responsible for providing benefits and support. Moreover, they need to learn how to reach those institutions. It turned out that in our fieldwork, many of the respondents had initially never heard of the PCSW and were referred to it by other organisations or by people from their local network. As such, they did not have any prior expectations on how the PCSW could support them. First, this shows the importance of being embedded in a social network in the host society for accessing welfare services, and second, it highlights the need for (correct) information on benefits and services by the PCSW itself. While it was not the focus of our research, our findings also raise questions on how many newly arrived immigrants eligible for social support might not reach the PCSW due to unawareness of the institution.

After having reached the PCSW, then, an important element impacting the access to welfare benefits put forward by newly arrived immigrant beneficiaries is (the quality of) the relationship and interactions with the social worker, who represents the face of the institution and acts as a gatekeeper of the access to it for the beneficiary (as studied in the previous parts in this book). While access to welfare services is the result of an interplay between multiple actors at different levels, this is not always perceived as such by the newcomer beneficiaries for several reasons. First, beneficiaries feel that they are to a large extent dependent on the discretionary power (both in terms of service delivery and information provision) of the social worker. Moreover, access to certain benefits or services are perceived to vary between PCSWs. As a consequence, the usage of benefits is felt to be strongly dependent on the social worker or PCSW, a perception that can be attributed to both differences in the knowledge of services and benefits on the beneficiaries' side and actual differences in services provided by social workers and municipalities. Newcomer beneficiaries may then experience feelings of arbitrariness regarding the provision of benefits and services. An additional difficulty for many newly arrived immigrants is their limited knowledge of the language, which also impacts the communication with the social worker and their understanding of rights and procedures concerning the access to social benefits. This can be exacerbated by internal policies imposing the beneficiaries to communicate in one of the national languages, even if they are not sufficiently able to. These difficulties can be attenuated to a certain extent by having high sociocultural and language capital. Knowing how to obtain information, speaking a common language, and/or having a social network allows for a better knowledge of rights entitlement and thus for better access to PCSW services and benefits. Even so, our findings suggest room for improvement in the degree of fit between the newcomer beneficiaries and the PCSW, especially when it comes to overcoming language obstacles.

NOTES

1. This does not necessarily mean that the majority of newly arrived immigrants are refugees, but might rather be related to the way the fieldwork was accessed. Indeed, many organisations and associations we contacted in order to connect us to possible participants work for a large part with refugees. Also, other forms of migration (being a citizen from the European Union, family reunification, regularisation, …) do not necessarily give access to social benefits. To give an idea of the migration profile of non-EU-migrants, in 2019 the main motive for obtaining a first residence permit were family reasons (45%). On respectively the second, third, and fourth places we find educational reasons (17.5%), paid activities (12%), and international protection (11.5%) (Myria: https://www.myria.be/nl/cijfers/migratie-in-belgie, accessed on 02/06/2022). Regarding the profile of beneficiaries at the PCSWs, numbers of the Federal public planning service for social integration (PPS SI) show that 13% of all beneficiaries receiving a social integration income in 2021 were refugees (PPS SI: https://stat.mi-is.be/, accessed on 13/07/2022).

2. LRIs are small collective or individual reception structures managed by the PCSWs (mandated and funded by Fedasil). Newly arrived immigrants can access them either at the end of the application for international protection in cases where there is a high probability of obtaining international protection or after obtaining the status during the period of searching for a permanent accommodation. Normally they are entitled to two months to look for accommodation, renewable up to two times. This means they have in total six months' time to find accommodation. As residents they receive support on a broad range of domains by social workers that may be working in the LRI or in general/devoted services at the concerned PCSW.

3. In the following chapters we will only focus on the beneficiaries' experiences at the 'regular' PCSW as opposed to the LRI (unless specifically stated otherwise), although it must be mentioned that the respondents did not always make a clear distinction between the two.

4. Cultural capital is defined by Lamont and Lareau (1988, p. 156) as '[i]nstitutionalised, i.e., widely shared, high status cultural signals (attitudes, preferences, formal knowledge, behaviors, goods and credentials) used for social and cultural exclusion'.

5. Social capital is defined by Bourdieu (1986, pp. 248–9) as, 'The aggregate of the actual or potential resources which are linked to possession of a durable network of more or less institutionalised relationships of mutual acquaintance and recognition – or in other words, to membership in a group – which provides each of its members with the backing of the collectively-owned capital, a "credential" which entitles them to credit, in various senses of the word.'

6. Upon arrival (or after receiving a positive answer in case of an application for international protection), immigrants entering Belgium have to register themselves in the foreign nationals register at the municipality of where they will be residing. After their registration and usually a home visit by the police (in order to ensure the given residing address is correct), they can apply for a residence permit.

7. Dial-a-bus is a bus that usually operates in sparsely populated areas with no regular public transport services and has to be booked in advance.

REFERENCES

Bourdieu, P. (1986). The forms of capital. In J. G. Richardson (Ed.), *Handbook of theory and research for the sociology of education* (pp. 241–258). Greenwood Press.

Choi, S., Davis, C., Cummings, S., Van Regenmorter, C., & Barnett, M. (2013). Understanding service needs and service utilization among older Kurdish refugees and immigrants in the USA. *International Social Work, 58*(1), 63–74.

Essex, R., Kalocsányiová, E., Rumyantseva, N., & Jameson, J. (2021). Trust amongst refugees in resettlement settings: A systematic scoping review and thematic analysis of the literature. *Journal of International Migration and Integration, 23,* 543–568.

Heidinger, E. (2022). Overcoming barriers to service access: Refugees' professional support service utilization and the impact of human and social capital. *Journal of International Migration and Integration, 24,* 271-312.

Hernandez, D., & Rossel, C. (2015). Inequality and access to social services in Latin America: Space–time constraints of child health check-ups and prenatal care in Montevideo. *Journal of Transport Geography, 44,* 24–32.

Koning, E. A., & Banting, K. G. (2013). Inequality below the surface: Reviewing immigrants' access to and utilization of five Canadian welfare programs. *Canadian Public Policy, 39*(4), 581–601.

Lamont, M., & Lareau, A. (1988). Cultural capital: Allusions, gaps and glissandos in recent theoretical developments. *Sociological Theory, 6*(2), 153–168.

Levesque, J.-F., Harris, M. F., & Russell, G. (2013). Patient-centred access to health care: Conceptualizing access at the interface of health systems and populations. *International Journal for Equity in Health, 12,* 1–10.

Lipsky, M. (1984). Bureaucratic disentitlement in social welfare programs. *Social Service Review, 58*(1), 3–27.

Ma, A., & Chi, I. (2005). Utilization and accessibility of social services for Chinese Canadians. *International Social Work, 48*(2), 148–160.

Moynihan, D., Herd, P., & Harvey, H. (2014). Administrative burden: Learning, psychological, and compliance costs in citizen-state interactions. *Journal of Public Administration Research and Theory, 25*, 43–69.

Nawyn, S. J., Gjokaj, L., Agbényiga, D. L., & Grace, B. (2012). Linguistic isolation, social capital, and immigrant belonging. *Journal of Contemporary Ethnography, 41*(3), 255–282.

Ricketts, T. C., & Goldsmith, L. J. (2005). Access in health services research: The battle of the frameworks. *Nurse Outlook 2005, 53*, 274–280.

Simich, L., Beiser, M., Stewart, M., & Mwakarimba, E. (2005). Providing social support for immigrants and refugees in Canada: Challenges and directions. *Journal of Immigrant Health, 7*(4), 259–268.

CHAPTER 10
THE NEWCOMERS' PERCEPTION OF SOCIAL ASSISTANCE PROVISION AND ITS ORGANISATION

ADRIANA COSTA SANTOS AND YOURI LOU VERTONGEN

This chapter aims to explore newly arrived immigrants' perceptions of the PCSW services they receive. Three aspects of this perception will be analysed: services, practices, and self-perception. The first part looks at the perception of the rights and services at the moment of registration at the PCSW. The second part will analyse the representations that newcomers have of the concrete practices of social workers, who are responsible for opening up rights and who embody the face of the institution being in the front line of contact with newcomer beneficiaries. This section will be analysed from the perspective of the notion of *appropriateness* (Parkhurst & Abeysinghe, 2016; Weber *et al.*, 2004) of the services provided in relation with the expectations preceding the access to them. Finally, the third part analyses the impact of the (perceived) practices of PCSWs' social workers on the beneficiaries' perception of themselves. This part will be approached from the angle of the notion of *deservingness* (Ratzmann & Sahraoui, 2021; Laenen *et al.*, 2019; Laenen, 2018), imported into street-level bureaucracy literature to analyse the conditions under which citizens are willing to share access to welfare resources. This notion appears to be a relevant analytical tool for studying the moral considerations by which social workers would determine access to social support for migrant beneficiaries (van Oorschot, 2008; van Oorschot *et al.*, 2017). The notion of deservingness was often studied from the perspective of the street-level bureaucrats. In our fieldwork, we observed that it was an important feature to analyse the interactions between the social workers and the beneficiaries, from the perception of the latter. Hence, in the present chapter we propose to examine deservingness from the perspective of the beneficiaries, namely through the discussion of the discursive processes by which the migrant beneficiaries try to give substance to this notion (Halluin-Mabillot, 2012).

To introduce the subject of perceptions, it seems important to recall, as we saw in the previous chapter, the decisive aspect of *accessibility* (Russell *et al.*, 2013) in the relationship between newly arrived immigrants and the institution. Indeed, newcomer beneficiaries' perception of the PCSW institution and social workers' practices seemed to be largely determined by the way they understand its functioning and logic. It is worth mentioning what was also established in the previous chapter: due to the lack of understanding and knowledge of the Belgian social welfare system, most of the beneficiaries we met did not seem to have precise expectations of what the PCSW could offer them a priori when they encountered the institution. The moment of registration at the PCSW, often described as a moment of struggle, stress, and complexity, inevitably impacts the development of their attitudes and perceptions of the PCSW, the evaluation of appropriateness of the services as well as of their own deservingness. In our research, we observed that this complexity to cope with the institutional requirements seems to be exacerbated in the Brussels Region's case studies, probably resulting from the size of the PCSW and the workload that is associated (discussed in Chapter 5 dedicated to the challenges of service delivery).

1.   PERCEPTION OF THE INSTITUTION AND THE SERVICES

In previous chapters, we discussed the service delivery and implementation of social policies for newcomer beneficiaries of the PCSW, from the perspective of social workers and managers. To recapitulate, in addition to the financial support granted through the social integration income, there are additional financial and social aids intended to enable 'a life in conformity with human dignity' as stated by Art. 1 of the PCSW's organic law of 1976. These aids are supposed to be individualised and tailor-made to the specific needs of the beneficiaries. As far as newcomer beneficiaries are concerned, this may include training or language learning programmes, as well as the provision of specific material and financial aids.

Following the logic of the 'active welfare state', this aid is granted in return for a 'readiness to work', which must be performed by the beneficiary (Franssen, 2006), and that is concretised in the contractualisation of the financial aid through the signature of an Individualised Social Integration Project (ISIP), as discussed in Chapter 2. This contract then determines a series of tasks and missions to be accomplished by the beneficiaries (such as following classes, registering at public employment services, and applying for vacancies) in order to keep their right to the PCSW's benefits. These services and policies are subject to interpretations and representations that are present on the beneficiaries' discourse. This is what we will analyse on the following section.

1.1. The PCSW as a provider of financial assistance and ad hoc complementary social aids

From the very first contact with the institution, the PCSW is mainly described by newcomer beneficiaries as a provider of financial support to start a new life in the host country. This financial aid function, although described by several beneficiaries as 'a minimum' (Wallonia, C, beneficiary, 21/05/2021), is considered as an important tool for economic stabilisation that should enable them, in the long run, to become emancipated and gain autonomy in the host society. Many discourses of migrant beneficiaries are based on the idea that the 'PCSW pays for [their] life' (Brussels, B, beneficiary, 23/09/2021) and they consider this aid as an opportunity to facilitate their settlement in the host country and to realise their new life project.

> I thought and I still think that the PCSW is more for financial aid. I was also literally told that if a file is opened for you at the PCSW, you are entitled to financial help. They don't give help for, say, just an address, or just looking for work or anything like that. Either you can do that independently, or the whole package is given like that. (Flanders, A, beneficiary, 01/02/2022)

Second, beneficiaries mentioned the possibility of getting ad hoc social assistance. As mentioned above, these social benefits are supposed to be individualised and thus tailor-made following specific needs of the beneficiaries. Some of our interlocutors were aware that, in addition to the integration income, which amount is legally established, they can request other types of aid, such as the reimbursement of bills not covered by the medical card, assistance with school fees, or the purchase of a computer or furniture (in addition to the legally determined installation grant).

In this sense, most part of the beneficiaries consider the PCSW support (as a financial and complementary social aid provider) as an indispensable but temporary step to their settlement in Belgium.

> PCSW helps you to the level you want, until you say it's enough. [...] They are like parents; they teach you to walk, and that feels good. PCSW does the same. When you come to Belgium, you can't do anything, and you don't know the language. They do everything for you until you know the

language well and you have a job. Then you can do what you want and for me, that's enough. (Flanders, C, beneficiary, 18/01/2022)

However, the interviews with newcomer beneficiaries show that in several cases the information on the possibility of receiving ad hoc supplementary aids primarily comes from exchanges with other PCSW social workers, other beneficiaries, or citizens, rather than from the social worker of reference. Consequently, and as already seen in previous chapters, the granting of these supplementary aids is associated with a random possibility that can be requested but that is never guaranteed. Thus, the granting of these social aids is perceived as not being based on a logic of equity between PCSW beneficiaries.

When I told her [the social worker] that I don't have furniture at home, she gave me a discount voucher, while other people told me that I would receive 1,300 euros [legal amount of the installation grant] to buy furniture. She gave me this paper, I had to go to the shop to buy on my own and then there would be a price reduction. I didn't understand so I didn't use it and returned it to the social assistant. I thought that if I take the discount card, I will lose the 1,300. (Brussels, C, beneficiary, 01/12/2021)

The access is often understood to be approved or refused without recognising an underlying logic, or the sole logic of convincing the social worker of the need for such assistance. As we will further develop in the next section, most respondents perceive this assistance as a form of 'favour', the granting of which is associated with the discretionary power of social workers, rather than an actual 'right'.

1.2. Perceiving imbalance of power

Although the function of financial aid is cited first and foremost by the newcomer beneficiaries interviewed, it should be noted that social workers also have the task of facilitating access to a series of services according to the beneficiary's 'state of need' assessed during the social enquiry. In this sense, the PCSW has in its missions to promote other aspects of integration of newcomer beneficiaries, such as further education or integration into the labour market (Degraef, 2013).

The PCSW services foresee that granting is conditional on a series of tasks (listed in the ISIP contract) to be performed by the beneficiary. These tasks serve to justify the aid they receive, but also to encourage beneficiaries' emancipation, to 'activate' them (Duhant, 2021:8-12). The beneficiary is thus responsible for regularly presenting to the social worker proofs of the fulfilment of these tasks. However, while some of the recent reports and literature indicate that individualised contracts are well received by newcomer beneficiaries because they allow individualisation of support (see, for example, Caldarini, 2018), many of the newcomer beneficiaries we met during our research reported that they were not able to understand the content of the contracts they were led to sign, barely remembering what was mentioned in the contract, as the following interview excerpt shows:

> I don't remember anything about it [the contract] because I couldn't speak the language. She [the social worker] said what I had to sign. I asked what it was that I was signing. She said [...] that my Dutch was not so good [enough] so I would not understand. I believed them and said 'Ok' and I sign. (Flanders, C, beneficiary, 18/01/2022)

Moreover, many of the beneficiaries interviewed reported that they did not perceive either the 'negotiated' or individualised aspect of these contracts. According to them, the contract has been drafted by the social worker and the beneficiary simply must sign it:

> Yes, this is mandatory [to sign the contract]. Because the PCSW's income is for the integration. [...] Between us and the PCSW it is legal. (Wallonia, I, beneficiary, 04/05/2021)

In other words, while these contracts are presented in official policy by the social workers as having been negotiated and agreed with the newcomer beneficiaries, for most of them, the content of these contracts appeared to be somewhat standardised or imposed by the social worker, as an obligation in order to obtain the financial aid. The newcomer beneficiaries' perception of these contracts and its content as not being in a negotiated form reflects the imbalance of power between the beneficiaries and the social workers (Gustafsson, 2013). As observed in related literature, this perception of power dynamics requires the beneficiary to anticipate the social workers' expectations over him or her in return for the support received (Van Parys & Struyven, 2018; Van Parys, 2016; Nothdurfter, 2016). This perception of the social workers' practice will be further developed in the following section.

2.   THE PERCEPTION OF SOCIAL WORKERS' PRACTICES

Two elements appear to be central to the analysis of the perception of social workers' practices. First, we observed the centrality of the relationship with the social worker and the way it contributes to perceiving the exercise of discretionary power. Second, we analysed the perception of social activation practices as a form of control, in tension with the goal of autonomy and emancipation. These two elements will allow us to focus on the 'appropriateness' of service delivery, as it is narrated by newcomers.

2.1.   Perceiving discretion: the central role of social workers

As earlier described in the present book (see Chapter 8), the social workers have a determining role in limiting the response to the request made by the beneficiaries or, on the contrary, will seek to identify additional needs favouring their integration. This discretionary power can be manifested in the way the social worker will decide to strictly apply the rules for granting assistance and thus refuse to grant it when the conditions for obtaining it are not fully met, or on the contrary, to interpret these rules in a broader way thus favouring the allocation. Discretion, from the point of view of the social workers, seems to be a way of overcoming the bureaucratic aspects of social work and engaging in forms of social justice – here specifically addressed to newcomer beneficiaries, whose deservingness is assessed in different forms. In the fieldwork with beneficiaries, many respondents testified that the allocation of the ad hoc social aids – arising from discretion and detection needs – was perceived as random and inequitable ('some received this, while others received that'). When they compare with one another the aids they receive and see that it is differentiated, they conclude that there is no underlying logic in the granting of these aids. From their interpretations of granting and refusal, we observed the centrality of the social worker in the perception that the newcomer beneficiaries have of the institution and its practices. Thus, discretion is mostly perceived as a matter of the 'kindness', the competence, or the personality of the social worker.

> The social worker said no, you can't have it now. I said: 'But everybody has it and I don't!' He said no […] He is not nice, he is not nice. Maybe it is not only with me. (Wallonia, O, beneficiary, 05/06/2021)

In other words, while social workers consider the tailor-made and individually adapted aspect of ad hoc complementary social assistance to be a matter of equity, the beneficiaries, for their part, often perceive it as a marker of a form of inequality of treatment, of which the social worker, rather than the institution itself, would be primarily responsible.

The perception of the attribution of these complementary social aids as not being part of any underlying logic tends to consider them as a 'favour', as previously mentioned, rather than as a right. Thus, from the point of view of the beneficiary confronted with discretionary practices, obtaining social assistance appears to be arbitrary, dependent on the 'goodwill' of the social worker. Conversely, refusing to grant assistance will be perceived as a lack of goodwill, competence, or in some cases justified by an overload linked to the latter's workload.

> At a certain moment we had a big argument. She [the social worker] said she didn't understand me [...] But at that moment there was someone who spoke my language and who works at the PCSW. I asked if [that person] could not help us to make the communication easier. She said that this was not possible and that if I wanted someone, I would have to arrange this myself, and that she only wanted people who spoke Dutch and not someone who spoke another language. At that time, I did not know anyone who spoke Dutch. [...] She did not want to use the person at the PCSW who could speak the language, nor someone who could speak another language except Dutch. (Flanders, C, beneficiary, 24/01/2022)

> My wife [who is ill and has since passed away] just asked [her social worker] to intercede to stop [home delivery of meals] because she was no longer able to pay for it. And the assistant said 'No, no I can't, you have to do it yourself.' So, my wife was stressed. [...] Most of the time, the PCSW works very well, but sometimes there are malicious people [social worker] who may not play their role and do harm. (Wallonia, M, beneficiary, 27/08/2021)

> I told her [the social worker] for example that I had a meeting with the lawyer on Thursday and asked if she [the social worker] could pay for the train ticket. She answered that I had to request a train ticket two days in advance, and I asked on Monday. On Tuesday and Wednesday, I sent more e-mails. I didn't get anything until Friday. It was always like that with her. You had to call her ten times, send ten e-mails to her and the interpreter, but you don't get an answer. Then she would get mad with me and say she didn't have time. (Flanders, D, beneficiary, 01/03/2022)

In the views of most part of the interviewed newcomers, dealing with a 'good' social worker will allow them to receive help adapted to their needs, whereas a 'bad' social worker will only be able to provide help of less quality and therefore less adapted to the recipient's needs.

> My assistant has 73 people in her files and I feel I am the only one with her. 73 people and I feel, she is free, she has time for me. She can manage 73 people and I didn't feel it. If I sent her an email, she didn't tell me, 'I'm busy. No, I have other people that I need to take care of.' No. I feel like I'm the only person and I have only this assistant. She did a great job. (Flanders, C, beneficiary, 21/01/2022)

Moreover, we find that dealing with different agents (for example, in the context of support distributed among different services) reinforces the idea that differences in the treatment of beneficiaries are due to moral considerations (Kobelinski, 2012), to the personality of the social worker or to his or her perceived level of investment in the support of the beneficiary.

> [Can you tell me why you prefer dealing with S. – a social worker from an NGO – rather than with V. – the PCSW social worker?]
> I don't know exactly but she [S.] is a nice person. She listens and she is a woman too. When you tell her about something, she does everything she can to do it. So, when you have this, you don't think about something else because your troubles are already dealt with. (Wallonia, B, beneficiary, 08/07/2021)

The feeling of injustice and arbitrariness seems to be amplified in these cases, consequently reinforcing the perception of the centrality of the role of the social worker's personality, competence, and 'goodwill' in the process of obtaining the social assistance.

> [Does the PCSW pay for your education?]
> […] Yes, everything. The school sends the bills straight to the PCSW. They also pay [for the public transports]. In [previous municipality] not. If I had to go to [another city] for example, I had to pay for that myself as well. I paid for everything. They only paid when I had to go to the lawyer or to interviews [for the asylum procedure], otherwise they didn't. (Flanders, D, beneficiary, 01/03/2022)

> I would say that this is a chance to have such a good [social worker] because sometimes, you can have someone who know all the regulations about refugees and she does not make your task harder whereas sometimes, you get new people who make your task harder. (Wallonia, C, beneficiary, 10/05/2021)

In other words, the discretional functioning of the PCSW institution is perceived through the relationship that newcomer beneficiaries forge with the social worker(s) in charge of their support. As the distinction between the rule and the discretionary power of the social worker appears blurred in the minds of the beneficiaries, the discretionary power, when it is perceived, appears therefore to represent arbitrariness. This representation of the relationship will also have an impact on the perception of the procedures and tasks in terms of practices of control.

2.2. Perceiving control

In addition to preparing the content of the ISIP contract, the social workers have the function of monitoring or controlling the proper execution of the project by the beneficiary. If necessary, social workers oversee suggesting sanctions to the beneficiaries who do not follow the terms and conditions set out (see Van Parys, 2016; Nothdurfter, 2016; Ellis, 2007). The tasks reported in the ISIP recover several aims: settling – newcomers being often asked to get their administrative situation settled as a first step (for example, having a health insurance and a bank account); integrating (for example, following language courses, enrolling in the PES or applying for vacancies); proving eligibility (for example, bringing proof of not having another income); or proving compliance with the duties (for example, bringing receipts and certificates). They are mainly perceived by the social workers as involving the beneficiaries in the grip of their own autonomous future rather than confining them to a passive role of being assisted. However, many newcomer beneficiaries admit feeling overwhelmed by administrative requirements and other responsibilities, especially upon arrival. As mentioned above, they often declare to sign all the documents presented to them, without knowing or understanding their content due to a lack of language knowledge. Our fieldwork reported to the fact that, from their point of view, some tasks are often puzzling and perceived as an unnecessary administrative burden.

> [When asked to estimate the amount of time spent per week complying with PCSW's requirements]
> Every day. The PCSW, the municipality, for me I have a lot of appointments. Every day, every day. I have many, many, many appointments. Now, I write here in the agenda. Just yesterday, we have what? We have the 6th, the 7th, the 17th, the 11/05, the 22/05, the 31/05, the 27th, all these are appointments. (Wallonia, I, beneficiary, 04/05/2021)

Also, according to some beneficiaries, the way the procedure is organised, linked to the number of appointments for bringing proof, or even the inadequacy of the schedule, can represent an obstacle in their quest for autonomy instead of a step towards it, as the following excerpts illustrate:

> Before I left [a PCSW in Wallonia] I talked with the assistant. I said 'I'm going to go to the University of Brussels […] in order to start studying law, so I want to finish with the assistant with the CPAS of [municipality in Wallonia].' He made a lot of obstacles for me, because […] when there is a student who benefits from a social income from the PCSW, you can't change the PCSW. […] He [the PCSW] made some […] obstacles for me, so I couldn't study well, the way I planned to do. (Brussels, E, beneficiary, 27/09/2021)

> The [the service for socio-professional integration] was a very good help in very difficult moments. But every time I had mandatory appointments, I had to go to the school first to ask for an exemption. It was hard because then I had to catch up on classes. Then when I arrived at the PCSW, 10 minutes before the appointment [the social worker] cancelled, so I missed the appointment and the classes. The objective was to help me to do my training, but I was prevented from doing it because I always had to come [to appointments]. (Brussels, G, beneficiary, 11/02/2022)

Moreover, we observed that the demand of 'proving compliance', which aims to get the beneficiaries to prove that they are effectively cooperating with the institution, 'wisely' spending the money, or proactively seeking a job, are perceived by some of the beneficiaries as *control* tools. These kinds of tasks are then associated to a projected 'lack of trust' that is also present in the description of the questions beneficiaries are subjected to by the social worker. The following extracts are an example of this negative feeling of being mistrusted:

> In order for them to give you your money, the PCSW asks, when the year is over, that for any purchase I have to make I keep all the store tickets. […] The tickets, all of them, every year, every expense. […] You have to keep everything! […] They [the PCSW] look at everything […] how this money you spend. The house, the electricity, the water, everything, everything, your expenses, in the store, your clothes, your shoes,… […] That's why when you are dependent you have nothing, you have to do all that … but when you work, it's over. (Brussels, G, beneficiary, 05/02/2022)

I heard from many Syrian people in my previous city the same about this assistant. She needed to know everything and asked us everything. 'Are you going there? Why? With whom? What will you be doing?' Like she didn't trust us. (Flanders, D, beneficiary, 06/03/2022)

It is to note that in our fieldwork, control practices are first understood by beneficiaries as a way of ensuring that the community's money is distributed wisely. Nevertheless, they often interpret social workers' attitudes through moral considerations. Controlling is therefore interpreted as not trusting that one will make a 'good' use of the received money.

[Is there anything you think is missing in the support of the PCSW?] Having trust. Not questioning everything. Not everyone is the same, maybe there are those who take advantage, but there are also those who are honest. [You have the feeling that they didn't trust you?] Yes. [...] She [the social worker] literally said that. She said she didn't believe anything about my story. (Flanders, A, beneficiary, 01/02/2022)

Some newly arrived immigrant beneficiaries describe these moments of control as 'harsh' and 'lacking a human approach', or as going against the perspective of empowerment of the PCSW beneficiaries.

When they need us to do a paper, to do something, to do a document, they don't ask. They stop the money, and so we need to go to the PCSW, we ask 'Why did you stop the money?' – 'Because ah, you have to make this paper of request of commune, make this paper ...' [...] Why don't you ask? How do I know you need that paper? [...] It was really something that was very mean. (Brussels, I, beneficiary, 14/09/2021)

Accordingly, these controls (and potential sanctions) are sometimes then perceived as a marker of a form of 'infantilisation' or even 'humiliation'. Some respondents mention a negative impact of the PCSWs' practices on their self-esteem and independence. While the most part of newcomer beneficiaries understand these controls as being legitimate in relation to the financial aid they receive, some of them oppose the notion of control to the need for social support. The social activation practices that, as presented in the previous chapters, are considered by social workers as a way of empowering beneficiaries, are therefore re-interpreted by beneficiaries who do not feel 'activated' but rather 'controlled'. Therefore, our interlocutors are aware of the conditionality of the rights, which reflects on demonstrating to the social worker their willingness to be active. This perception tends to evolve with the beneficiaries' experience within the PCSW, for instance when meeting different interlocutors with different missions that can be reflected in the level of 'help' and 'control' they exert.

2.3. General satisfaction and appropriateness

These elements of analysis on the immigrant beneficiaries' perceptions of services and practices of the PCSW help us to understand how they evaluate the institution and whether they find it is adapted or not to their needs. This general satisfaction can be understood through the concept of 'appropriateness', which postulates that the accessibility of a service is linked to the adaptability of the service to the needs expressed by the beneficiaries (see, for example, Parkhurst & Abeysinghe, 2016; Weber *et al.*, 2004). In other words, to be perceived as accessible, the service must be able to meet a specific need of the beneficiary.

First, in general, the impact of the PCSW in the lives of the beneficiaries is first and foremost described as positive – 'it is important to be thankful, as they [the PCSW] provide us the possibility of paying for living' (Brussels, G, beneficiary, 08/02/2022) – and it is considered necessary in order to be able to start a decent life in Belgium.

> It is difficult to come to Belgium without money. Without the PCSW I wouldn't have managed. A friend of mine did not get money and food from the PCSW [...]. We don't have family here [in Belgium], we don't have anyone. [...] They [the PCSW's] provide help for everything, until people say they don't need the help anymore. (Flanders, D, beneficiary, 25/02/2022)

Second, we have seen that, for many newcomer beneficiaries, being supported by the PCSW was seen as an essential but also temporary step in their integration process. It seems, therefore, that the ultimate goal of being supported by the PCSW is, in the long run, not to have to depend on it anymore. From this point of view, the appropriateness of the PCSW support is assessed by the beneficiaries based on the possibility of becoming emancipated in the long term and being able to manage on their own. This element is justified in the discourse of the beneficiaries by several arguments such as wanting 'to live independently and not being dependent on assistance' (Brussels, G, beneficiary, 02/02/2022). Moreover, some of them perceive the goal of emancipation as not having to comply with PCSW conditions, mainly due to the assumption that the administrative burden is an obstacle rather than a tool to achieve this goal, or at least a waste of time. For example, some beneficiaries mentioned the annual obligation to register in employment agencies, even if they are not looking for a job, or the demand to bring several applications as proofs, even if the jobs were not particularly relevant to the beneficiaries' will and skills, or the need to bring empty payslips to prove that they did not work that month.

> For example, if I want to go on holidays, the PCSW condition is that I have to be back within 28 days. If I stay longer, they will reduce my living wage or support. [...] This was not mentioned in the contract. [...] This condition is too difficult. First, I would go to Vietnam to visit my family, that is far. And second, now with COVID, if I go to Vietnam I have to go in quarantine. (Flanders, A, beneficiary, 28/02/2022)

This allows us to understand that a double point of view is expressed among the newly arrived immigrant beneficiaries. On the one hand, the PCSW assistance is perceived as an important help, an opportunity to obtain financial support and to free oneself from the material distress when they start to settle into the host society. In this sense, the assistance of the PCSW is associated with a temporary springboard towards effective autonomy in the host country. Yet, on the other hand, the fact that this aid is organised with a heavy counterpart seems in some cases to be perceived as an obstacle to the possibility of really asserting oneself as autonomous. However, when some newcomers express their will of 'independence' or 'autonomy', it was also much larger than the only fact of not being submitted to the PCSW administrative requirement. It was also about being able to work in order to live a decent life, having their own house, or being able to provide for their family.

> For example [the PCSW] gives 900 euros. I don't need 900 euros to stay at home. Give me 1,200 euros and I do something [...] in Belgium. It's better. [...] I don't want to take 900 euros to do nothing. I prefer to take 1,000 euros and [work]. [...] I don't want to stay at home. When we work, it is better for us. (Wallonia, O, beneficiary, 05/06/2021)

Third, as observed in the precedent section, the overlap between the social workers' functions of 'help' and 'control' is also put forward by many beneficiaries in their perception of the 'appropriateness' of the services. The discourse in the following quote from Brussels illustrates to what extent the social worker's function of control overlaps with the function of 'help' and counselling.

> [The social worker] collects what we want the money for, what we do, what
> we had built [...] and organises the papers to follow what we do, but ... not
> accompanying, not noticing efforts, but just controlling. They look at what
> we do, let's say, just have an eye on what we're doing: 'Ok we got this, you
> have already finished this, you must do this now, this is the time to study
> another level, or you must find a job, just follow this.' But not really ask
> what we want to do. (Brussels, B, beneficiary, 01/12/2021)

Let us observe the case of M. (Brussels, F, beneficiary, 31/03/2021) who
compares the services received by two different PCSWs. He states that the first
PCSW he was registered in (Brussels) was, in his opinion, not appropriate. He
had just obtained his refugee status after a three-years-long asylum procedure.
Tired by this long procedure, he felt that the tasks to be accomplished were too
demanding to be understood and done properly ('you have to take language
courses and training and a job, and to come once a month') and without him
feeling free to take his time to have a plan before starting to accomplish it.
He says that he had to go quickly even if he did not know 'where', or he would
risk losing financial aid. When M. moved to a new PCSW (Wallonia), he had
the impression that the social worker was content to give him money, without
looking at what he was doing with it and without accompanying him daily.
In both cases, what emerges from his assessment of the service is the fact
that the approach is not collaborative: the accompaniment is either heavy
by controlling the tasks; or lacking supervision or counselling. His needs
do not seem to be considered in the two approaches favoured by the social
workers who supervise his case.

Moreover, the difficulty of expressing needs, the controls, and the absence
of negotiation about one's project, can be experienced as a stress factor linked
to the fear of missing a task, leading to a loss of income.

> There was a strange thing, a constant worry. When you get the school
> results, you have to send them to the PCSW after the first term [...] but
> the thing, maybe they don't know, is that the university is always late.
> They start sending emails that are heavy, it's like they accuse you, it's like
> they push to a fear on you, if you don't do that, you're going to have these
> consequences. (Brussels, G, beneficiary, 02/02/2022)

Finally, the perception of whether or not the service is appropriate seems to
be strongly linked to the knowledge and understanding of the PCSW system.
For example, some beneficiaries were sanctioned for unknowingly violating
one of the stipulations of their contract (for example, by failing to bring in

a study certificate) and thus found out what they were allowed or not to do after they had violated one of the stipulations of the contract and received a warning. Some of our interlocutors explain in this sense that a person coming from abroad and not knowing the codes and functioning of the host society needs more information to be oriented correctly.

> Sometimes the judgment is either that 'Why don't you know that you have to do that?', and other times the judgement is 'Of course they don't know because they come from another place.' So, it depends, it is double judgement. (Brussels, J, beneficiary, 29/09/2021)

They then mention some specific needs of newcomers in terms of orientation and information that could be understood by them, considering that '[e] verything has to be relearned and they can't assume that we already know it' (Brussels, H, beneficiary, 15/09/2021). Some of our interlocutors emphasise the need for a specific approach that takes into account the migration pathways of the beneficiaries, as opposed to a generalist approach that would treat all beneficiaries in the same way, which would be tantamount to discriminating against those beneficiaries who are less knowledgeable about the system, their rights, and the practices of the institution. In the coming section, we observe how being a beneficiary of the PCSW is perceived by newcomers, and how this perception is anchored in their interactions with the institution.

3.   SELF-PERCEPTION OF NEWCOMER BENEFICIARIES

As introduced in the precedent sections, we assume that self-perception of newcomers is constructed and negotiated in the relationship they establish with the institution, through the central figure of the social workers. Following Martiniello and Rea's 'migratory careers' framework, 'success and the failure of a career must be analysed by taking into account the values and norms of the host society and of the society of origin' (2014, p. 1085). Hence, during settlement, the newcomers' representations of success and failure vary between *here* and *there*, but also they evolve and are negotiated over time and space, along with identity changing, in 'a simultaneous learning process of a practice and of a change in social identity' (p. 1083). In our fieldwork, we observed two main elements of newly arrived immigrants' self-perception in their experience within the PCSW: the impact of downward social mobility (Franz, 2003), in terms of comparison between the social status in Belgium and the one preceding migration, and the discursive construction of 'deservingness' of social benefits.

3.1. Perceived social status: a perception of downgrading

First, in the discourse of our interlocutors, we find that being a beneficiary of the PCSW and being dependent on financial aid can be perceived as a form of downward social mobility compared to their perceived social status preceding migration:

> [when you are receiving social assistance] you always feel that you are nothing, that you are a loser [...] Because I could not do anything. I could not work, just go to school. [...] At this time, I was thinking that I already had an education, I already had a profession, but I was not speaking the language and the language is a very difficult obstacle. (Wallonia, B, beneficiary, 12/07/2021).

The negative consequence upon newcomers' self-perception can also be impacted by the newcomers' experience of social assistance in their country of origin. Later in the same interview, the newcomer quoted above compares her situation as a PCSW beneficiary with a form of disability:

> [Do you mean that when you received money from the PCSW for the first time, you felt a bit uncomfortable – odd – is that it?]
> Yes, [I felt] like a disabled person because the State was helping me. My mother is disabled in [my country of origin] and I know that at this point she cannot work. But before she worked nevertheless [...]. And so, for me, I don't agree with giving money just like that. (Wallonia, B, beneficiary, 12/07/2021)

Then, the awareness of downward mobility seems to be even more present as the financial aid from the PCSW is considered as a strict minimum that barely allows them to meet their essential needs.

> It is very difficult. Frankly, very difficult. [...] Because you must pay everything. For example, the rent, the heating oil, the electricity. Also, the water. And the prices are going up. And the amount is too small for all this, this is difficult [...]. But we must get along with it you see. (Wallonia, K, beneficiary, 21/09/2021)

> It is difficult to say because ... this income ... you can live with it. You cannot say it is not enough but ... just the minimum. You can cover the minimum yes. [...] The problem is that I am alone, and I have a problem to reunify my family. [...] Sometimes I have to send something to my

family too so that is why I can say that [the social integration income] is not enough yes. (Wallonia, C, beneficiary, 21/05/2021)

In these cases, we find the feeling of being 'doubly downgraded': having a low socio-economic status, but also the status of being assisted or dependent on a state income. In addition, in our fieldwork this new (low) social status appears to create new difficulties, such as perceived discrimination in the housing market and problems to find adequate housing, as the following interview extracts attest:

The most difficult thing at the PCSW is when you get your positive [decision on the application for international protection] and you need to look for a house. [...] If you call and say you're still with the PCSW, they don't want you. If you don't know anyone and do not receive help from the social worker, it is very difficult. [...] The renting prices go up like crazy, also the issue of foreign-language speakers, not having a job yet [...] But even when you work, foreign-language speakers do not get there. (Flanders, D, beneficiary, 06/03/2022)

I found [an advertisement for] an apartment, when I was in the PCSW of [municipality]. And I went to the appointment, and I say 'Hello, I come for the apartment' and he [the owner of the apartment] said 'What is your salary?' And I say, 'I am at PCSW.' He said 'Excuse me' and I cannot enter the apartment to see. I said 'What!?' He said 'No.' So I went to the appointment, and I did not enter. I stayed outside. (Brussels, A, beneficiary, 11/03/2021)

Moreover, being subjected to control and sanction mechanisms that are often interpreted as a 'lack of trust' and representing the discretionary power of the social worker as a form of 'goodwill', may lead to the beneficiary's self-perception as devalued on the social scale. Nì Raghallaigh (2013, p. 96) studied the feeling of being mistrusted by caregivers in aid interactions in the migratory path. According to the author, this specific context needed to be seen as an 'interaction' between individuals' experiences in their home country and the difficulties on integrating within an unsettled context. What seems to be at stake in our fieldwork, is that the beneficiary's ability to carry out a social integration project is questioned and the tasks he/she has to carry out may be perceived as infantilising or paternalistic.

And then I came [to the PCSW] and said 'I'm still waiting for my money, but it hasn't arrived.' And I remember, there was a woman who said to me 'But it's not your money, it's your help! Ok? Say thank you!' Thank you, but if you really want to help me, help me to get out of the PCSW! (Brussels, G, beneficiary, 11/02/2022)

When I pay for something, the PCSW knows. I set an example for my friend. He likes alcohol. So, he bought once […] some alcohol and after the PCSW […] took an appointment with him [and] said 'Why did you buy the alcohol? We gave you the money to eat, and just to eat.' He asked how they knew about it. They [the PSCW] said 'You paid with your bank card, […] we see everywhere.' And that there is no private with the bank cards, when it is at the PCSW, there is no private. When you pay for something outside, they see. […] I don't like that. Yes, because you give me 300 euros, ok, I agree with that, I'm happy. But leave me alone […] Let me [do what I want to do with the money]. […] They [the PCSW] say no. […] I don't like it. (Wallonia, O, beneficiary, 05/06/2021)

The lack of respect is when you go to the PCSW and they put you in a stereotype, they think that these people who are at the PCSW, who are migrants, that they come to pick money and do nothing, they are going to say to themselves that they know your profile […] they put you in this profile […] I fought to get where I am, not to be in this profile. I studied to find this respect; I did two years of qualification training, I presented my final project, I worked well. (Brussels, C, beneficiary, 17/09/2021)

This element is probably not specific to newcomers' beneficiaries (see, for example, Engbersen, 1999). However, what can be indeed specific is the fact that the stigma and the paternalistic discourses around the 'social excluded' that are common to PCSW's beneficiaries are mixed in our fieldwork with the stigma related to migration. To this social status, which is generally negatively perceived by the newly arrived immigrant beneficiaries, is added the status of a foreigner, unfamiliar to socio-cultural codes of the host society.

Authors have shown that this perception of oneself as socially devalued is reinforced by interactions within the institution and by the stereotypes about migrants that they perceive in the 'host society mood' (Al-Rasheed, 1992, p. 546; Cohon, 1981, p. 256), what is to say their own view of the public opinion about migrants' reception in the host society. In this regard, Valenta assumed that 'the interactions, relations and networks that immigrants engage in may be a source of integration, self-confirming, social anchorage and emotional support [but also] sources of ethnic misrecognition and discrediting' (2008, p. 215). This leads us to analyse another relevant feature of social interactions during resettlement: the impact they might have on social recognition and prestige.

> They [the people in a previous city] think we are different from them. They think we come here to receive money, but that is not true. I come from a rich family in Syria. I never took the bus, we always took the car, I went to a private school, we had a cleaning lady. We don't come here to receive money. Before the war I could go by myself to Europe, because my dad had a lot of money. It's really dangerous to come here and it costs a lot of money. I don't come here to go to the PCSW and receive money. We couldn't stay in Syria because of the war. (Flanders, D, beneficiary, 01/03/2022)

As the quote illustrates, while the tendency of feeling socially devalued appears in most of our respondents' discourses, it is even more present among the individuals whose migration path has led to an important economic downgrading. It is then to note that in the case of immigrants with significant socio-cultural capital, they tended to particularly underline the limits of the PCSW's services and the institution's inability to offer them a project that would allow them to recover from this downgrading.

> You know my status is very special. Because I am in architecture, I was a professor in university [in the country of origin]. It is very difficult for the PCSW to find you a training or a job, you know. It's very complicated for them. If I was the … the ordinary people, they would have found this very easily already. If I was an ordinary man, if I had no degree, if I had no document to work, it is easy for them to find something … I don't know like cook, like … I don't know. But now I don't know, my case is a little bit more complicated. (Wallonia, K, beneficiary, 21/09/2021)

In line with earlier findings in the German context of Brücker *et al.*, (2021), this interview excerpt shows the difficulties encountered by some of our interlocutors with degrees in their country of origin when they are only offered jobs that fall short of the skills they acquired during their studies or their professional situation prior to immigration (see also Dustmann & Frattini, 2013). What seems to be problematic in their case is to get out of a downward spiral of social mobility through diploma equivalences and training before entering the labour market. As observed on Chapter 6 of the present book, the fact that vocational trainings seem to be privileged over longer university studies may induce newcomers to take functions that do not correspond to their precedent skills and studies. Therefore, we ascertained that some longer educated newcomers are only offered jobs and functions that fall short of their real skills, what seems to contribute to their negative perception of their status as welfare beneficiaries.

Finally, the access to labour market presents a tension between the PCSW's mission and the willingness of newcomer beneficiaries to find an employment situation that is adapted to their skills and former socio-economic status. According to the goal of 'social activation', most of immigrant beneficiaries interviewed emphasise gratefulness of having a financial income while they are trying to overcome the need for training and qualifications to enter the labour market. Nevertheless, some newcomers with lower educational background stated their desire to be quickly integrated into a socio-professional pathway through Art. 60 or PCSW's devoted services and regret that they are held back by the need imposed by the institution to learn the language first. At the same time, some others, especially those with a strong socio-cultural capital that allows them to understand the system and the rights associated with it, mentioned the need to go to the PCSW with a well-reasoned plan for the future, to avoid being pushed in a direction they do not want to go, for example, to do 'manual labour jobs' or a professionalising training focused on working immediately instead of engaging in longer studies to recover from a partial recognition of diplomas. In other words, 'You have to have plans because if you don't have plans, the PCSW will push you to work' (Flanders, C, beneficiary, 07/01/2022).

3.2. Negotiating deservingness

In the precedent sections, we observed that the perception of the discretionary practice as 'arbitrariness' appeared to question their own 'deservingness' of social benefits. During the interactions with social workers, newcomer beneficiaries are aware they must demonstrate that they deserve the received support by complying with the institution's rules and by showing a proactive attitude. From the point of view of the institution, this can be a normal issue of 'rights and duties'. But newcomer beneficiaries also develop their own understanding of deservingness. Such understanding is articulated around two main types of discourses.

First, we find an argument that consists in demonstrating that one is indeed deserving by insisting on the 'springboard' function of the social assistance received. Accordingly, financial support is thus necessary to allow them to rely on a sustainable integration in the labour market in order to eventually be able to contribute and reinvest in the host society. In other words, the idea is that newcomer beneficiaries see the PCSW services they receive as a transitional period allowing them to manage settlement in the host society.

I have eaten the Belgians' money, then I will be able to contribute. (Brussels, E, beneficiary, 28/09/2021)

> The PCSW can help me, but they also have their conditions and I need to follow them. If I earn enough [by myself], I can live independently. That is better, because then I have more freedom. (Flanders, A, beneficiary, 28/02/2022)

From this point of view, benefiting from PCSW services is justified because it will allow them to contribute to the host society later on. The beneficiaries thus develop an argument centred on the fact that thanks to the financial aid and social guidance, they will one day be able to become independent, to integrate the labour market in a sustainable way, and therefore to no longer depend on the PCSW.

> There is always [the problem of] the language. The [Belgian] State helped me so I can have time to learn the language and one day, I will be able to contribute to the [Belgian] State to give back all it gave to me. I hope I will be able to [do it so] one day. Because at the beginning this is the PCSW and who is behind the PSCW [...]. I hope that I will find a job to pay back all they gave me. (Brussels, B, beneficiary, 01/10/2021)

Gratefulness is associated with the 'springboard' discourse. As the support of the PCSW appears to be inevitable until the beneficiaries have enough resources and knowledge of Belgian society to 'fend for themselves', they intend to prove that they will strive to become independent as soon as possible. Therefore, this vision of the PCSW as a springboard to autonomy is accompanied by an argument that migrant beneficiaries will thus be ready to contribute to society as soon as possible.

> We are very grateful for the PCSW. We come with no money, no clothing. Without the PCSW we would stay on the streets. (Flanders, D, beneficiary, 06/03/2022)

> I don't really agree that they give money like that without asking me if I can do something [in return]. [...] It doesn't bother me today if the PCWS says 'We're going to help you [...] but you have to work anyway.' I know now I'm doing something; I am working. [...] I am doing something, that we feel we are helping the [Belgian] State. You don't get money if you don't do anything. (Wallonia, B, beneficiary, 12/07/2021)

Second, beneficiaries also develop discourses and attitudes that allow them to distance themselves from actors deemed 'non-deserving'. While they try to portray themselves as active and self-sufficient, in a temporary state of dependency but eager to work, contribute, and get out of the welfare system, they point to and criticise the perceived 'laziness' of some other newcomers, as the following excerpt illustrates:

> They [the perceived 'laziness' immigrant beneficiaries] should do the same as what I did. I would say that they should go to the PCSW immediately and they should work and learn. When you get an appointment, you have to go right away. [...]. The more you do, the better it goes. Everyone will be happy for you too. If you don't listen, you will lose time. If you don't go to appointments or don't go to school, it will cause you problems. [...]. Of course, if you don't do anything, they won't help you because you're stupid. If you stay home, don't listen to anyone and weep to get money then it won't work. I hate such people. [...]. It is not good if you never listen and just sleep. (Flanders, C, beneficiary,18/01/2022)

In these discourses, the moral hierarchy between 'deserving' and 'non-deserving' coincides with the one established by the institution and the social workers. This can suggest that newcomers undertake a form of reappropriation of the stigmatising discourses against people considered as 'undeserving'. By reaffirming this hierarchy, immigrant beneficiaries distance themselves from these negatively perceived attitudes and, doing so, eventually demonstrate that they deserve the help provided by the PCSW. Similar considerations can be found in the self-judgement they develop as beneficiaries of the PCSW, hence not independent, not 'normal', or not a good example for their children, for example.

> I know that today I'm doing a training, but you can also think that this way the state helps me to learn the language and one day I'll be a normal person. (Wallonia, B, beneficiary, 12/07/2021)

> If I do like this [working and being independent from PCSW], if you have children, he will see you how to fight for your life, so they will learn from you. If I stay in the house, I will do this, cook, and I will [watch] movies, and he will grow up [learning the example] like this. But I don't want this so I have to fight and my children they will grow up the same like me. (Wallonia, B, beneficiary, 21/10/2021)

These excerpts can therefore be interpreted as a reverberation of dominant discourses as they are incorporated within the PCSW and embedded by newcomer beneficiaries. This idea echoes Dubois' (2010) argument that recipients of social benefits come to 'strategically' endorse the discourse and moral considerations defended by the institution providing social assistance in order to get into its good graces and continue to benefit from its services. This idea also echoes the work of Halliun-Mabilot (2012), although in her case it is not the state institutions providing social assistance but the non-governmental associations that support refugees in their asylum demands. The author's observations show that the associations, caught between the growing demand for efficiency in the processing of asylum applications and the state's imposition of a hierarchy between deserving and undeserving people, rely on moral considerations to construct discourses that allow them to present asylum seekers as having to receive their refugee status as a priority. They thus invite applicants to reproduce a discourse that conforms to the institution's expectations of them in order to offset, as effectively as possible, the policy of systematic suspicion developed by the institution. In our fieldwork, it is unsettled whether the dominant discourses are reappropriated as a strategy to correspond to the social workers' expectations – what we could probe, taking in account the fact that allocation of rights is often associated to 'goodwill' – or if it is simply embedded in newcomers' own representations of 'deservingness'. Yet, we can observe that representations are in any case built *in relation*, it is to say, in the present case, during the interactions between beneficiaries and the institution. Thus, we here assume that the figure of the 'deserving' beneficiary as it is reproduced both in the social workers' and beneficiaries' discourses, is in any case built, negotiated, and thus performed, considering that beneficiaries are not 'passive recipients' (Weller, 2018, p. 51). The beneficiaries may indeed share – at least in some respects – the goals defended by social workers or reproduce discourses as a strategy of compliance. This idea will be further developed in the next chapter (Chapter 11) on the strategies deployed by newcomer beneficiaries to deal with social services, which reveals some of their agency despite the power imbalance of the relationship with the institution.

CONCLUSION

This chapter aimed to analyse the perceptions developed by newcomer beneficiaries of the PCSW. Three aspects of this perception were analysed. First, the perception of the PCSW services – where the aid is seen as a very positive and essential, hopefully temporary, springboard to an emancipated future. Second, the perception of the social workers' practices – where the discretionary practices and the controls are embedded in the centrality of the relation with the social worker and impacts their understanding of the institution within unbalanced power dynamics. Third, the perception the newcomers have on themselves as beneficiaries of PCSW, impacted by downward social mobility and the social construction of 'deservingness', developed in interaction with the social worker. The analysis of these three dimensions of the newcomers' perceptions leads us to identify three main tensions present in the discourses of newcomer beneficiaries about the service delivery at the PCSW.

First, in what concerns the appropriateness of the services as it is addressed by newcomers, considering the general positive appreciation of the aid provided by the PCSW as an important tool and as a temporary step for emancipation, newcomers assess the institution's adequacy in terms of its ability to promote autonomy and effective integration in the mid-term. This question is, for instance, addressed on self-perception discourses by the newcomers' will to recover their former social status, for instance by being supported on finding a job in adequacy to their skills. Indeed, we observe that the capacity of entering the labour market and finding a durable employment situation is often considered by newcomers as a set of skills that they are eager to develop while receiving the financial aid of the PCSW. Nevertheless, the adequacy of the support from the PCSW on this aspect is barely mentioned or questioned. At the same time, many respondents seem to evaluate the 'appropriateness' of services through the criticism of the controls they experience. Those respondents put forward the overlap between the social workers' roles of 'help' and 'control', where the latter seems to override the former. We have seen that the perception of the control procedures, associated by some beneficiaries to an unnecessary administrative burden, appeared to be questioned when confronted with the PCSW's goal of promoting autonomy of the beneficiaries. Here we find a tension between the aim of autonomy (which is shared by the institution and its beneficiaries) and the procedures of control that are associated to this aim. Conversely to the expected, in some cases, control procedures seem to hinder the achievement of autonomy. We can say in these cases that the institutional praxis fails to achieve its objective, on the way it is perceived by the target public.

Second, many respondents address the specific needs of newcomers in terms of orientation and information to discover a whole new system, thus they emphasise the need for a specific approach for new immigrants. This evaluation of 'appropriateness' of service delivery is opposed to a generalist approach that would treat all beneficiaries in the same way, which would be tantamount to discriminating against those beneficiaries who are less knowledgeable about the system, the rights and practices of the institution.

Finally, when addressing the newcomers' self-perception in relation with the institution, we ascertained that the social construction of deservingness plays an important role within the interactions between the social workers and newcomers. We found that most of the newcomers recall the dominant discourses and reaffirm the moral hierarchy between deserving and non-deserving, while portraying themselves as beneficiaries of the PCSW. Therefore, it is worth noting that if the representations and expectations of newcomer beneficiaries are elaborated, influenced, and realised in the context of interactions with the street-level bureaucrats, newcomers come to have to 'tell' (and negotiate) their deservingness while demanding social guidance and support. This may take the form of a match with – or a re-appropriation of – institutional discourse, sometimes focusing on the need to demonstrate that these aids are a springboard for the future, enabling them to give back to Belgian society what it has granted them; sometimes demonstrating that they are active people, who deserve the aid, 'not like others'. Strategies of newcomers will be discussed in more depth in the next chapter.

REFERENCES

Al-Rasheed, M. (1992). Political migration and downward socio-economic mobility: The Iraqi community in London. *New Community, 18*(4), 537–549.

Brücker, H., Glitz, A., Lerche, A., & Romiti, A. (2021). Occupational recognition and immigrant labor market outcomes. *Journal of Labor Economics, 39*(2), 497–525.

Caldarini, C. (2018). *Projet Individualisé d'Intégration Sociale: vers un accompagnement de meilleure qualité* (Rapport des groupes focus avec un échantillon de citoyens bénéficiaires). CPAS Schaerbeek.

Cohon, J. (1981). Psychological adaptation and dysfunction among refugees. *International Migration Review, 15*(1-2), 255-275.

Degraef, V. (2013). *Recherche-Action sur l'accompagnement des personnes dans les CPAS bruxellois* (rapport final). Université Saint-Louis Bruxelles.

Dubois, V. (2010). Chapitre 10/Politiques au guichet, politique du guichet. In O. Borraz (éd.), *Politiques publiques 2. Changer la société* (pp. 265–286). Presses de Sciences Po.

Duhant, V. (2021). Quelle est votre demande? Résistances éthiques à l'activation. *Les Politiques Sociales*, (3–4), 27–35.

Dustmann, C., & Frattini, T. (2013). *Immigration: The European experience.* In D. Card, & S. Raphael, *Immigration, poverty, and socioeconomic inequality (Eds.)* (pp. 423–456). Russell Sage Foundation.

Ellis, K. (2007). Direct payments and social work practice: The significance of 'street-level bureaucracy' in determining eligibility. *The British Journal of Social Work, 37*(3), 405–422.

Engbersen, G. (1999), *Publieke bijstandsgeheimen: Het ontstaan van een onderklasse in Nederland.* Stenfert Kroese.

Franssen, A. (2006). L'État social actif et la nouvelle fabrique du sujet. In I. Astier, & N. Duvoux. (Eds.) *La société biographique: Une injonction à vivre dignement* (pp. 75–115). L'Harmattan.

Franz., B. (2003). Bosnian refugees and socio-economic realities: Changes in refugee and settlement policies in Austria and the United States. *Journal of Ethnic and Migration Studies, 29*(1), 5–25.

Good, A. (2011). Tales of suffering: Asylum narratives in the refugee status determination process. *West Coast Line, 68,* 78–87.

Gustafsson, A. (2013). Social assistance among immigrants and natives in Sweden. *International Journal of Manpower, 34*(2), 126–141.

Halluin-Mabillot (d'), E. (2012). *Les épreuves de l'asile. Associations et réfugiés face aux politiques du soupçon.* EHESS, coll. « En temps & lieux ».

Kobelinsky, C. (2012). Sont-ils de vrais réfugiés ? Les tensions morales dans la gestion quotidienne de l'asile. In F. Didier, & J-S. Eideliman (Éds.), *Économies morales contemporaines* (pp. 155–173). La Découverte.

Kretsedemas, P. (2005). Language barriers and perceptions of bias: Ethnic differences in immigrant encounters with welfare system. *The Journal of Sociology & Social Welfare, 32*(4), Article 8.

Laenen, T. (2018). Do institutions matter? The interplay between income benefit design, popular perceptions, and the social legitimacy of targeted welfare. *Journal of European Social Policy, 28*(1), 4–17.

Laenen, T., Rossetti, F., & van Oorschot, W. (2019). Why deservingness theory needs qualitative research: Comparing focus group discussions on social welfare in three welfare regimes. *International Journal of Comparative Sociology, 60*(3), 190–216.

Martiniello, M., & Rea, A. (2014). The concept of migratory careers: Elements for a new theoretical perspective of contemporary human mobility. *Current Sociology, 62*(7), 1079– 1096.

Ní Raghallaigh, M. (2013). The causes of mistrust amongst asylum seekers and refugees: Insights from research with unaccompanied asylum-seeking minors living in the Republic of Ireland. *Journal of Refugee Studies, 27*(1), 82–100.

Nothdurfter, U. (2016). The street-level delivery of activation policies: Constraints and possibilities for a practice of citizenship, *European Journal of Social Work, 19*(3–4), 420–440.

Parkhurst, J. O., & Abeysinghe, S. (2016). What constitutes 'good' evidence for public health and social policy-making? From hierarchies to appropriateness. *Social Epistemology, 30*(5–6), 665–679.

Picozza, F. (2017). Dublin on the move: Transit and mobility across Europe's geographies of asylum. *Movements, 71,* 71-88.

Russell, D. J., Humphreys, J. S., Ward, B., Chisholm, M., Buykx, P., McGrail, M., & Wakerman, J. (2013). Helping policy-makers address rural health access problems. *Australian Journal of Rural Health, 21,* 61–71.

Valenta, M. (2008). *Finding friends after resettlement: A study of the social integration of immigrants and refugees, their personal networks and self-work in everyday life.* Fakultet for samfunnsvitenskap og teknologiledelse.

van Berkel, R., & van der Aa, P. (2012). Activation work: Policy program administration or professional service provision? *Journal of Social Policy, 41*(3), 493–510.

van Oorschot, W. (2008). Solidarity towards immigrants in European welfare states. *International Journal of Social Welfare, 17*(1), 3–14.

van Oorschot, W., Roosma, F., Meuleman, B., & Reeskens, T. (2017). *The social legitimacy of targeted welfare: Attitudes to welfare deservingness.* Edward Elgar Publishing Limited.

Van Parys, L. (2016). *On the street-level implementation of ambiguous activation policy: How caseworkers reconcile responsibility and autonomy and affect their clients' motivation* [PhD dissertation, KU Leuven].

Van Parys, L., & Struyven, L. (2018). Interaction styles of street-level workers and motivation of clients: A new instrument to assess discretion-as-used in the case of activation of jobseekers. *Public Management Review, 20*(11), 1702–1721.

Weber, M., Kopelman, S., & Messick, D. (2004). A conceptual review of decision making in social dilemmas: Applying a logic of appropriateness. *Personality and Social Psychology Review, 8*(3), 281–307.

Weller, J. (2018). Les figures de l'usager dans les réformes de modernisation des services publics. *Informations Sociales, 4,* 46-56.

CHAPTER 11
DEVELOPING FORMS OF AGENCY: HOW DO NEWCOMERS DEAL WITH SOCIAL SERVICES

JÉRÉMY MANDIN

The previous chapters have shown that the relationship between newly arrived immigrants and the PCSWs' social workers is 'structurally asymmetrical' (Demazière, 1996, p. 7) in the sense that:

> Even if the protagonists are both assigned to a face-to-face [interaction], the professional seems to occupy a position of power and to have a capacity of intervention on the situation of the unemployed [beneficiary] that are not reciprocal [...]. (Demazière, 1996, our translation)

Social workers are central interlocutors of the beneficiary in the access to social aid functioning as gatekeeper to social assistance. Indeed, as seen in previous chapters, not only is he/she responsible for informing the beneficiary about their rights, social workers are also in charge of collecting the information to decide on the allocation (or not) of a social benefit, proposing a response to the hierarchy and following up cases. Social workers can also apply sanctions to the beneficiary (Chapter 8). Social workers also have room for discretion in applying the PCSW's guidelines and – as Chapter 8 has shown – are often trusted by their hierarchical superiors.

However, despite the unbalanced power relation, the bureaucratic encounter between social workers of the PCSW and the newcomers can still be considered a two-sided interaction. If social workers are in a position of power when compared with the position of the beneficiary, a part of their work is dependent on the level of collaboration of the beneficiary in – for example – providing relevant and correct information. As Chapter 8 has shown, social workers adapt their work and their decisions to how they perceive their interlocutor and their situation. For example, a newcomer showing 'active' and 'collaborating' attitudes is likely to be perceived more positively, which can make the interaction with social workers easier and facilitate the access to certain benefits. These different elements then raise the question of the agency that newcomers have (or not) in their interactions with social workers. In other words, while Chapter 8 demonstrated that the way in which social workers use their discretionary power can have an impact on the assistance that beneficiaries receive, we now examine the capacity (or lack of capacity) from the perspective of newcomer beneficiaries to influence the relationship with social workers, to have their needs met, and to develop their autonomy.

1. FROM COMPLIANCE AND COLLABORATION TO ASSERTIVENESS

A crucial aspect of the relation between newcomers and PCSWs' social workers is that newcomers – at least when they arrive at the PCSW – largely depend on PCSWs' financial aid or non-financial services and support to fulfil basic necessities such as housing or food (see Chapter 7). Services such as the integration income are indeed designed as a last resort safety net for people who do not have access to other forms of income. In this sense, the participation of the newcomer in the relation with the PCSW is largely 'non-voluntary' (Lipsky, 2010, p. 54; see also Wright, 2003, p. 256) as beneficiaries do not have alternative solutions. Because they do not have alternative solutions, beneficiaries have little choice but to comply with the administrative process and with the requirement of social workers. For example, if – as described in Chapter 12 – newcomers can be critical towards the practices of control from the PCSW's social workers, they nevertheless have little choice but to submit to it. In the quote below, a newcomer describes how – while finding them useless – he had to answer the questions of his social worker during his first meeting.

> [I ask BF if he had to give some information for the integration income application. He says yes and starts enumerating the questions he had to answer during his first meeting with the PCSW social worker]
> In [your country of origin], do you have an apartment or a house? No.
> *Do you have money? No.*
> *Can't your family help you? No.*
> [When I ask him his opinion about these question he answers that he found them useless]: 'I come to the PCSW because I don't have money!' (Wallonia, L, beneficiary, 07/06/2021)

This echoes the observation from Howe (1990, p. 141) about the claimants of unemployment benefits in Northern Ireland:

> Basically, they cannot withdraw from the service should the costs become too high, for they have no other recourse. Trapped in this way, claimants must sustain the relationship with the SSO [SLB] even if the costs become very high. (Howe, 1990, p. 141)

One of the results of the necessity to sustain the relationship with their social worker in order to be able to keep a secure access to the PCSW's services is that the large majority of beneficiaries adopt a compliant attitude when interacting with social workers.

The compliance with the administrative process and with the demands of social workers can, however, be performed in different ways. Variations are present in the forms that collaboration with social workers can take.[1] Newcomers can develop 'active' forms of collaboration with their social worker by trying to anticipate – or better, exceed – a social worker's expectations. Some expectations can be explicitly expressed by social workers and formalised in the ISIP (such as learning the language or finding a job) but other expectations (such as showing a positive and active attitude) are more subtle and need to be interpreted by beneficiaries who know that they have to perform in specific ways when interacting with social workers. Showing willingness and commitment in the search for a job, for example, can help newcomers to demonstrate to social workers their 'good faith' as well as to reassure them on the fact that the newcomer shares the same sets of expectations (such as a rapid integration on the job market or a willingness to learn a national language). By presenting themselves as 'collaborating' beneficiaries and by being recognised as such, newcomers are aware that this can contribute to establish good relations with social workers and facilitate interactions.

> Yes, of course he agreed [moving to another city to try to find a job]. Because he likes when I am searching for something. When I don't stay at home. He likes when someone is positive. They don't like when someone is always negative. (Wallonia, O, beneficiary, 05/06/2021)

For newcomers, putting forward a 'determined' and 'trustworthy' attitude can also help opening new possibilities of negotiation with social workers. This is illustrated by the quote below where a respondent explains how he obtained from his social worker to have more time between his convocations to the PCSW.

> I had meetings every week with the social worker when I arrived here in the PCSW. Every Wednesday morning, at ten. First, she helped me for the

money. [I had to meet her] every week like that. I said to her 'Wait Madame, I have to work!' […] I said, 'Not every week! Every Wednesday, I have to take time to come here but I have to work!' She said 'No problem, A. I understand. [your previous employer] explained to me that you are a good worker, you don't need any translator to speak French … Go to work, go to work ok!' With me, she was very nice. (Wallonia, N, beneficiary, 14/10/2021)

Engaging in proactive forms of collaboration with social workers and anticipating their expectations can then be a way to obtain more autonomy from the institution and more space to make their own choices in terms of socio-economic integration.

Newcomer beneficiaries can also engage in more 'limited' or 'minimal' forms of collaboration with their social worker. This means only fulfilling administrative requirements or sending documents and information that are directly required by social workers.

[About an amount of money he received from the Walloon Family Allowance Fund]
My social worker did not see it [the money] because she said nothing. I have the money and I use it as I want as far as the money goes […] She did not tell me anything [about the possibility to have the allowance or the incompatibility with PCSW income]. So I said nothing [to her] either. She only asked me if I am still attending my training. I said yes. She said that I have to send the papers saying that I have a training contract. (Wallonia, B, beneficiary, 12/05/2021)

The quote above illustrates that engaging in more 'limited' forms of collaboration is not necessarily the result of a form of passivity (Dubois, 2010). Indeed, as the quote shows, opting for such limited forms of collaboration is sometimes expressed as a way to respond to what is perceived as a lack of professional commitment from social workers' part. In this case, the beneficiary describes his reticence to inform his social worker about the allowance as a response to the fact that his social worker did not inform him about the existence of the allowance in the first place. This suggests that the degree of collaboration shown by newcomer beneficiaries can also depend on the level of commitment of social workers. The quote also illustrates that avoiding sharing information – as long as social workers do not ask for this information – is also a way to limit the control that social workers have over the newcomer's life.

The data collected during the fieldwork shows that the vast majority of the newcomers adopt a compliant attitude when interacting with social workers.

As mentioned above, this compliance can be explained by the structural constraints faced by newcomers – such as the need for material support, their perception of the imbalance of power, and the blurred distinction between legal rights and aids conditioned to the discretionary power, due to the centrality of social workers in the access to such support. However, this compliance can also be explained by the fact that newcomers either interiorise and/or share with social workers some representations of deservingness that might converge with the ones circulating within the institution (see Chapter 12). Therefore, they tend to adapt their attitudes accordingly when interacting with social workers.

In a limited number of cases, however, interviews show that newcomer beneficiaries can also go beyond mere compliance with the terms of social workers and develop strategies to try to mitigate the power unbalance characterising their relation with social workers and to cope with social workers' discretion.

In his ethnographic study of unemployment in Northern Ireland, Howe (1990) analyses the relations between beneficiaries of income support benefits and the administration. He notes that, when beneficiaries are interacting with the officers, they are engaged in a role relationship (Kelvin & Jarrett, 1985, p. 84) where they are expected to display a certain set of behaviours including subordination, acquiescence and humility (Howe, 1990, p. 140), which – according to the author – most claimants conform to. However, Howe also noted that some of them (a minority) could break with this social role and become what he calls 'assertive' claimants who

> may attempt to negotiate the role relationship [street level agents] in ways which confer individualistic advantages [...]. Generally speaking, such claimants become sensitised to the fact that their relationship to the SSO [social security office] and its staff is not predetermined but can be manipulated. When, or if, this happens, these claimants begin to perceive the situation in a new light, and become aware that, *within limits*, it is possible to play a more active and ambitious role. (Howe, 1990, p. 140; emphasis in the original)

A similar dynamic seems to be at play here. One way for newcomers to become more assertive in their relation with social workers is to make reference to what they perceive as 'the law' or 'the rules' to contest a decision:

> When I register to the PCSW, the PCSW has to give me my rights without discussing, this is normal. We also have duties [to the PCSW]. You have to

go do your integration [integration course], you have to … this is normal. But when someone does the integration [course], does everything but has no rights … Also when I [mention] the law, that based on this article I am asking for this and this, [my SW] said, 'How can you know more than me? I am from Belgium, you, you are a foreigner, you cannot talk like that!' (Wallonia, I, beneficiary, 04/05/2021)

Making reference to the law has three effects in the quote above. First, it allows to switch the perception of PCSW support as a favour (see Chapters 9 and 10) and to redefine it as a right. Second, it contributes to redefine the position of the newcomer in the interaction by showing competences and understanding of the regulations. Third, by making reference to the law, newcomers also make a distinction between what depends on the law and what depends on social workers' discretion. This distinction allows newcomers to – as Howe (1990, p. 140) puts it – 'perceive the situation in a new light', to perceive the power dynamics existing within their relation with social workers differently. Newcomers who adopt more assertive attitudes generally accept final decisions when they are clearly identified as the result of the application of the rules. What is sometimes contested, however, is the discretionary power of social workers when it is perceived as an obstacle to a fair and objective evaluation of the demand:

When my wife died, it was difficult. When I called the assistant for the funeral, to help with the expenses, and to change the situation, for me not to be the household second anymore [and to be able to receive the social integration income]. And [the SW] told me on the phone that it was a very serious situation and that it will be very difficult before even doing and submitting the application, and she told me she was really sorry. But then, the authorities are looking at the rules, the law and they gave a warning that we are in another level and so we had the income for social integration. Effectively [the help for the funeral's expenses] was not included, this we understood. But what we did not understand is that every time we submitted an application to the assistant [the SW], she started to deny [the possibility of a support] before analysing and submitting the demand. (Wallonia, M, beneficiary, 27/08/2021)

Making a distinction between the law (or what is perceived as the law) and social workers' discretion often requires for the newcomer to have a certain level of understanding of the functioning of the institution. The knowledge and competences accumulated by newcomers can then impact their understanding of the function of social workers within the institution as well as their understanding of their own agency when dealing with the institution. In this perspective, some respondents were more confident in their capacity to argument and to make their own demands to the PCSW:

> I went to the council,[2] but I was prepared, I wasn't stressed. [...] I said [to the president]: 'I know what I want, this is for the better, let me go to University.' This is also a question of human rights to let people study [...]. I will have my degree and with my degree I will have a job which will allow me not to return to the PCSW, to contribute, to give back what you gave me. [...] So when they see how I defend myself, they know I will not fail at school! They have to support me for University. Well, at the end it's him [the president] the boss, I can't decide. Then they told me, 'Ok'. I explained to them why. (Brussels, G, beneficiary, 11/02/2022)

As the quotes above illustrate, newcomers sometimes use the reference to 'rules' as a way to mitigate the impact of their social worker's discretion upon their life. In this context, an important element of attention is the way in which the 'rule', which is the set of legal provisions governing access to social assistance in Belgium, is approached differently by social workers and beneficiaries. While for the former it is perceived as a constraint to access rights and must be challenged – through discretionary and even moral commitment – to guarantee social assistance (Chapter 8), for the latter it is, on the contrary, a tool that can be used to limit the discretionary power of social workers and to ensure, as a consequence, equity.

As Howe (1990, p. 163) argues, becoming assertive in front of social workers is the result of a learning process that also depends on the specific situation of the claimant. More specifically, our data shows that developing assertiveness depends on the type of capital (Bourdieu, 1986) that immigrants have at their disposal and that is usable in the Belgian context. Our material suggest that specifically cultural capital is important when it comes to exerting agency. Instances of assertiveness were generally encountered during interviews with newcomers who had a good knowledge of the language spoken in the PCSW. This did not only concern immigrants who were native speakers of one of the contact languages used in the PCSWs but also those who studied one of these languages during their studies or learned it in Belgium. Adopting an assertive attitude in front of social workers also generally requires a certain degree of understanding of the regulations and of the administrative processes. Some newcomers – because of their education and profession in the home country – were more comfortable with dealing with administration upon their arrival in Belgium. Others also could develop their understanding of the PCSW's administrative processes from their own experience with the institution.

Besides cultural capital, newcomers also use their social capital, which represents the person's network of social connections and social obligation (Bourdieu, 1986, p. 47) to collect information that can be used when interacting with their social worker. The importance of having a social network in challenging social workers' decisions is illustrated in the following quote:

> When I made the request for a laptop [and got rejected], I didn't sit still and I used a lot of my contacts. I received a response from [name], she is not a PCSW assistant, but she helps students. She informed me that I am entitled to an 80/20 ratio which I can get through them. [...] After asking around a bit, I went back to my assistant. I said what I had heard and that I am entitled to a laptop where apparently the PCSW pays 80% and I pay 20%. Finally, she suddenly changed her answer and said that I am entitled to a laptop. (Flanders, C, beneficiary, 20/01/2022)

In fact, it appears that the social capital acquired by newcomers in Belgium is often a crucial tool to develop assertiveness as well as to develop forms of resistance (as we will see in the next section). To a certain extent, social capital can compensate the lack of cultural know-how (language skills, administrative knowledge, and so forth) that immigrants might experience when interacting with the PCSW (see Chapter 11).

2.   COPING WITH STREET-LEVEL BUREAUCRACY: TYPOLOGY OF RESPONSES TO OVERCOME DIFFICULTIES

Until here, we analysed different attitudes that newcomers can adopt when interacting with PCSWs' social workers. As mentioned throughout this book, the relation with social workers is of critical importance for newcomers' access to social benefits. Newcomers are largely – but not exclusively – dependent on social workers regarding the access to information, the relevant formulation of their demands, and the transmission of their demands to the relevant authorities. Newcomers can also be dependent on social workers in receiving other types of non-financial support, such as help with paperwork. Therefore, when difficulties arise in the relation between social workers and newcomers, it can have an important impact on the access of the latter to much needed support. As we saw, despite being limited by the unbalanced power dynamics in favour of social workers, newcomers still have a form of agency in this relation. In this section, we will analyse different types of responses that newcomers put in place when facing difficulties in their relation with social workers. Such responses depend on the type of attitudes that the beneficiary develops in relation with their social worker studied before (compliance, assertiveness).

2.1. Mobilising cultural and social capital: negotiate, protest, and bypass

A first response that we encountered during the fieldwork was to *try to resolve the difficulty directly with the social worker* through practices of negotiation or through practices of more frontal protest. In some cases, newcomers can adopt a compliant and collaborating attitude for the resolution of a problematic situation or to try to overcome difficulties with the social worker through negotiation, as the following quote illustrates:

> One time in a volunteering job, I got a lot of money that I didn't expect, it was 800 euros. […] And I kept it secret, I didn't tell them [PCSW] because it's a volunteering job and we have decided before: anytime that we're going to work as a volunteer, this money is for me. And all of a sudden, she [the social worker] told me: 'Give me your bank card, we need to check it'. […] She told me: 'You got this money, why didn't you tell me?' […] And she told me 'Sorry but we need to discuss this with the PCSW' and she said it in a gentle way, in a nice way, 'We're going to discuss this and we're going to have a decision. I try but you have to keep in mind, maybe we're going to take this money from you.' I said 'I don't refuse to pay it back. You have the right and you pay me every month. But is there any way to try to keep this money?' She told me 'Yes, there is a way. You can ask the person you worked with to give us a proof that you deserve this money so we cannot take it from you. Otherwise, we'll have to take it from you.' […]. Then I went to [volunteer coordinator] and they did really nice, like an email to PCSW and she called them and communicated with my assistant. She justified and they gave me the decision that I will not pay it back. […] (Flanders, C, beneficiary, 21/01/2022)

In the quote above, showing a compliant attitude by accepting a priori the principle of being penalised cannot be reduced to a sign of total submission to the logic of the institution, as it is also a way for the newcomer to open the possibility for a (positive) resolution of the problem. This echoes what Dubois (2010) describes as 'the strategic dimension of docility' in his study of the interactions at administration desks of French Family Benefit Offices (CAF). For the author an 'ostensible allegiance to institutional morals can take a strategic dimension' (Dubois, 2010) in the sense that beneficiaries can use it – for example – to try to attract the indulgence of the institution's agents or to mitigate the effects of a possible sanction. The data collected during the interviews shows, however, that attitudes of compliance and collaboration are not always used as a strategy but also illustrates the fact that beneficiaries can also genuinely share – at least some – of the objectives of social workers such as the building of a relation of trust based on the respect of the rules. Attitudes of compliance and collaboration can also be favoured in a context where newcomers largely perceive the PCSW's support as a favour (see Chapters 9 and 10).

Trying to overcome a difficulty can also take another form with newcomers protesting against the social worker's decision.

> Most of [newcomer] families do not speak French well. But they are also afraid because they are foreigners [...]. They are not like me when I say that the PCSW does wrong. [...] The [social worker] said that this is wrong and that [my husband] benefited from the PCSW's rental deposit and that he has to give 950 euros. But this is not true. We have proofs. I brought my proofs to the PCSW and I talked to the [social worker] and I said: 'Is this normal to say such things?' She has to present some proofs [if the social worker argues] that she gave the PCSW's rental deposit to my husband. (Wallonia, I, beneficiary, 04/05/2021)

> We consider PCSW as our god [...] even when [PCSW] is yelling at you, you don't dare yelling, [PCSW] can break you. In my community, we are afraid. You go to the PCSW to access your rights, not to get friends. You can't let people step over you. If you don't know, you ask. It is important not to be afraid. There are NGOs [non-governmental organisations], get close to them, they have time to listen to you and to inform you about your rights and your relation with the [social worker]. What is the link between you? The law between the PCSW and the person who receive. [...] First, you need some self-confidence. (Brussels, G, beneficiary, 11/02/2022)

These quotes illustrate that protesting is not always easy for newcomers. It requires some resources and some competences, such as being able to speak a contact language, knowing how to express and/or file a complaint, or having sufficient confidence to go against a PCSW's decision. It also often involves specific practices, such as the collection of proofs mentioned in the first quote. Similar to what have been observed in other migration contexts (Lafleur & Mescoli, 2018, p. 492) the collection of evidence and, more generally, the meticulous conservation of PCSW documents, letters, and emails was a relatively common practice among newcomers, especially for newcomers who had limited skills in French or Dutch.

> We have this thing, we make an archive. For example, I have papers from the commune, from PCSW … we have an archive. We are afraid of this thing because maybe one day the PCSW will ask me a paper which is … which goes back to 2015, and this happened already and you don't find this paper online or you ask for the paper and they tell you 'No, it's your responsibility to find, it's your responsibility to keep these papers.' Now, I have boxes and … it's for all refugees. We are afraid of losing the papers. (Brussels, B, beneficiary, 23/09/2021)

This illustrates the ambivalent dimension of the use of 'proofs' within the PCSW. One the one hand – when required by social workers, proofs are an instrument of control that also transfer part of the responsibility of the access (or lack of it) to social benefit on the shoulders of beneficiaries. On the other end, the conservation and collection of proofs can be used by beneficiaries to negotiate with social workers.

A second response to the difficulties experienced in the relation with social workers is to try to *bypass* such relation. Bypass refers here to taking contact with another actor (institutional or not) to try to get over the discretionary power of social workers. One way to bypass the blockage with social workers is 'vertical', which refers to social workers' hierarchy. It is important to note that, as described in detail in Chapter 7, the regulation allows the possibility to contest a PCSW's decision through a procedure of appeal. Chapter 8 also shows how social workers themselves sometimes advise newcomers to make such appeals. However, the formal appeal procedure primarily concerns the PCSW's decisions and is therefore less effective for other types of difficulties such as conflicts with social workers. An appeal can be formulated against an unjustified refusal – which can then cover a complaint against the social worker's work of completing the file with the right demands – but not against a conflict with the social worker. From our interviews, it seems that only a few respondents have asked the transfer of their file to another social worker. In one instance, a respondent who encountered difficulties in their relation with their social worker obtained such a transfer. This transfer was possibly bringing other difficulties for the newcomer:

> So I asked to … and then somehow they change the assistant. Because they said that that assistant he had a lot of problems in files on him and they

assigned another assistant for me and I was her first file to process you know. She knew nothing. She was always afraid. She was always anxious when I talked to her. She was almost crying. (Brussels, G, beneficiary, 14/12/2021)

More generally, the data we collected during the interviews with newcomers showed that newcomers rarely try to appeal to social workers' hierarchy. This can be explained by different factors, including the difficulty to identify and contact a relevant interlocutor linked to a lack of understandability of the institution, but also by the fact that the hierarchy can be perceived as relatively supportive of social workers.

Bypassing can also occur in a more 'horizontal' way, when newcomers seek and/or find support with other social workers or other workers of the PCSW. While formally asking for a new social worker can be problematic when difficulties arise, some circumstances such as a prolonged absence or a change of personnel can – temporarily or not – provide the newcomer with a new interlocutor. This change of interlocutor can help resolve some problems, as is illustrated in the quote below.

Because, the application files for the family benefit, first, we were not informed about it. That's her [the SW] responsibility to inform us but she was always running away, telling that she did not know us. But we have been lucky because there were other assistants who were nice and who respect the law and do their job. So, during [the social worker's] absence for two or three months, some other assistants have transmitted our application that was still pending. And the children have had their benefits. (Wallonia, M, beneficiary, 27/08/2021)

Newcomers can also seek support and advice from other workers of the PCSW in the framework of activities organised by PCSWs in cities for newcomer beneficiaries, such as information sessions or weekly workshops. During these activities, newcomers can make contact with the PCSW's other workers and ask for advice or for support regarding their personal situation as illustrated in the fieldnotes below taken at the end of a weekly workshop organised by a PCSW that was aimed specifically at newcomers:

At the end of the session, while most of the participants left, S. comes to see O. and A. [the PCSW's worker in charge of the workshop] and starts to talk to them discreetly. She explains that she will move soon to another apartment which is at the sixth floor of a building and that she is looking for a lift to rent. She says that a company made her an offer at 175 euros for half a day of use.

'Is it ok?' S. asks

'Well, it is the price' confirms A. who explains that this is the price that she herself had to pay when she moved.

S. then talks to O. and asks her if it would be possible to have some support from the PCSW to cover the cost of the lift.

O. [who is not in charge of S.'s file] answers that she will check if S. can have some support for renting the lift. (Wallonia, A, beneficiary and social worker, 08/02/2022)

This example illustrates what Dubois (2010, p. 15) calls 'the ambivalence of the relationship with the institution'. The relationship with the institution Dubois argues, 'Is a factor in producing both a "social bond" and coercion in the sense that it contributes to helping people with difficulties face their situation and keeping them in their "place".' We can then add to Dubois' observation that institutions such as PCSWs can also provide opportunities to build relations of solidarity either between beneficiaries and the staff or between beneficiaries themselves as it can occur during the type of activities mentioned above. Such relations of solidarity can then be used by newcomers to find allies who can help accessing services.

Bypass strategies can also be developed with actors outside of the PCSW. Indeed, the newcomers we interviewed were often in contact with workers of other organisations involved in the integration of immigrants. One type of practices that was encountered in the field was the fact to ask for the support of such workers who often have a good knowledge of the welfare system and who have the capacity to understand the administrative work of the PCSW's social worker. The support provided by this type of actors can be limited to information or advice, but some newcomers ask for more direct support in the relation with the PCSW.

E.: [...] some [social workers] were causing trouble and ... I don't know. So yes, we saw the difference from one social worker to the other. Researcher: Did you try to make an appeal when there was an appeal? E.: No, we did not even know that we could do an appeal but we just complained to our acquaintances and to a woman who worked ... who we knew from the reception centre. We complained and she came with us [...] and after that, the problem was solved. (Wallonia, B, beneficiary, 09/02/2021)

No, I did not have many discussions with her [the PCSW's social worker]. We did not get along. At the beginning I wasn't understanding everything.

I was with [an NGO]. Once I started to adapt and to take my business into my own hand, I started to want to go [to the PCSW] alone, to do this, but I never got in touch with her [the PCSW]. So I went regularly to [the NGO] to say that it was not working, that I was not able to contact her [the PCSW's social worker], that I need help, she is not here, etc. [...]. They had the contact of this assistant. First she did not answer but then, they wrote an email and she answered. (Brussels, E, beneficiary, 11/03/2021)

In the first quote, the newcomer found support from one of the workers met previously in the reception centre. In the second quote, the support came from relations developed with a local NGO. This – and in particular the first example, illustrates that newcomers build different forms of capital during the migration process. Coping with the international protection system and the migration procedures can help to develop knowledges and competences (cultural capital) that can be used afterward. In the same perspective, by going through institutions and meeting professionals at different stages of the migration, newcomers develop social relations from which they can get support (social capital) when PCSW's social workers are not complying with their tasks. Regarding the specific question of the interaction with PCSW's social workers, while this social capital could help to unlock specific problematic situations, it was not necessarily followed by an immediate transfer of knowledge and competences to the newcomers themselves. In other words, the social capital of newcomers (their social networks in Belgium) was not always converted into more cultural capital (knowledge and competences usable within the PCSW). In this perspective, such social capital was also contributing to reproduce a form of dependence of the newcomers.

Finally, the data collected during the fieldwork show that many other actors can help newcomers in their difficult relations with social workers. Authors have described the importance of 'brokers' in immigrants' access to welfare (Ratzmann, 2019, p. 212 and sq.). Such actors have been described as 'intermediaries' or 'bridges' involved in the relation between beneficiaries and street-level bureaucrats. In this context, brokers 'play an important role in creating substantive access to benefits and services at the local level' (Ratzmann, 2019, p. 214). Among the actors mentioned during the fieldwork we find, for example, lawyers, friends, family members, volunteers from associations. or doctors and nurses.

Our research then shows that social capital is an important element not only to ensure the access to welfare in the considered case studies as analysed in Chapter 7 and Chapter 8, but also to cope with the power dynamics that characterise the relation between PCSW social workers and newcomers.

More specifically, it suggests that this social capital is largely dependent from the insertion of immigrant beneficiaries into what has been conceptualised as 'arrival infrastructures' (Meeus *et al.*, 2019) which allows immigrant to access resources and forms of capital that can be used to mitigate the power unbalance with social workers.

2.2. Coping with difficulties: endure and avoid

When newcomers face difficulties in their interaction with social workers, they can also adopt responses that are more passive than the responses listed above. One possible response is to simply *endure* the difficulty and wait for the situation to resolve itself without trying to actively protest or resist the social worker's decisions:

> I heard that there were others who did file a complaint against her [social worker], and that the person was transferred to another place because of those complaints. But I never filed a complaint against her, I didn't want to touch her personally. (Flanders, C, beneficiary, 24/01/2022)

Enduring a difficult situation can also be seen as a temporary strategy to be held until the material situation of the newcomer changes:

> I keep them out you know. And I spent the rest of time surviving, it was better than that. Then meanwhile I was staying with my ex-girlfriend, I found another apartment with the same landlord […] So I called him like 'Hi Frederika, I am looking for an apartment. I know that you have a small one in [another municipality] and I want to get the f* out of [municipality where he was at the time].' Because I wanted to have access to PCSW [of the other municipality] and I knew that PCSW usually support you to find a job, you know. And I at that time started studying […] I thought that I have a very good reason to stay, to stay depending on the welfare till I realise my [master's studies] project. (Brussels, G, beneficiary, 14/12/2021)

In some cases, this type of response can be linked to the fear of facing more problems in the case of a complaint. Such fear can be informed by previous negative experiences of others (friends, family) with resisting a social worker's decisions. One respondent, for example, refrained from filing a complaint about not receiving various benefits after a friend did the same with a negative outcome:

I did not file a complaint because I was scared to do that. They would not have accepted my complaint. My friend had the same problem in [other municipality] and they didn't accept what he said. They opened a case for him and told him he had to leave the municipality. My friend did not receive money for one year, that's why he filed the complaint. (Flanders, C, beneficiary, 10/05/2022).

As mentioned previously, having social and/or cultural capital can be of paramount importance in determining whether to protest or not against a social worker's decisions. The lack of these types of capital may lead then to a passive response, as becomes apparent in the following quote by the same respondent as in the previous quote:

When I didn't agree with a decision, I told the social worker, but she said, 'This is the rule, we cannot do anything.' I didn't know where else to go, so I didn't do anything. (Flanders, C, beneficiary, 10/05/2022)

Enduring difficulties in the relation with the PCSW does not necessarily mean staying passive in all aspects of socio-economic integration. Indeed, as we saw earlier in this book, benefiting from the PCSW is largely perceived as something temporary, and finding a job is perceived as a priority for newcomers. In this context, some newcomers can be encouraged to try to accelerate their integration in the job market (even at lower conditions than expected) in order to be able to leave the PCSW as soon as possible, rather than to try to solve the difficulties they encounter with the institution.

When I asked my question [...] she [the social worker] answered very aggressively, very fast, she wasn't happy to be here, so it was very difficult to talk with her [...]. She was one reason I told myself: 'Ok, keep in mind that you have to leave this thing [the PCSW] as soon as possible.' First I was quite relaxed, I said I have time to learn French, do everything ... but then I had the feeling that I really needed to leave the PCSW as soon as possible, find a job fast, anything. (Brussels, E, beneficiary, 27/09/2021)

Finally, another response that we encountered during the fieldwork was for the newcomer to *avoid* the interactions with social workers. Indeed, some newcomers experienced high anxiety and stress due to the negative interactions experienced with social workers. In some cases, this anxiety translated in the newcomer's apprehension regarding the meetings with their social worker, as is illustrated in the following quote:

> The problem is that I work part-time now and my daughter goes to school. Certain things for school I have to request through the PCSW. It happened to a friend of mine, so I'm afraid that I will be sent to the PCSW by the school for certain requests. […] If needed, I will ask then for another assistant. (Flanders, C, beneficiary, 24/01/2022)

In a certain number of cases encountered in the field, the relation with social workers was characterised by the experience of various forms of violence. Very often this violence was symbolic in the sense that it was exerted through the discussion with the social worker and it contributed to reinforcing the social worker in their position of domination. These situations were very difficult to live for newcomers who were in a precarious socio-economic situation and produced experiences of psychological troubles, sometimes requiring medical attention. In this context, some of the people we interviewed described how they would later avoid getting in touch with their assistant in order to avoid a negative experience.

> Researcher: 'So you said that you were avoiding to see [the social worker] again.'
> E.: 'Yes, the frustration that we experienced.'
> Researcher: 'But how do you do when you have a question or when you need assistance?'
> E.: 'Sometimes, I had some psychological troubles and I contacted a psychologist and he told me that if I had more difficulties … because at this time, I was receiving a lot of bills and I was not daring to go [to the PCSW] because I knew that [the social worker] would tell no […].' (Wallonia, M, beneficiary, 27/08/2021)

The quotes illustrate how avoidance can also be a way of coping with the psychological costs – in this case the stress created by the anticipation of the interaction with the social worker – of the administrative process (Moynihan *et al.*, 2015). Avoiding the interactions with social workers can take different forms, either strict limitation of the interactions to what is necessary to ensure the access to benefits but also – as illustrated in the quote above – refraining to ask for support. Avoidance can have a high cost for newcomer beneficiaries as it can contribute to cut them from some forms of social support that they would otherwise be entitled to. This response against the difficulty encountered with social workers was concerning only a minority of respondents among our sample. Moreover, it is not always possible to avoid all interaction when, for example, beneficiaries are called by their social worker for an appointment.

Most of the time, avoidance was limited to the fact for the beneficiary to refrain from asking for support.

To conclude, in this section we saw that newcomers develop a diversity of responses to cope with social workers' discretion. Negotiation and protest are certainly part of the repertoire that newcomers can use, even if it often requires forms of cultural capital (contact language skills, administrative knowledge, and so forth) that is not always available to newcomers. Other strategies, however, can be developed on the basis of the social capital that newcomers have built since their arrival in Belgium. Indeed, the contacts they created with local actors as well as their enrolment (voluntary or mandatory) in different institutions provide resources that can be used to try to bypass – or at least mitigate – the discretional power of social workers. Finally, experiences of frustration and violence when interacting with social workers can also lead some newcomers towards responses including the avoidance of the contact with the institution. This last response leads us to the question of non-take-up that we will address in the next section.

3.   NON-TAKE-UP

In the final section of this chapter we will discuss the issue of non-take-up of benefits and its different forms. The notion of non-take-up designates 'the phenomenon that people or households do not receive the (full amount of) benefit to which they are legally entitled' (van Oorschot, 1991, p. 16). Non-take-up of benefits can take many forms. The researchers from the Observatoire des non recours aux droits et services (The Observatory of Non-take-up of Rights and Services), identified different types of non-take-up (Warin, 2016, p. 4):

- **Non-take-up by non-knowledge**: when the beneficiary does not have knowledge of the existence of the benefit.
- **Non-take-up by non-proposition**: when the benefit is not activated by the agent despite the beneficiary being legally entitled to receive it.
- **Non-take-up by non-reception**: when the beneficiary knows the benefit, asks for it but does not receive it.
- **Non-take-up by non-demand**: when the beneficiary does have knowledge of the existence of the benefit but does not ask for it.

Despite the fact that the phenomenon of non-take-up started to gain political and academic attention in the 1990s in Europe and that research was subsequently developed on this subject (see, for example, van Oorschot 1991,

1996; van Oorschot & Math, 1996; Warin, 2012, 2016, 2018; Noël, 2016), to our knowledge, no studies have focused specifically on the non-take-up of immigrant beneficiaries. In a report about the non-take-up of the Income of Active Solidarity (RSA) in France (the French equivalent of the Belgian Integration Income), Warin (2011, p. 8) explains that the rate of non-take-up of the RSA is proportionally more important among non-EU-foreigners than among French citizens. In Belgium, a report on the trajectory of care of drug users of foreign origin (Derluyn *et al.*, 2008) suggests that this population has a lower rate of take-up of certain types of care services (such as residential care services) when compared with the drug users of Belgian origin. In the following paragraphs we will analyse non-take-up practices of newcomers in Belgium as it emerged from our fieldwork.

It is important to keep in mind that for this research we selected respondents that were or have been benefiting of the PCSW services. This necessarily produces a bias in what regards an analysis of non-take-up in the sense that our research does not take into account newcomers who have not – for any reason – accessed PCSWs' services despite being entitled to do so. As described in Chapter 4, for newcomers with a precarious residence permit, benefiting from social aid can mean being at risk of losing their residence permit.[3] However, as demonstrated below, the fieldwork still provided insights about some non-take-up practices. The analysis is structured following Warin's framework presented above (Warin, 2016).

3.1. Non-take-up by non-knowledge

As described in Chapter 9, information is a central element for an effective access to PCSW social benefits, while many newcomers do not have clear and exhaustive knowledge of the different services offered by PCSWs. For newcomers, one element that limited the capacity to access the PCSW's services was the lack of language skills upon their arrival in Belgium. The consequence is that some of the people we met during the interviews discovered some of the services well after their arrival, realising that they were not using a benefit that they were entitled to for many months. This situation is illustrated by the following discussion with a young man who discovered several months after his arrival and settlement in Belgium the possibility of asking for an installation benefit:

> I ask BF. how he learned about the existence of [the installation benefit]. He explains that he learned about it by his brother. He asked for help first to his brother and then to the PCSW. His social worker did not tell him about this benefit.

I ask him what he thinks about that. He says that this is not normal. He explains that during the first meeting with the social worker, he received several leaflets with information but he could not read them because of his lack of language skills. Maybe the information about the installation benefit was on these leaflets he says. (Wallonia, L, beneficiary, 07/06/2021).

Because social workers are central in the access of newcomers to information, non-take-up by non-knowledge can also be analysed as forms of *non-take-up by non-proposition* where social workers fail to propose to the beneficiary a benefit to which they would potentially be entitled:

[answer to what the beneficiary would change about the PCSW]
Be honest about what people are entitled to. It is painful when they don't get what they're entitled to or have to ask for it themselves, because often they're entitled to the things they ask for. It is important to get clear information. (Flanders, D, beneficiary, 06/03/2022)

The quotes above concern non-take-up of a PCSW service but some of the newcomers we met were also not aware of the existence of the PCSW when they arrived in Belgium and thus did not take up social support when they were entitled to. For the newcomers that we met during the fieldwork, this specific case of non-take-up (because of the lack of information about the existence of the PCSW) also depended on the type of arrival in Belgium. Newcomers who applied for international protection and who went to a centre for asylum seekers were generally already in contact with a social worker in the centre. In this context, their direction to the PCSW once their status was recognised was relatively straightforward and immediate. In comparison, we encountered newcomers who followed different pathways of arrival with less direct access to the PCSW. This was the case for one of our respondents who has not been in a centre despite his application for international protection, but was living with one of his brothers since his arrival. In his case, he searched for a job for several months before finally contacting (upon his brother's advice) a PCSW once the resources of his brother became too scarce to provide for him. We also encountered the case of women who arrived in Belgium through family reunification and who had to suddenly leave their partner – sometimes after being victims of domestic abuse – or whose partner passed away. Without a proper knowledge of the Belgian welfare system, some of the women we met in this situation had to rely on family members of friends for several months – without any forms of income – before learning about the PCSW. In both cases, several months of potential resources have been missed because of the lack of knowledge about the relevant institutions. As we have seen earlier in this book, non-take-up by non-knowledge can be favoured by the fact that PCSW rarely engage in active external communication towards the potential beneficiaries, and in particular newcomers.

3.2. Non-take-up by non-reception

Our fieldwork provided examples of non-reception due to human error from social workers when accomplishing the tasks of which he/she is responsible for. Among such errors, social workers can forget to process a request or to file a request with an external entity:

> I asked my assistant for rent subsidy and she said 'Ok, I will do that for you, you can come here to the secretariat and sign and that's all.' But now that's been six months of waiting and I sent an email to the rent subsidy and they replied 'You have no file with us, we don't have your name.' And I emailed my new assistant and she said 'You can reapply, I will send again.' But I have been waiting for six months. (Flanders, C, beneficiary, 07/01/2022)

> I have been on the waiting list for social housing for three years. After three years my brother-in-law came to Belgium, and I requested social housing for him as well and also asked the assistant where my name was on the list, but I was not on the list. The assistant forgot to send my application. (Flanders, D, beneficiary, 06/03/2022)

Finally, newcomers also experience forms of 'temporary' non-reception due either to the temporality of the administrative process (such as delays in requests) or to sanctions. This temporary non-take-up, also described as 'frictional' non-take-up (van Oorschot & Math, 1996, p. 7), can constitute challenging conditions for newcomers who – for most of the people we met – had very few if any financial resources when arriving in Belgium. In this context, the weeks between the first meeting with social workers and the attribution of the integration income were often described as very difficult because of the incapacity to meet very basic material needs (such as food) and the necessity to rely on food offered by local NGOs when it was not provided by the PCSW itself.

3.3. Non-take-up by non-demand

The cases of non-take-up described above are mainly caused by elements that are outside of the newcomers' control. However, the data collected during the interviews show that some instances of non-take-up can have a more voluntary and strategic dimension. Sometimes non-take-up by non-demand is caused by the avoidance of contact with social workers or the PCSW, for example after a bad experience with social workers or the institution, as explained above.

> I always tried to have, to have minimum contact with the PCSW. Super minimum. But I didn't even ask for any benefits like Basic-Fit or food or transportation … Yeah, transportation I did but I am really, I was really minimising any contact with PCSW because it gave me a lot of stress. (Brussels, G, beneficiary, 14/12/2021)

In the quote above, the psychological costs related to the administrative burden (Moynihan *et al.*, 2015) of the beneficiary also plays a role in the instance of non-take-up. In other cases, non-take-up by non-demand occurs when newcomers know about a benefit but choose not to demand it without experiencing specific difficulties with the PCSW. Newcomers can refrain to demand support from the PCSW because of the fear to lose their residence permit, as mentioned already. For example, one of the newcomers met during the research explained that he could ask for PCSW's support but that he did not because, when he arrived, a desk agent of the city explained to him that – as a beneficiary of family reunification – this could prevent him from renewing his residence permit in the future.

It is important to note that, because of the criteria of selection of our sample, the instances of non-take-up we met rarely concerned the integration income but rather some other – more peripheral – services from the PCSWs. For example, several newcomers mentioned their choice not to ask for the rental deposit that the PCSW can provide as a support to the housing costs:

> Researcher: So did you also asked the PCSW for the rental deposit?
> F: Yes, but then, they explained to us that this rental deposit, they will take it from our income, from the money they give us and in our case we had some little savings with us. We decided that this [the PCSW's rental deposit] was not necessary, that we would pay our rental guaranty and they could just give us our money. Because if we signed this contract, we wouldn't be able to leave the house fast enough. (Wallonia, C, beneficiary, 10/05/2021)

In the quote above, the non-take-up can be interpreted as a form of strategic choice as it is a way for the newcomer to stay able to change house more rapidly. In other cases, however, newcomers described their refusal to ask for a benefit as a moral choice.

She [the social worker] came more than one time to check the house, to check if everything was ok. I said I didn't need anything and everything was fine. I had everything I needed, I'm not going to ask for more. Some people do, but not me. For me, that's not important. (Flanders, C, beneficiary, 18/01/2022).

A.: 'Yes, but sometimes it's special, you can take the ticket and give it to the PCSW for a refund.'
Researcher: 'And you did this?'
A.: 'Sometimes, yes. But I am a shy person and I can't always go and say, "Hey hello, I want to be reimbursed".' […]
Researcher: 'Can you explain this to me? Why?'
A.: […] 'I am not used to somebody giving me money. It's difficult for me. […] When I need something, I ask to my family. That's the first time that somebody was giving me money. I did not want to accept it but I have no choice.' (Wallonia, O, beneficiary 05/06/2021)

The two quotes above translate the feeling of discomfort that many of our interlocutors described in relation to the situation of asking for public support. This feeling was also linked with an 'ethic of individual responsibility' (van Oorschot & Math, 1996, p. 9) that was shared by the large majority of the newcomers we met and that – as illustrated above – sometimes led to practices of non-take-up (although often limited to specific services). These practices, which contradict the suspicions of 'welfare shopping' and 'opportunistic behaviour' that are sometimes associated with migrants, also illustrate the political dimension of non-take-up (Warin 2010). Indeed, as Warin (2010, p. 11) notes, 'Non-take-up is not exclusively the result of forms of passivity and inaction. It also expresses forms of disinterests and disagreement. In this perspective, non-take-up by non-demand goes beyond the question of the effectiveness of the PCSW's services (its capacity to deliver its services), but interrogates its very pertinence.'

CONCLUSION

This chapter addressed the capacity of newcomers to develop forms of agency in their relationship with social workers. This capacity for agency needs first to be contextualised within the structural asymmetry of the relationship where it is social workers who have the power to intervene over the beneficiary situation. In the same perspective, the agency of newcomers is limited by the fact that – beyond the difficulties that newly arrived immigrants have to face in terms of accessibility – PCSW's services are designed as last resort safety nets and that newcomers do not usually have alternative options to cover basic needs.

It was observed in this chapter that newcomer beneficiaries can adopt different attitudes when interacting with social workers. The attitude that was the most common among our interlocutors was a compliance with the administrative procedures and the demands of social workers. We show, however, that compliance can be performed in different ways by newcomers. Newcomers can develop 'active' forms of collaboration with social workers by trying to anticipate or exceed the social workers' expectations. Newcomers' beneficiaries can also engage in more 'passive' or 'minimal' forms of collaboration with social workers, by choosing to limit such collaboration to the fulfilment of minimal administrative duties and to develop strategies of integration outside of the control of social workers. In both cases, our chapter shows that the collaboration with social workers cannot be interpreted as a purely passive attitude and already involves forms of agency. Some newcomer beneficiaries can also stop – often temporarily – to comply with social workers' terms and adopt a more assertive attitude in their relationship with social workers. This assertiveness is possible when newcomers cease to consider social benefit as a favour and start to consider it as a right based on rules. To social workers' discretion, newcomer beneficiaries can then oppose what they perceive as 'the rule'. For newcomers in Belgium, it was observed that the possibility to perform such assertiveness is highly dependent on the skills and resources they have at their disposal. The language skills but also the capacity to understand regulations and law are indeed central, which suggest the importance of locally usable cultural capital in the capacity of newcomers to influence the relation with social workers.

Beyond these different attitudes the research also found different types of responses that newcomers can have when a difficulty arises in the relationship with social workers. These responses include instances of negotiation, protest, or bypass but also more passive responses such as enduring or avoiding the relation with social workers. This chapter illustrates how such responses are informed by the types of capital (social and cultural) that newcomers can mobilise locally. Cultural capital appears to be central for negotiating and protesting social workers' decisions/requirements. The research also highlights how social capital is also a crucial element enabling newcomers to act upon their relationship with social workers. Such social capital can be constituted outside of the PCSW (among friends, or NGOs, for example) but also within the PCSW and its different services. This last point suggests a dual experience of the PCSW as a place of control and constraints and as a place where resources can be found.

Finally, it has been found that – despite the common representations of immigrants as welfare profiteers – the relation of newcomers with PCSW was also characterised by situations where the former did not access benefits or services they were entitled to. Some of these instances of non-take-up were informed by a lack of information or by the failure of the institution to provide some services (due to administrative errors, delays, and so forth). In some cases, however, newcomers also expressed their lack of access to certain services as the result of their own conscious choice of not demanding such services. In some cases, non-demanding can be informed by structural constraints or by the fear of negative impact on the newcomers' situation but, in other cases, newcomers can renounce to certain services on the basis of moral considerations. In these cases, non-take-up expresses forms of disinterests and disagreement, which also illustrates how newcomers can interrogate the very pertinence of PCSW's services.

NOTES

1. It is important to note here that if these different forms of collaboration are distinguished here for the sake of the analysis, they do not always appear as distinct in the field. Indeed, newcomers can resort to different forms of collaboration on different matters and thus alternate between then.
2. We recall that in the social benefits application procedure, beneficiaries are allowed to present their case to the committee, mainly if they do not agree with the decision taken.
3. As mentioned in Chapter 4, this concerns, for example, foreigners who have a recent residence status for family reunification, as stated in the immigration law of 15 December 1980. Newcomers can generally be informed about this risk by the Immigration Office, PCSW's social workers, or agents from the commune of residence.

REFERENCES

Bourdieu, P. (1986). The forms of capital. In J. E. Richardson (Ed.), *Handbook of theory of research for the sociology of education* (pp. 46–58). Green Word Press.

Demazière, D. (1996). Des réponses langagières à l'exclusion: Les interactions entre chômeurs de longue durée et agents de l'ANPE. *Mots, 46,* 6–29.

Derluyn, I., Vanderplasschen, W., Alexandre, S., Stofels, I., Decorte, T., Franssen, A., Kaminski, D., Cartuyvels, Y., & Broekaert, E. (2008). *Trajectoires de soins des usages de drogues d'origine étrangère.* Academia Press. https://dial.uclouvain.be/pr/boreal/fr/object/boreal%3A153603

Dubois, V. (2010). *The bureaucrat and the poor: Encounters in French welfare offices.* Routledge.

Howe, L. E. A. (1990). *Being unemployed in Northern Ireland: An ethnographic study.* Cambridge University Press. https://doi.org/10.1017/CBO9780511735318

Kelvin, P., & Jarrett, J. (1985). *Unemployment: Its social psychological effects.* Cambridge University Press.

Lafleur, J.-M., & Mescoli, E. (2018). Creating undocumented EU migrants through welfare: A conceptualization of undeserving and precarious citizenship. *Sociology, 52*(3), 480–496. https://doi.org/10.1177/0038038518764615

Lipsky, M. (2010). *Street-level bureaucracy, 30th anniversary edition: Dilemmas of the individual in public service.* Russell Sage Foundation.

Meeus, B., Van Heur, B., & Arnaut. K. (2019). Migration and the infrastructural politics of urban arrival. In B. Meeus, B. Van Heur, & K. Arnaut (Eds.), *Arrival infrastructures: Migration and urban social mobilities* (pp. 1–32). Palgrave MacMillan.

Moynihan, D., Herd, P., & Harvey, H. (2015). Administrative burden: Learning, psychological, and compliance costs in citizen-state interactions. *Journal of Public Administration Research and Theory, 25*(1), 43–69. https://doi.org/10.1093/jopart/muu009

Noël, L. (2016). *Rapport thématique: Aperçus du non-recours aux droits sociaux et de la sous-protection sociale en Région bruxelloise.* Observatoire de la Santé et du Social de Bruxelles-Capitale.

Ratzmann, N. (2019). *Caught between the local and the (trans)national EU citizens at the front-line of German welfare policy* [Phd, London School of Economics and Political Science]. http://etheses.lse.ac.uk/3982/

van Oorschot, W. (1991). Non-take-up of social security benefits in Europe. *Journal of European Social Policy, 1*(1), 15–30. https://doi.org/10.1177/095892879100100103

van Oorschot, W. (1996). Les causes du non-recours [Des responsabilités largement partagées]. *Revue des politiques sociales et familiales, 43*(1), 33–49. https://doi.org/10.3406/caf.1996.1728

van Oorschot, W., & Math, A. (1996). La question du non-recours aux prestations sociales. *Revue des politiques sociales et familiales, 43*(1), 5–17. https://doi.org/10.3406/caf.1996.1725

Warin, P. (2010). *Qu'est-ce que le non-recours ?* La Vie des Idées.

Warin, P. (2011). *Le nom recours au RSA: des éléments de comparaison* (Working Paper 13). Observatoire des non-recours aux droits et services.

Warin, P. (2012). Le non-recours aux droits. *SociologieS,* novembre. https://doi.org/10.4000/sociologies.4103

Warin, P. (2016). *Le non-recours: définition et typologies. Actualisé en décembre 2016* (Working Paper 1). Observatoire des non-recours aux droits et services.

Warin, P. (2018). *What non-demand demands: On the non-take-up of social welfare.* Books & Ideas. https://booksandideas.net/What-Non-Demand-Demands.html.

Wright, S. E. (2003). *Confronting unemployment in a street-level bureaucracy: Jobcentre staff and client perspectives.* University of Stirling. http://dspace.stir.ac.uk/handle/1893/259

CONCLUSION PART III

JÉRÉMY MANDIN

As gatekeeper of the access to social services, social workers have significant power over newcomers' integration in Belgium. The second part of this book analysed in detail how this power is institutionally organised and how it is perceived and performed by social workers in the interactions with newcomer beneficiaries. The third part of the book approached the same relation from the perspective of the newcomers.

Chapter 9 addressed newcomers' perspective on the accessibility of PCSW's services, starting from the emergence of certain needs to the actual reception of appropriate services. Our research allowed to identify different ways through which newcomers became beneficiaries of PCSWs. These different ways imply different experiences in terms of access, from the refugee who is referred to PCSW by social workers from reception centres or LRI, to the newcomer who has arrived with the family reunification programme and who is referred to PCSW by a friend after a divorce. Despite this diversity of pathways of access, our research shows the importance of being embedded in a social network (either through institutions or through personal network) in the host society for accessing welfare services. Another result brought in Chapter 11 is that – among the newcomers we interviewed – the majority did not have a precise idea of the type of services offered by PCSWs before their first contact with the institution. Being registered to a PCSW is not necessarily enough to ensure access to services. Here, the circulation of information appears as key, especially for newcomers who do not have the appropriate cultural capital (language skills, administrative know how, and so forth) to have a good understanding of the numerous services of the PCSW. Four main channels of information are mentioned during the interviews with newcomers: PCSW social workers, other professional/organisations, newcomers' network of friends or relatives, and knowledge gained by newcomers during previous experience. Social workers are one of the most important providers of information for beneficiaries. However, our interviews with newcomers show significant differences in the ways social workers inform their interlocutors. Many interlocutors pointed out the limited and fragmented nature of the information they received from their appointed social worker. In this context, and despite the fact that they sometimes provide incorrect information, secondary channels such as friends or other professionals are often crucial for newcomers to access some services. Chapter 9 shows how newcomers perceive their access to services as being mainly dependent on the discretionary power of social workers. Put differently, they perceive their access as a matter of favour rather than a matter of rights.

Chapter 10 moved to the question of the access to PCSW to the question of newcomers' perception of the institution. Three dimensions of these perceptions have been addressed: newcomers' perception of PCSWs' services and their appropriateness, newcomers' perception of social workers' practices, and newcomers' perception of themselves as beneficiaries. Regarding newcomers' perception of the appropriateness of PCSW services, the interviews show a form of tension in the way beneficiaries describe the institution and its action. On the one hand, the vast majority of the interviewees tend to express a positive appreciation of the support provided by PCSWs. Such a support is perceived as temporary – as a sort of springboard – by newcomers who typically express their aspiration for autonomy and proper access to work during the interviews. On the other hand, newcomers also often express criticism regarding the practices of control and sanctions applied by social workers. Such controls are perceived by some newcomers as obstacles rather than support to achieving effective autonomy. In this perspective, newcomers sometimes perceive the institutional praxis of PCSWs as contradictory with its objective of supporting the autonomy of beneficiaries (an objective that many newcomers agree with). Regarding the perception of social workers' practices and discretion, many newcomers perceive the personality, competences, and goodwill of social workers as critical factors to the access of social services. In this context, while social workers' discretion is often perceived by social workers as a way to provide more equity, it can be interpreted by newcomers as a form of inequality of treatment. More generally, many respondents also emphasise the need of a specific approach for new immigrants as opposed to a more generalist approach that would tend to produce discriminating effects against newcomers who are less knowledgeable about the system. Regarding newcomers' perception of their situation as beneficiary, Chapter 10 shows that becoming a PCSW beneficiary is often accompanied by an experience of downward social mobility. Our research also describes newcomers' perspective about 'deservingness'. We found that most newcomers express definitions of deservingness that present elements of convergence with the definition of the institution (such as the necessity to be proactive) and thereof also reaffirm the moral hierarchy between 'deserving' and 'non-deserving' beneficiaries. Still, from the point of view of newcomers, deservingness is also experienced as something that needs to be performed in front of social workers in order to 'prove' that one is justified to benefit from social services.

Finally, Chapter 11 addresses the question of the agency of newcomer beneficiaries by looking at how newcomers can engage with the structurally asymmetrical relationship with social workers. This engagement was analysed through three dimensions: the attitudes that newcomers can adopt in front of social workers, the responses that they can develop to cope with difficulties in the relation, and finally the possibility of non-take-up practices. It has been found that the vast majority of newcomers are actually developing compliant attitudes when engaging with social workers. Compliance cannot be understood as a purely passive attitude, however, as it can be performed in different ways: through a form of active collaboration with social workers or through more minimal forms of collaboration. Some newcomer beneficiaries can also adopt – often temporarily – more assertive attitudes in front of social workers. Becoming more assertive often requires perceiving PCSWs' services not as 'favours' but as 'rights', based on 'rules'. This illustrates the difference of perspective that social workers and newcomers can have about the rules. While for the former, rules are sometimes perceived as a limiting factor in providing adequate support to newcomers, for the latter, it can constitute a resource to try to mitigate social workers' discretion and therefore ensure equity. The capacity to develop assertive attitudes is not evenly distributed among newcomers. Indeed, cultural capital (under the form of language skills, administrative know-how, and basic understanding of regulations) appears to be of importance to developing such attitudes. Chapter 11 then described a variety of responses that newcomers can adopt to cope with difficulties in interacting with social workers. These responses include negotiation, protest, bypass, and also more 'passive' responses, such as enduring or even avoiding the interactions with social workers. Here again, our research found that the type of responses that newcomers can have are highly dependent of the type of capital that they can mobilise locally. The research shows how being embedded in social networks in Belgium is important for the capacity of newcomers to cope with difficult relations with social workers. Chapter 11 then addresses the question of non-take-up by describing how – despite the common representation of immigrants as social welfare profiteer – newcomers do not necessarily benefit from services they are entitled to. Beyond the instances of non-take-up that are independent from newcomers' choice, the research also found that newcomers can also, on some occasions, consciously renounce to certain services based on moral considerations.

PART IV

CONCLUSION

HANNE VANDERMEERSCHEN AND PETER DE CUYPER

The aim of this book was to provide a better understanding of the social assistance to newly arrived immigrant beneficiaries, through the case study of Public Centres for Social Welfare (PCSWs) and their service delivery to newly arrived immigrants in Belgium. In doing so, it contributes to the literature on the intersection between the welfare state and migration governance. Belgian PCSWs, as similar institutions elsewhere, play a crucial role in granting access to social benefits to newcomers and, more generally, in their settlement and integration process. Moreover, the assistance and support provided as well as decisions taken by welfare institutions such as the PCSW in Belgium can have a long-term influence on the lives of newcomers. However, at the onset of this research little was known about the practices and interventions with newcomers in terms of assistance provision, the policies that regulate them, and other influencing factors. Beyond a documentation of the Belgian assistance provision, this research contributes to a broader in-depth understanding of the dynamics between immigrants and the welfare state from policy to practice. Moreover, by including the study of migrants' own experience with welfare institutions, it brings a multi-stakeholder perspective to the subject matter and contributes to the emerging but still insufficient literature on the functioning of welfare systems from the perspective of recipients.

The detailed analysis presented in this book relied primarily on a large-scale qualitative data collection, based on 197 interviews with staff and newcomer beneficiaries in PCSWs. The results reflect an analysis at three levels, more particularly the organisational/management level, that of social workers, and that of the newly arrived immigrants as beneficiaries. Combining these levels of analysis, we were able to address a gap in the literature, as mentioned above, since earlier research called for analyses bringing the perspective of staff and perceptions of beneficiaries together (Raeymaeckers & Dierckx, 2013). Also in our own literature study, we detected a need for a more comprehensive and nuanced understanding of service provision to newcomer beneficiaries and the challenges and pitfalls it entails. A quantitative survey among PCSWs (at the management level) was conducted as well in order to complement and cross-check our findings from the qualitative study, bringing data triangulation into our research design.

This study fulfilled three research aims. A first aim was to map the practices regarding the granting of rights and social activation interventions targeting newly arrived immigrants. Second, we shed light on the factors influencing social workers' choices and decisions regarding social benefits and social activation targeting newcomers. Third, we provided an analysis of the accessibility of social welfare for newcomers and of their experience with a welfare administration. As a general theoretical framework, we relied on the concept of accessibility, as well as on the existing literature on street-level bureaucracies, and more specifically at the intersection of welfare and migration (see Chapter 1).

This book first presents a set of introductory chapters, introducing the theoretical and methodological framework and providing more insight in the specificities of the research context. Second, the core of this book consists of three parts, addressing subsequently the social assistance for newly arrived immigrants (Part I), the decision-making process (Part II), and the experiences of newly arrived immigrants in terms of access to the welfare services (Part III), with Parts I and II relying on the accounts of the PCSW and its staff and Part III presenting the perspective of immigrant beneficiaries. In what follows, however, we transcend this division, combining the different points of view gathered throughout our study, and thereby presenting a more complex and multi-layered overview.

The conclusion has been built as follows. In the first three paragraphs, we come back to the original research aims as described above. We shortly summarise our key findings with regard to each of them, bringing the perspectives of all actors, ranging from the 'system' to the users, together. In a fourth and fifth paragraph, we discuss main findings related to two additional themes that emerged from our study, that is, the question of equity and the high price of support.

1. INSIGHTS ON THE PRACTICES OF GRANTING OF RIGHTS AND SOCIAL ACTIVATION INTERVENTIONS TARGETING NEWLY ARRIVED IMMIGRANTS

The findings presented in this book indicate that PCSWs have two main ways of organising their services towards newcomers. One way is dealing with newcomers' demands and the related files directly at general social services; another way is to manage these records first at specialised social services, before being transferred to general social services. Both approaches were prevalent in the field, having a specialised service or sticking to an overall generalist approach, as well as some configurations keeping the middle. Regardless of (not) having a specialised service, a considerable share of PCSWs state to have social workers specialised in working with newcomers.

PCSWs also rely on partners to execute service delivery for newcomers. A vast number of partners were mentioned, but the exact patchwork differs from municipality to municipality. A recurring partner are the regional centres for integration. However, cooperation with these organisations is on average less intense than one could expect based on the complementarity in terms of expertise and the common focus on integration in society of both organisations.

Going back to the internal functioning of the PCSW, throughout this book it was explained that different levels are at play in the decision-making process on the allocation of social benefits, with social workers, managers, and/or directors and a deciding committee each having their own specific role. An emphasis on tailor-made support, and decisions on a 'case by case' basis was observed as a common thread throughout our findings. Clearly, there are rules and policy lines set, but they do not cover (nor aim to cover) all possible situations encountered in the field. Moreover, negotiating the rules to some extent is part of the process. While the entitlement to an integration income is rather fixed (by law) and conditions are rather straightforward, complementary aids (in addition to the social integration income) need to be argued.

Our analysis revealed the importance of discretion in the social assistance provision to newcomer beneficiaries at PCSWs. However, the use of discretion requires the engagement and motivation of the social workers and presupposes they acknowledge their discretionary power and take responsibility in performing it. Indeed, the discretionary power of social workers gives them the possibility to engage with the rules in different ways. They can strictly adhere to the rules – which may lead to allocating lower aid – or engage more with the rule – finding spaces of interpretation to increase the social aid. As a result, the extent to which discretion is performed differs largely between social workers and between services at the PCSW, which can affect the outcomes for beneficiaries as well. These findings confirm the value of 'street-level bureaucracy' as a theoretical framework for the analysis of service provision to newly arrived immigrants, as (different forms of) discretion, in particular, indeed turned out to be fundamental in the decision-making process leading (or not) to access to rights.

Specifically with regard to labour market activation, our mapping of practices revealed that social workers act as gatekeepers to employment, with newcomer beneficiaries not only having to be willing but also to be ready for work, or, in other words, they need to be considered employable by social workers at the PCSW. Even though there is cooperation with the public employment service and other organisations in terms of labour market activation, the PCSWs are the primary actor in charge of beneficiaries' journey towards employment. Labour market activation tends to occur later for newcomer beneficiaries, with other (intermediate) goals being prioritised first, and social workers often (felt they have to) temper newcomers' expectations with regard to employment prospects as well.

2. FACTORS INFLUENCING CHOICES AND DECISIONS OF SOCIAL WORKERS

While some room for interpretation of the legal framework for social assistance is necessary to make a tailor-made support possible, it also comes with its own risks, since discretion and other factors than mere 'facts' influence the judgement of social workers. As described in the literature, these factors fall into two main categories: institutional aspects (the process of professional socialisation of social workers in the services frequented by immigrant beneficiaries) and the personal characteristics of social workers. Among the factors influencing the approach of social workers that strongly came forward in this study is the way in which they evaluate the attitude of the beneficiary, that is, how he/she is viewed, perceived, based on personal moral positionings as well as institutional expectations. Such assessment is based on moral and relational aspects and may reflect some (cultural) prejudices of the social workers and reveal unbalanced power dynamics, putting beneficiaries at the mercy of the judgements produced on them. In our research, we observed that beneficiaries' attitudes will be positively assessed when they 'collaborate' and demonstrate 'willingness', motivation, and commitment. Examples of the expected attitude of 'deserving beneficiaries' – as perceived by the social workers – are responding to the convocations, bringing the needed documents, being honest, understanding what is being asked, and why the aid is or is not granted, accepting and following the advice of the social workers, engaging in socio-professional integration initiatives, showing the willingness to learn the national language concerned, and so forth. In practice, these types of behaviour function as prerequisite for accessing and maintaining the social rights at the PCSW. This is line with the literature on 'welfare deservingness': accessing rights is also an issue of proving to deserve them.

In this process, the assessment of the attitude of the beneficiaries by social workers (and of other social actors involved in the decision-making process at PCSWs) can have real consequences in terms of the support that the former can (or cannot) receive. In the literature review presented in Chapter 1, we learned how the decisions of street-level bureaucrats in a context in which there is a structural tension between 'care' and 'control' inherently carry a risk of differential treatment, or even discrimination, thus potentially reproducing – rather than reducing – social inequalities (Lotta & Pires, 2019; Maynard-Moody & Musheno, 2012; Raaphorst & Groeneveld, 2019; Thomann & Rap, 2018). However, in our study we observed that an increased engagement of social workers in supporting the demands of 'deserving beneficiaries' and 'defending a case' can lead to more favourable decisions, thus making discretionary practice, paradoxically, a potential tool of social justice towards the most vulnerable populations such as newcomers – therefore challenging the restrictive welfare policy framework. Nevertheless, the possibility of this happening depends on the level of awareness of social workers of their discretionary power, as well as their choice to make this extra commitment to (and take on more responsibility for) the cases they manage, instead of strictly adhering to the rules and minimum standards they have set.

From the point of view of newcomers, deservingness is also experienced as something that needs to be performed in front of social workers in order to 'prove' that one is justified to benefit from social services. During the interactions with social workers, newcomer beneficiaries were found to be aware that they had to demonstrate that they deserved the received support by complying with the institution's rules and by showing a proactive attitude. Beneficiaries also develop discourses and attitudes that allow them to distance themselves from actors deemed 'non-deserving'. However, the 'case per case' approach – and the discretion practiced in the concrete realisation of it, as well as the lack of transparency about rules (cf. infra), also comes with a feeling of arbitrariness among immigrant beneficiaries, as will be discussed later in this concluding chapter.

Our findings demonstrate the importance of attitudes of deservingness – and therefore the crucial role of the relationship operating between social workers and welfare beneficiaries – in understanding the dynamics of local social service provision to immigrants. This is in line with earlier findings from Ratzmann and Sahraoui, who point out, 'Moral judgements play an important role in street-level bureaucrats' use of discretion' (2021, p. 441), regardless of its outcome.

3.   ACCESSIBLE SERVICES FOR NEWCOMERS?

The analyses revealed a number of problems in terms of accessibility for newcomers. Without being exhaustive, here we highlight four main challenges that were identified in this volume.

First, a major stumbling block is currently (a lack of) needs detection for newcomers. Social workers and managers explain that the vast amount of administration is time consuming, which by consequence leaves less time for discussing other aspects. This argument needs to be understood in the light of the context of time pressure and high workload, which characterizes many PCSWs (and are also a common feature of many street-level bureaucracies). Need detection is challenged by time pressure, by social workers' strategy to avoid extra work (as working with newcomers is already considered to be time consuming), by language issues, by beneficiaries not knowing what to expect and/or what to ask for, among other things. The extent to which needs detection actually occurs in practice varies largely between social workers. Failing to invest in (or have room for) problem detection also results in an accrued imbalance between what is considered 'actual social work' – increasingly difficult to achieve – and administration – which corresponds more and more to the work carried out by the social workers of the PCSWs, as they point out. The lack of needs detection is a problem of availability of service delivery. Yet, needs detection was also identified as a precondition to make adequate referrals: one can only refer to a partner to offer support if the need for support is identified first (think of needs as diverse as legal advice, psychological counselling, help with schoolwork for the children, and so forth).

A second large obstacle with regard to accessibility is related to language. The access to, and use of services and benefits is greatly influenced by language, as it depends on the possibility of reciprocal understanding between social workers and beneficiaries. Language-related inequity experiences have been stressed in the literature, and language has been shown to contribute to the social stratification of access (see, for example, Brubaker, 2015; Cederberg, 2014; Holzinger, 2020; Ratzmann, 2021). Our study indicates that language problems affect the quality of service delivery at the PCSW, in line with earlier findings from Van Robaeys and Driessens (2011) in a PCSW in a Belgian city as well. In our study, language problems were found to affect mutual understanding, making it difficult to touch upon 'deeper' issues (involving issues related to psychosocial wellbeing, for example), and hence impacting the support given to newcomers. Failing to understand one another in a detailed way affects the content and nuances of communication, and hence the quality of the service delivery, and the appropriateness of the support. However, while many respondents pinpoint the issue of language, generally there is no systematic or structural solution offered to it. Instead of relying on a professional framework offering guidance about when to use certain tools or strategies (ranging from Google Translate to professional translation), personal opinions, preferences, practical considerations, and ideology seem to guide choices in practice, resulting in a variety of approaches in the field. While many social workers stress the importance of beneficiaries learning the regional language as a matter of integration (which is mentioned as an argument for relying on the regional language as much as possible), other social workers go further in organising translation and contacting an interpreter, highlighting the importance of good and nuanced communication. Practical problems with regard to interpreting services also play a role, such as missing or defective structural agreements, time-consuming procedures, financial costs, the lack of availability of certain languages or dialects, and the increased duration of conversations with interpreters. Yet, the interviews with beneficiaries have demonstrated the importance of adequately dealing with language problems. Indeed, while language was not necessarily identified by newcomers as the principal factor influencing their relation with PCSW, interviews have nevertheless illustrated how the difficulty to deal with language affects services (think of missing out on information about the existence or availability of services, miscommunication, shyness to ask for things, etc.).

Another challenge in service delivery at PCSW for newly arrived immigrants affecting the accessibility of the PCSW regards the understandability of the system of aid, and of the PCSW as an institution. Based on the accounts of the social workers, it is challenging to make sure the beneficiaries understand what PCSW stands for, what help they can get, what the goals are, and so on. This knowledge cannot be taken for granted, and even less with newcomer beneficiaries. This was confirmed in the testimonials of newly arrived immigrants, explaining they did not know what to expect, and mentioning difficulties to obtain information (and their dependence on their social worker for it, see further). As discussed in Chapter 1 presenting the literature review and theoretical framework, these challenges relate to the accessibility of the service as well, and more particularly to dimensions of approachability (transparency, outreach, information, and so forth, see Levesque *et al.*, 2013) and availability and accommodation (organising the service in such a way that it suits the context from which the beneficiary comes, see Russell *et al.*, 2013), among other things.

Last, the analyses also revealed that the awareness of challenges for newly arrived immigrants differs largely between social workers as well, impacting service delivery. More generally, we noted that there was little reflection upon the accessibility for immigrants, and little questioning of the 'system' and common practices in that sense. This affects the appropriateness of service delivery, one of the dimensions of accessibility as presented in the framework of Levesque *et al.* (2013, see Chapter 1), as awareness is a precondition to tackle problems.

4. QUESTIONING THE EQUITY OF THE ASSISTANCE

The experiences of newcomers revealed a strong dependence on their social worker, not only for granting support, but also for obtaining information. The analysis showed it was hard for newcomer beneficiaries to know their rights. Access to information is difficult, with no systematic overview of rules, conditions, or entitlements available. There is little transparency in terms of rights and conditions, as, currently, predominant sources of information are the social worker or one's social network. In addition to the lack of transparency, also a lack of equity was brought forward by the newcomer beneficiaries. They did not perceive the system as fair nor as being built on consistent rules. Instead, newcomer beneficiaries spoke about the support they received in terms of being 'lucky'. The findings showed beneficiaries perceived the assistance and support they received as a matter of favours rather than rights. The present book brings here a contribution to the literature of street-level bureaucracy by showing that the relation between rules and discretionary power can be interpreted differently by street-level bureaucrats and by (newcomer) beneficiaries. Our research showed that while PCSWs' social workers often consider rules as limiting factors in the access of rights and discretionary power as a resource to provide more adequate support, from the perspective of the newcomers, rules can constitute resources to mitigate the uncertainty related to social workers' discretion and therefore ensure better equity.

The dependence on the social worker brings up the question of automatic take up of social rights, as this would indeed solve a number of problems in the field, and improve equity. It is, however, a double-edged sword: discretion is necessary for the way the PCSW works and is often used to the advantage of beneficiaries – but as it is now, it leads to a perception of arbitrariness – and to inequity in the facts as well. The literature review presented in Chapter 1 taught us that discretion and the resulting risk of discrimination and reproduction or reinforcement of social inequalities can in turn create a perception of injustice in bureaucratic processes among immigrant beneficiaries (Lafleur & Mescoli, 2018). Here, too, the findings lead us to conclude this occurs in Belgian PCSWs as well.

As mentioned repeatedly above in the discussion on discretion, social workers need to find a balance between working in a tailor-made way and sticking to policy lines to ensure equity. Yet, an ambivalence in this sense is present among decisions and actions of managers, directors, and committee members as well. In the fieldwork, there was a recurrent discourse of managers, directors, and the committee stating that they promoted or safeguarded equity by having a more neutral position, more overview, and so forth. However, they also emphasised the importance of taking decisions at the individual level, 'doing what is best for a particular person'. Both discourses – of working in a tailor-made way and to ensure equity – are present in the field, and both seem to guide practice; it is not always clear how they articulate to each other, nor in which situations which of both applies. Furthermore, our analyses cast some doubts about equity being unequivocally promoted by the committee. The committee has considerable discretion in terms of decision-making, while their professionalism – or at least the professionalism of some members, not the entire committee per se – is sometimes questioned in interviews. Even though the committee can indeed level out differences between social workers, its own objectivity – or even fairness? – was disputed to some extent as well. Indeed, our analyses revealed how prejudice and a lack of expertise, among other things, introduce bias into the decision making. While the existence of a deciding organ hierarchically overpowering social workers was not questioned as such by our interviewees, based on our findings, it seems the quality of social assistance would definitely benefit from a committee composition based on relevant professional background.

5. THE SUPPORT OF THE PCSW COMES AT A PRICE: LEARNING COSTS, PSYCHOLOGICAL COSTS, AND COMPLIANCE COSTS

In Chapter 1, we referred to the concept of 'administrative burden' (Burden *et al.*, 2012; Moynihan *et al.*, 2014), which comes down to the costs that citizens experience when interacting with public administration. The administrative burden consists of learning costs, psychological costs, and compliance costs, and has an impact on the access and use of services. Based on the accounts of immigrant beneficiaries, we can conclude that support from the PCSWs often comes with a large administrative burden for immigrant beneficiaries. Examples are numerous, and all three types of costs – learning, psychological, and compliance – were encountered in the field.

To start with, the support granted at the PCSW – which is often described as something that is 'given' – represents psychological cost. It is associated with downward social mobility, often even a 'double downgrade': receiving financial aid from the PCSW implies having a low socio-economic status, and simultaneously comes with the status of being assisted or dependent on a state income (which in turn leads to new difficulties, for example the struggle to find adequate housing due to discrimination practices against PCSW beneficiaries). The latter applies for other, non-migrant beneficiaries to a large extent as well, yet for some of the newcomer beneficiaries, the difficulties are exacerbated by the contrast with their social status and/or financial situation in their home country (depending on their educational and professional background before migration). Findings also indicate that many interviewees experienced a feeling of discomfort for having to ask for public support. Moreover, for newcomers, the stigma and the paternalistic discourses around the 'social excluded' that are common to PCSW's beneficiaries were mixed in our fieldwork with the stigma related to migration.

For example, we could read in Chapter 10 how the 'controls' that are part of the system (for example, controls of the need for different types of support, the expected transparency about financial expenses, and submitting proof of willingness to work such as proof of job applications and proof of language school attendance) can weigh on some of the newcomer beneficiaries, perceiving it as a lack of trust, or even as infantilising and/or burdensome. It is both time and energy consuming, and count as compliance costs, and sometimes as psychological costs as well. Social activation practices that are often considered by social workers as a way of empowering beneficiaries are therefore re-interpreted by beneficiaries, who do not feel 'activated' but rather 'controlled'.

In spite of the common representations of immigrants as welfare profiteers, the analyses revealed that there are also situations in which newcomers did not access benefits or services they were entitled to, especially complementary types of aid. The reasons for non-take-up varied. In some cases, the non-take-up was the result of a lack of information or a failure of the institution to provide some services (due to administrative errors, delays, and so forth). In other cases, newcomers also expressed their lack of access to certain services as the result of their own conscious choice of not demanding such services.

Such instances of conscious non-take-up were informed by different factors such as the fear of a negative impact on the own (newcomers') situation, or as a strategy to avoid contact after a negative experience with the social worker/PCSW and to reduce stress from dealing with the PCSW (from the perspective of the newcomer). In a (limited) number of cases, newcomers also engaged in non-take-up practices for moral reasons, often in order to remain able to cultivate a positive perception of themselves (as someone who does not systematically ask for support, for example).

Examples of learning costs can be found throughout this book as well, such as the difficulties experienced by the newcomers to understand the system (both the PCSW as well as the social security system more generally) and to get information about entitlements to complementary aids. In brief, we can conclude that the affordability of support – one of the dimensions of accessibility in the insightful framework of Levesque *et al.* (2013), as presented in Chapter 1 – currently falls short for the target group of our study.

On a more general level, throughout this volume it became clear how a strong power imbalance affects the service delivery to the newly arrived immigrants. As beneficiaries, people are in a strongly dependent position, which is exacerbated for newcomers, for example through their unfamiliarity with the system. We found many examples illustrating the unfortunate position of newcomer beneficiaries in terms of power balance, and, on most occasions, the situation seems unquestioned. To give just a few examples, in Chapter 10 it was shown how newcomer beneficiaries were signing documents such as the ISIP contract[1] – written in Dutch/French – without really knowing or remembering the content. Also, they were not aware of the 'reciprocal' and individualised nature of the document – which it is in theory – but rather perceived it as an imposed or standard document, necessary to sign in exchange for support. It is also the social worker (and not the beneficiary) who decides on the (non-use) of a translator to facilitate the conversation, and, as mentioned above, newcomer beneficiaries are dependent on their social worker for information to a large extent (while newcomers have less prior knowledge about it to fall back on). In sum, if PCSWs wish to improve their accessibility for newcomers, reducing the administrative burden – which is closely related to, and an expression of the power imbalance between the institution/the staff and its users – would be a fruitful way to start, even though the actions of social workers are strongly influenced, and limited, by a large work pressure and case load, as well as by the weight of their own administrative duties.

Despite the power unbalance that is at the core of the relation between PCSWs' social workers and newly arrived immigrants, our research shows that the latter still remain capable of developing forms of agency in order to secure access to social support. This agency can take different forms, from the type of attitude that newcomers adopt during their interaction with social workers to the type of responses they can develop to cope with a difficult situation. The agency that a newcomer can develop when interacting with PCSWs' services remains dependent on the amount and the type of capital that they can mobilize locally. While the possession of certain forms of cultural capital (local language skills, administrative literacy, and so forth) certainly makes the access to adequate support easier, our research shows that the lack of such capital can sometimes be compensated by the use of social capital in order to overcome difficulty of access. In this perspective, the importance of local social networks (of friends, acquaintances, and family members, but also non-PCSW social workers) appears as an important factor of access for some newcomers.

In conclusion, this book has shed light on the implementation of welfare policy towards immigrant beneficiaries on the ground, by reporting on the experience of both social workers and other institutional social actors, as well as that of the newly arrived immigrants themselves. Through this analysis, and in particular by combining a plurality of perspectives, it has been possible to highlight the complex functioning of service provision for newcomer beneficiaries and the challenges this entails. Street-level bureaucracy and the resulting discretionary power of social workers are crucial in this process, as are the relational dynamics between them and immigrant beneficiaries, with a set of specific factors playing a key role. Moral judgements of deservingness, practices of (in)equity, varied forms of agency operating within a paradoxically strict yet porous structural framework are among them. The detailed description and in-depth analysis we have produced through our research and this book – beyond the theoretical contribution to the literature on the intersection between welfare and migration governance through the prism of street-level bureaucracy – can be useful material for policymakers to rethink aspects of the functioning of welfare services towards immigrant beneficiaries in order to make them more accessible for them, as well as to optimise the possibilities for rewarding social work for the professionals involved.

NOTES

1.   ISIP stands for Individual Social Integration Project (PIIS in French, GPMI in Dutch) and represents a 'contract' established between the PCSW and the beneficiary of the aid, specifying the objectives of social integration (engaging in studies or training, active search for employment, and so forth) pursued by the user with the support of social workers from the PCSW. It lists the mutual rights and duties of the beneficiary and the competent PCSW.

REFERENCES

Brubaker, R. (2015). Linguistic and religious pluralism: Between difference and inequality. *Journal of Ethnic and Migration Studies, 41*(1), 3–32.

Burden, B., Marx-Freere, M., & Soss, J. (2012). The effect of administrative burden on bureaucratic perception of policies: Evidence from election administration. *Public Administration Review, 72,* 741–751.

Cederberg, M. (2014). Public discourses and migrant stories of integration and inequality: Language and power in biographical narratives. *Sociology, 48*(1), 133–149.

Holzinger, C. (2020). We don't worry that much about language: Street level bureaucracy in the context of linguistic diversity. *Journal of Ethnic and Migration Studies, 46*(9), 1792–1808.

Lafleur, J.-M., & Mescoli, E. (2018). Creating undocumented EU migrants through welfare: A conceptualization of undeserving and precarious citizenship. *Sociology, 52*(3), 480–496.

Levesque, J.-F., Harris, M. F., & Russell, G. (2013). Patient-centred access to health care: Conceptualizing access at the interface of health systems and populations. *International Journal for Equity in Health, 12*(18), 1–9.

Lotta, G., & Pires, R. (2019). Street-level bureaucracy and social inequality. In P. Hupe (Ed.), *Research handbook on street-level bureaucracy. The ground floor of government in context* (pp. 86–101). Edward Elgar Publishing.

Maynard-Moody, S., & Musheno, M. (2012). Social equities and inequities in practice: Street-level workers as agents and pragmatists. *Public Administration Review, 72,* S16–S23.

Moynihan, D., Herd, P., & Harvey, H. (2014). Administrative burden: Learning, psychological, and compliance costs in citizen-state interactions. *Journal of Public Administration Research and Theory, 25,* 43–69.

Raaphorst, N., & Groeneveld, S. (2018). Double standards in frontline decision making: A theoretical and empirical exploration. *Administration & Society, 50*(8), 1175–1201.

Raeymaeckers, P., & Dierckx, D. (2013). To work or not to work? The role of the organizational context for social workers' perceptions on activation. *British Journal of Social Work, 43*(6), 1170–1189.

Ratzmann, N. (2021). Deserving of social support? Street-level bureaucrats' decisions on EU migrants' benefit claims in Germany. *Social Policy & Society, 20*(3), 1–12.

Ratzmann, N., & Sahraoui, N. (2021). Conceptualising the role of deservingness in migrants' access to social services. *Social Policy and Society, 20*(3), 440–451.

Thomann, E., & Rapp, C. (2018). Who deserves solidarity? Unequal treatment of immigrants in Swiss welfare policy delivery. *Policy Studies Journal, 46*(3), 531–552.

Van Robaeys, B. & Driessens, K. (2011). *Gekleurde armoede en hulpverlening. Sociaal werkers en cliënten aan het woord* [Coloured poverty and care. Social workers and clients speaking]. Tielt: Lannoo.

ABOUT THE AUTHORS

Adriana Costa Santos is a PhD researcher in social and political science at the Centre de recherches et d'interventions sociologiques (CESIR), University of Leuven – Saint-Louis – Brussels.

Michelle Crijns is a former researcher on migration and integration at HIVA, University of Leuven (Belgium). She now works as a participatory grantmaker at the Wilde Ganzen foundation (the Netherlands).

Peter De Cuyper is a migrant integration expert and research manager at the University of Leuven, HIVA – Research Institute for Work and Society.

Abraham Franssen is Professor of Sociology at the University of Leuven – Saint-Louis – Brussels. He teaches in particular the analysis of public action and the sociology of collective action with research focusing on the analysis of public action in the field of social policy, education, and youth. His work is characterised by its participatory methodology and its action research approach, through the implementation of the group analysis method.

Angeliki Konstantinidou is the Junior Network Officer of IMISCOE (International Migration Research Network) at the Centre for Ethnic and Migration Studies (CEDEM) of the University of Liége. She is also a PhD candidate at CEDEM and at the Centre for European Studies and Comparative Politics (CEE) of Sciences Po Paris.

Jean-Michel Lafleur is Senior Research Associate at the FRS-FNRS (Fund for Scientific Research) and Associate Professor at the University of Liège (Centre for Ethnic and Migration Studies). He is also the Coordinator of the IMISCOE Research Network.

Jérémy Mandin is a researcher in social sciences and anthropology at the Centre for Ethnic and Migration Studies (CEDEM) of the University of Liège.

Carla Mascia is a postdoctoral researcher at the Université libre de Bruxelles. Her research focuses on the street-level implementation of migration policy, social inequalities, and the impact of colonial past.

Elsa Mescoli is post-doctoral researcher and Associate Professor at the University of Liège, Faculty of Social Sciences, CEDEM – Centre for Ethnic and Migration Studies.

Roberta Perna is post-doctoral researcher in political sociology at the Complutense University of Madrid and member of the Steering Committee of the ECPR Standing Group Migration and Ethnicity.

Marije Reidsma is a senior researcher at HIVA – Research Institute for Work and Society – at the University of Leuven.

Hanne Vandermeerschen is a research expert in migrant integration at the University of Leuven, HIVA – Research Institute for Work and Society.

Youri Lou Vertongen is a doctor in political science and guest professor at the Université Saint-Louis Brussels. His research focuses on collective mobilisations around migration issues in Belgium and Europe.

Printed in the USA
CPSIA information can be obtained
at www.ICGtesting.com
LVHW020309060124
768263LV00005B/313